The Screenplay Business

The development of a film screenplay is a complex and collaborative process, beginning with an initial story and continuing through drafting and financing to the start of the shoot. And yet the best ways of understanding and managing this process have never been properly studied. *The Screenplay Business* is the first book to do exactly that, addressing such questions as:

- How do film scripts get written, and what are the tensions between creativity and business?
- How can the team of the writer, producer, director and development executive work together most effectively?

The Screenplay Business presents a theoretical and practical framework for understanding the business of independent script development, and encompasses ideas about creativity, motivation, managing creative people, value chains, and MBA leadership theories. This book will help producers and writers to nurture their stories through the long development process to the screen. It explains the international film business, and contains new research and extensive interviews with leading industry figures, including practical advice on how to run script meetings and handle notes; how to build a sustainable business; and how to understand what happens when a script is written.

The Screenplay Business is a new key text for academics and students researching film and media, and indispensable reading for anyone working in film screenplay development today.

Peter Bloore is a produced film screenwriter; a media business consultant specializing in business strategy, creativity and drama development; and Senior Lecturer in Creativity at the University of East Anglia. He is currently co-writing a new screenplay and working on a novel.

The Screenplay Business

Managing creativity and script
development in the film industry

Peter Bloore

Routledge
Taylor & Francis Group

LONDON AND NEW YORK

First published 2013
by Routledge
2 Park Square, Milton Park, Abingdon, Oxon OX14 4RN

Simultaneously published in the USA and Canada
by Routledge
711 Third Avenue, New York, NY 10017

Routledge is an imprint of the Taylor & Francis Group, an informa business

© 2013 Peter Bloore

British Library Cataloguing in Publication Data
A catalogue record for this book is available from the British Library

Library of Congress Cataloging in Publication Data
Bloore, Peter.
The screenplay business : managing creativity and the film industry / by Peter Bloore.
p. cm.
Includes bibliographical references and index.
1. Motion pictures - - Production and direction. 2. Motion picture authorship. 3. Motion picture industry - - Finance. I. Title.
PN1995.9.P7B58 2012
384'.8 - - dc23
2012011935

ISBN: 978-0-415-61332-3 (hbk)
ISBN: 978-0-415-61333-0 (pbk)
ISBN: 978-0-203-14371-1 (ebk)

Typeset in Baskerville
by Saxon Graphics Ltd, Derby

This book is dedicated to the memory of Peter Herring, an inspiring art teacher who encouraged schoolchildren to express their creativity, and helped me to believe in myself.

Contents

Figures

Tables

Boxes

Preface

No film script is written in a vacuum.

The screenwriter may be sitting on his own, typing away on the computer and dreaming up new stories, but in his mind is the influence of the producer, director, development executive, potential financiers, and the echoes of many past films and screenplays. These factors shape the script and the completed film in a million different ways, so why don't we admit it and think more carefully about it?

This book came about as a result of twenty-five years of working in the film industry, both as a screenwriter and as a director of television and short films. I have experienced at first hand the life of a professional writer, with various projects in development with different producers. I have known the trials and tribulations of getting films made, and seen what it is like for producers and sales agents raising finance at the festivals and markets of Cannes, Los Angeles and Berlin.

By 2005 I had also become a university lecturer, and as the course director of the Media MBA at Bournemouth University I was writing up the curriculum for a Masters film business module. It became apparent that none of the books available about the film industry and scriptwriting really covered the reality of development and the independent film business, especially in the UK. There were over a hundred books in print on how to write screenplays, and over forty books on how to produce, and yet none of those books really dealt with the development *process* as I knew it. When I moved to the University of East Anglia and started teaching screenwriters on the MA in Creative Writing and film-makers on the MA in Film and TV Studies, it was clear that new writers and directors had no way of finding out what it was really like to work in development. If they knew more about development maybe it would help them nurture their own stories from genesis to audience, without falling into the many elephant traps waiting on the way. At the same time in my work as a freelance media business consultant I could also see that many people working in the hectic world of film lacked the time and space to reflect on what they were doing, and listen to other people's experiences.

So I had the idea of writing a book to try to fill those gaps. It would be aimed at people already in the industry or else studying the industry and hoping to be in it; including writers, directors, producers, development executives, academics and students. It would examine the whole development process; look at the fluctuating relationships between the writer, producer, director and financiers; propose some models and typologies for analysing films; and consider the entire issue of what is really *meant* by creativity in film and television. And here is that book. It has taken many years to research, two years to write, and has benefited from the input and generosity of many interviewees, fellow academics and industry friends.

As I said, no film script is written in a vacuum. This book is now going to try and fill that vacuum, so that we can understand what *really* happens when a script is written.

Acknowledgements

I have interviewed many people for this book, some formally (using recorded interviews) and others informally or 'off-the-record'. Without their generous time and patience this book would not exist, so my gratitude to them is immense. I would also like to thank all those industry people who gave me 'off-the-record' interviews that have not been directly quoted but have hugely informed my research. In general it is the screenwriters and directors who have been more reluctant to be interviewed or who have requested anonymity. This is maybe because they rely on producers and development executives for their next jobs, and so are reluctant to speak too openly.

Where they have been quoted in the book all interviewees have had the opportunity to read the selected text, to correct errors of fact, and have had the option to anonymize themselves for certain quotes. Interviews have been edited to remove some repetitions, hesitations and verbal ticks where they interfere with the flow of the text (such as 'like', 'I mean', 'you know', 'seriously', 'sort of', 'basically', 'right?'). Various colloquial versions of the word 'said' (like 'I went', 'I go', and so on) have been replaced with the word 'said', because that is what was meant. Otherwise major edits have been shown by an ellipsis (…).

Quotations from third-party sources are referenced with a footnote, so if there is a quotation without a footnote then it is from one of the original interviews made for this book (full details are in the bibliography).

I have tried to avoid using gender-specific words; however, where it is unavoidable the word 'he' regrettably has been used to include both men and women. This is a shame since many of the most successful producers, development executives and writers are in fact women.

A big thank you has to go to the universities that I have worked for over the last few years. At the time of writing the university system in England has had research funding and student funding cut massively by central government, and to compensate for this the universities have been obliged to charge fees directly to students at higher levels than before. In all the media coverage it seems to have been overlooked that as well as teaching students universities provide time and space for critical reflection, and are permanently funding research and book writing by paying the salaries of their academic staff and supporting their work with research grants. Therefore I would like to thank the University of East Anglia for my post as Senior Lecturer in Creativity; for my annual personal research grant (thanks to David Peters-Corbett and John Charmley); and for the supplementary research fund of the School of Film and TV Studies (thanks to Brett Mills, Keith Johnston and Su Holmes). Without that support this book would never have been written. The same is true of the majority of academic books, and also quite a few novels and books of poetry (like those written by my colleagues who are teaching Creative Writing at UEA). So next time the politicians of any party are threatening to cut funding for humanities education and research, please don't forget the much wider impact that our universities have on our cultural and intellectual life.

I would like to thank all of the interviewees cited in the bibliography, and I would also like to thank the people who have supported my work over the years, or advised me on writing this book, especially Nik Powell, Stephen Jukes, Rebecca O'Brien, Angus Finney, Jon Cook, Sarah Golding, Mark Jancovich, Chris Brady, Ivan Mactaggart, Guy Undrill, Michael Lengsfield, Patrick McGrady, Norman Lancaster, Val Taylor and Giles Foden.

Many thanks to Aileen Storry and all her team at Routledge for her strong vision, editorial judgement, patience and unwavering faith. Thanks also to my parents, who were always there for me but let me find my own way over the years. And above all, thanks to Jane Greenwood, for her love and endless support, for her help on the manuscript, and for putting up with me for so long.

Peter Bloore
29 February 2012
Wingfield, Suffolk

Introduction

A world of stories and money

'You'll never guess what happened on the train this morning ...'

'I had this really weird dream last night ...'

'Did you hear what's happened to John?'

Every day we tell each other stories. Sometimes we are reporting what's happened, and sometimes we are making it up. It happens all over the world, in every culture and in every race. We instinctively understand the process of storytelling: the set-up, the buildup, and the pay-off. And if the story goes down well, or it gets a laugh, then we repeat it and perhaps embellish it to get a better laugh, or a cry of surprise.

When we are not telling stories we are consuming them: from the morning newspaper to the book at bedtime, from the novel on the train to the film in the cinema. At home and in the workplace we repeat stories of what has happened in the past, and those stories reinforce the way we behave and what we expect from those around us. It could be said that shared experience, repeated through storytelling or symbolized through images, is at the heart of the development of culture: both national culture and organizational culture. Stories are really the bedrock of our identities, and as social creatures we endlessly use them to try to make sense of our experiences and our place in the world.

Imagine listening to an amazing story being told in a cavernous darkened room, flickering with light, and surrounded by lots of fellow human beings all enraptured by the unfolding of the story. Everyone wants to know what happens next, even if they have heard the story a hundred times before. Is it a painted cave in Lascaux in south-western France, forty millennia ago; or is it a blind storyteller speaking in a Mediterranean hall-palace in the eighth century BC; or is it a busy multiplex cinema on a Friday night? In a way there is no difference – it is all storytelling and all trying to make some kind of sense of our existence. Film may be an internationally popular form of entertainment, worth billions of dollars annually,[1] but at heart it is still a form of storytelling using performance, moving pictures, language and music.

But storytelling is not a one-way process: a single moment of 'telling'. It is an interaction between a narrator and an audience, because above all we *respond* to stories. That is what makes them so exciting and so engaging. Part of the story lives in our minds and in our own emotional experience of it. There is a proven neurological basis for this. In the late 1980s scientists at the University of Parma were studying the frontal lobes of the brains of macaque monkeys, and in particular the neurons which are responsible for hand and mouth actions. They discovered that some motor neurones would activate when the monkeys picked up food, but that other motor neurones would also respond when they saw *another* monkey picking up food. They called these *mirror neurons* because they are responding to (or mirroring) an outside action.[2] They also seem to activate when the monkeys hear things, as well as when they see them. Using functional MRI brain scans this research has been repeated in other studies of monkeys, and crucially in the human brain as well.

This has profound ramifications for our understanding of humanity, because if we experience other people's actions and experiences neurologically, just by watching them happen, then these same mirror neurons may be partly responsible for empathy, the ability to respond emotionally to other people's feelings and experiences. And from empathy flows compassion, guilt, anger at injustice, altruism, and potentially all moral behaviour.[3] As the discoverer of mirror neurons, Professor Giacomo Rizzolatti, explains:

> It would seem therefore that the mirror neurone system is indispensable to that sharing of experience which is at the root of our capacity to act as individuals but also as members of society. … Moreover our capacity to appreciate the emotional reactions of others is correlated to a particular group of areas that are characterized by mirror properties. Emotions, like actions, are immediately shared; the perception of pain or grief, or disgust experienced by others, activate the same areas of the cerebral cortex that are involved when we experience these emotions ourselves.[4]

These recent discoveries seem to support the thinking of the twentieth-century French philosopher and literary critic René Girard,[5] and even further back the eighteenth-century Scottish philosopher David Hume, who wrote: 'No quality of human nature is more remarkable, both in itself and in its consequences, than that propensity we have to sympathise with others.'[6]

These mirror neurons don't just make us human. They mean that our brains are hardwired to respond to stories about other people, and emotionally to mimic what we see. This underlying principle was recognized as far back as ancient Greece and Aristotle's Poetics, where he discusses the importance of *mimesis* – a term that has been interpreted to mean representation, imitation, receptivity and self-expression, and the origin of our word 'mimicry'. The reason stories touch us is because they make the audience identify with the events and the characters, empathizing with them by responding to the mimesis of dramatic role-play.

Significantly, mirror neurons are triggering a non-linguistic emotional response, and film is primarily a visual and experiential medium, using pictures and sound to create another world. Even more than the theatre that Aristotle was writing about, cinema is speaking directly to those mirror neurons in our brains, manipulating our empathy and drawing us into experiencing a different emotional world, outside our normal lives. This may explain the cathartic power of film storytelling and its ability to engage spectacularly with audiences all over the world, regardless of cultural boundaries.[7] As the film director Alexander Mackendrick eloquently put it:

> Cinema deals with feelings, sensations, intuitions, and movement, things that communicate to audiences at a level not necessarily subject to conscious, rational and critical comprehension. Because of this the so-called 'language' the film director uses may, in fact, make for a richer and denser experience. Actions and images speak faster, and to more of the senses, than speech does ... cinema is not so much non-verbal as *pre*-verbal.[8]

Compared to film, no other art form costs so much, encompasses so much risk and unpredictability, and is enjoyed by such a large and international audience. And yet film is really just selling an experience, and the audience takes away only the *memory* of the experience, rather than ownership of the product (the DVD comes later, as an opportunity to *re*-experience). And that experience rests in our minds and in the responses of our mirror neurons.[9]

The storyteller and the businessman

For centuries storytellers were able to invent and deliver stories as they wished, with perhaps a bit of influence from their patrons, or motivated by the simple desire to please their listeners. But a new dynamic emerged with the development of professional theatre, first in ancient Greece and later reinvented in Elizabethan England, that of a group of performers developing a corpus of new work and competing against other companies (in Greece for a prize, and in London for income from the ticket-buying audience). To help win that competition they used spectacle (scenery, props, costumes and music) to help build the immersive and mimetic emotional experience. In fact, the latest special effects proved to be the downfall of Shakespeare's Globe Theatre. It burnt down on 29 June 1613 when a theatrical cannon fired during a battle sequence in the play *Henry VIII* set fire to the thatched roof.

So why was this such a big change for storytelling? The answer is that theatrical spectacle needed money, invested upfront to pay for the props, costumes, special effects and sets. And that was on top of paying the writer for the script and the acting talent for their performance. 'The play's the thing', perhaps, but it required a very risky level of investment. The audience had not yet seen the new play, so the investors would not know whether it was going to be a success, until it was performed on the first night. To help counter that risk Shakespeare and his company repeated their back catalogue of successes, adapted other people's stories, resuscitated characters like Falstaff, designed plays around popular actors, and even produced sequels to Shakespeare's more successful plays ... exactly the same tactics used by the Hollywood studios for the last century. And Shakespeare's business acumen did not end there. Nowadays, as well as a writer credit he would also get an executive producer credit, because he was a co-owner of the Globe Theatre and one of the shareholders of the Lord Chamberlain's Men theatre company (which had the right to perform his plays; an early example of intellectual property rights based on exclusivity, to try to defeat the opposition).

The theatre world of Shakespeare highlights the origin of the modern commodification of performance-based storytelling, and marks the start of the tense dynamic between theatrical creativity and commerce, artistic risk and financial risk. Behind the creative and mimetic interaction between the storyteller and his audience (with all those invisibly firing mirror neurons) is the inevitable business relationship between the storyteller and his financier: the money that makes the storytelling possible. Eventually the Romantic movement of the early eighteenth century intensified that debate with the growth of the cult of the heroic artist's personal vision, and the perceived importance of creative freedom from commercial and societal restrictions.[10]

And that conflict is what this book is really all about. How *do* modern film scripts get written, and what are the tensions between the creative and the money? Or is the process so symbiotic that it becomes ultimately impossible to separate them? And then there is the problem of people. Film-making is widely known to be a very collaborative process, but it also involves a huge number of specializations. A film can get stronger as more people contribute and bring their own strengths to it, but it can also get more diluted and confused, so at the heart of development and film-making is the thorny question of when do you agree to compromise on your vision to 'get the film made'? And when precisely does collaboration become compromise?

The aims of this book

This book is *intended* to be thought-provoking, and even radical. Instead of only looking at film books and practitioner interviews, it also steals ideas from creativity theories, psychology, motivation, value chain models, and

MBA business and leadership theories. It is, after all, a book about creativity, and that sometimes involves wandering off and looking in unusual places for weird stuff, and seeing what works. Some of these business ideas have too rarely been brought into the film and media sectors. Some of the ideas might not work for everyone in the film industry, or work only in part, but hopefully some of them at least will make people think harder about what they do and how they could encourage creativity at work. In a way, it can be treated like a crash course MBA in film business and script development, aimed at sparking ideas and deeper reflection.

The book proposes some generalized typologies and frameworks about how the industry works, which will hopefully cause debate, disagreement, and over time the development of better frameworks. Without typologies it is hard to teach people about the sector, and harder still for people in the sector to analyse and understand their workplace. They will not be perfect but hopefully they will be the start of a process, in the same way that a treatment is the start of a process to a completed film.

The main part of each chapter explains ideas and concepts gleaned from interviews and experience, often incorporating analysis and theories from other fields. At the end of each chapter is a box or two, containing *case interviews* – an interview or excerpts from several interviews providing insights into a key theme raised by that chapter or by the wider research. The aim is to create a good balance between strong rational narrative and more discursive anecdotal reality. Due to lack of space one or two voices have been chosen for each chapter, but they usually reflect the views of other interviewees as well.

The book aims to avoid long case studies explaining what happened on an individual film, in part because other books have already done this, and in part because every film is so different that it is often difficult to draw out general lessons from individual anecdotes.

Two final disclaimers. First, this is *not* a book about Hollywood. It will concentrate on the independent film marketplace, emphasizing Britain and Europe (perhaps future research could widen this to include other regions, especially Asia). The Hollywood system has already been widely studied and written about, and most films funded in the UK are developed for the independent marketplace rather than studio production. The Hollywood Studios operate a very different business model (as Chapter 2 explains, they are vertically integrated businesses funding production to supply the permanent distribution machine), and Hollywood development is more dominated by the talent management system and the power of certain key agents and their clients. The differences between the independent film business and the studio model are thoroughly explored in several chapters (especially chapters 2 and 12), but the overall emphasis of this book will be to understand independent films and their marketplace.

Second, this book is *not* going to tell you what a good story is, or how to write it. This book *is* going to tell you how to identify and work with the right people, how to access funding and build a sustainable business in development, and how to escape development hell. Or at least make it less like hell and more like an enjoyable creative and professional experience.

This is a book about people and collaboration, creativity and commerce, big ideas and massive egos, and above all the long and very risky game of script development.

Let the story begin …

Part I

The complex world of film development

Part I of the book deals with the film business, how films are financed, and how this affects development and creativity. It looks at the people who work in development; the creative triangle of the writer, producer and director; and the pressures that the development process and commerce will exert on their relationship. It also looks at how the development executive and script editor fit into the process.

Part II looks more at business theories about managing creative people and teams, and considers how they might be applied to the film industry. What is the best way to manage the development process to create a film that is both successful and creatively satisfying? And how can producers and their development executives build profitable and sustainable businesses, based on strong relationships with creative talent? Taken as a whole the book tries to answer the question:

How can the creative team of the writer, producer, director and development executive work together most effectively?

1   The bigger picture
How films are developed

I have just spent three months negotiating one writer's agreement, where not a word has been written on the script. By the time we lawyers have finished I sometimes wonder if they will still want to work together.

(Anonymized media lawyer)

What is film script development?

Tell me the story so far …

These are the words that Alfred Hitchcock used to say every day to screenwriter Evan Hunter as they sat down to work on their adaptation of Daphne du Maurier's short story *The Birds*.[1] So, what *is* the story so far? This chapter will provide an introduction to the process and business of screenplay development. Subsequent chapters will then analyse the wider business of film finance and distribution, before returning to development in more detail.

The development of a film script is a long and complex process, beginning with the initial story concept and continuing through drafting and financing, hopefully to the start of the shoot. Initially, it is often creatively driven by the writer, but it is a team effort and is managed by a producer or development executive. No professional script is developed in a vacuum and the context is money: to pay for the writing of the script and the production of the film. And yet the best ways of understanding and managing this important development process have until now not been properly researched and studied. First, here is a working definition of independent film development:

Screenplay development is the creative and industrial collaborative process in which a story idea (either an original idea or an adaptation of an existing idea, such as a play, novel, or real life event) is turned into a script; and is then repeatedly rewritten to reach a stage when it is attractive to a suitable director, actors and relevant film production funders; so that enough money can be raised to get the film made.[2]

The reason that the definition refers to development being an *industrial* process is that it requires interaction with the film industry, with an eye to the eventual market. Film is one of the most expensive art forms, and that requires investment. The development process requires payment for acquisition of the rights to the story and payments to the writer for his work. Production then requires further massive investment; and without it there is no product or art form, since an unproduced screenplay has virtually no inherent value.

Aristotle argued that a play does not need to be performed to have impact on an audience, because it can still be read as a text; however, with film the visualization of the text by the director is considered vital. A film is *made*, not written. That process of making involves the screenwriter dreaming it up, the producer raising the funding, the actors playing their parts, the director calling the shots, the film editor reassembling it, and the distributors and cinemas marketing it and getting it out there to the audience. This industrial collaboration of different creative and commercial agendas is one of the many things that makes the film business so fascinating and complex. But the value chain does not end there, because films are also dependent on reception for their reputational value, including critical reaction and audience response (through box office figures and DVD sales). The problem with development is that the producer is trying to predict what the audience may choose to watch and enjoy in several years' time; and yet like many cultural industries that audience's eventual choices are predicated on a complex and conflicting mixture of motivations – including subjective personal taste, response to marketing influence, trends that are current at the time, peer influence, and even a sense of differentiation of the self from others.

To go back to the definition, the inclusion of the word *relevant* before production funders is important because different types of funders want different things from a film project: for example the arthouse specialist production funders want a certain type of script, supported by certain directors and actors; whereas mainstream production funders want other types of script and other actors attached. An actor with huge value in the specialist marketplace may have no impact at all in the blockbuster mainstream marketplace. Crucially, if there is a mismatch between the project, the talent attachments and the size of the budget, then it can prevent the film making it into production, as shown in Chapter 3. Therefore the producers and development executives should have the finance sources and the market for the films very much in their minds during development. It helps for the professional writer also to be aware of this context, and how his collaborators are thinking. Whilst the industrial context should not be allowed to stifle creativity, it pays to be aware that the vision of the script will *only* be realized through this market. It also helps for the student of film to be fully aware of these tensions, and to understand that no completed film has been made without influence from them during the process.

Strictly speaking development *can* be done by a single writer working entirely on his own, but since it is an industrial process it is usually *a collaborative team activity* (involving maybe more than one writer and incorporating the feedback of a script editor, director and other stakeholders), and managed by a producer (and possibly a development executive) who is responsible for the money-raising element. Good development involves open constructive feedback to make the story stronger and the characters more compelling. It shouldn't be about producers and executives telling writers what is wrong or how to fix it – it should be a collaborative journey to make the story as good as it can possibly be, through rewrites and polishes and detailed discussions. In practice it can often end up confrontational, destructive and divisive, but that is where the skill of an experienced and skilful producer and executive comes in – to try to keep it on the rails. This journey is one of the key themes of this book.

The idea and the option

The idea for the story sometimes comes from the writer, but just as often it comes from the producer. It is either an original idea, or based on an *underlying source* like a stage play or novel or real-life story, which has caught the producer's or development executive's attention. Around 50 per cent of projects developed in Hollywood are based on adaptations.[3] In interviews for this book Film4 executives estimated that in the UK it is closer to 40 per cent, and BBC executives suggested their current slate was about 40–50 per cent adaptations.[4]

The producer then either buys the film rights to the story idea (or underlying source material), or else he buys an *option* of the rights. An option is a smaller amount of money, paid up front or in instalments, in return for the exclusive right to develop the project into a screenplay for a set period of time; with an agreement to pay a much larger fee for the acquisition of all film-related rights on the first day of principal photography of the film. The producer does not yet own the rights, but he has an option over them which means that the writer cannot allow anyone else to develop the project. The option often requires renewal payments every year or every eighteen months to keep the rights holder happy, and sometimes these renewals may get more expensive or be contingent on other targets being passed. This all depends on the deal negotiated by the writer's agents, powerful gatekeepers/intermediaries who defend the writer's interests. Having obtained the rights or a window on those rights the producer then employs a screenwriter to transform them into a treatment and then a screenplay.

This means that the screenwriter often does not hold the rights (or the option) to the story that he is working on – the producer does. And if the screenwriter *has* come up with the original idea then the producer will ask him to assign or option the rights of the idea to the producer, as protection that the writer will not then go and work with a different producer on the project. But here is the catch-22: if the project idea is owned by the producer or production company or studio, and not by the writer, then the producer usually has the power to replace the writer if they so wish. Here lies the inherent insecurity of the writer – in order to get a film through development (and get paid themselves), and then financed for production by the producer, they have to give away their rights to the project and potentially their creative ownership of its future direction. In short, to get paid they have to accept losing control. This is why a fruitful and trusting relationship between the writer and producer is so vital. To try and avoid this catch-22 some writers will develop a screenplay without payment (known as a *speculative* or *spec. script*) and sell it only when they think it is strong enough for them to get better deal terms and resist losing as much control to the producer (maybe even gaining themselves an executive producer credit).

The advantages to developing a script based on an adaptation is that the overall tone, structure and ending of the story are probably apparent from the outset, and the producer and development funder have a clear idea of what they are going to get at the end of the process. If the book or play has been very successful there may even be a loyal fanbase that could be expected to pay to see the film (as long as the film is sufficiently faithful to the fans' vision of the original). A novel also gives actors more to read about their characters and their motivations, and this may help convince them to commit to the project (a screenplay often has to leave various subtexts and motivations unsaid because it can only describe what is shown, whereas a novel can often describe the interior life of a character). All of this makes it easier for the producer to raise development funding on an adaptation. But the two substantial downsides are that, first, the producer is paying for the option as well as the work of the screenwriter on the adaptation, so his costs are higher; and that, second, there is a time limit on the process and if the option *does* expire before the film is made then the producer is left with nothing in return for his investment because he does not own the underlying story.

Another possibility for the agent representing the novel or play is not to go for an option at all, but demand a full assignment of rights in return for a much larger amount of money (with a turnaround opportunity for the writer to get the rights back after a specified number of years). Another deal point for writers with a successful underlying work is to demand that the title of the film adaptation must match the title of the book, to facilitate cross-selling of the book when the film comes out (the reason producers sometimes resist this is because they want the ability to change the title if required for marketing purposes).

Intellectual property and the labyrinth of rights

There are other existing books on contracts and *intellectual property* (IP) in film and the media,[5] so it is enough at this stage to say that licensing content is highly complicated and becoming more so, as a result of the current fragmentation of markets and the proliferation of media platforms. A completed film's value is optimized by exploiting the different factors of time (different exploitation windows offer the chance to see it immediately for a premium or after a delay); repeat consumption (via different platforms, such as cinema followed by DVD); exclusivity (only available at the moment on one platform); and differential pricing.[6] As shown in Fig. 1.1, the film that is being exploited in these multiple ways can then also have multiple rights holders, only one of which is the writer (others include financiers, producers and distribution licence holders).[7]

Agents acting for the writer have to try and predict what these future rights might be worth, and negotiate a commensurate fee for the writer and share in future revenue, and this is all before the screenplay has even been written (the potential value of DVD and online consumption of movies and TV was at the heart of the strike by the Writers Guild of America in 2007–2008). The agent's legitimate need to protect the writer's interests results in potential problems for the producer in the early stages of development: first, the producer's lawyer's fees; second, the time spent negotiating terms

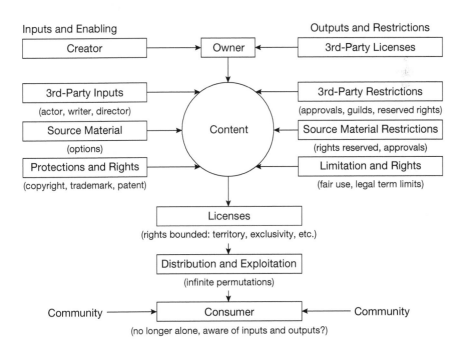

Figure 1.1 Licensing content is complicated (Ulin 2010)[8]

with the writer's agent; third, the cost of the option or assignment fee; and finally, a badly handled option negotiation process can damage the emerging relationship and trust between the writer and producer. Therefore producers with an existing long-term relationship with a writer sometimes try to get at least the basic treatment informally worked out before negotiating a formal option with the agent; otherwise a lot of time and money could be lost before they even know if they have an idea worth running with.

The backstory: screenwriters in Hollywood and Europe

Historically, the weakness of the position of writers goes back to the fact that they came late to the world of film, and have suffered from a lack of status ever since, especially in Hollywood. The movies started life as a silent fairground attraction where spectacle was the key and writers were superfluous, as the ethnographer Hortense Powdermaker explains:

> The high point of these early movies was a train moving through space, a fire engine dashing down the street, or people running down a road. When they lengthened to four or five reels, writers began to trickle into the industry. They assisted the director in getting a story and wrote titles to accompany the action. The 'talkies' obviously made writers more necessary. Today they are an accepted part of the production of every picture, from low-budget Western to the high-budget A film. They came, however, into a medium in which the essentials were still movement and action and their main job was the creation of plots. Characters were secondary and important primarily as mannikins to keep the plot moving.[9]

The literary tradition of Europe arrived in Hollywood with the wave of immigrants fleeing the Second World War, especially from Germany and Eastern Europe. This caused a temporary improvement in the status of the writer, boosted further in the 1950s by the decline of the studio system and the rise of the independent producer. Ironically, Europe was also responsible for the subsequent growth of the auteur tradition (where the director is seen as the author/auteur of the film, not the writer) which again sidelined the role of the writer and helped give rise to the writer-director role, which came to dominate European arthouse development. So power shifted from the producer to the director/writer-director, and then eventually back to the producer again, without ever settling in the hands of the writer. The 1970s to the 1990s saw the rise of a small number of powerful screenwriters in Hollywood, whose agents played the game of encouraging script bidding wars between producers and studios, but while fees and executive producer credits for a small number of players grew, the average screenwriter remained on the periphery of the business, especially in terms of power and influence. As a result, while screenwriters in Hollywood remain a key part of the business, they are always highly dependent on other people to finance, interpret and visualize their work; and in turn they may feel alienated, sidelined and frustrated, in part because of lack of control over their fortunes and creative lives.

In the UK and Europe film writers often come from a background in theatre or television, where the role of the writer is more highly valued. However, in film the director still gets the possessory credit, such as: 'a film by'. A writer accustomed to working in TV at a senior level, with higher status and more authorial control, can feel exploited and used by the film development process because of the cultural emphasis placed on financiers' notes and the director. There can also be a conflict when, having done a couple of drafts, the TV writer feels that they have done their work – they do not expect the endless rewrites that are in general more common in film than they are in television. As the BBC's Head of Film Christine Langan puts it:

> The writer may feel that they're doing a lot of the running, for the longest period of time, with notes coming from everywhere; and then when it comes to the crunch, they have the quietest voice in the mix. They don't actually get into the crucial moments in the edit, and they're somewhat dispensed with. ... I really remember people talking about the voice of the writer. No-one ever talks about the voice of the writer anymore. Very rarely.

However the writer does have clear power over the producer in two key ways. First, the producer always requires a new screenplay to take into the financing marketplace, so without the writer they have nothing (as shown in Box 1.1). This is why building long-term relationships with writers (and directors) is vital to being a successful independent producer. Second, the producer's option is usually only for a limited amount of time, and if the underlying idea belongs to the writer then the rights will eventually revert back, so that he can try to take it to a different producer (although the catch-22 returns and he will have to sign his rights away again to get the new producer to take it on). Therefore the writer's power rises every time a contingent option renewal comes around.

Box 1.1 Going fishing: a simple overview of film finance

The writer creates the screenplay (the hook),
but the hook needs a bait (the director).
The hook and the bait catch the fish (the actors),
and with the fish you can make dinner (a financed movie),
and not starve (at least not this year).

But without that first hook the producer has nothing ...

Note: with specialist arthouse film-making the director (the bait) is perhaps more important than the need for name actors in the package, but the general principle still holds.

So what are the key stages of work for the writer, after the initial commission? The writer creates an *outline* of about eight to ten pages, which is part of the development process and is usually not shown outside the company; and then a detailed *treatment* (a.k.a. a *step outline* or *scriptment* or *scene breakdown*) of possibly forty to sixty pages. Note that there is eventually a *synopsis*, which is usually written *after* the script is completed and used for pitching purposes, but confusingly this is also sometimes called a treatment. During the course of interviews for this book some producers and writers said that too little time is spent on the treatment, and the writer moves on to the first draft too quickly. They recommended spending longer at the treatment stage and working closely together on it, to ensure a shared coherent vision of the story and the type of film they are making together (see the case interview with agent Julian Friedmann in Chapter 14).

The completed first draft is delivered by the writer to the producer and development executive and they give their feedback notes so that the writer can move on to the next draft. This process of redrafting and polishing can continue for years, with feedback also coming in from financiers and attached talent (directors and actors); and sometimes with new writers being brought in, either to replace the first writer or to do credited or uncredited dialogue polishes. A project which spends too long in this process can end up being *over-developed* – subject to so many different opinions and notes that it loses its focus, direction and individuality – or it can lose all momentum as financiers' executives change and leave the project in limbo – a situation known in the business as *development hell.* Some projects get dropped completely, in which case they are known as *shelved* or *on the shelf;* however, some projects still come back into development from here, especially if the writer becomes successful on another film. Chapter 5 examines these development stages in detail, and analyses the power relationships between all the players involved.

The problem with screenplays: a literary blueprint for a visual art

Film and TV dramas are narrative forms using *external* representations (like dialogue, expression and action) to represent internal emotional life. Subtexts are used to reveal discrepancies between the external behaviour and conscious or unconscious inner life and motivation. By contrast, many novels and poems in the last century have become less concerned with narrative and more concerned with representing *internal* life and feeling (for example, using literary techniques such as stream of consciousness or unreliable narrators. This trend in the novel is perhaps no coincidence, as the emergence of film and television as the predominant narrative mediums has freed novels from having to be narrative forms. In the same way art became more abstract and experimental after the development of photography, because representation had become less important than message and vision).

The screenplay may be describing those external representations of the film story, but the writer still has to think through the internal life of characters in order to represent the external in a way that illuminates the internal. In the completed film the actor's performances and the director's *mise-en-scène* can draw the audience's attention to subtextual meanings; but it is sometimes harder for the screenplay writer to represent subtexts without the clumsy use of dialogue parenthesis or explicit stage directions.

At the heart of screenplay development is the strange disjunction that the writer is creating a literary artefact, which is judged partially in literary terms (an evocative and spell-binding page-turner has a good chance of getting made) but is then a blueprint for a visual work of art. The dialogue will make it to the screen, but the prose style and dramatic description will not. It will then be read by financiers who will use it to judge whether to invest a large amount of money in the visual work. Furthermore, many development executives come with university degrees in literature, and are trained to deal with words, not images.

Like watching film, reading is an experiential activity in which the mind is emotionally interpreting the material, but the trap is that some screenplays that read well may not always end up as good films. It is like employing a painter for the ceiling of the Sistine Chapel on the basis of a written description of which subjects are going to be included. This is why the track record of the attached director is so important, because it gives the financier a clue as to what it will *look* like. In much the same way, Pope Julius II commissioned Michelangelo to paint the Sistine Chapel on his reputation and past work (in fact, the artist then completely rewrote the commission, which started as just the figures of twelve apostles against a starry sky). And yet, and here is the crux of the problem, most screenplays are written and developed *without* the eventual director attached, so the financier is reading a literary blueprint written by someone who is not going to carry out the job. That is why it is important for the producer to attach the director as early as possible in the development process (and why writer-directors get a lot of work); and why the creative triangle of director, writer and producer is so important. The visual style that the director has used in the past helps the financier to interpret what the film may look like in the future. As we have seen, this is another reason why adaptations of novels are so popular: the detailed emotional and visual descriptions of the novel give the financiers and acting talent a clearer idea of what the film may look and feel like than the hundred-page screenplay (which is often predominantly dialogue).

After all the screenwriter's creative efforts, and many months slaving over a hot computer, the screenplay is ultimately just a selling document for other people: the director and producer. Perhaps that is why many screenwriters hold a grudge about feeling like jobbing hacks rather than artists. So now it is time to look at the scriptwriter's patron and champion: the entrepreneur that is the producer.

The creative producer and development

The film producer does not usually invest his own money in film production – he or she has to go out and raise money for the script from the marketplace. In the case of a producer with a studio deal he has to persuade the studio's executives to invest in it, and in the case of an independent producer he has to persuade a variety of third parties to invest in it: often a mixture of broadcasters, equity investors, banks, and different international distributors (buying or pre-buying films for their own country's territories).

In many languages the verbs 'to produce' and 'to create' are similar, and from the beginning of the film industry the role of producer has involved both financial and creative work. However, there is a distinction between those producers who *mainly* want to deal with the financial deal-making aspect of the job (who sometimes have the title executive producers) and those who also like to be *very* involved in creative decisions throughout development, casting, filming and editing. The latter sometimes refer to themselves as being *creative producers*, and might be more intrinsically film-motivated than business-motivated. They may be more likely to initiate script ideas and then find the right writer and director, as David Puttnam did on *Chariots of Fire, Local Hero* and *The Killing Fields*.[10] Most producers are somewhere on a continuum between these two positions.

Alejandro's Pardo's 2010 paper *The Film Producer as a Creative Force* does a great job of discussing the creative contribution of film producers over the years, including the rise in academic and industry appreciation of the role of the creative producer in the 1990s. The auteur theory of the French magazine *Cahiers du Cinema* argued in the 1950s that the artistic authorship of the film belonged to the director, and as a result for many years sidelined academic recognition of the creative roles of the writer and producer. However, many of the great producers have had an over-reaching vision and influence that is visible throughout their films, regardless of the director at the helm, and Pardo explains:

> At times, however, it happens that the question of whom the dominant creative vision belongs to becomes a little blurry, especially in the case of those directors and producers who possess genuine creative talent and a marked personality. Proof of this is the appearance of the category of *producer-director* used for defining both directors (Capra, Wilder, Hitchcock, Preminger, Pollack, Spielberg or Eastwood) and producers (Selznick, Kramer or Lucas), whose common characteristic centres on their role as the principal authors of their films, beyond the specific work of direction or production that they have fulfilled.[11]

Actually, very few producers would say that they are not creative producers and most financial producers would argue that they *are* creatively involved, but it is a question of degree and involvement with the writer and director during development.

Sometimes producers employ a *development executive*. They work with the producer to source and develop a slate of several script projects, including researching and helping to attach writers and directors, and providing creative advice to the producer and writer on the different drafts of the screenplay. This may include advice on composition, story structure and character development (there is a full analysis of the roles of the development executive and script editor in Chapter 6). How much autonomy and control the development executive has over the development and management of projects on the slate varies massively from producer to producer.

But not all producers employ development executives. In the UK the creative producer could be said to divide into two development types: the *sole creative producer* and the *creative team producer*. The sole creative producer does *not* usually use a development executive to manage the writers, but instead wants to be very hands-on in all the discussions with the writer from the start of development onwards. There may be an assistant, who may do some script reading and general administrative tasks, but the choice of projects and the supervision of the writer rests with the producer. As a result the sole creative producer does not develop large slates of projects, but concentrates on a small number (maybe two or three active at any one time), because otherwise there would not be the time to work closely with the writers. This is the model of a constant dialogue and discussion between the producer and the writer at all stages of drafting, rather than the formal process of the writer delivering a draft and then receiving notes from the producer before rewriting. On some projects the producer may employ a freelance script editor for a few weeks to provide creative advice on the script's development, but it is unusual for them to stay on board the project for long. This kind of producer works regularly with the same teams of writers and directors, but it is not really a scaleable business in that it cannot be built up or sold on, and the producer may find it hard to attract investor funding into the company or a slate. However, by keeping overheads and general outgoings low, and not employing a regular head of development, they can be in production every few years and still make a good living, especially by occasionally working with other larger companies, such as Working Title. UK examples include Andy Paterson, Sarah Radclyffe, Gareth Unwin, Colin Vaines and Damian Jones.

By contrast, the creative team producer *does* employ a development executive, and that executive has more autonomy over sourcing and developing projects. There is a bigger slate of active projects, perhaps six to eight, and a number of further relationships with creative writers and directors are being regularly maintained in the hope that a suitable project for the company will eventually emerge. There will probably also be an assistant and maybe a work experience runner. However, the producer is still very creatively involved, and will often be in script meetings with the writer and the development executive. UK examples include David Heyman (Heyday Films), David Thompson (Origin Pictures), Duncan Kenworthy (Toledo Productions), Andrew Macdonald (DNA Films), Barnaby Thompson (Ealing Studios), Christian Colson (Cloud Eight), Mark Herbert (Warp Films) and David Parfitt (Trademark Films). Some production companies will also develop projects for both television drama and film, such as Nira Park's Big Talk, Andy Harries' Left Bank Pictures, Douglas Rae's Ecosse Films and Stephen Garrett's Kudos Pictures. The income and turnover of TV development and production help support the film development activity. Furthermore, some producers are linked to a distribution company that can release the film in its home territory, either through ownership or an output deal (more on this in Chapter 2).

After a big success some producers choose to move from working as *sole creative producer* to *creative team producer* as and when they can afford a larger slate of projects and the staff salaries, but others choose to remain small and 'hands-on'. Problems sometimes emerge when the sole producer tries to grow the business and employs a development executive but does not give them sufficient autonomy to operate, preferring to remain very 'hands-on' (this can be frustrating and confusing for the development executive and for writers with projects on the slate).

Sometimes there are two producers working with one development executive, so that between them there is more chance of getting one film made a year (necessary to help cover the extra outgoings of the development executive and the office). They may work together on some films or on their own for other films. Examples of two producers working closely together include Alison Owen and Paul Trijbits at Ruby Films; Rebekah Gilbertson and Nicole Carmen-Davis at Rainy Day Films; Kate Ogborn and Lisa Marie Russo at Fly Films; and Gail Egan and Andrea Calderwood at Potboiler Productions/Slate Films. Due to the extra capacity and support structure, this size of company sometimes finds it easier than the sole creative producer to attract slate development funding from European or national subsidy funds, or from private investors.

The role of executive and associate producers in development

Executive or associate producers are not usually very involved in script development and writers' meetings, unless they are also part of a studio or broadcaster. There are four broad types of executive or associate producer.

First, there are the executive producers whose main role is to raise funding *after* the script is highly developed. They may give their own script notes, but do not usually have a development executive. They are sometimes freelance or separate from the company, and sometimes paid a *finder's fee* if they bring production funds to the film.

Second, there are those executive producers who are 'friends' of the project and whose attachment helps attract finance or needs rewarding by a formal credit (for example, powerful source writers, key cast, managers, etc.). In the US this can sometimes include spouses and close friends of the producer or director. Again they come on board when the project is already well developed, and they will not usually employ development executives.

Third, there are those producers who are employees of broadcasters, studios, public funds or private tax-finance-driven funds who demand a producer credit (or executive or associate producer credits) on films their organizations support. They are not independent producers, first because they are salaried employees (therefore not independent), second because they are greenlighting funds with their organization's own money rather than raising it from third parties, and finally because they are working with other producers who are the main producers responsible for identifying and developing the projects from their earliest stages and are primarily in charge of delivering them. These *employee executive producers* are often working with a development executive (who may be bringing projects to the company), and sometimes quite a large number of other employees including in-house lawyers and accountants. Their script notes carry a lot of influence in the final drafts and the run-up to production, because their approval may lead to budget finance.

Finally, a small number of powerful screenwriters and actors in Hollywood have agents who are able to negotiate them an executive producer credit, both for prestige and a chance of extra recoupment and influence (in 2002 over two-thirds of screenwriters nominated for Oscars also had producer credits).[12]

Co-producers, strictly speaking, refer to a producer from another country who is helping to co-finance or co-produce the film as a result of some location filming or use of talent in that country. They sometimes give script notes, but other times make a purely financial contribution and come on board relatively late. However, the proliferation of people wanting a producer credit means that sometimes co-producers are just executive producers under another name (because there are already too many executive producers with that title).

Line producers are responsible for the shooting and production management of the film and are not usually involved in development because they are usually brought on board during pre-production.

There is also a distinction between the totally independent producer and the producer who has an *output deal* or *first look deal* at a studio, something that will be covered in Chapter 12.

The reason for going into these different roles in detail is that we can see that different projects may go through different types of producer and receive different levels of creative engagement from the producer and development executive.

Introducing development funding: the numbers and the risk

Having acquired the rights or an option over the screenplay, the producer then needs to cover the development costs, either by investing his own money or by raising money from others. The writer tends to get paid a proportion of their fee upon signature of contract, more on delivery of treatments and first and subsequent drafts (if the writer is not replaced), and the balance on first day of principal photography (this is the majority of their fee). Development funding for the producer needs to cover these writer's payments, the costs of paying any underlying option agreement, fees for script editors and other consultants, travel, entertainment (vital in a relationship-based business) and legal costs. As the project gets closer to production there may be fees for casting directors, location managers, director's recces, budgets and schedules. Of course in real life the producer also has to pay the rent, business overheads, and try to keep the company and himself going. Plus the producer attends development meetings, gives script notes, and works on financing the film budget. Many development sources in the UK are reluctant to pay for the producer's time and overheads; however, the US studio system does (an independent producer without a first look deal may expect to get between $25,000 and $40,000 for a development fee).[13]

Another funding option for a producer with a good track record is to try to get a first look deal with a distributor, studio or broadcaster. In return for development funding and some overhead costs the producer guarantees to give the financier a first look at any projects he is developing, before he shows them to other finance sources (plus another look if the package changes after they have passed first time). These deals are more common in the US (although some European mini-studios now use them too); there is more on studio first look deals in Chapter 12.

So how *much* money is invested in development, and for how long? Usually the more expensive the prospective film the higher the development budget, to reflect the higher expertise of the attached producer, writer and director. Estimates suggest that the average European film with a budget of £1.75m–£3.5m costs about £44,000–£130,000 to develop, and larger films with a budget of £6m–£9m cost up to £260,000 to develop.[14] A film can be in development for anywhere between one and ten years, with the mean average duration being 3.4 years (regardless of whether the film is made).[15] In the US the film development process is more process-driven, professionalized and better paid, and this is reflected in a spend on development of 5–10 per cent of a film's total budget in the US, as opposed to just over 4 per cent of a film's budget in the UK.[16] Total investment in UK film screenplay development was recently estimated at £50m per year, covering 1,700 films in active development.[17] By contrast Hollywood invests a staggering thirteen times more money, at nearer £650m per year.[18]

Only 16–20 per cent of films developed in the UK and Europe reach production,[19] and in the US it is lower, at 10–20 per cent (nearer 5 per cent for the studios, because they have more projects in development).[20] But recoupment is handled differently in the US because the studios treat development as an overall annual fixed cost, and a portion of this is allocated to *each* film as an above-the-line budget cost, at about 8–10 per cent of the total budget.[21] Therefore the films that *do* get made pay for those that do *not*. Since the studios are integrated and are receiving income from distribution, this is achievable and even tax efficient (they are writing income against legitimate development costs). Independent UK producers cannot do this, partly because they are usually not distributors. They get paid on first day of principal photography and they cannot charge development costs on one film to another film's production budget because the film's financiers would understandably resent paying for the development of other failed scripts.

In short, if the individual project in development does not get made, the development investment does not get paid back. For example, assume there are five projects on a slate, each costing £50,000 to develop, resulting in a development budget of £250,000. Only one film gets made, and on first day of principal photography the costs get paid back (£50,000), along with an extra 50 per cent premium (£25,000), which is the usual deal (plus 5 per cent of producer's net profits after distribution, but, as Chapter 2 shows, the profits may not add up to much). So with £75,000 coming back to the company, the development slate is still £175,000 in the red. The producer would need to get four of the five projects made to recoup the cost of the development slate (and that is before any interest payable on the money). This is a far higher conversion rate than most producers have (*conversion* means converting a project from development into production). This is one reason that producers are reluctant to drop a project from the slate: if they do not produce it, they can never get back the money and time they invested in it. They may be able to charge some development costs against the tax payable on their production fee, but that may be only a minor benefit (and may apply to their company investment but not to third-party investors in development).

Therefore it is difficult for the independent producer to raise development funding from non-industry equity sources because it is very high risk; it cannot be recouped from other projects on the slate; it gets tied up for a long period of time; it is only repaid with only a small premium (profit) when the film shoots (too small for the level of risk involved); and the investor probably does not even get much of the profit share of the completed film (after distributors and other parties have taken out their costs and fees). It could be argued that more investors would put money into development if a greater share of the back-end profit from the film was guaranteed from the outset. Instead, development investment is potentially all spend and no income (the only real advantage is the potential tax write-off for some high-net-worth investors).

Furthermore, a private investor putting money into film production can guarantee that within the next year or so he will get to visit the film set, meet the actors, go to the film's premiere, and above all impress his friends at dinner parties by being able to drop into the conversation 'the film that I am producing'. So even if the film loses money, he has both reputational and personal benefit. However, the private investor putting money into development is not guaranteed any of the above. After many years it is perfectly possible that none of the films he is investing in will get made, so there is no reputational benefit, and a good chance of some leg-pulling from his more financially astute friends when he has to write the whole thing off. Rather than bragging about it at dinner parties, he may be more inclined to try and forget that it ever happened.

There are many reasons why projects can fail, or go into the limbo of development hell, not just the fact that the script doesn't quite creatively come together or that financiers don't like it enough. Sometimes the option over the underlying work expires; or the development funding dries up and the writer will not do any more unpaid drafts; sometimes the executive who loves it at a studio or other financier goes to a different job; sometimes a director or key actor leaves the package or loses their 'heat' and 'currency' in the market; sometimes a similar film goes into development or production elsewhere; sometimes the entire financing and economic landscape changes due to circumstances beyond the producer's control; and sometimes the moment for that particular film has simply passed because the tastes of the financiers or the public mood have changed. Many of these problems come down to timing – which may be beyond the producer's control.

Another problem can be that the cumulative development costs of a film can simply become too high for them to be recoupable on the production budget (for example, a project often accrues a previous producer's development budgets, especially if the option has lapsed and it has gone into turnaround. This means that it returns to the underlying writer, then is re-optioned to a new producer, but still has to repay some of those historical development costs, known as *turnaround fees*, when it goes into production). The cumulative development costs make it unviable and price the script out of the production-funding marketplace.

Given the multiplicity of reasons why films can fail to raise development funding or then fail to get made, it is perhaps unsurprising that a lot of development funding is from public sources with a cultural or public good remit rather than private investors or commercial organizations. There are just too many potential downsides to development.

Hurdles and gatekeepers

In most cases an agent is required to present the project in the first place, since most producers (and broadcasters) will not accept scripts that do not come through an agent (it is both legal protection for them and an additional filter to prevent them from being inundated with 'no-hope' projects). Therefore, for a new writer the first hurdle is getting an agent to represent them, although once found an agent can be invaluable in advising on the best producers to approach for that type of project.

The next hurdle for the writer is to get a producer interested: most development funders do not usually accept direct approaches from writers or their agents because they want to see a reputable producer already attached to the project (they feel that having a producer on board increases the chance of it getting into production and therefore the development investment being repaid). The final hurdle is the executives employed by the development financiers, who will make their subjective judgement on the quality of the idea, its likelihood of going into production, the track record of the producer and writer, and the match between the project and the brand of the financing organization. A detailed analysis of film types and their prospective development funders is given in Chapter 3.

This means that there are no less than three sets of gatekeepers for the writer between the script idea and getting paid: the first is the agent; the second is the producer who has to champion the script, plus his development executive and script readers (who produce summary reports and recommendations for successful producers before they read them); and the third is the development funder. And all this before the script itself gets written, as shown in Fig. 1.2.

Of course not all scripts actually get external development funding. Sometimes the script is commissioned by the producer without development finance from an outside source. Many development funders are also production funders, and a producer does not want to expose the idea to the production finance market too early (and possibly get rejected). Therefore, a producer will fund the first couple of drafts in-house if they can, especially if it is an original idea rather than an adaptation.

Alternatively, the writer can do all the work, without working with a producer and without being paid. *Spec. script* is short for a speculative script, and means that it is written without the commission of a studio, production company or broadcaster, either in the hope of selling it after the script is well developed or using it as a writing sample to demonstrate the writer's skills. (Note that if it is being developed as a writing sample then it should be crafted as such, targeted at the film genre the writer most wants to break into, and ideally suitable for TV jobs as well as film ones; for example, genres such as comedies, psychological thrillers and typical TV drama formats.) The advantage of the spec. script for the writer is that there are no collaborators or restrictions on what can be written; but the disadvantage is that he then has to try and interest and attach a producer, who has not been involved from the outset and may not feel sufficient ownership.

On some low- and ultra-low-budget projects there is no development funding and the writer ends up doing a lot of speculative work, yet the producer usually still insists on a full assignment of rights. A suggestion

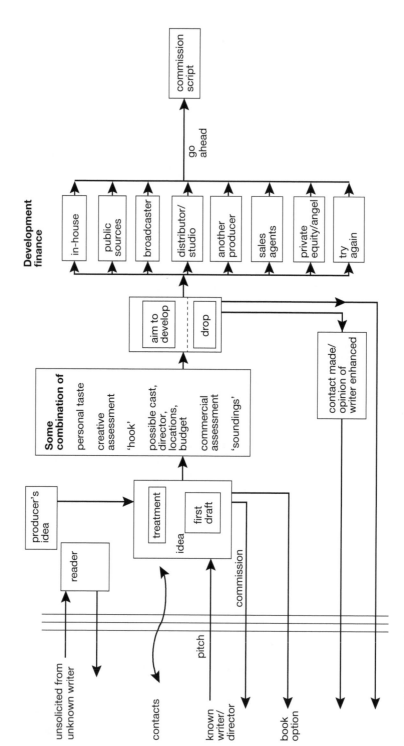

Figure 1.2 The initial hurdle of development (Finney and NFTS, 2010)[22]

from some writers is that if the development budget is small or non-existent then the producer should not expect to buy out the writer and the writer's work should be considered as a contribution-in-kind and treated as an investment in the project and rewarded with appropriate influence, increased profit-share, and possibly an associate producer credit.

The point where Fig. 1.2 ends (commissioning the main draft of the script) is where this book really starts – looking at the ongoing relationships and hurdles, as the script goes through many more drafts. Each time a draft is delivered the same evaluation process kicks in (including personal taste, creative assessment and industry soundings). Usually the element of subjective personal taste dominates the feedback. Within the 'soundings' section of the figure comes the vital role of trusted readers, both formal (agents, script editors, publishers, producers) and informal (partners, friends, children, etc.). As successive script drafts are delivered, more and more industry influences and feedback come to bear, with increasing emphasis on the attached package of actors and director, until the film is either dropped or goes into production.

The figure shows the importance of the finance market in deciding which projects to progress into development. No project should be developed by a producer without an awareness of what the market will be for the finished film or programme, so it is vital to see how the rest of the film industry works before looking at development funding in more detail. That will be the subject of the next chapter.

Case interview with producer Andy Paterson

*Producer Andy Paterson (*The Girl with a Pearl Earring, Restoration, Hilary and Jackie*) has developed his own way of working closely with writers, and he is involved from the outset in very detailed discussions of every element of the story and how it will be visualized. It means that by the time the writer formally starts to write, the story has already been worked over in a lot of detail. This working method fits the single project producer better than the slate producer, because he or she can only work on a relatively small number of projects at a time.*

The notion somehow that the world needs movies is a very bad place to start. Because actually television needs product, film doesn't. Television has hours to fill, cinemas would quite happily fill themselves with American movies and there is really no need for British films to be made. So the only reason to start developing something is if there is a story that you feel has to be told as a movie, is a movie that the world will want to see, and is a movie that you can make that nobody else should make. I remember pitching a very commercial idea to an American distributor, and they listened and said – it's really not a bad idea, but it's not what we want from you. We do that kind of stuff. We don't need you to be developing some big genre piece. What we want from you is the thing that nobody is going to bring to us ...

What we do is find stories which we somehow find compelling, fresh, stories we have to tell. And they will, by definition, be things that are hard to sell because they haven't been done before. What distributors want are ... films that audiences will go and see. Our task in development is to find great stories, and they will be, I hope, fresh, original. By definition, therefore, hard to market because you're trying to sell something to people and they don't know what it is. It's the heart of the problem with movies that you buy them before you know what they are. There are very few commodities where you put your money down at the box office, having heard a bit about it, but without having tested the product. So, my worst development decisions have come when I've decided I *ought* to do something, rather than remembering that what I do is find stories that I have to tell, and have to find a way to do.

Why might this idea not work?

Everything for me starts with trying to be as ruthless as I can about figuring out what the story can be, because the worst thing you can do as a producer is to get excited about an idea. You know, I'm a reasonably good salesman when it comes to going into a room and telling people a story. I mean I've done it for twenty years, I kind of know how to boil that story down, get people excited about it. And actually, sometimes the worst thing you can do is get some development money. Because then you're off on a roll.

So, the starting point for me these days is to try and get to the absolute heart of how a story works as a movie and to see if there are any fundamental flaws in there, because once a writer is committed and is off there writing the first draft it's an awful lot of their time, your time, development money; and the greatest failure is to get to a point on a script where you think – I should have seen that this could never be a movie.

So the first thing is to try and prove to yourself why you *shouldn't* tell the story. Certainly to take some time between first hearing the story and deciding whether it passes what we used to call the 6 a.m. test of whether, when you haul yourself out of bed in the middle of production you really know why you're doing it ... every morning you're going to get up, facing huge obstacles, and walk into a room with a lot of actors, and you'd better be really excited about both the scene you're going to do and how that scene fits into the movie. So, I try and take some time between hearing an idea, thinking about an idea and taking action on an idea.

Working closely with the writer

We do a lot of talking. Outlines are useful but I do believe that you ought to be able to *tell* the story. I have to go into a room and, again and again and again, find a way of casually pitching the story to somebody without them realizing that they're being pitched, and just get them hooked into it. And the more you can keep that story in your head, the more you can understand where the beats are or what the questions are, where the tension in the story comes from, the more likely it is to go the distance.

I really don't like the notion that what we do is say to the writer – okay here's the commission, go off and write the draft, come back and we'll give you notes. What I think the process from the idea to the movie should be is a gradual step by step by step. ... We work on the story, we talk out the story, we try and figure out what the story is trying to do, what kind of movie it is, what it is that's going to make it exciting. That may lead to a treatment that becomes an extended treatment, and it gradually expands out into a screenplay. So you're not just sending somebody off into the darkness for three months and then getting back a draft.

2 Show me the money

The business of film and the value chain[1]

> I think someone who has writing talent and who also understands how the television, film, and games industries work, will be more successful as a writer. They understand that you're not writing for the public, you're writing for the people who can invest money.
>
> (Julian Friedmann, writers' agent)

The value chain concept

It's a long journey from the first idea for a script to the public seeing a finished movie, and a lot of money and risk is involved along the way. As the film business academic Jason Squire put it: 'In no other business is a single example of product fully created at an investment of millions of dollars with no real assurance that the public will buy it.'[2]

To understand film development it is important to have a clear understanding of how the film industry works, and to do that it is worth using the MBA business concept of the *value chain* and the *value system*. This is an excellent technique to understand any industry and the companies collaborating in it, to see how different players fit together or compete with one another.

A value chain is *a connected series of activities, that work together to create and deliver a product to customers.* These activities could include research and development, manufacturing, packaging, marketing and distribution. Then there are the support services that help these activities to happen, such as human resource management, accountancy, information technology, legal services and so on. Sometimes all these activities are carried out by the same company (through different departments or subsidiary companies), and sometimes by separate companies or freelancers.

The term 'value chain' was codified in 1985 by Michael Porter from Harvard Business School, in his influential book *Competitive Advantage: Creating and Sustaining Superior Performance.*[3] Strictly speaking, a value *chain* represents those activities carried out within a single company, as shown in Fig. 2.1, and a value *system* represents those activities being carried out by a series of different businesses or freelancers, all working together (as shown

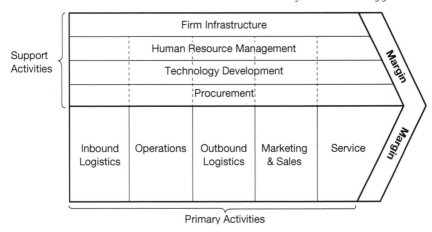

Figure 2.1 The value chain (Porter, 1985)[4]

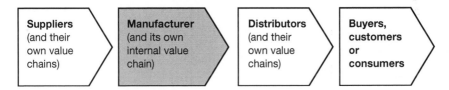

Figure 2.2 The value system: multiple collaborators, supplying and delivering value (adapted from Porter, 1985)[5]

in Fig. 2.2). Most industries go through cycles of either employing individuals in-house (chain), or else outsourcing and buying in those services (system), according to the economic conditions or business trends at the time.

The profitability of the central manufacturing company is largely determined by what it pays for what it buys from suppliers (known as *upstream*), what its own manufacturing costs are, and what it charges for what it delivers to its distributors and customers (known as *downstream*). Note that each company collaborating in the system probably has its own internal value chain (containing support services, logistics, marketing, etc.) which it has to manage.

Studios vs. independents

The value chain and system have already been applied by business academics and consultants to various sectors, including the car industry, food processing, broadcasting, luxury goods, and the retail sector in general.[6] It can also be applied to the film industry, but it's important to draw a distinction between the way studios work (in the US and in some countries in Europe), and the way that the independent film producer works.

In the studio system a film is often developed, financed, produced, distributed and exploited mainly without leaving a single integrated company or its subsidiaries: in other words, a simple corporate value *chain*. Of course, each film is different, and parts of the process may still be outsourced by the studio; for example, most of the people working on a film shoot are freelancers who are not permanently employed by the studio (camera crew, actors, directors and so on). Often an independent producer will develop a film, and then bring the script to the studio for the funding of production and carrying out of distribution. Non-US examples of studios include the French companies Pathé, UGC, Wild Bunch (with distribution also in Italy, Germany and Benelux), Gaumont, and Vivendi-owned StudioCanal (who bought and absorbed the distributors Optimum in the UK and Kinowelt in Germany); in Canada E1 and Alliance (plus distribution in UK through Momentum and Spain through Aurum Films);[7] in Japan Shochiku; and in Australia Village Roadshow. A representation of the studio value chain is shown in Fig. 2.3.

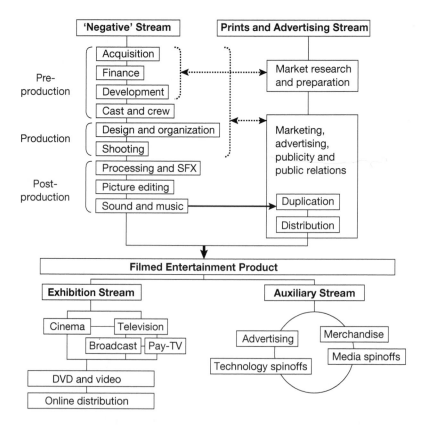

Figure 2.3 The filmed entertainment value chain, particularly applicable to the studios and spin-off merchandising chain (Vickery and Hawkins, 2008)[8]

So what about the independent film? An independent film is basically *not* a studio picture, and its development finance and production finance is provided by *more than one source*. The producer and a number of different financiers share some or all of the investment risk.[9] Therefore the independent film operates in a value *system*, because the film is not made and delivered to its final audience by a single company (the studio), but by a system of companies, businesses and freelancers, all working on different elements of the production and exploitation process, and adding value in different ways along the chain. Furthermore, once the film is exploited the money handed over by the consumer (in return for a cinema ticket, DVD purchase or online download) is subject to various revenue shares or commissions as it passes back through the value system, which then complicates the revenue flow.[10]

As part of operating within a multi-player value system, independent films are usually acquired, marketed and distributed by different distributors in different territories in the world. The independent distributor *chooses* which films to buy the rights to distribute and may decide to acquire in advance of the film being produced (the pre-sale) or may wait until after the film is completed. Occasionally, an independent film is picked up by a Hollywood studio to distribute in several territories, or even the world. Herein lies the weakness of the independent producer or financier, because they usually do not control distribution and therefore the income stream.

The independent film value chain model

A key part of competitive business strategy involves aligning an organization with its strategic environment, so it is vital for those running businesses in the film industry fully to understand the value chain they are working in, especially in times of radical change.[11] Therefore there has been a rise of interest in the concept of the film value chain, probably as a result of changes in the economies of film financing and distribution which threaten existing business models (for example, technological convergence, the decline of DVD sales and the projected rise of digital downloads).

However despite the increasing use of the film value chain by writers, consultants and lecturers, until 2009 there had been few attempts accurately to codify the chain and explore its complexity, especially within the independent sector as opposed to the studio sector. In May 2009 a version of the independent film value chain model in Fig. 2.4 was devised by the author and published in a paper called 'Re-defining the Independent Film Value Chain'.[12] It was tested through teaching sessions at a number of UK universities and executive short courses, and this revised version has incorporated feedback from media business consultants, executives, MBA students and film practitioners. This chapter analyses the chain in detail under a series of subheadings. Strictly speaking it is a value system, because it is examining the independent sector where there are separate cooperating

The Independent Film Project Value Chain

By activity. Conventional European or US independent non-studio film, with multiple financiers and distributors. © Peter Bloore 2009/revised 2012.

Library ('long tail')
Distributor: reissues during first licence
Distributor: sells new licence after reversion
Producer: remake/sequel (back to start)

Element	Development	Financing and Pre-sales	Production: Shoot and Post	International Sales and Licensing	International Distribution	Exhibition and Exploitation	Consumption
Players (organizations or freelancers) (listed in approx order of creative power and influence)	Screenplay writer, Source writer (if any), Producer, Talent agent, Talent manager, Development exec... Director (as part of package and collaborating with writer), Script editor, Development financier, Director and maybe key cast (if attached as part of the package, especially in later stages of development). The development stage often lasts longer than other stages, and is high risk. A report in 2007 found that only 18% of films developed in the UK reach production. The money is re-paid on first day of shoot out of production finance, and funders do not usually share much in the final revenue. Some development funding is available from public subsidy bodies, especially in Europe.	Producer(s), Production company, Director and cast (as part of package), Talent agents/manager, National distributor, National broadcaster, National/subsidy finance, International pre-sales (via sales agent), the writer, Equity financiers (cash-flowing pre-sales or gap), Co-prodn funds/ prods, Exec./Assoc. producers, Tax break financiers (where relevant), Completion bond, Insurance. The most complex stage of the process, where multiple stakeholders have to be made to say 'yes' simultaneously. This period includes 'soft pre-production': recces and more casting.	Director, Cast, Producer, Cameraman, Crew, Editor and staff, Financiers (in general), CGI/special effects, Writer, Completion bond, Line producer, Production company staff, Studio/location, Support services, Post-production and facilities, Post-production supervisor, Film labs (reducing), Insurance (Note: Director, financiers and producers are sometimes all involved in final edit sign-off). This is the process of actually making the film. There is some reduction of costs due to digitization of entire production and post.	International sales agent and maybe Producer (marketing and selling the unsold distribution rights licences to the completed film; and receiving sales commission and sales expenses recoupment). Collection agencies (gathering relevant international revenues and returning it to the financiers, for a fee). This is the selling of the completed film, and the delivering of it to those who have pre-bought it. International film markets and festivals (Cannes, AFM, Venice, Berlin, MIP, Sundance) provide platforms and sales opportunities for sales agents.	Distributor/Territorial rights holders – for each territory in the world. (Some distributors only buy a portion of rights for that territory, or buy them all and license some to third parties. They may pay for the territory rights (advance), pay for prints and advertising (p&a), and then keep a proportion of exploitation revenues to recoup those costs. The distributor in each territory then controls the marketing and release of film, not the producer. In the US studio model national distributors are often owned by the studio, and marketing control retained.) 'Spin-off' secondary product/merchandising: other companies sometimes acquire these rights, the production of which may have their own value chain.	Windows of exploitation are as follows (in current approx order of value, but likely to change): DVD and VHS sales/rental pay-TV (satellite and cable); Cinema (a.k.a. Exhibitor) Free TV (PSB or Advertising) Video-on-demand (VOD) Online download (rent or own) (Note that windows are mainly controlled and negotiated by the national distributor, not the producer.) Physical distribution services (reducing, to be replaced by digital storage and transfer management). Library rights (see box above). Exploitation of 'Spin-off' secondary products/ merchandising: toys; computer games; books/ screenplay; soundtrack (CD or download). These may involve various profit shares.	Consumers (and word of mouth), Film critics, influencing consumers (formal, and also informal via internet and bulletin boards). Note: This is usually the first time the film or spin-off secondary product is seen by the end consumer, and where its true value can be assessed and realized – after many years and many millions of pounds have already been spent on creating the product. Note: however US studios often use test screenings, prior to the end or post-production. Recoupment corridor: The money handed over by the consumer for a cinema ticket, DVD purchase, or online download, is then subject to revenue shares, marketing cost deductions, and commissions as it passes back through the chain to the financiers and producer.
Support Services (hired in for indie production, but often in-house for studios)	**Marketing** Studios with permanent marketing staff may employ marketing techniques and feedback at the development stage of the process. However, most indies and European companies usually do not.	**Marketing** PR during shoot for early marketing, and create a reserve of pictures. Preview screenings.	**Marketing**	**Marketing** (working across every stage of the value chain) Marketing creates sales info for use at international markets and trade papers. Word of mouth.		Marketing for each territory and for each exploitation avenue. Usually distributor driven. Separate exhibition marketing for cinema/chain as a leisure destination. Separate retail marketing for DVD stores.	**Marketing** Some US studios carry out ongoing market research during the release, aimed at testing behaviour and response.

Lawyers and Accountants and Consultants (working across every stage of the value chain)

Figure 2.4 The independent film project value chain[13]

companies; however, the term 'value chain' has been used here because over time journalists and academics in the media sector have dispensed with the distinction between the value chain and system, and refer to them both as the value chain.[14]

The order of the listing of 'players' in each segment

Film finance and production is a highly complex and collaborative process, including a range of private and public organizations and freelance individuals (*the players*). The players named in the boxes have been approximately listed in order of creative power and influence, with the most powerful at the top. However, this is a subjective generalization since each film varies substantially. This is an addition to previous film value chain models, because it enables it to be read in terms of shifting levels of creative value and influence/power during the process. For example, it can be seen that some players (like the writer, the producer and the director) shift in influence from segment to segment (for example, from development to post-production, as discussed in Chapter 5). This order of listing does *not* reflect their financial input or their entitlement to income.

Development

Development has been shown as a separate segment from production (unlike some other film value chain models). This reflects three issues: first, a lot of time and energy is spent in development, incorporating different players to production; second, financing often comes from a different source from production financing (and in Europe often involves public subsidy funds); and third, independence of development can be one of the definitions of an independent film. Sometimes development can be said to include *packaging* the project (by attaching actors and other talent), and budgeting and researching the shoot. However, detailed recces and *soft pre-production* (preparation before a formal greenlight for production) has here been included within the *financing and pre-sales* section. This is because the diagram needs to reflect the shift in power and influence between the script development stage and the packaging stage, due to the entry of new collaborators in the chain.

It is important to note that the chain as a whole clearly shows the distance between the development process and the end consumer of the film, and as a result marketing departments and distributors rarely influence the creation of the independent films they will eventually exploit. This separation can be said to be one of the weaknesses of independent film-making compared to studio film-making, and it is an issue that will be returned to later.

Financing and pre-sales

This is the stage where the film is financed by the producer using money from third parties, including a range of collaborating businesses, advisers and investors, in return for rights to exploit the film and/or equity (share of profits). This is the most complex stage of the process, where the leadership and negotiation qualities of the main producer are most vital in ensuring that multiple stakeholders have to be made to say yes simultaneously. Each of the investors may bring with them business needs and creative views that can massively affect the completed film. Above all, they and their lawyers are interested in their recoupment position. *Recoupment* is a film industry expression meaning repayment, usually applying to income from the sales and exploitation of the film that is used to pay off investors in the production budget of the film.[15] The recoupment position is how one investor recoups compared to other investors. *Recouping in first position* means that you are recouping before the other investors. Recouping *pari passu* means that you are recouping at the same time and in equal amounts as other investors within that arrangement. *Pari passu* is a Latin phrase which literally means 'with equal step', and indicates that you are sharing something out equally, as children do when they say 'one for you and one for me'. There will be more on the vexed issue of recoupment later.

Pre-sales refers to the process where a film is sold, in advance of being made, to distributors in some territories in the world, on the strength of the perceived value of the attached director and cast. The producer receives a contract stating a minimum guarantee of income from the distributor, including 10–20 per cent of the fee upfront and the rest on delivery of the film to the distributor (meaning that the producer then has to use equity or bank borrowing with interest to cashflow production, until the second payment on delivery). This was a key part of independent financing throughout the 1980s and 1990s; however, pre-sales have become more difficult since the 2008 recession because distributors have become reluctant to pre-buy films, due to lack of credit from their parent companies or from banks, falling broadcast fees in Europe, the international rise of internet piracy and illegal downloading, and the connected decline in the value of the DVD market (DVD sales fell by 20 per cent in all major pre-sales markets in 2008, and more in 2009[16]). Increasingly, foreign rights are being sold after the film is completed, where there is less risk for the distributor (they can actually see what they are buying) and where their money (possibly borrowed from a bank and incurring interest) is being tied up for a shorter period of time before recoupment through actual distribution. This has left some producers unable to complete the upfront financing of their films, and the production end of the film industry may remain unstable until the national and international value of DVD, the internet and video-on-demand (VOD) is more clearly known and therefore predictable (hopefully giving distributors the feeling of security of knowing how much to pay for the rights). Furthermore, the global financial crisis has meant that many banks have closed their film divisions or are reluctant to lend against risky pre-sales.

Production: shoot and post

Quite simply this is the segment where the film is shot and edited, and the largest numbers of creative and technical freelancers are involved. *Post-production* includes the whole editing process including the addition of computer-generated special effects and music. The shoot is usually the point at which the director is most powerful; however, this may be reduced during the edit and post-production process, since the financiers are concerned to protect their investments and get involved in creative decisions. Often the director, financiers and producers are all involved in approving the final edit, and who has the sign-off is often a closely fought contractual issue.

International sales and licensing

This is the point at which the completed film is licensed internationally to distributors in each country or group of countries (known as territories). Those distributors pay an advance to receive the film and have the rights to exploit it over a specified period of time (known as a *window*). Usually the distributors agree to return a share of the profits of the distribution of the film back to the original financiers of the film (after their distribution and marketing costs and sometimes their advance has been recouped).

It has been decided in this value chain model to show sales and licensing as a separate segment, because sales agents are neither part of production nor included in the role of the distributor. Often overlooked by other film value chain models (and indeed some overviews of the film industry), the sales agents add value to the chain, take commissions from the recoupment corridor, and are a crucial part of the business-to-business marketing element of the chain. Including sales agents here in the chain helps to illustrate the complexity of recoupment. As shown, *pre-sales* (international sales contracted or estimated before production) are often a part of financing production (bank financing can be raised against them), so sales agents are also shown as players in that segment; some of them even invest equity in production.[17]

In the studio system many international sales are either handled through automatic output deals, where foreign distributors have a deal to take all of a studio's projects in their territory, or else foreign distribution is handled by a subsidiary of the studio (reducing the need to show sales agents in the studio model of the value chain).

International distribution/exhibition and exploitation

This is the process whereby the distributor markets and exploits in each territory, sometimes selling on portions of the rights. The *windows* (or time-sensitive opportunities of different types of exploitation) could be listed as follows, in the current order of value to the distributor (rather than the timing of exploitation): DVD/Blu-Ray sales and rental; pay-TV (satellite and cable); airline in-flight screenings; cinema (a.k.a. the exhibitor); free TV (PSB or advertising); video-on-demand streaming (VOD); and finally online download (to rent or own). Due to changing business models that order of value is changing, especially as the DVD sales decline is replaced by online download or VOD, which may become the largest source of income. Since the turn of the century the duration of the cinema window has been shrinking in order to try to get films onto the DVD shelves quickly, whilst the cinema campaign is still strong in people's minds.[18] Some companies have even experimented with *simultaneous releases* or *day-and-date releases* (where cinema release is simultaneous with premium subscription pay-TV or VOD).[19]

Those not used to the film industry may be surprised to see that cinema box office is not the area of highest value, and indeed cinema often makes a loss for the distributor, because of the level of marketing costs incurred at this stage. The box office figures published in newspapers/media are only the beginning of the income stream (they are also a gross take figure and do not take into account tax, fees and marketing costs). Instead, the cinema release is usually a loss leader: a prestige activity that drives DVD and download potential, and fulfils the terms of some output deals. These output deals between studios/distributors and the subscription TV companies (like HBO, Showtime and Starz in the US, and BSkyB in the UK) have become an increasingly important source of regular income for studios and independent distributors in the US. The cutting back of output deals by the pay channels in 2009–2010 may have helped to speed up the closure of New Line Cinema, Miramax, Fine Line, Picturehouse, Warner Independent and Paramount Vantage.[20]

Studios are able to set global release patterns and windows for their films, because of their control of local distributors. However, in the independent sector the windows are mainly controlled and negotiated by the national distributor who has acquired the rights to distribute the film in that territory, in discussion with the exhibitor and other exploitation rights owners. Furthermore, it is the distributor who finances and controls the prints and advertising (p&a) campaign to the final audience, and therefore who decides how widely the film is released, *not* the producer.

In the UK the underlying weakness of the business model for the producer is that the exhibitors hold onto so much of the exhibition income (about 66 per cent, compared to 50 per cent in the US); and much of the balance of that is absorbed by the distributor through fees or recouping distribution costs. Income for the producer from exploitation is further reduced by the current dominance of BSkyB over pay-TV (and that broadcaster's preference for studio fare), and the reluctance of BBC and Channel 4 to acquire completed British films that they do not co-produce.

The production of *spin-off secondary products* or merchandising (such as toys, computer games, book/screenplay, soundtrack) is sometimes carried out at this distribution stage, and might not involve the original film's producer or financiers (although some profits may go back to them, according to individual deals). These secondary products may involve their own separate value chains and various revenue shares, especially since they may be sold in different retail outlets from the film itself (for example, record shops, toy shops, clothing shops, etc.). Again, the US studio system keeps tight control of this, and may plan it from the development stage, whereas independent films come to it late, if at all.

Consumption

The consumer has been included as the last segment of the value chain, which is not usual practice in many other value chain diagrams. This has been done because the consumer is fulfilling two key value-related functions: first, purchasing the product, allowing financial value to return down the chain (customer consumption); and second, influencing the long-term 'library' value and reputation of the film, which is very much a product of the response of the general audience (box office figures and word of mouth) and published critical voices (these include formal 'approved' media critics, such as in reviews on television or in newspapers, and informal 'unapproved' critics, such as on internet websites or bulletin boards). As Graham Vickery and Richard Hawkins have pointed out:

> The unique economic features of the film and video industries stem from the 'experience goods' characteristics of these products, whose market performance depends on complex interactions between psychological, social and cultural factors. ... The realisable value of a film is determined largely by intangible assets that have very special characteristics. Consumer perceptions of the personality and talents of individuals associated with a film can play a crucial role in determining the value of the film.[21]

Including the consumer in the chain is also in keeping with reception theory in cultural studies, which states that the audience is not merely a passive recipient of meaning, but is involved in the creative reception and 'decoding' of the text or film.[22]

Library rights

This value chain shows library rights as a separate segment, coming back from the completed 'first run' of exploitation of the relevant windows to re-impact earlier in the value chain. The film can then be re-exploited in two ways: first, for the duration of the distribution licence, it can be re-exploited by the distributor (for example, a second release of the DVD, perhaps in a collector's edition); second, once the distribution licence expires and the rights revert, the producer may then be able to sell (via a sales agent) a further distribution licence (to the same distributor or another one) for another period. This is often as part of a package of films, rather than as an individual property. A repeat theatrical release is rare, until a significant anniversary of a classic is reached (say ten or twenty years); however, a re-release onto a newly developed technological format has become quite normal. A director's cut of a film is an example of library rights exploitation, because there is no need for a major injection of capital (there may be some re-editing and re-mixing costs, but usually these are minimal; and digital technology is reducing them even further).

Library and reissue rights are potentially an area of extra value for film and television programmes compared to some other media products (such as newspapers and magazines), partly because of the long shelf life of a successful film and partly because the distribution of the completed product is generally licensed, rather than carried out by the originating company (with the exception of studios).

A separate section within library rights (of particular interest to those who are working in development) are the remake or prequel or sequel rights. These are retained by the producer and/or key financiers, and are not granted to distributors. The original writer will also usually benefit, to varying degrees according to the original contract. However, this part of library rights leads back to the very start of the value chain and the development of a new script (even in the case of a remake, which often involves a change in geographical and cultural setting). The reason why investors like remakes and sequels is that there is apparently less risk involved, because the concept has already been tested and the market for the film should be more predictable.

Risk

Generally speaking, the earlier (further to the left) you are in the chain (towards development and production) the higher the potential risk for the capital investor, due to the distance in the recoupment chain from the money paid by the consumer.[23]

What are integrated companies?

The model clearly demonstrates visually and textually a number of issues and weaknesses in the independent model that film industry insiders have long been aware of.[24] These include the large number of collaborating individuals and organizations; the complexity of the multi-player independent financing process (making it prone to setbacks when a player drops out); the separation of the producer from distribution and marketing; the vacillating power of the writer; and the fact that lawyers and accountants appear to have the most stable jobs in the industry (because they can earn money at every stage of the value chain). Cooperation between the players along the chain is certainly not inevitable or causal, and in his book on the independent film industry Angus Finney makes the point that because there are so many cooperating players required to produce a film the inherently fragmented chain is often on the verge of disintegration, especially at the financing stage:

> The strategic effect of what could be termed a 'disintegrated model' is that each element in the chain is heavily dependent on the next player/operator's partnership and cooperation in order to drive a project forward. A network of varying interacting players have to be attracted, managed and, in many cases, forced into focussing and delivering specific commitments and activities in order for a film project to proceed. The risks are extreme. In addition, the seed idea, and early sunk costs in a concept, idea and writer's work to produce a realisable screenplay, is six, highly complex stages away from contact with the end-user, the film consumer.[25]

To counter this problem, some producers try to establish long-term relationships with other finance companies, sales agents and distributors in the value chain, in order to simplify the financing and production process, either informally (ongoing relationships) or formally (joint ventures, purchases, mergers, output deals).

This ultimately leads to the strategic possibility of *integration*, which is when a company (or a consortium of companies) owns players at different points in the value chain, and is therefore able to earn money in different places.[26] There are two types of integration. *Vertical integration* involves operating in *different* segments in the value chain, for example owning both a production company and a sales agent, and therefore receiving income when the film is produced and also when sales commissions are earned. *Horizontal integration* involves owning several players in the *same* segment of the value chain – for example, at the exploitation end of the chain one company could own many media outlets to show the same film content in different exploitation windows (such as a DVD label, a TV channel and a website where films can be downloaded). This is illustrated in Fig. 2.5, which redraws the value chain to demonstrate the different types of integration.

Integration is particularly relevant to the film industry, because there are different commissions and profit shares taken by different players in the chain. The more a company can access these different revenue streams, the sooner it can earn money to offset against the expense of production, and the longer it can continue to profit from exploitation. The classic film industry example of vertical integration is the way that the Hollywood Studios in the 1920s and 1930s owned the actors, the directors, the production studios, the distribution network and the cinema chains. This meant they controlled the upstream suppliers and the downstream distributors, ensuring massive profits, consistency of product, huge control over how the films were marketed, and high entry barriers for potential competitors. This continued until a US Supreme Court decision against Paramount Pictures in 1948, which prevented all the studios from owning and operating cinema chains on the principle that it was anti-competitive. However, the industry was de-regulated again by Ronald Regan in the 1980s, and after that the studios again acquired cinemas.[27]

An example of successful film integration via acquisition was the European company PolyGram Filmed Entertainment, which in the 1990s operated across fourteen countries and pursued a strategy of owning or having deals in key territories with production companies, sales agents *and* distribution companies. Some of this was vertical integration (developing and financing films that could then be sold and distributed in-house), and some of it was horizontal integration (owning PolyGram Specialist Video and part-owning the Sundance TV channel). The integration strategy enabled distribution marketing departments to be involved in the decision as to which films should be greenlit for financing in the first place, thus reducing the distance between the development/production section of the chain and the exploitation section of the chain. It also entered the library section of the chain by acquiring and exploiting the third largest film catalogue in the world, containing 1,500 feature films and over 10,000 hours of television programming.[28] This provided the sales agents with films to sell before the newly produced product came onstream.

However there are potential downsides of integration, including increased company overheads, a larger workforce (with all the associated employment costs), the need for different skill sets to operate successfully in the production and distribution sectors, and overall extra managerial complexity (especially if the integrated firm is spread across a number of different geographical locations and time zones), at which point some selective outsourcing could enable an integrated company to become more efficient and cost effective.[29] Furthermore, a distribution arm attached to a production company can lead to a loss of guaranteed money upfront from pre-sales to the distributor (which would help reduce the financial risk at the production stage).[30]

Some UK distributors are becoming more closely involved in production, most recently Revolver Entertainment (after the success of distributing *Kidulthood* it set up the production company Gunslinger to produce youth films like *Shank, Sket* and *Anuvahood*); and Vertigo Films (which produced

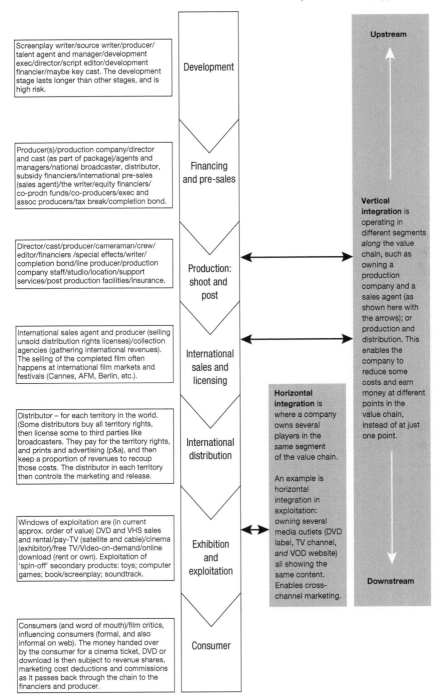

Figure 2.5 The independent film project value chain: shown vertically to demonstrate types of integration.[31]

Streetdance 3D, Monsters and *Horrid Henry (3D)*, as well as owning a German post-production company (The Post Republic) and being a partner in the sales company Protagonist Pictures, a joint venture with Film4 and financier Ingenious Media). So the move towards integration is perhaps coming first from distributors looking to secure strong content rather than from producers looking to secure distribution. At the time of writing, the UK Film Policy Review has recommended closer cooperation between producers and distributors, initially on a project-by-project basis, including specific funding to encourage joint venture projects which will lower distributors' costs but ensure a greater share of distribution income to the producer.[31]

The other possible integration is with sales agents. There are about thirty-five sales companies in the UK, most of them employing five to six people, but some of them much larger.[32] There are more sales agents in the UK than in any city outside Los Angeles,[33] so it is a logical move for UK producers to form closer links with them, in order to earn money from sales commissions and to benefit earlier in international recoupment, or for producers and sales agents to integrate more formally than just occasional output deals. UK producer Jeremy Thomas started this back in 1998 by forming sales agent HanWay Films to help sell the films produced through his production company Recorded Picture Company (HanWay Films now also represents Ecosse Films and a further library of some 500 arthouse films). However, others argue that production and sales are very different businesses with different core competencies and the crucial question is where final decision-making power rests: with the producer or the sales agent? Both of them will want the freedom to choose their own products and express their own taste, and there is a danger that the producer may force the sales agent to represent his films at markets where the agent may believe that other third-party acquisitions may fare better.

Either way, some sales agents have already become more involved in controlling production: during 2009–2011 there was a growth in sales agents with access to equity or minimum sales *guarantees* (as opposed to just estimates) for production financing, to help them secure the higher status projects to then sell internationally, including Summit (with the *Twilight* trilogy) and IM Global (*Paranormal Activity*). Some sales agents even have their own US distribution, for example Lionsgate, Focus (via Universal), The Weinstein Company, Exclusive (via Newmarket) and Summit.[34] Again, the integration is being initiated by other players in the value chain than the producer. The question is whether these sales agents/producers would consider getting involved earlier, by investing in the high risk of development of non-franchise films.

What does the film value chain model not show?

Any value chain model as applied to the film industry has several limitations, including being unable to represent the importance of reputation and personal relationships, timescale and, above all, the levels of investment and recoupment at different stages.

Reputation

Value chain models do not show how competitive advantage is gained by those businesses that rely upon branding, softer people skills, specialist knowledge and contacts.[35] This could be said to be particularly true of the film and TV sectors, where great value is placed on experience, trust and personal relationships.

Timescale

The value chain diagram gives the false impression that the same amount of time and effort is spent in each segment. Fig. 2.6 approximates the average time actually spent within each segment (this is indicative, since every project varies massively).

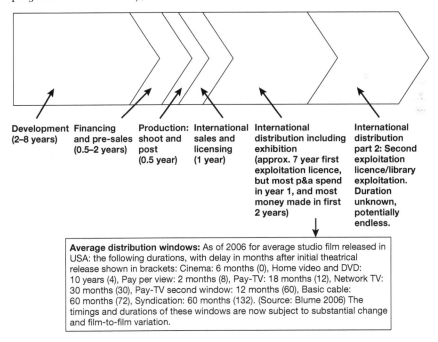

Development Financing   Production: International International   International
(2–8 years) and pre-sales shoot and   sales and   distribution including distribution
             (0.5–2 years) post   licensing   exhibition   part 2: Second
                           (0.5 year) (1 year)   (approx. 7 year first exploitation
                                                   exploitation licence, licence/library
                                                   but most p&a spend   exploitation.
                                                   in year 1, and most   Duration
                                                   money made in first   unknown,
                                                   2 years)   potentially
                                                                          endless.

Average distribution windows: As of 2006 for average studio film released in USA: the following durations, with delay in months after initial theatrical release shown in brackets: Cinema: 6 months (0), Home video and DVD: 10 years (4), Pay per view: 2 months (8), Pay-TV: 18 months (12), Network TV: 30 months (30), Pay-TV second window: 12 months (60), Basic cable: 60 months (72), Syndication: 60 months (132). (Source: Blume 2006) The timings and durations of these windows are now subject to substantial change and film-to-film variation.

Figure 2.6 A rough estimation of the film value chain according to time spent within each segment, as a proportion of the total project

Levels of investment and recoupment

The vast majority of investment is during production, which is notably the smallest segment in terms of timescale (see Fig. 2.6). However, levels of investment in different segments vary so much from film to film that any visual representation of an average would be highly misleading.

The value chain diagram does not attempt to show the flow of income and the order of recoupment; because the value chain concept as designed by Michael Porter was intended to analyse business strategy, competitive advantage, cost advantage (reducing internal costs in product manufacture by managing internal and external relationships), and buyer value (reducing costs and increasing the perception of value for the buyer).[36]

Not everyone in the film value chain receives income in the same way, or even always in one single way. For example, some players (like production crew) are paid flat fees upfront from production budgets before the product is completed. Some players (like equity financiers) earn income from revenue streams coming from actual sales of the finished product (but only after exhibitors, distributors and sales agents may have taken their commissions and expenses from that revenue). The timing and levels of these deals vary from film to film. Other players (like producers, key acting talent, writers and directors) are entitled to receive both: they are paid flat fees during production, but then also share in revenue when certain levels of income are reached and equity investors in primary positions are paid off (they may also receive separate fee deferral payments at some stage during the recoupment schedule). This is a departure from conventional industry value systems, where a supplier company would only be paid a flat fee for providing goods or services, and would not also expect a share of the manufacturing company's profits. This staged introduction of profit shares, sometimes at different moments during the recoupment process, interferes with the clarity of the accounting process and even the long-term profitability of the production company or film financier; as well as making the profitability and *return on investment* (ROI) of an individual film much harder to quantify. Furthermore, some players (like sales agents) may receive a percentage commission on selling the film, as well as a repayment of any expenses that they have incurred during the exploitation of the film (for example, the sales agent's marketing expenses).

Purely as an illustration of the complexity of this process, Fig. 2.7 and Fig. 2.8 show different examples of typical recoupment charts, showing the order of recoupment of investors (imagine the chart to be like a bucket filling up with water from below so the lines at the bottom get paid off first). Fig. 2.7 (which shows both a fictional independent budget and recoupment schedule) is taken from Davies and Wistreich's 2007 book *The Film Finance Handbook*. However, it is a simplification of total income, because it shows only what the financiers receive, which is net income, *after* the deduction of sales costs and commissions, distributor's p&a costs, exhibitor's take, and other commissions (these deductions largely occur before the film financier receives the income).

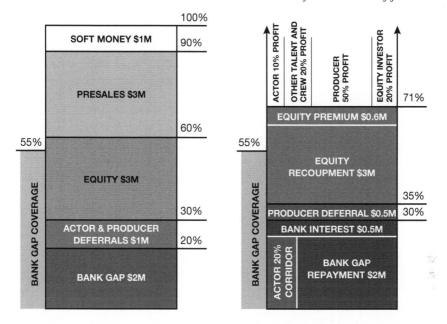

Figure 2.7 A fictional example of an independent film budget investment chart (on the left) and recoupment chart (on the right) (Davies and Wistreich, 2007)[37]

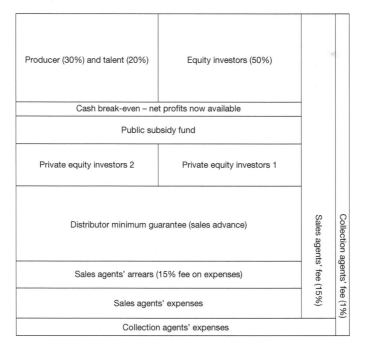

Figure 2.8 A typical independent film recoupment chart (Finney, 2010)[38]

Figure 2.8 is adapted from Angus Finney's 2010 book *The International Film Business*, and it does show more of the deductions of the sales costs and fees (although not distributor's prints and advertising costs and exhibitor's take). A detailed breakdown of the levels of typical fees and costs is shown in Fig. 2.9, also from Finney's book. It is worth remembering that every sold international territory will have its own version of this recoupment chart, to allow for the distributor's different contract.

These figures are attempts to indicate a typical deal, but in reality every film is different, according to the negotiation of the individual financing and recoupment structure; and the US studio system is different again.[39]

It is important to understand that the producer receives most of his income on the first day of principal photography (his fee is usually about 3 per cent of the budget), simply because the recoupment positions of the financiers and the fees and costs deducted by distributors, exhibitors and sales agents mean that the profit share from the exploitation of the film does not add up to much (this is known as *producer's net profit*, in that it is net of these fees and costs). This could be said to disincentivize the producer from being very active during distribution, because in order to survive they are instead busy preparing the next script to go into production, so that they can get paid again. However an integrated company may change this dynamic, because the producer is motivated by being able to benefit more quickly from distribution income.

The importance of retaining talent in the company and the value chain

For the producer every single film is a new script and a new start, with the exception of movie franchises where there is a returning star and storyline. Therefore it is the producer's relationships with writers and directors that provides some form of continuity for the business, but as a result of the multi-player and freelance nature of the production business producers often find it very difficult to retain writers and directors across many films. This is made worse by the financial power of the studios to lure key talent away to other film projects, especially in the US. This increases the producer's value chain fragmentation because teams have to be formed anew for each new film, reducing the ability to learn as a group during the process, build ongoing trust, and ensure consistency of product. However, some producers in the UK have built successful careers out of forming close links with key directors or writers. Examples include producer Rebecca O'Brien, director Ken Loach and writer Paul Laverty; producer Simon Channing-Williams and director/writer Mike Leigh; producer Andrew Eaton and director Michael Winterbottom; producer Duncan Kenworthy and writer Richard Curtis; producer Mark Herbert and director/writer Shane Meadows; producer Andrew Macdonald, writer John Hodge and director Danny Boyle (and latterly producer Christian Colson and director

Danny Boyle). In some of these cases the director is integrated into the production company and made a company director, which can help strengthen the relationship.

It could be said that securing an ongoing and close relationship with key creative talent (especially writers and directors) should therefore be the key strategic aim of most independent film producers. It is the difference between either building a secure business with a track record and a realizable future potential or making an ad hoc series of individual film productions. This should be at the heart of a development strategy, both for the company and for individual projects, and is also a central theme of this book.

Model: an independent movie

Assumptions:

i)   US distribution is through major specialist arm
ii) Foreign sold/handled by an international sales company
iii) Back end is a 50–50 split between financiers and producer re net profits (after negative cost of the film has been repaid and all fees/costs have been paid out...)

	US side of exploitation	Revenue flow
Fee	US distributor: interest and overhead charge on advance (override) 10% minimum, can be as much as 18–20%.	
Fee/cost	TV sales (30–40% of income given to distributor).	
Fee/cost	DVD duplication and marketing costs (royalty to you of 15–20% unless you can achieve a better deal).	
Fee/cost	Prints and advertising costs against the theatrical release in all territories with interest and override.	
Fee	35% distribution commission against rental figure of between 40 and 50% income stream to distributor.	
	Foreign sales side of exploitation	
Fee	10–25% sales commission on all foreign territories, 5–10% against the US sale.	
Fee/cost	$150,000 minimum sales and marketing costs in foreign (but likely to be $200,000).	
Fee	1–1.5% collection agent on all revenues collected.	
	Individual distributor deals in 'foreign'	
Fee	Distributor: interest and overhead charge on advance (override): 10% minimum.	
Fee/cost	TV sales (30–40% of income given to distributor).	
Fee/cost	DVD duplication and marketing costs (royalty to you of 15–20% unless you can achieve a better deal).	
Fee/cost	Prints and advertising costs against the theatrical release in all territories, with interest and override.	
Fee	35% distribution commission against the rental figure of approximately 30–45% income stream, but as low as 25% in the United Kingdom.	

Figure 2.9 The cost of recoupment: fees and commissions charged on the exploitation of a typical independent film (Finney, 2010)[40]

In the current time of dramatic technological and economic change the theoretical tool of the film value chain, as defined in this chapter, is useful to provide an insight into the past, present and potential future workings of the film industry, and consider how changes to the value chain may alter new business models. However, every film is different and would have its own variation of the chain (and a slightly different value chain could be posited for ultra-low-budget and no-budget films, especially when they are self-distributed in the home country by the producer).

The next chapter looks at the different types of film that are made within this value chain, and how that influences the sources of development funding that would be approached by the producer.

Case interview with producer Julie Baines: Wait until the script is really ready ...

Producer Julie Baines founded Dan Films in 1994. She has worked with directors including Nicolas Roeg, Peter Bogdanovich, Frank Van Passel, Michael Winterbottom, Mika Kaurismaki and Deepa Mehta. Julie most recently produced Christopher Smith's Triangle, *a psychological thriller starring Melissa George.*

> I learned very early on as a producer not to send out scripts too early. Even if you can see how the screenplay may be developed further in the future, other people generally can't. And why should they? They've not been party to all the discussions that you have had. And talent attachments are crucial these days. Financiers consider projects in a completely different light and will make decisions if they think the project is really going to happen – and happen soon. Without attachments, they will track the project and tell you to come back when you are further advanced.

This point of view was influenced by the time she spent as Head of Production at The Film Consortium (one of the UK's Lottery film finance franchises) when she was receiving projects looking for production funding:

> I had producers coming to me with projects for production finance so I saw it from the other side of the fence, which was incredibly valuable. One of the things that used to annoy me more than anything was a producer submitting a project with a casting wish list of huge names, that you knew they would never get. And often they would say that they were still working on the script and would have

another draft in a month. So why am I reading this now then? Why do I want to read two drafts of this project in one month? Once I've read the first version, my judgement is coloured. If I read the (hopefully) better version in a month's time, then I am totally fresh to the story and it stands more chance of my appreciating it.

3   A new analysis of types of film and film development funding

> I'm very aware as a creative person that those who control the means of production control the creative vision.
>
> (George Lucas, producer and director)[1]

Defining three types of film

The above quote from producer and director George Lucas goes to the heart of the battle for control between the creative and the money man. Which leads to the question: which kinds of company tend to invest in which type of movie, and why? This book now aims to answer that question by creating some typologies to help distinguish between different types of movie and their funding sources.

In general, typologies are useful because they simplify our thinking and help analyse and categorize complex areas of creative and business activity; but their weakness is that they can over-simplify some of those complexities, and emphasize integration and similarity over difference and individuality. Given this disclaimer, and the fact that every film is in some way different and unique, there are broadly three types of film, which we will call *specialist* (including auteur-driven films), *conceptual* (genre-driven), and *Anglo-Hollywood* (studio-driven). These same three types exist in other countries (although Britain is unusual for making so many films directly with Hollywood, because of the shared language and acting pool). It is very important to understand their differences, because they have a direct impact on the development process and the way development funding is raised. Chapter 12 proposes a similar typology of US films (Fig. 12.1).

This typology is looking at British films on the definition that they are culturally set in Britain, or reflect the experiences of British people in other countries, *regardless of the funding source*. Some successful British writers and producers are also working directly on full studio films, culturally *set* in the US, which therefore fall outside this table.

When considering where a particular film fits into the typology it is important to look at the intent of the film-maker, the track record of the director and actors, the choice of financiers and their brand (see Table

3.1), and the target audience for the film (see Box 3.1). Sometimes an independent British conceptual film is picked up by a studio for distribution in some countries, for example *Tamara Drewe*, which was picked up by Sony Pictures Classics for the US. But studio acquisition for distribution in some territories doesn't make it into an Anglo-Hollywood film in this typology because it wasn't *mainly funded by a studio* for its own international distribution machine. In the case of *Tamara Drewe* it was sold by sales agent WestEnd films to independent distributors around the world. *Tamara Drewe* is primarily a conceptual film, independently funded and distributed, with some financial support from the BBC; however, it is influenced by Anglo-Hollywood comedies in style and tone (and later the marketing campaign too).

The UK has historically lacked strong companies operating consistently in the conceptual category, in part because successful British producers and talent are attracted by job offers to work in Hollywood. However, recently this film category has started to attract interest from Film4 and BBC Films, and it may be an area of growth for future UK distribution-integrated businesses (Chapter 2 mentions the work of Vertigo Films and Revolver Entertainment). France has traditionally had some successful companies in the conceptual category, such as the French mini-studio EuropaCorp, which was founded by director Luc Besson specifically to make French conceptual mainstream films without relying on studio production or development funding. EuropaCorp has deals with US distributors and an integrated international sales agent.[2]

Being part of a typology, all these statements are generalizations and many films blur the categories. However, they do have their uses for categorizing film types, financing and target audience. It could be suggested that new columns could be added for intermediary films (such as conceptual films that get picked up and distributed by US studios after development and production). However, that would make the model too diffuse to be meaningful as a categorization, and it is more interesting to look at how films can occasionally move between categories during their development and release. An example of this is *Slumdog Millionaire*, which started as a specialist auteur film (developed at Channel 4's Film4 and Celador Productions), based on a novel adapted by a predominantly arthouse writer, albeit with a track record of occasional cross-over to mainstream (Simon Beaufoy, writer of *The Full Monty*). However *Slumdog* had a higher concept than most auteur films, taking it into the conceptual category. Director Danny Boyle had worked across all three categories of film, and the final budget was $15m. By the end of production it was jointly funded by the British TV company Celador ($10m) and studio division Warner Independent Pictures ($5m).[3] This means *Slumdog* straddles the line between conceptual and Anglo-Hollywood. However, it had no name cast (in Hollywood terms it was still low budget), and was not expected to be a big international earner, even after it was completed and screened. In fact,

Table 3.1 The three types of British film

	Specialist (a.k.a. auteur/art-house/directorial)	*Conceptual* (a.k.a. genre/high concept)	*Anglo-Hollywood*
Type of film	Director-driven, and sometimes actively auteur film-making. Specialist because they are non-mainstream. Some are genre-based, but most are arthouse or cross-genre, with challenging subject matter. Targeted at film festivals and arthouse cinema chains. Often made by director-writers. Creative risk-taking is quite likely, because audiences and funders expect it.[4]	Films with a straightforward pitch or concept; including genre (thrillers, horror, romantic comedies, etc.). The genre is more important than the name of the director, and the film is marketed on the pitch. Between 2005 and 2010 there was a steep rise in UK films 'with a distinctive hook, genre or style', both in number produced and income at box office.[5]	Also conceptual, but funded largely by a US studio and aimed at the US market and the studio's own international distribution network. A hybrid between a British story/setting and the sensibility/structure of a US mainstream film. Shot in Britain with predominantly British talent (perhaps one or two names for the US marketplace). Creative risk-taking generally unlikely, but budgets large so higher overall risk.[6]
Aspiration	Aspire to make art and win awards. Expected to appeal to a narrower audience segment than mainstream films. Some hope to 'cross over' into the mainstream, but this is rare.	Aspire to be mainstream (some hope to be Anglo-Hollywood in their commercial projections). They are not intended to get awards.	Manufactured to be internationally commercial and mainstream.
Level of realism	Realistic (sometimes 'kitchen sink'), or hyper-reality (due to artiness).	Hyper-reality (due to concept or genre, or both).	Realistic or hyper-hyper-reality.
Examples	*The Wind That Shakes The Barley; Red Road; Fish Tank, An Education; Tyrannosaur, Submarine, Bright Star;* anything by Mike Leigh and Shane Meadows. A small number of them break out and become internationally lucrative (from *Chariots of Fire* to *Trainspotting*, and more recently *The King's Speech*), but these are the exception. Most are low budget and rely on the home market and a small number of European territories.	*The Inbetweeners Movie; Calendar Girls; Made in Dagenham; Kidulthood; The Queen; Chalet Girl; Horrid Henry; Shaun of the Dead; Lock Stock and Two Smoking Barrels;* teen films in the vein of the *Twilight* franchise; and youth music films like *Streetdance 3D*.	Examples include many of Richard Curtis's romantic comedies (or Brit-coms) from the 1990s (*Notting Hill, Four Weddings, Bridget Jones's Diary*); the bigger budget Jane Austen adaptations; *Kinky Boots, Shakespeare in Love,* and franchises like Harry Potter, Nanny McPhee, Narnia, and James Bond. The British production company Working Title accounts for many of these films, financed through their output deals (first with PolyGram Filmed Entertainment and now Universal Studios).

	Specialist (a.k.a. auteur/art-house/directorial)	Conceptual (a.k.a. genre/high concept)	Anglo-Hollywood
	Anglo-Hollywood specialist: There are a small number of specialist films funded by Hollywood on bigger budgets and aimed at awards kudos: for example *The English Patient*, *The Hours*, *Remains of the Day*, *Never Let Me Go*, *Atonement*, etc. They are usually adapted from famous novels with respected directors or highly auteur UK-based directors like Terry Gilliam or Tim Burton. They are in this column because of the type of audience they are aimed at.		See also Anglo-Hollywood specialist sub-section in left-hand column.
Director	Auteur or auteur-esque, must have clear distinctive vision and the broadcaster must want to form a relationship between their brand and the director and/or cast. Michael Winterbottom, Ken Loach, Shane Meadows, Andrea Arnold, Jane Campion, Mike Leigh, Paul Greengrass (before the Bourne trilogy), etc.	Directors are sometimes big names, sometimes arthouse directors looking for a bigger budget, and sometimes first timers, including experienced commercials directors or TV directors.	Most Anglo-Hollywood film directors have previously been successful auteurist or conceptualist directors, and will usually go back to those forms. For example, Mike Newell, Stephen Frears, Anthony Minghella, John Madden, Roger Michell, Danny Boyle, Paul Greengrass, Joe Wright, etc.
Audience type: (see below for more details)	Mainly avids/buffs, with some aficionados. Mainstream plus only on rare cross-over films, and on Anglo-Hollywood-specialist.	Mainstream plus, and some mainstream. Few aficionados.	Mainly mainstream, mainstream plus (to a lesser extent aficionados and avids on 'must-see' films, but generally they will reject them as 'selling out' to the US).

when Warner Brothers decided to close down Warner Independent Pictures, they still thought the film was a risky proposition and believed it would go straight to DVD in the US, without a theatrical release;[7] so they sold half their rights in the film to Fox Searchlight (including US distribution rights), a decision they were to regret when it won eight Oscars and went on to make in excess of $140m in US box office, and over $30m in DVD sales.[8] Certainly, *Slumdog Millionaire* was a cross-over success, but it was an exception to the norm and it is usually safer to develop and produce films assuming that they will stay within a category.

Three types of audience

The audience typologies in the bottom row of Table 3.1 are based on UK Film Council research from the 2000s, and are broken down in Box 3.1.

Box 3.1 Different categories of cinema-goers, based on research by the UK Film Council/Stimulating World Research[9]

Mainstream audiences are unlikely ever to view anything other than major 'Hollywood'-style blockbusters. Escapism is a central driver of their reason to visit a cinema. Very unlikely to seek out 'foreign' or specialized films. This is the vast majority of the UK audience.

Mainstream plus audiences are generally mainstream, but see some more specialized films on a few occasions per year. Cinema attendance can be as infrequent as once a month. A less mainstream film that has earned itself the status of a 'must-see' can appeal to them over and above mainstream fare. These films will typically be US or English, offbeat but upbeat, accessible and with a familiar cast (e.g. *About Schmidt* with Jack Nicholson, *The King's Speech*).

Aficionado audiences tend to view a mix of films, including major foreign language titles, and can be encouraged to become even more adventurous in their viewing choices. May portray themselves as more discerning than other film-goers, describing themselves as 'anti-Hollywood' – even though they still predominantly see mainstream American films. Compared to mainstream types, Aficionados are more likely to make an effort to seek out specialized films that have caught their attention. Aficionados will see all the same specialized films as mainstream plus audiences, as well as specialized films that are foreign, more thought-provoking and have unfamiliar casts. They are still likely to reject the more extreme examples of specialized material.

Avids or 'Film buffs' avoid mainstream films in favour of more extreme, esoteric and difficult subject matter (specialized) films. They go to the cinema twice a week, attend film festivals, collect rare DVDs and follow particular directors/actors. They may like films that do not fit neatly into any genre. They will discuss and analyse films. They will see mainstream films for different reasons than other audiences (e.g. to appreciate the special effects in *The Matrix* or *Avatar*). Most university film studies students fall into this category.

Summit avids are the most widely knowledgeable and tend to work in the film industry or film education/journalism.

Specialist avids tend to be the most obsessive, often dismissive of films they do not deem worthy of consideration and have a pronounced collector mentality.

Scattergun avids enjoy film as one (albeit important) component of their varied cultural diet.

The producer (and maybe the writer) need to be focused about which of these audience groups they are targeting; and therefore what typology of film it is (Specialist or Conceptual or Anglo-Hollywood). Following automatically on from this is whether the right type of director is attached for the type of film, what the budget size is, who the likely financiers are, and, finally, what p&a spend is required to reach that audience segment, and which distributors would therefore be suitable to handle the release (deep enough pockets and requiring strong relationships with the correct types of exhibitors). If none of the target distributors want to handle the film there may be something wrong with the script or package rather than with the taste of the distributors. And the size of the potential audience of specialist films is much smaller: in a major survey in 2011 in the UK it was found that of engaged and committed cinema-goers 31 per cent mainly or only go and see specialist indie films, whereas 69 per cent go mainly or only to see blockbusters.[10]

How the three types of film are financed

Financiers often have their own brands or brand associations, and their choices of budget level are also sometimes limited by the amount of money they can afford to invest. So let's look more closely at which organizations will usually fund which type of film (Table 3.2).

It is crucial for the producer to make sure that a film's budget matches its value in the film sales marketplace, either financially or via brand association, and this chart could help assess where a film may sit. The usual problem is when specialist films end up being made for too large a budget, and are then unable to recoup (or even unable to get out of development and into production).

Three types of development finance (and the strings attached)

The reason for going into so much detail with this typology is that the three types of film are usually developed from different sources, as we can see in Table 3.3.

Table 3.2 How the three types of film are financed

	Specialist	Conceptual	Anglo-Hollywood (and Anglo-Hollywood specialist)
Finance source	Independently produced by very small companies (two or three employees).	Independently produced by very small or small companies, or in Europe sometimes integrated mini-majors like Canal Plus.	Produced by studios, usually through very established production companies, though sometimes smaller ones if they trust the producer.
Budget size	Auteurist films dominate the UK low-budget market. They are low to medium budget, with the majority funded by the home territory (usually broadcasters).	Wide variety of budget sizes, from ultra low to high. The more expensive ones often lose money, because they are competing directly with Hollywood product and lack the studios' ability to attach stars (to secure domestic TV and DVD income), invest in global marketing campaigns, and recoup directly from integrated distribution and exhibition.	Usually large budget because of the need for big names to drive a US release and big production values. However, they will also have to recoup their studio-funded international distribution campaigns.
Broadcaster?	A domestic broadcaster is usually vital. Crucially, broadcasters back them for brand association with the director or adapted work, rather than the expectation of big box office profits (they have to pay for TV programming anyway, and film finance is a subsidiary of overall drama programming).	These films are not driven primarily by the auteur film-maker, but by the concept of the script and the package (cast and director) usually matched against the financing power of the marketplace (predicated by sales agents, through pre-sales or estimates used by the producer to access equity funding). However, in the last five years UK broadcasters Film4 and BBC have taken more interest in conceptual films, especially those with a youth or more auteurist edge (see below).	A domestic broadcaster is not necessary at the funding stage. Usually broadcast rights are sold on after production, as the result of a distribution deal between the broadcaster and the studio or its output-deal-connected distributor.
Why and how do they back the film?	These films are made for artistic prestige, more than commercial returns. Films are funded on the director's reputation/art potential.[11] Dependent on broadcasters BBC and Channel 4 and public subsidy. Surprisingly few private investors put money in here (because it is comparatively safe, if the right director is attached at the right budget level), but they tend to be attracted to conceptual films.	These films are made for a mixture of art and commerce. For low budgets the genre is vital (such as horror or thriller). For larger budgets the package is vital, because pre-sales or sales estimates are needed to secure funding (often non-industry equity). The package is the actors, as attracted by the director. Sometimes investment is from larger sales agents, like Summit, and recently some UK distributors	These films are made because the studio needs product for international distribution. These projects are often developed and financed and distributed in large part by US studios (and sometimes the larger sales agents), who will also receive the majority of the eventual profits. Therefore they are developed with an eye to production and the audience market. These films rely on the US domestic box office to

	Specialist	Conceptual	Anglo-Hollywood (and Anglo-Hollywood specialist)
		have also part-financed production, such as Vertigo (*Streetdance 3D*, *Horrid Henry 3D*, *Monsters* and *The Sweeney*) and urban youth-oriented Revolver Entertainment (*Sket* and *Shank*). Until 2010 the UK Film Council Premiere fund encouraged this sector; however, the move of lottery funding to the more culturally focused BFI may reduce support for this sector in favour of specialist films. Non-film investors are sometimes tempted by the promises of profits at Anglo-Hollywood level.	recoup a large part of their investment, with the rest of the world being marketed off the back of the US success. However, foreign is now sometimes starting to account for more than 50 per cent of income.
Main gatekeepers	Film executives at BBC and Channel 4 and executives at the National Lottery production fund (previously UK Film Council).	Equity financiers, talent agents, sales agents and executives at the National Lottery production fund. Also involved are European mini-studios like Canal Plus and Pathé, and some UK distributors (see above). In the last few years Film4 at Channel 4 have backed more genre films, especially those with a youth angle, including *Attack the Black*, *The Inbetweeners Movie*, *How to Lose Friends* and *Shaun of the Dead* (developed at Film4 but eventually acquired after production by ITV). BBC Films were involved in *Made in Dagenham*, *Streetdance 3D*, *The Awakening* and *In The Loop*.	US studio executives and UK companies with formal output deals with them, or strong track records and relationships.
US studio involvement	Specialist US studio[12] divisions will sometimes acquire for US distribution, but will not invest in production unless the director has an international reputation or the subject matter appeals.	Specialist US studio divisions will sometimes acquire for US distribution, but rarely invest.	US studio always involved: either via specialist divisions or the main studio.

Table 3.3 How the three types of film are developed

	Specialist/auteur	Conceptual	Anglo-Hollywood (and Anglo-Hollywood specialist)
Who has the idea?	Often a director-originated idea, often that of a director-writer. When writer-originated the attachment of a suitable director is vital to appeal to the right broadcasters.	Either a writer-originated idea or producer-originated idea or existing story (book or play or life story). Director employed to suit the international marketplace, especially pre-sales.	Usually a producer-originated idea (sometimes writer-originated), or existing famous novel or stage play, with a suitable name writer and director employed to suit US studio backers.
Who runs the development process?	Probably developed by a producer and writer or writer/director team, without a production company development executive. Script feedback from broadcaster development executives. Occasional use of script editors, but this is not usual. Marketing information unlikely to be considered. The director is given considerable autonomy (some say too much) because of inherent faith in the director's vision.	During development there may be large input from in-house development executives. Script editors often used. Notes from sales agents will be taken seriously, because they are often a part of the financing process. Marketing information used, if obtainable, but many of these companies lack access to it.	Large input from development executives and distributors and marketing departments from an early stage. Script editors invariably used. (Note that Anglo-Hollywood specialist films are in this column, rather than the Specialist column, because of the development process used. In the first typology they are in the Specialist column because of the intended target audience.)
Development funding?	Sometimes starts as a spec. script or adaptation, or small investment from the producer, then funding from broadcaster development or public subsidy (national or European via the EC's MEDIA fund).	Starts as spec. script or adaptation, then funding from broadcaster development or public subsidy (national or European via the EC's MEDIA fund) or equity investor.	Development funding requires major investment from the studio or major production company with TV income or studio links or a major development slate (equity or subsidy or both). They do not usually receive subsidy or broadcaster funding (more possible on an Anglo-Hollywood specialist film).

	Specialist/auteur	Conceptual	Anglo-Hollywood (and Anglo-Hollywood specialist)
Development budget	Relatively low development budget, sometimes with the writer or director working for a long time on spec. With bigger name arthouse directors and writers it can go up (indicative budget: £10k–£50k, or up to £80k with experienced talent).[13]	Possibly an expensive option payment, and usually a mid-range 'name' writer in the genre, so a mid-range development budget (£25k–100k).	The project often starts as an expensive book or play or high concept, requiring an expensive option payment, and needs a very experienced and expensive 'name' writer. Possibly several different writers over time, adding up to a high development budget (£75k–£200k). Some projects stall because of the high development costs attached to the previous development of the film.
Replacement writer or the use of anonymous script polishers?	Very unlikely to replace the writer.	Replacement writers are quite possible, and becoming more widespread. Anonymous script polishes are unusual.	Standard practice to replace the writer, and use anonymous script polishes.

As shown in Chapter 1, development funding is high risk and low return, and even if the film is successful there will be little or no profit above the dividend received on the first day of principal photography. Given these terms, banks or independent equity investors are wary of getting involved; so most development funding in the UK and Europe is dependent either on publicly funded broadcasters or on national or European public subsidy funds. So what are the strings attached to these two routes of funding? Broadcasters investing in development and production are generally inclined to support those auteur film-makers and specialized films that they wish to associate with their own corporate brand. They eschew home-grown conceptual films (which are often therefore the hardest to raise development funding for), preferring to buy in US mainstream films with more recognized stars.

Public development funds also have intended or unintended consequences on which projects are developed. For example, some funds (such as the regional film funds) require projects with a local cultural bias; others favour the attachment of a distributor or sales agent (such as the Europe-wide MEDIA public subsidy fund, and the defunct UK Film Council Slate Scheme), which may stifle creativity at the early stages; and others still culturally favour arthouse films and writer-directors rather than conceptual films (as some broadcasters do). Furthermore, if the public fund takes the project on to production it can sometimes have complicated committee-based greenlighting systems or legal requirements.

In both broadcaster development and public fund development the track records of the producer and writer come under close scrutiny. It is generally difficult for the writer to apply directly to these funds (unless they are very established), and alternatively there are only a small number of new talent schemes and competitions run by some national subsidy funds. This is why many new writers end up writing their own projects in their own time as speculative scripts and then get them placed after they are reasonably complete.

The UK is dominated by the power of the four 'gatekeepers'[14] of film development and production in the UK: the BFI Film Production Fund with National Lottery funding (previously the UK Film Council), BBC Films, Film4 and Working Title (mainly making Anglo-Hollywood specialist and mainstream films with Universal or StudioCanal). These gatekeepers unintentionally create a false market that most producers need to navigate, prior to the industry marketplace of sales and financing and the consumer marketplace of the paying audience. In other words they take into development those films that are also likely to get production funding from their own funds. Three out of four of the above gatekeepers are specialists in their leaning, which warps the development marketplace away from conceptual and mainstream films. Although it is not talked about widely in the industry, the inescapable conclusion is that films are initially developed by producers for particular gatekeepers, and therefore the nature of funding and the internal gatekeeper financing marketplace may affect the final script. It is only a small number of successful producers, who can raise development slate funding or an output deal with a studio or broadcaster, who are able partially to free themselves from this effect. (Again the UK suffers from the lack of well-financed integrated companies which might otherwise develop mainstream scripts and directors. At the time of writing some of the proposals of the UK Film Policy Review may help to remedy this problem, by allowing producers to reinvest development money recouped from successful production.)[15] It has been suggested that this situation causes a lack of diversity and plurality in film development, and that the sector may benefit from a publicly funded development fund that enables the independent producer to option and develop projects (especially with risky new writers) without committing to a likely production funder and altering a project to suit the corporate brand and arthouse taste of the gatekeepers (see Chapter 14 for more suggestions about this).

By contrast, in television drama development there is no public Lottery funding, but there is a broadcasting schedule to fill and therefore a demand for broadcast hours per year. The gatekeepers at the BBC and Channel 4 are augmented by drama gatekeepers at ITV and BSkyB (the latter currently do not invest in film, but do invest in drama), and a far greater acceptance throughout the TV sector of the power and relevance of genre and audience demand. This may be one reason why British TV dramas have been recently exported and franchised internationally with greater consistency and regularity than UK films,[16] and why more and more British film producers are also developing TV series and serials alongside their feature film slate. Examples include Ecosse Films with *Monarch of the Glen* and *Mistresses* for BBC TV; Revolution Films with the *Red Riding* trilogy for Channel 4; and Warp Films with *This Is England '86* for Channel 4 (a rare example of a spin-off TV series from an arthouse feature film, probably driven by the broadcaster's desire to continue to work with auteur director Shane Meadows). The power of the returning TV series to drive turnover and cashflow then helps the company to continue to develop film projects by helping cover company overheads and paying development costs.

Conclusion: Make the film for what it is worth

Different types of film get developed, produced and distributed by different types of company, and are aimed at quite specific audiences. The producer and writer need to be aware of getting the right match between these financing companies and their own project, as well as between the target audience and the film. The choice of development funder could be the most important choice that the producer and writer ever make: it will influence the final script and the completed film. Another important issue is whether the type of film (and the size of its likely audience) really matches the projected budget. As usual, this is the old issue of commerce vs. creativity.

At the end of the day the producer continually has to ask himself the following question:

> *Am I developing and making the film with the right people, and for what it is worth in the financing marketplace (not necessarily the consumer marketplace); or has the likely cost of the cast, the director, or the shoot, pushed it beyond what I can sell it for?*

The professional writer and development executive should also consider this maxim during development, so that the cost, ambition and scope of the story match its likely value in the marketplace for that category of film. A low-budget conceptualist schlock horror film cannot support complex crowd scenes or too many different locations (which is why these films classically revolve around a small number of people trapped in a haunted castle/house/island/train/underground bunker). And creative experimentation has a cost attached – for example, a film script that maybe changes genre half-way through, or challenges audience expectations with radical narrative twists, is perfectly acceptable to part of the market; but only at the right price tag and with the right director in the driving seat.

In the next chapter it is time to examine in detail the development roles of the screenwriter, the producer and the director, and their general character types and personalities. This will help lead into issues about managing creativity and development in Part II of the book.

Case interview: How the producer chooses development financiers – matching the brand of the financier to the project

The small number of gatekeepers to development funding means it is important for the producer to know the company he is approaching, especially its brand match with the project and its director, as various interviews carried out for this book have shown. For example, producer and writer Peter Ettedgui emphasizes that a film will be intentionally or unintentionally changed by the company that is funding development:

> To some degree every financing company has a brand, based on certain values, or if they don't have a brand they are aspiring to one. It may be a more auteur-driven brand, it may be more commercial, or more genre-based, or it may be more linked with period films. If, say, you are thinking of approaching Film4, you know that they tend to look for projects which are more personal, based on original material, perhaps a little more idiosyncratic or left-field, and less dependent on perceived commercial factors. The perception is that

they are on the side of the film-maker, and represent a greater degree of artistic freedom. And if you go to a studio like Disney to raise finance money you go in knowing that this is the 'Mouse House', with a brand built on wholesome values and family fare. So when we had [the film] *Kinky Boots* in development at Disney we knew full well that we could not push the more risqué aspects of the film's subject – we had researched the world of drag queens, fetishism and transvestism, but we knew that we wouldn't be able to portray the more lurid details of this life in a Disney-backed film. Whereas, had we made the film with Film4, we would have portrayed this world more authentically, probably working with a different writer and director; but it wouldn't have been such a crowd-pleasing comedy by nature. What I'm saying is when you as a producer go out to raise development or production money for a project, your first job is to know which financier is appropriate for the kind of film you want to make. It's absolutely essential as a producer that you know what your film is, because only then can you make sure that everyone else is on the same page.

So the money has strings attached – the source is expecting input and influence, to make the film match that organization's own needs and brand association. Producer Andy Paterson agrees and argues that the choice of development funder is the producer's first vital decision, and that influences most of the later decisions.

My task is to try and find a way of getting that story onto the screen. … And that is a process of enabling, but it's also a process of protection. So from the very beginning you'd better have a sense of the kind of people that might understand the story (including the simple dynamic of how much this movie's going to cost vs. what it's worth, because there's really no point developing something that is incredibly expensive if it's necessarily a very limited audience). … You don't want to make the catastrophic commercial decision right at the beginning, just so you can get some money to write the script. … One of my many jobs (as a producer) is to match the source of development money with the project in such a way that when the notes come in, you will already feel that you're trying to make the same film. So mis-selling at any stage in the process could be disastrous … you've got to be very careful about matching the funding and the executives with the project and the writer. And I try to be really open with the writer about how it works. Sometimes you can over-protect writers, and if you're going to write in the movie business there's not much point being protected, you need to *understand*. I've always found that writers thrive on understanding how the process works in all its awful levels, because then they don't get shocks a year and a half down the line when they've already put their heart and soul into a script and you turn round and go: 'Well you know of course the people who gave us the money didn't want that story in the first place, they want you to take out this and change that and do that, because actually they want a different movie.' That's not protection, that's just feeble.

Paterson's concern is that some development financiers may take the idea and gradually turn it into what they want, rather than what you intended.

If you go and pitch it to the wrong people [for the film], say those people are going to want to make a very commercial version; and there's plenty of people out there thinking all along that they'll let the writer go a certain distance, but what they're going to do then is make changes. And if you want to make a really commercial film, then great, go pitch it to people that know how to do that, but know what you're doing.

The producer also needs to negotiate with the funding source, if their feedback and notes are not what was expected:

If the notes are somehow suddenly widely different from everything we've spoken about on the project, then I have at least the moral authority with the people giving the notes to say: 'That's not what we talked about, that's not what you bought.' If the script just isn't working, that's a different thing. Sometimes you'll get notes that go: 'This isn't what you sold me, this just isn't working.' And then you have a different situation, you have to deal with the writer and say: 'This isn't delivering what we promised, and why is that?' And that's as much my problem as the writer's problem.

Case interview: Development and the writer-director

Some interviewees mentioned that they thought writer-directors were favoured over the original writer for development funding. Development consultant and lecturer Phil Parker argued that to date original writers have not had a big enough slice of the development budgets from the National Lottery, BBC and Channel 4. Producer and screenwriter Peter Ettedgui agrees and says that original writers do not get enough access to development because of the current habit of broadcasters and public funds in the specialist sector to back writer-directors rather than writers:

> The belief of many executives and companies (in the specialist sector) is that films should be conceived and developed by the figure of the writer-director. The inherent flaw in that process is that while they may be fine directors, very few writer-directors really know how to write. This may be partly because they haven't studied screenwriting; but it's also because the notion that they are the author of the film creates a certain arrogance – that the strength of their directorial 'vision' transcends the basic requirement to tell a story and keep the audience hooked. Such auteurs are sometimes frankly not that good at collaborating with writers. The result is that writers are often locked out of this whole area of indie film-making, where they could really be cutting their teeth; and that's why you find most of our finest writers learning their craft and plying their trade in theatre and television, rather than film.

Script editor Sarah Golding agrees that most writer-directors are more one than the other....

> I don't think I've ever come across anybody who was equally good at both writing and directing, that I can think of... I've worked with writer-directors who are better writers (more rarely); or better directors (more commonly). Whichever way round it works, the director when they're writing has to try and think of themselves as writers at that moment, and not think of themselves as directors ... Somehow a document has to be produced that goes out there and attracts the money. And that has to be a crafted, written document,

which is sometimes quite hard for writer-directors who have got an incredibly strong vision and know everything that's happening and have filmed the whole thing in their head many times. But to put something on paper that conveys that intense vision is a struggle. ... If people were seeing the film, instead of reading it as though they were reading a book, it wouldn't be a problem. It's to do with the nature of how we read things, and assess their suitability to be made into films.

4   The creative triangle

Building development relationships

> The studio wanted to make a horror film, but they didn't tell me that. They chose me to direct and I chose collaborators like the Director of Photography from *The English Patient*. We were making an art-house film, not a horror film. It was bound to end in tears.
>
> (Asif Kapadia, director of *The Warrior, Far North, Senna*, discussing the film *The Return*, starring Sarah Michelle Gellar)

Introducing the creative triangle

Now that we have a clear concept of how the independent film industry works, and how development funding is raised, the next few chapters will start to address the following crucial question:

> *How can the creative team of the writer, producer, director and development executive be made to work together most effectively?*

If the producer can manage these relationships correctly, then there is a better chance of getting successful films developed and financed, and as a result building a successful and sustainable company.

Many interviews were carried out for this book, with writers, producers and script executives, and the message emerged loud and clear that the surest way to build a film with a coherent vision was to encourage a strong and trusting relationship between the writer, producer and director. Emphasis was laid on the importance of communication, trust, and a shared mission and vision of the *type* of film that is being made. As the French producer Jean-Luc Ormieres once said: 'The most important thing is the team of producer, writer and director. The stronger the relationship, the more we will be creative, and the stronger we will be in the marketplace.'[1]

This could be represented as a creative triangle (see Fig. 4.1) where communication is clear and power is equally shared.

Screenwriter Tony Grisoni admits that it is pragmatic for the writer to support the creative triangle concept, because the writer is the one who is most liable to be replaced (as he explains: 'You can be dropped out like a

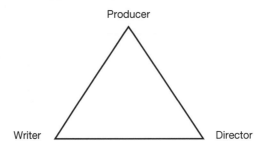

Figure 4.1 The film creative triangle[2]

spare part of a machine, and replaced by a different cog'). He argues that if the writer is always afraid of being replaced then he may not take the risks that are necessary for originality and creativity. But Grisoni also explains that a strong triangle protects all three people and the film itself from too much interference from finance sources, which can have a wider creative benefit:

> I think that together you will make a better film. The guiding tenet is 'we are making this film *together*, and we will make our own mistakes. We'll make as good a film as we can. ...' Lars Von Trier (the Danish film director) once called it the holy triumvirate. I'm in danger of stretching the religious metaphor to breaking point, but I do think people who come together to make a film do make an act of faith in the spirit or the core of that film.

Screenwriter Rob Sprackling agrees, and suggests that one of the problems with the Hollywood system is their culture of replacing the writer and therefore destroying the creative triangle:

> If you get a producer that really believes in the writer, and the director that understands the writer, then everyone's working off the same page. If there's mutual respect and trust then you're much more likely to come up with something good than if everyone is doing their own thing. When it comes down to it, I think it's very difficult to get a movie to be good if you constantly sack the writers, because the writer is the original creative voice. If you want to get rid of your original creative voice, what are you saying?

Duncan Kenworthy, the producer of the comedy *Four Weddings and a Funeral*, also mentions the importance of the triumvirate, as expressed in this interview with the film journalist Tim Adler:

> It was easy to get up a head of steam on *Four Weddings*, because Mike Newell (director), Richard Curtis (writer) and I all had similar

backgrounds, reading English at Oxbridge. We spent probably eight months doing nothing but talking about it, and I am convinced that this had an awful lot to do with the final film. Within the central triumvirate of director, producer and writer there was no ambiguity. It always amazes me how much ambiguity a script can hide. You think that everybody reads the script in the same way but they don't. A script is in many ways an unsatisfactory blueprint for a film because it hides so much, much more than it reveals. In some ways the producer's job is to be the best interviewer in the world, getting the writer and director to talk and be absolutely in tune.[3]

So this is something that producers and writers and directors always have to ask themselves: *are we all making the same type of film?* This needs to be clear from the outset, and is not something that can be fixed in the editing room, because the fault-lines and problems will always be there.

The creation of a strong triangle is complicated by two key issues. The first is personal: writers, directors, producers and development executives all tend to have certain psychologies and character types, which can sometimes be in conflict with one another (as this chapter will explore). The second issue is power, because over time the development process causes power to shift from one member of the triangle to another, complicated by the arrival of powerful newcomers and financiers who disrupt the relationships of the triangle (as the next chapter explores). Both these issues need very careful management by the producer.

The writer: a classic creative type

The study of personality types is a branch of *differential psychology* which tries to analyse and describe the differences and similarities between people, creating a classification of their general psychological characteristics: the consistent patterns of thought, emotion and behaviour.[4] The problem with personality types and character traits as a methodological approach is that people change throughout their lives, under the influence of upbringing, society, culture, education, workplace, and so on; and most people are a complex bundle of different and sometimes conflicting character traits. However differential psychology is increasingly gaining mainstream acceptance and there does seem to be a difference between the *type* of person that becomes a writer and the type of person that becomes a producer; and again the type of person that becomes a successful director. Understanding these generalized differences may help cast light on the complexity of maintaining strong relationships during the development process.

Many writers could be said to be the classic lone creative person: working in a spare bedroom and wrapped up in an imaginary world of their own creation. Chapter 8 examines the personality traits of creative people in more detail, but like other creative people, writers tend to be more than averagely intelligent, independent, self-motivated, inquisitive, lateral-thinking, tolerant of ambiguity, willing to take intellectual risks, confident and full of self-belief (although perhaps at the same time insecure and anxious). They have the mental facilities of visualization, remote association and manipulation of images, perhaps through metaphor and poetic description.[5]

Screenwriters have strong domain-specific knowledge (in this case writing ability and film literacy), and some at least are good at self-management (professional writers tend to work around fixed daily routines). Most film writers are freelancers, operating outside a company structure and averse to the kind of supervision and bureaucracy that working in a company would bring. This reflects their instinctive unconventionality. They are not particularly motivated by money (although that doesn't mean they don't want to be paid), but they *do* want the respect of their peers, and for their vision and ideas to be seen and respected. On the downside they can be non-conformist, dreamy, difficult, impulsive, defensive, arrogant, stubborn, rebellious, unreliable, obsessive, and react personally to criticism and praise. Above all, they want to feel that they are in control and don't like to feel that they're being managed, which can cause a problem for the producer whose job it is to manage them.[6]

They are often obsessed by their writing, so there may be a long-suffering partner who has a sensible job to keep them afloat, or else they do their writing in the evenings whilst holding down a job in the daytime. They are compelled to write, in the same way that artists are compelled to paint and draw, just to get their ideas out of their heads and down onto the page. The act of creative thought can be obsessively all-encompassing and even ecstatic, wiping out the world around them in favour of the world inside their minds. This trance-like state has been noticed by many observers of creative people, and creativity theorist Professor Mihály Csíkszentmihályi labelled it as *creative flow* in his influential 1990 book *Flow: The Psychology of Optimal Experience*, and its sequel: *Creativity: Flow and the Psychology of Discovery and Invention*. He explains that:

> Concentration is so intense that there is no attention left over to think about anything irrelevant or to worry about problems. Self-consciousness disappears, and the sense of time becomes distorted. An activity that produces such experiences is so gratifying that people are willing to do it for its own sake, with little concern for what they will get out of it.[7]

Unlike some creatives, writers are fascinated by other people – their lives, situations and worlds. Humanity is their resource and stories are their stock-in-trade, so their intellectual preoccupations are often balanced by empathy and concern for the human condition.

The director: a charismatic leader

A writer may be dreamy and creative at home, and may need to be charismatic and strong in meetings, but he does not have to be a *leader*. However, a director does. He has to convince other people to back him with millions of pounds, and then convince a large team of actors and crew that he will give them both creative freedom and strong leadership over the intense period of the shoot. The best directors are undoubtedly creative, but unlike writers they cannot lock themselves away in a garret and do it all on

Table 4.1 Why different industry players find it convenient for the director to retain cult power and auteur status (Epstein, 2006)[8]

Player	Reason for supporting director power
For the Hollywood studios	For the studios it is convenient for the director to have credit, even if they have legal ownership of authorial status and distribution rights. A helpful buffer between the stars and the studio – and a 'scapegoat' if it all goes wrong. Adds an aura of artistic endeavour.
For the producer	For the producer the director is central to attracting cast. Auteurism gives further credence to the director's track record and persuades investors to commit. The director engenders trust. Less questioning about the identity of the rest of the team.
For the talent agencies in Hollywood	Agents can use director clients to build packages with other clients: stars, literary properties, writers, etc.
For film reviewers, critics and academics	Directors provide a focus for their commentary and criticism.
For the director	Auteur status ensures the director gets good fees; high status (including DVD commentary, film festival and awards appearances, etc.) and artistic status; it also helps support the director's leadership and engineer the consent of cast and crew.
For the writer	On the plus side, the director helps the writer get the film made and get paid. On the downside, writers stand more to lose than many other players: directors are a challenge to authorial status, potentially able to derail their vision, and sometimes the source of the irritating 'a film by' credit. And the director gets paid more for less time on the job.

At almost every turn, inside and outside the community, they work to lend an aura of aesthetic dignity to the community's own perception of itself.
(Edward J. Epstein)

their own. However, as Table 4.1 shows, *auteur theory* and its cult of the vision of the film director helps give other people that confidence in their leader.

Business theories about leadership give some insight into the likely character traits of the successful director. Leadership is usually divided into two broad types: *transformational leaders*, who inspire and transform their followers by focusing on the big vision and charismatic leadership; and *transactional leaders*, who are more micro-managerial and rewards-based, using organizational bureaucracies and clear targets and goals.[9] Film directors tend to be transformational leaders, but because they need simultaneously to control and empower a large team of experts they also have to create a fine balance between being *authoritarian* (demanding the final decision), *directive* (letting people know what is expected), and *participative* (consulting and allowing creative involvement). Like many successful leaders, directors have a lot in common with a sub-division of transformational leaders known as *charismatic leaders*, who exert especially powerful effects on followers by virtue of their commanding self-belief and vision (see Box 4.1).

Box 4.1 Charismatic leadership (adapted from Conger and Kunungo (1988), and Greenberg and Barn (2003))[10]

The following characteristics are common in charismatic leaders (and some film directors):

- Narcissistic and succeed through belief in themselves rather than in others
- Often invoke strong reactions, which can be positive or negative
- Expressive behaviour and eloquence (tone of voice, expressions and body language engaging and captivating. Dynamic presence)
- Self-confidence in the correctness of their position and judgement. Unlikely to publicly air doubts or fear of failure
- Personal risk-taking (even if it involves a risk to their own position. Gamblers)
- A sense of vision of the future, even a sense of destiny
- Extraordinary behaviour (unconventional, sometimes extravagant). Their ways when successful elicit admiration, when unsuccessful criticism
- Successful change agents (opposition to the status quo. They want to make things happen). Ruthlessness/freedom from internal moral conflict (convinced about own rightness. Sometimes candid and forthright in reprimanding subordinates. Capable of transference of blame. They maintain a clear conscience, even when firing employees)
- Environmental sensitivity (realistic about constraints and resources)
- Better at change and innovation than administration
- Followers can become over-reliant and dependent on the leader (problems of succession planning within organizations – bad at training successors, potentially due to fear of being replaced by them)
- Some motives and strategies can be unethical – the charismatic leader may operate outside norms of behaviour and morals.

There are pros and cons amongst these character traits of *charismatic leaders*, but some of the ones that may be downsides in a long-term corporate environment could be upsides in running and controlling a short-term high-pressure film shoot. Some charismatic leaders also have a strong element of narcissism as a character trait. The so-called *narcissistic leader* was developed as a formal leadership concept by the American psychoanalyst and leadership theorist Dr Michael Maccoby (2000) and psychiatrist Dr Roy Lubit (2002), based on Freud's concept of the personality trait of *narcissism* (named after the Greek myth of the self-absorbed young man, Narcissus, who fell in love with his own reflection). We all have a degree of narcissism (it is part of our sense of identity, self-esteem and security), but it can be extraordinarily useful in a leader. Narcissistic leaders can charm their superiors, manipulate people effectively, communicate ideas, forge quick superficial friendships, make tough decisions quickly, and generate enthusiasm in others; but in the worst cases the character trait can also lead to egotism, vanity, conceit, paranoia, selfishness and grandiosity.[11] Sometimes it is the producer's job to anchor the director to reality, and act as the Sancho Panza to his Don Quixote. Dr Lubit has suggested that these positive and negative traits can be categorized into *productive* or healthy narcissistic leaders, and *unproductive* or destructive narcissistic leaders, as Table 4.2 explains.

This is not to say that all film directors are totally narcissistic, but that some of these character traits are often present, and for good reason,

Table 4.2 A comparison of the behaviour of productive and unproductive narcissistic leaders (Lubit, 2002)[12]

	Healthy narcissism	*Destructive narcissism*
Self-confidence	High outward self-confidence in line with reality	An unrealistic sense of superiority ('grandiose')
Desire for power, wealth and admiration	May enjoy power	Pursues power at all costs, lacks normal inhibitions in its pursuit
Relationships	Real concern for others and their ideas; does not exploit or devalue others	Concerns limited to expressing socially appropriate response when convenient; devalues and exploits others without remorse
Ability to follow a consistent path	Has values; follows through on plans	Lacks values; easily bored; often changes course
Foundation	Relatively secure self-esteem. Possibly healthy childhood with support for self-esteem and appropriate limits on behaviour towards others	Relatively insecure self-esteem. Possibly traumatic childhood undercutting true sense of self-esteem and/or learning that he/she doesn't need to be considerate of others

because at the start of the shoot the director is required to stamp his confident authority quickly on a large group of people with a large number of egos and get everyone moving in the same direction towards a coherent vision. There is only a fine line between an inflated sense of 'grandiosity' and an epic movie-maker. As creativity expert Raymond Nickerson points out: 'the line between self-confidence and arrogance is a fuzzy one, as is that between a willingness to take reasonable risks and irrational disregard for possible consequences of actions'.[13]

The director's task of leading large groups under time and resource pressure means they have to be authoritarian, assertive and towards the extroverted end of an *introvert/extrovert* continuum. This contrasts with the writer, who may be more *ambiverted* (inspired by social interaction, but needing time and space alone) or towards the *introverted* end of an introvert/ extrovert continuum.[14] Many of the problems identified above in relation to *destructive narcissism* occur over a longer timescale, and compared to business leaders directors have many advantages: there is a clear stated goal (finishing the film), short timescale, and the high motivation of the production team can be largely taken for granted (high pay, *Maslowian high self-actualization* (see Chapter 8), and the high-pressure nature of the film production business weeds out people who do not perform or are not self-motivated). In addition, the majority of the team will be broken up in seven weeks, at the end of the shoot, so there is no need for the director or producer to form a long-term group dynamic or culture (unless you are a film-maker who works regularly with the same crew, like Stephen Soderbergh, Mike Leigh or Ken Loach). Therefore the director is able to be totally autocratic, even narcissistic, and the contingent situation of the shoot means that these attitudes are not just acceptable but respected. But those same traits could be a problem during the long game of development.

When the director meets the writer

The style of direction required on a film shoot does not always match the participative smaller team dynamic of development. The autocratic charismatic leader is a distinctly different character type from the lone creative writer, and writers may not respond well to a dictatorial style. Theories about managing creative people (see chapters 8 and 9) are unequivocal that dictatorial attitudes and control procedures do not encourage creativity. Therefore the director has to be encouraged to switch from the necessary autocracy required by a film shoot to a far more gentle and encouraging role as a member of the development team.

A director in a development meeting may also be under time pressure, especially if he is still finishing the edit on another film, or publicizing an existing film, or if he has several other projects in development.

However, there are other concrete reasons why the writer may consciously or unconsciously resist the arrival of the director. The writer has been working on a screenplay for longer, whereas the director has just come on board and read the screenplay for the first time. The writer may feel that the director has been foisted upon him, because the choice of director is made by the producer under commercial pressure, sometimes without consultation or approval of the writer. The new arrival is also threatening his nurtured relationship with the producer and development executive ('Will they listen to him more than me? Will they prefer him to me, and maybe even replace me?'). More crucially, the writer is having to hand control of his unchallenged vision of the film over to someone else. Will their visions match one another, or is this the beginning of the end?

So the arrival of the director needs careful handling, and sometimes it is up to the producer or development executive to try to influence the director's behaviour at this stage, by preparing him for the meeting with the writer and vice versa. Failure to do so could embitter or alienate the writer; result in him intentionally or unintentionally not doing his best work; and cause the kind of creative stalling that many projects hit at this stage of the development process.

But the writer also cannot be over-protected. The director has to be able to raise any genuine issues with the script, so that they are resolved quickly and not temporarily glossed over. His feedback may be the product of a fresh pair of eyes, rooted in the experience of making other films, or may be about how to visualize key sequences and transform them from the literary form of the screenplay page to the big screen. Furthermore, many writers are simultaneously nervous and excited by the arrival of the director – this is the person who could make the film happen. To have got the script to the point where a bankable and serious director comes on board is a major achievement in itself, and a strong relationship with this director may also help get future scripts made in the future.

In these first meetings the producer is also testing out the director, to see if his ideas for the film match the vision that he and the writer have been working on; and the producer will also be talking to his contacts in the industry to assess whether attaching the director will add the necessary momentum to get the project financed. Producer and ex-development executive Ivana MacKinnon explains:

> It's very useful to really know what that film is before you get to that point (the arrival of the director) and then to find someone who also *shares* the vision for that film. ... I think it is a harsh reality for writers in the film industry that at first they are absolutely at the heart of everything and at a certain point they are sidelined, because the director takes it and the director has to make it their own. And unless the writer and the director can forge a powerful relationship, well, the producer can keep having a go at the relationship with the writer and keep trying to get them involved, but ultimately the producer has to also leave that director to make the project into their own vision, otherwise it's

impossible. Try and get as much communication as possible between the writer and the director is the only thing you can do, and try and make sure that they are both trying to make the same film.

All the interviewees for this book emphasized this same point – that the vital thing is to encourage honesty and open communication to ensure a match between the vision of the writer, director and producer so that they are all trying to make the same type of film.

Thus the producer or development executive is a vital mediator at this stage, and how they prepare for and manage the writer and director relationship can be vital for the whole project. This is examined in more detail in the case interviews at the end of this chapter, but ultimately the buck stops with the producer, who is also often a creative himself, and *also* a leader, and *also* another character type again.

The producer as entrepreneur

If the director has to be a leader, then so does the producer, as screenwriter Rob Sprackling explains:

> It's the writer's job to have the creative vision, the director's job to realize that vision and the producer's job to get the money and get the film made. ... If you don't have one key person who is determined to make it happen, then it will not work and not get made. The team must have a leader – you need to trust the leader and believe that after all the work they are able to get it made. The producer has got to be that leader.

The producer is very hard to fit into the typology of a character type, because he has a complex parcel of different skill sets and leadership styles that are required at different stages in the development, selling, production and exploitation of a film, in addition to the longer term strategic management and financing of a company or distribution business. The producer has to be both a *transformational leader* when inspiring financiers to spend millions on the film, and a *transactional leader* when using closer managerial skills to operate the production company, the legal negotiations and the production management side of the shoot. In terms of wider business strategy, independent producers generally fit into being responsive, manipulative (especially of external power circumstances), bargaining, intuitive and entrepreneurial, rather than using detailed long-term planning or rational analysis (their finance and business environment is too interdependent and chaotic).[15] Remember, the film producer does not usually have instant access to money, unless he is a studio or broadcaster executive. He has to go out and raise the money for the script from the marketplace. This makes producers first and foremost *entrepreneurial*, in that they are launching a new venture every time they try to fund another film.

According to the *Oxford English Dictionary*, part of the etymology of the word is the French *entreprendre*, to undertake, and amongst the definitions is: 'one who undertakes; a manager, controller; champion'. This neatly sums up the fact that the producer has to be a manager, but also a champion for other people. Typical entrepreneurial personality traits include independence, risk-taking, creativity, innovativeness, proactiveness and the ability to live with uncertainty. Boxes 4.2 and 4.3 show these general character types and skills in more detail. Like some creative people, entrepreneurs also tend to be *sensation-seekers*, a heritable personality trait that creates a need for novel experiences, enjoying the excitement of risk and embracing jobs that bear personal, financial and career risk (see Chapter 8 for more on sensation-seekers and creative people).[16]

Box 4.2 Summary of the character traits of entrepreneurs, adapted from Burns (2011)[17]

Character traits of owner-manager entrepreneurs: (relevant to most film producers)

- Need for independence – 'to be your own boss'
- Need for achievement – money is usually the badge of achievement, but sometimes peer or public recognition rather than money
- Internal locus of control (ability to exercise control over your environment and therefore destiny). Sometimes this leads to control freakery and micro-management
- Ability to live with uncertainty and take risks. Therefore sometimes prone to short-term incremental decision-making, rather than long-term planning.

Character traits of entrepreneurs in growth businesses and serial entrepreneurs (some relevant to film producers, some less so)

- Opportunistic – exploiting change for profit. Prepared to sell the business and move on to something else. Sometimes they get bored and move on to the next opportunity too fast
- Innovative – spot an opportunity in the marketplace and develop to exploit it. This requires an ability not just to embrace change, but to instinctively favour it
- Self-confident – believe in own judgement, sometimes to the point of being delusional
- Proactive and self-motivated: drive, determination, seek out opportunities. Long work hours – but they *enjoy* doing the work
- Tend to learn by doing, not by training (which may explain why some film producers resist the need for formal training courses on film production)
- Visionary, with flair – good for motivating others, helps to make own luck
- Willingness to take greater risks and live with more uncertainty – can put their own house on the line to make something succeed.

Box 4.3 Summary of the characteristics of entrepreneurs and innovators (Quinn, 1985)[18]

- They are fanatics who are often described as possessed or obsessed, even to the exclusion of family or personal relationships. As such they perceive the probability of success as higher than others around them. This commitment means that they persevere despite setbacks
- They have long-time horizons, and are prepared to work for many years trying to get a particular project to succeed. They therefore avoid early formal plans and proceed step by step
- They try to incur few overhead costs, work from low-rent offices, work overtime, and invest resources directly into the projects
- Instead of being formal strategists and planners, they adopt solutions wherever they can be found
- They usually work as a one-man band or run their own small company. Therefore there is no need to answer to committees, boards or corporate bureaucracies, so they can personally respond quickly and flexibly to any problem. This speed of response helps conventional entrepreneurs respond to market need or technological innovation, and in film it increases the producer's capacity to redesign the financing plan quickly if a financier drops out or an opportunity suddenly presents itself
- Motivated by rewards like peer recognition, power or independence as much as money; and as a result they do not panic or quit when others motivated purely by money may do so.

The summaries in boxes 4.2 and 4.3 use words like 'proactive', 'delusional', 'fanatical' and 'committed', and the producer will need these traits, because the odds of financial success are so stacked against him. Film business journalist Tim Adler[19] suggests that to get an idea of the odds against film success, consider that for every ten ideas only one gets turned into a treatment; and out of every ten treatments only one reaches first draft. Of the ten first-draft scripts only one will be developed further; and out of ten well-developed scripts only one will get selected for development and possible production by a financier/broadcaster/studio. Out of ten of those at the financing stage only one will get made. But then exploitation starts. Out of every ten films produced roughly five lose money, four eventually recoup after several years, and one will be a comparative hit. But as we saw in Chapter 2, the hit will probably not earn the independent financier or producer any more money than the failure, once the distributors and exhibitors have taken out their costs and fees, which may make the outsider wonder why anyone becomes a producer in the first place.

With at least some producers the answer is that they are more passionate about films and creative vision than they are about how much the movie makes them financially. It could be said that many UK film producers are what are called *lifestyle entrepreneurs*, meaning that they are primarily motivated by a passion for the product, in this case films, rather than by a desire to make profit (which is secondary, and more a part of survival than a goal in itself). The term lifestyle entrepreneurs was explored by Professors Allan Williams and Gareth Shaw at Exeter University, arising from their study of non-economically motivated entrepreneurs in tourism (see Box 4.4).[20] It unfortunately sounds demeaning, because the word lifestyle is sometimes associated with superficiality, so perhaps *passion entrepreneurs* would be a title with a more positive slant.

Indicative of their overriding passion for film is that producers are more likely to be found at film festivals than at executive business seminars. This is by way of contrast with the conventional entrepreneur, who is usually more obsessed with business in general, may launch several different businesses in totally unconnected sectors during a career, and is driven by the goal of profit and business growth.

Box 4.4 Some characteristics of lifestyle/passion entrepreneurs[21]

- Motivated by quality of life rather than growth
- Very limited growth orientation
- Under-utilization of resources and capital investment
- Irrational management and non-return-on-investment-based decision making
- Limited marketing and product development expertise and activities
- Under-utilization of information and communication technologies
- Reluctance to accept professional advice or external involvement
- Motivated by survival and sufficient income to maintain their way of life
- Low training on management
- Unwillingness to let go or to sell their ventures
- High dependency on distribution partners for their earnings – even when this is detrimental to profitability and competitiveness.

> The vast majority of entrepreneurs are independent minded and have difficulty in participating in clusters or accepting external advice. This applies particularly to lifestyle entrepreneurs who are not profit motivated.
>
> Peters et al., 2009

In small business start-ups there is a similar research distinction between the *growth firm*, set up with the intention of expansion, and the *lifestyle firm*, set up primarily to undertake an activity that the owner-manager enjoys and to provide income but not growth or expansion (so there is no need for strategic management or the acquisition of other businesses).[22] Occasionally a lifestyle firm can change into a growth firm accidentally, but the difference is in the entrepreneur's original motivation for starting the business. This may go some way towards explaining why many UK film producers do not build up and sell on big businesses. They stay small and take on each project individually because that is the way they like it (much to the frustration of government initiatives aimed at making the industry larger and more sustainable).

What happens when they are all together in a team?

There has been a lot of research about how teams work most effectively, and one of the key factors is allocating the right roles to the right people. One way to understand the different team roles of producer, writer and director is by using the business team roles system proposed by Meredith Belbin (see Box 4.5).

Box 4.5 Summary of Belbin's nine team roles (Belbin, 1981, 2004)[23]

- **Plant:** Highly creative people, *planted* in the team. Provide seeds of ideas from which major developments grow. Innovators and inventors. Solve difficult problems. Usually prefer to operate independently at some distance from other team members. Tend to be introverted and react strongly to criticism and praise. Allowable weaknesses: up in the clouds, inclined to disregard practical details
- **Shaper:** Challenging, dynamic, thrives on pressure, highly strung. The drive and courage to overcome obstacles. Competitive. Charismatic and extroverted. Allowable weaknesses: prone to provocation, impatience
- **Resource investigator:** Extroverted, enthusiastic, and communicative. Explores opportunities, and develops contacts. Allowable weaknesses: liable to lose interest after initial fascination
- **Coordinator (or chair):** Mature, calm, confident, and a good chairperson. Clarifies goals, promotes decision-making, delegates well. Strong sense of objectives. Allowable weaknesses: ordinary intellect or creativity
- **Completer finisher:** Painstaking, conscientious, anxious. Searches out errors and omissions, delivers on time. Allowable weaknesses: perfectionist, worries about small things, reluctant to 'let go'
- **Monitor evaluator:** Sober, unemotional, strategic and discerning. Sees all options, judges accurately. Hard-headed. Allowable weaknesses: lacks ability to motivate others
- **Implementer (or company worker):** Conservative, dutiful, disciplined, predictable. Organizing ability, practical common sense, hard-working. Turns ideas into practical actions. Allowable weaknesses: lack of flexibility, unresponsive to unproven ideas
- **Team worker:** Socially oriented, rather mild, sensitive. An ability to respond to people and to situations, and to promote team spirit. Allowable weaknesses: indecisive at moments of crisis
- **Specialist:** Expertise and in-depth knowledge of a key area for the team goal. Allowable weaknesses: tendency to focus narrowly on their own subject.

Belbin created these categorizations as a result of a research programme at Henley Management College during the late 1960s into the effectiveness of management teams and the complementarities of different roles. He argued that if there are too many people in a team with similar characteristics then the team may not function effectively. For example, if there are too many creatives, or *plants* as he calls them, then nothing will ever get finished. But too many *completer finishers* or *monitor evaluators*, and maybe nothing would ever get started. He argues that certain strengths are associated with *allowable weaknesses*, and an effective team is made up of diverse people with complementary skills and attributes, where one person's weakness is supported by another person's strength. A number of imperfect people could end up making perfectly functioning teams. For example, highly creative people are often not very interested in implementing long-term projects or running financial modelling spreadsheets, so you need a team in which different people take over different parts of the project. The same is true of the film development team, and Box 4.6 shows how some of the Belbin team roles could be applied to writers, directors and producers.

From this research Belbin developed a widely used series of tests to assess personality traits, so that leaders can allocate team roles more effectively. Since initial publication in his 1981 book *Management Teams: Why They Succeed or Fail*, the tests have grown in reputation and have been widely implemented in business. Belbin argues that they are not strictly psychometric tests (like Myers–Briggs tests), because they deal with a combination of traits, rather than measuring single and separate personality traits.[24] There is more on teams and how to manage them in Chapter 11.

Box 4.6 Belbin's team roles, as applied to film development[25]

Writers tend to be:

- **Plant:** Highly creative people. Provide seeds of ideas from which major developments grow. Innovators and inventors. Solve difficult problems. Usually prefer to operate independently at some distance from other team members. Tend to be introverted and react strongly to criticism and praise.

Directors tend to be:

- **Plant:** Highly creative (like writers)
- **Shaper:** Challenging, dynamic, thrives on pressure, highly strung. The drive and courage to overcome obstacles. Competitive. Charismatic and extroverted
- **Resource investigator:** Extroverted, enthusiastic and communicative. Explores opportunities, and develops contacts.

Producers should be (at different times):

- **Resource investigator:** Extroverted, enthusiastic (like directors)
- **Shaper:** Challenging, dynamic (like directors)
- **Coordinator (or chair):** Mature, calm, confident, and a good chairperson. Clarifies goals, promotes decision-making, delegates well. Strong sense of objectives
- **Completer finisher:** Painstaking, conscientious, anxious. Searches out errors and omissions, delivers on time
- **Monitor evaluator:** Sober, unemotional, strategic and discerning. Sees all options, judges accurately. Hard-headed
- **Implementer:** Conservative, dutiful, disciplined, predictable. Organizing ability, practical common sense, hard-working. Turns ideas into practical actions.

And in some cases, especially more *creative producers*:

- **Plant:** Highly creative (like writers and directors).

Box 4.6 clearly shows how many different team tasks producers are expected to carry out as part of their job, and each of those tasks requires different skill sets and character traits. It is hard to achieve all this in one person, and some successful producer teams have emerged by dividing the roles between two producers, such as the successful teaming at Palace Pictures and Scala Productions of creative producer Stephen Woolley, who specialized in working with directors and casting, and business producer Nik Powell, who mainly ran the company and raised production finance.[26] Not only is the producer's role multi-faceted, but so are the individual project's challenges. As producer and director Sydney Pollack declared: 'Every producer is different. It's been so different on every movie that I've worked on. For me, there is no definition.'[27] To get a deeper understanding of the varied role of the producer, it is worth reading two recent books of interviews with leading producers: Tim Adler's *The Producers: Money, Movies and Who Really Call the Shots,* and Helen De Winter's *What I Really Want To Do Is Produce.*[28]

This chapter has shown that the writer, producer and director are very different types of people, working in complementary but potentially conflicting roles. Put those three very different character types together and there is potential for disaster as well as success. This brings us back to the concept of the creative triangle. The value of strong collaboration in development and production was identified as long ago as the 1940s by anthropologist Hortense Powdermaker, the first dispassionate observer really to study Hollywood as a system and as a workplace. After cataloguing various case studies of disastrous development, Powdermaker then cited an anonymous example of a brilliant collaboration, where the three players in the team already knew one another, respected one another, communicated well and agreed on the kind of story they were trying to tell. Every stage of the script involved close collaboration between all three of them, and feedback from the studio executive, from outline to final draft. Powdermaker concluded:

> Ironically, this picture, made by the men whose goals and motivations were not limited to profits, was a big box-office hit and had far larger net profits than many films with only financial gains for goal. It also was praised as an exceptionally good movie. The economies of production which contributed to the net profits are obvious: the careful planning in advance; a producer, executive, director and writer acting rationally and towards the same end which was well defined in the beginning; the use of the story property purchased for the movie; the salary of one writer instead of seventeen; the saving on actors' salaries due to the speed of shooting made possible by advance planning and by the absence of major changes in the script on the set. … For all of them, front-office executive, producer, director and writer, the movie was more important than the assertion of their ego.[29]

However important the creative triangle is, nothing is static and permanent in the shifting and complex system that is script development. The triangle is hugely complicated by the fact that its three members also go through different levels of power and influence in relation to one another as the project goes through development and production, which can cause tensions, arguments and even split-ups. Understanding how and why this happens is crucial to managing the development process successfully; and that will be the subject of the next chapter.

Case interviews: How to help broker the relationship between the writer and the director

The arrival of the director sometimes starts to trigger a decline in the power of the writer. The writer can feel threatened by the powerful newcomer, and yet this is also the moment where the film takes vital steps towards becoming a reality. The writer has lived with the story, possibly for years, and this can lead to tension when it is time to hand it over to someone else. The director also needs to 'own it' and in this process of reshaping the script the director can sometimes appear oblivious to the thought and effort that has already gone into it.

A series of interview extracts from different writers, development executives and producers addressing this issue. (Note: these interviews were carried out separately.)

Tony Grisoni (screenwriter): When I've developed a screenplay with a producer, I wouldn't go further than a couple of drafts without a director. They have to become part of the team that's going to make this film, part of the vision. But the arrival of the director requires really careful handling – most of all because of me. That is where a good producer comes in.

Julie Baines (producer): If I've developed a script substantially and I am looking for a director, I don't want someone who wants to change the whole thing. Obviously I expect the director to put his or her own stamp on the project, but I had a recent experience where one of the directors we were interested in not only wanted to bring a whole new subplot into the story, which was unnecessary in my view, but also wanted to transpose it from the UK to India. I could see no reason at all for this. I always listen to other opinions, and if these ideas had been interesting and valid, I may well have entertained them, even if it meant doing a lot of extra work. But he seemed to want to make a different film to the one the writer and I wanted to make.

Neil Peplow (producer, currently Director of Screen Content at the Australian Film Television and Radio School): I was attracted to a particular script because of the writer. I loved that script, I wanted to develop it, and finding the best director is the next stage. So, the common sense check for me is: 'If I get this director on board will he or she significantly change this script that I loved at that first reading?' If it is yes, but he or she will get the film financed, that's when you decide whether or not to betray your initial instinct and go for the dollar (which I definitely wouldn't do, on past experiences); or you go with what attracted you in the first place, which was the writer's ability and talent and the underlying story that he or she is trying to tell.

Sarah Golding (development executive/script editor): Underlying everything can be a turf war about who is the author of the film, whether that is actually verbalized or not. And it's very strong in our film culture because of the predominance of the writer in television and in theatre. But the writers who work most often are the writers who work well with directors: and are collaborative and don't feel threatened. It's important to understand the simple equation that no director means no film.

Kate Lawrence (development executive): We tend to like the script to be in a place where it's pretty clear what this is, and then find a director who shares our vision. We typically try and bring a director in around the second draft stage so the screenplay is well enough developed that they can see what kind of film we are trying to make, but where the process isn't complete, so they will still have collaborative creative input into the second draft revisions and the polish. We would definitely want a director to feel involved in putting their stamp on a project.

Bringing the director on board

Sarah Golding: If I'm asked to manage that kind of situation then I talk to the writer about it in advance, especially if they're relatively inexperienced, so that they're ready for it and have an idea of what to expect. And one thing to put across is the fact that they need to allow time for the director to get as close to the script as everybody else is; to remember that the director's got maybe a year and a half less familiarity with the script than the rest of the team. And until you've really talked, you don't know whether the director wants to do the film for the same reasons that everybody else wants to, or whether he or she has been captivated by one or two things in it that particularly speak to him.

Neil Peplow: How you bring the director on board is to make sure the writer understands *why* that director has been chosen, has met that director, discussed why that director likes their script, and what they want done with that script. And if they seem to be on the same wavelength, then carry it forward. If the writer says I don't like that director, you've then got to make a judgement of: 'Will I be proud of what this director produces and have they got a track record which will help get this film made?' And then it's up to you whether or not you keep the writer. ... I always try to involve the writer in the decision of who the director should be; especially the level that I work at, which is low budget. There's not huge money in development, you're getting a modest option on a piece, and you're paying modest wages for the writers. If you suddenly block them out and you say: 'This is the director, you meet him on Tuesday,' then you're not going to get the best from them.

Sarah Golding: One of the things that starts everything off in a positive way and that should give the writer confidence is the fact that the director's coming onto the project because the writer's created a script which the director's interested in. It's a great starting point.

Olivia Hetreed (screenwriter): Happily for me I've always worked with directors who are very easy to work with and amenable and we had a very good and positive collaboration. But I realize that isn't always the case, and it would be better to be up front and say: 'What is it you think you're going to need to do here, and if you want to replace me, then let's have that discussion now, rather than find out at some horrible later moment?'

Kate Lawrence: It is an awkward moment, you never know quite how it's going to go, because obviously the writer doesn't want their work being torn apart by someone else, but the director does want to put their stamp on it and so will want some things changed. And you do have some meetings where for the first meeting they're saying: 'This is brilliant, this is wonderful,' and you say: 'Oh great, brilliant.' Then at the second meeting they're saying: 'So what I want to do is ...', and then they describe something that is completely changing what you've got, and then you think: 'Ah, okay, possibly not.' I think most writers are extremely well behaved but you can see stress levels rising, bit of clenched jaw, pen fiddling, and then generally you have a debrief with them afterwards, and try and get their absolutely honest opinion about what their concerns are. Then the producer's job is to be the intermediary and never put the writer in a position where the director takes over as the only voice on a project.

Neil Peplow: The writer can sit on his own in a room and develop a script in isolation, but you have to bring in the cold realities of the outside world, to speed that process up and get those decisions made. On one film we made, the writer wasn't convinced by the director we had attached, and I turned to him and said: 'Okay, let's find someone else. We are far down the line with this director, and the financiers who are potentially going to back the film will finance that director, but, let's look for someone else.' And I meant it – it wasn't a throwaway remark. At which point he considered the options, and said: 'No, actually, let's stick and let's work with this current director.' So it's just building a trusting relationship.

Anonymized screenwriter: Sometimes when directors come on board, either they want to rewrite it, or they want their person who rewrites all their films to come and rewrite it. So then that's a whole other set of challenges. And you know the producer may or may not keep faith, either with the writer or with the vision of the writer at that point, or they may just go 'Hey, well this is what we've hired and this is the way we're going to go with it and see what happens.'

Testing the vision

It is also important that the writer is not protected too much, at least from legitimate questions. Sam Lavender argues that writer, director and producer have to ask hard questions of each other from the outset, to test out the strength of the project and prove the fact that they are all trying to tell the same story. Without robust questioning of one another these issues may get missed, or buried until too late in the process.

Sam Lavender (Head of Development at Film4): You'd expect a director to do that – to ask hard questions of the script, having that set of fresh eyes come in and say: 'I actually don't buy this,' or 'I don't think that this bit works.' It's very important for a director to be honest upfront and ask the tough questions early. And the same really of (asking questions of) the director. Have exploratory conversations about a director's vision for the piece and ask in depth again and again: 'How do you cope with *this*?', 'How do you consider doing *this* at the budget?', all these kinds of questions. And before attaching that director you hope that you've come to an agreement about how to approach these things. ... It comes back to what I was saying about having as clear an understanding as you can about what the ambition for the film is, and if you haven't asked those clear questions upfront, then there's more leeway for it to come asunder.

Olivia Hetreed: I think there's a great deal of pressure on directors to have a voice, have a vision. I think they can be made to feel that unless they start demanding changes and moving things around, they somehow aren't doing their job. If they just turn up and shoot the script, then they won't be directing it enough ... they're being hired to give it a very specific flavour. I was talking to a writer who'd written one of the projects that was in this year's awards for everything, and he developed the screenplay with another director. Although the film is up for lots of awards and it was very successful and so on, the writer was still talking very wistfully about the other director's version and how that was going to be. And clearly that was really closer to his heart, as the film that he would have liked to have got made. ... It's not that it was a bad film, it just becomes a *different* film.

Getting the director's notes in advance

One way to manage the meeting of the director and writer is for the producer or development executive to get the director's notes first and discuss them with the writer before the meeting.

> **Sarah Golding**: Usually you wouldn't want to hear the director's notes for the first time in front of the writer. ... I would aim to get the ballpark notes from the director, so the writer doesn't arrive unprepared. I'd be talking to the writer about some possible solutions for the director, so the writer is able to respond immediately with thoughts about how to address the notes. I think the more people can get a head start before they meet, and come in feeling that they have some idea of what's going to be said, then the more comfortable everyone's going to be.

The approach where the director is always on board

Producer Andy Paterson gets around the problem of the arrival of the director by having him on board from the very beginning:

> **Andy Paterson**: My early movies were all with Mike Hoffman (director) and he was involved from the very start. So they were movies which were either written by him or developed with him in the mix and often leading the whole thing. Anand Tucker (director) and Frank Cottrell Boyce (writer) conceived the movie *Hilary and Jackie* from the beginning. They would walk on the beach, talk the story through, come and sit in my office, and we'd knock it around. Frank used to describe writing as 'the typing bit', because he wouldn't sit down and do that until he and Anand had figured out the story. Once that was all there, the speed that the script came out is amazing, because he writes dialogue like an angel. On *Girl with the*

Pearl Earring we brought Peter Webber (director) on quite late, but I knew Peter incredibly well and I felt that he was ready and passionate, and that he and the writer were going to get on, which was very important to me. ... So I find it works best when every development decision is taken with the actual people in mind and how they're going to work together.

5 The reality of development

Power and influence in a dynamic system

> Writers are in a unique position in the film industry, because they spend so
> much time on their own, having control over things. The best writers are
> the ones who understand that at a certain point they have to go out into
> the world and have to deal with compromise, and are excited by the
> collaboration model and not frightened of it.
>
> (Ivana MacKinnon, development executive and producer)

The triangle under stress

The creative triangle of writer, director and producer is infinitely complex
and unstable because it is part of a dynamic system involving a wider creative
team and financing network, that grows and shrinks as powerful newcomers
arrive and as existing members are replaced. Even those outside the team or
without formal power can still have influence – they may intentionally or
unintentionally disrupt, undermine or fail to deliver. Power and influence
shifts regularly within the team during this process. This chapter examines the
complex reality of development and proposes a graph of power and influence
to try to establish a typology of how and when these power shifts occur, to help
the producer and development executive to understand and manage them.
Box 5.1 shows different types of power and influence, and the chapter
examines the development process stage by stage and considers how these
types apply at different moments in the process to different players in it.[1]

**Box 5.1 Typology of sources of individual power and influence
(adapted from Handy (1985), and French and Raven (1959, 1968))[2]**

- **Physical power or force power:** Power from physical threats, bullying, force.
  Downside: people feel forced, demotivated. Method of influence: force.
- **Resource power or reward power:** Power from possession of resources,
  cash fee, salary, access to resource. Downside: people feel bought, possibly
  demotivating especially for creative people. Method of influence:
  exchange transactions, bribing, negotiating. The flipside of this is coercive
  power: removal of rewards, resources, etc.

- **Position power or legitimate power:** Hierarchical power from position in an organization; ability to reward and punish within the organization; control of flow of information, gatekeeping, control of access to social networks, right to organize and control. Downside: dependent on followers being compliant and not disruptive. Method of influence: rules, authority, procedure, punishment.
- **Personal power or referential power:** Power from personal charisma, popularity, influence, and perceived attractiveness. Downside: dependent on personal contact, continuing respect and popularity. Method of influence: logical persuasion, emotional persuasion, personal magnetism.
- **Expert power:** Power from expertise, meritocracy, past experience, peer respect. Downside: dependent on expertise being accepted, and continuing success; and it can be limited to narrow field of speciality. Method of influence: knowledge, expertise, respect.
- **Negative power:** Power from undermining other activity, by disruption, inactivity, discontent, distorting information. Downside: unofficial, destroys trust, risk of dismissal.

Most forms of power rely on the subordinate's perception of the influence of the leader. Some leaders use different techniques or a mixture of techniques depending on who they are trying to influence. In a cooperative environment (like universities) expert or personal power often has more influence than position power. Doctors rely on expert power over patients in GPs' surgeries, but in hospitals become more positional to control subordinates and nursing staff.

Film examples: A successful film director has personal power, expert power and short-term position power. A producer uses expert power and personal power to convince a writer to work with him, then resource power to pay him and try to control his output.

Stage 1: Original idea and treatment

The assumption in this chapter is that the writer is working with a producer from the outset rather than developing a speculative script on his own (where the writer retains control for longer but does not get paid). Who has the most power at the start of the project, the writer or the producer? It varies from project to project, but sometimes it is the producer: it is his choice which projects to put on his development slate, he may already have access to funding or relationships with funders, and it is often hard to get development funding without a producer attached, especially for a less known writer. In addition, if the producer owns the underlying rights to an idea or an adaptation (as opposed to it being the writer's idea) then he is again in a more powerful position and may be auditioning several suitable writers. However, sometimes the writer has more power, especially if it is a writer-originated project and there is a lot of heat around the idea, perhaps helped by the pitching powers of the agent or a bidding war. Lots of producers may want the project and the writer has more control to dictate better terms and more power over the early drafts of the script.

To convince a writer to work with him the producer has to use *expert* power, *personal* power and the *promise* of resources, and then use *resource* power to pay him and try to influence his output. Completion of the development agreement usually sees the writer lose rights to a project, because they are assigned or optioned to the producer, but in the short term he gains several things: control (because only he can write the first few drafts and at first he has a lot of creative freedom); peer esteem (because he is in development, ideally with a strong production company); and maybe payment (the producer may be earning nothing but still paying out to the writer).

This is a *negotiated exchange power transaction* where the copyrights and the expert skills of the writer are given in return for payment, but it is said to be *self-cancelling* because once the reward payments are completed the writer may stop work, even if the producer retains rights over the work for a further period. Furthermore the writer's payments may taper off during later draft deliveries (they are sometimes front-weighted towards the first few drafts). The other problem with exchange power transactions is that the recipient of the reward has to want it and be highly motivated by the desire for it, whereas writers, like many other creative people, are more motivated by their desire to tell the story and may even be de-motivated by external contingency payments (see Chapter 8 for more on the problem of extrinsic motivation/de-motivation). If the development relationship eventually breaks down, perhaps over creative differences or perceived non-fulfilment, the producer may initially use personal persuasion and charisma to try to win over the writer, but failing that may have to resort to legal force (the invoking of clauses in the contract to oblige the writer to finish or threaten to replace the writer, neither of which encourages creativity). It is therefore vital for the producer to develop a strong trust relationship with the writer, rather than have to rely on exchange power transactions or force transactions. At this stage the team is still small and relatively easy to control: only the writer, the producer, the producer's development executive (if there is one), and sometimes an optioned source writer who may also be involved in creative discussions.

There is a third power scenario, which is when a broadcaster or studio itself options the underlying rights to an existing story and then seeks the right producer and writer to work with to develop it. This is common in the US, but only occasionally occurs in the UK, perhaps with broadcasters or private equity funds.[3] One rare example is Vikas Swarup's novel *Q&A*, which was optioned by Film4 and eventually became the film *Slumdog Millionaire*. In this scenario the development financier is starting in the position of greatest power, and recruits a suitable producer, writer and, eventually, director. This means they also have the power potentially to replace any of them during development because they own the underlying rights and the others are under contract: a classic *exchange power transaction*. However, this is a simplification because the chosen producer, writer and director are usually well known and respected by the financier and therefore they in turn have *expert power* and *personal power*, and are part of an intended ongoing creative relationship across other films.

However the project starts off, this period of initial cooperation (once the contracts are agreed) is often fired by enthusiasm and high motivation, as screenwriter Sidney Howard (*Gone with the Wind*) explained:

> the first story conference is almost certain to end on a note of amiable optimism. The writer has a great angle on the material, the director is going to do a great job of direction, the star is going to be great in his or her role, a great picture is going to be made.[4]

The problems come as the team gets larger and a gap may occur between the concept of the intended masterpiece and the actual first draft.

Stage 2: First major drafts, with feedback starting

During the writing of the treatment and the first few drafts the writer is at his most powerful and influential. He has an almost god-like power over what happens and, to paraphrase the Bible, not a sparrow will fall from the sky without him knowing it and intending it to happen.[5] But this power will soon have to be left behind, starting when the writer delivers the first draft to the producer. Depending on your point of view, this is where the writer's control starts to slip away or where he starts becoming part of a more complex creative collaboration with a wider team. There is more on the giving of notes and the management of this process in Chapter 10 (from the producer's position) and Chapter 13 (from the writer's position). As we have seen, most professional writers are experienced enough to know and expect this loss of individual control, and know that the rewards from collaboration can be equally rewarding and creative, but nevertheless this is still a psychologically dangerous time for the relationship between the writer and the producer. The writer may be feeling a mixture of excitement, apprehension and insecurity about how the draft will be received, so it is important for the producer or development executive to read and respond quickly to it (even if this is only a holding response while a detailed response is worked out), so that he knows whether he is on target or not, because as writer and director Asif Kapadia succinctly puts it: 'The torture is not hearing back after you've delivered something. It just drives you nuts!'

The feedback on the first drafts will be from the producer, development executive and maybe other trusted voices, such as a formal or informal script editor, other trusted collaborators, partners, friends and so on.

However, they are all *internal* in that they are part of the project or trusted advisers. The next stage is when the feedback starts to come from *external* sources, who carry more power because they might fund the film itself. The decision about when to 'send it out' to development financiers belongs to the producer, and it is perhaps the most fraught question of the development process. Development financiers may also be potential production financiers, and the first impressions of a script often persevere. Once a script has been rejected by a finance source it can be difficult to successfully re-submit future drafts, unless a significant element has been changed, such as a new writer or director. There is also the question of whether to send it to all finance sources simultaneously or rely on personal contacts with individual executives.

As explained, some films are development funded by a financier from the outset, especially when they involve the adaptation of a successful underlying work. In this case the development financiers are involved in feedback notes from the first draft onwards, or even from the treatment onwards, and the distinction between this stage and the next stage (below) becomes more blurred. The adapting screenwriter has reduced power because of the need to be faithful to the reputation and fans of the original work, and possibly has to negotiate a constructive working relationship with the original work's author (they may have informal or formal approval of the script, and in which case may not allow the future renewal of an option).

Stage 3: Redrafting and multiple feedback: project attracting finance interest

So after sufficient drafts of the script the producer decides to 'send it out' to financiers and now the feedback comes in from a number of powerful external newcomers, who may eventually become part of the project, such as potential development financiers and their development staff; potential production financiers, including broadcasters or public subsidy financiers (including commissioning editors or film fund heads) and their development staff; equity financiers and their development staff; co-producers and their development staff.

These newcomers mainly exert *resource power* over the producer and the project because of their direct or indirect access to potential finance, so the producer has to consider their notes seriously. However, most of the powerful newcomers are salaried employees and themselves part of an organization, so may be subject to someone else's *position power* (needing to refer their decisions up the command chain for approval, to a senior manager or shareholders). They also have the capacity to exert internal *negative power* (where another member of their own organization does not want to back the project), and there is the strong influence of the organization's culture, brand positioning and market strategy. All of these may have a visible or invisible influence on the individual executives as they feed notes back to the producer and also try to decide whether they want to (or are able to) greenlight the film within their own organization's limited funds. The producer may choose what to filter out from these notes and what to emphasize, before passing them on to the writer (more on this mediation process later). Some of these financiers may commit if their notes are followed, but the problem is that this is a wooing phase and there is no guarantee that they will commit, even if the notes are taken on board (this could perhaps be called a *resource opportunity power*). The dilemma is: should the producer and writer agree to take on some notes that they feel may compromise what they see as their vision of the film, or should they reject the financier's notes and try to bring in other funding?

The multiplicity of funding sources is also potentially complicating, especially if they deliver conflicting script notes (the danger of 'too many cooks'), although some skilful producers use that multiplicity to play them off against one another and prevent any one financier from gaining too much creative control. Note that the writer is losing power, because his opinion is now one of many, and some of them are more powerful than his because they have money attached. This is also when the *transactional exchange* nature of his power becomes a problem, because at the request of the financiers he may be replaced or suffer the imposition of an additional dialogue polish writer (which is why a small number of writers also become executive producers: raising production money to try and gain resource power over the project and ensure their ongoing creative control). Again, the closeness of the writer's relationship with the producer is vital in preventing him from being replaced or usurped. Potentially there may also now be an independent script editor/script doctor (hired by the development financier or the producer), who may be advising the writer and whose opinion may also need to be taken into account (there is more on the contrasting roles of the script editor and development executive and how they affect the creative triangle in Chapter 6).

To make it harder, at the same time the script may go out to directors, on whose reputation and track record the script will eventually be funded (their power is through *expert power* and personal charisma). Very few funding sources will go far on committing to a project without knowing who the director will be, because the director brings so much of the vision of the film with them. This powerful latecomer to the development party may commit only after several meetings with the producer and writer, so again there is the question of how many of the potential director's notes to take on board to alter the script before the committal. And with the director comes his own trusted voices whose views find their ways into his notes (other writer friends, script editors, spouses, parents, children, etc.). The director's commitment to the project may be dependent on the timing of other projects to which he is already attached; and the producer's commitment to the director may be dependent on how effective the director's name is at attracting cast and production finance (as with all power, the director's power depends on the respect of others, on this occasion his standing with the controllers of *resource power*, the financiers). Directors often join or leave projects during the process, either at their own volition or other people's, each time triggering new rewrites and the arrival of a new directorial vision. Ivana MacKinnon (former development executive and now a producer) explains:

> There can be projects where there are a number of directors on board over time. So the writer has to form a relationship with a director who takes the project on and maybe does a draft with them and takes it in one direction, and then the director goes off for some reason and then there's another director who turns it in a totally different direction. I think that is completely heartbreaking for writers, because they invest in something and they start compromising their own vision to a certain extent to get a film made, and then actually they have to go in a completely different direction again, and that can be very difficult.

The same is true of attaching key acting talent, who may submit notes and ideas before deciding whether to commit to a project, especially on larger budget projects and where sales estimates are an important part of the overall financing (lower budget films with a known director may be greenlit by a broadcaster without the actors in place). The producer and writer have to decide what to incorporate and where the tipping point comes, beyond which they feel that the project is being damaged.

Figure 5.1 summarizes all these newcomer influences on the creative triangle, in a confrontational model that may reflect the way that a beleaguered writer may feel at this stage of the project, as his vision comes under multiple powerful influences and he has to sift through contradictory script notes to decide in what direction to take the script.

A more experienced writer and a collaboratively minded producer may argue that this is an over-aggressive representation, and that for the film to creatively survive development and production there needs to be a unity of vision within *all* these players so that they are all pulling in the same direction, and that it is the role of the mediating producer to get all the parties to identify with and internalize that vision (as shown in Fig. 5.2). However, eventually there will be disputes, and the power needs to rest somewhere within the team to resolve the disputes and make a decision about the creative way forward.

Wherever the power now lies, the writer may be subject to complex emotional reactions and insecurity as he receives all these feedback notes on a project that he used to control absolutely, and all of this needs to be carefully managed by the producer or development executive.

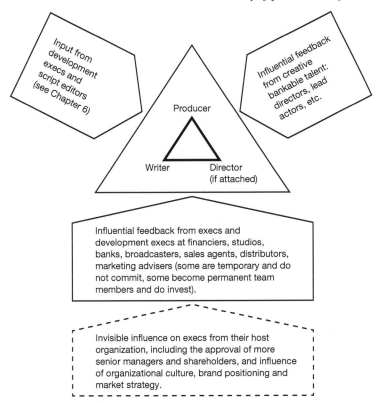

Figure 5.1 The triangle under stress: a simplified typology of newcomers to the development team and creative triangle, represented as confrontational elements

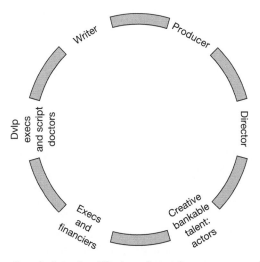

Figure 5.2 The perfect circle: a simplified typology of newcomers to the development team, represented as ideal collaboration

Stage 4: Final rewrites and shoot

During the final stages of financing a producer has to get all the funding sources to agree terms and greenlight the film. He sometimes has to push a film into pre-production in order to pressure the funders to commit and prevent the project from losing momentum or losing the window of availability on a piece of key talent. It is in this context that the final rewrites are done, where the producer is focused on completing the funding, and the power of the director and the financiers over the script is at its highest. The writer's power has now almost disappeared, and this is where he is most likely to be replaced for a dialogue polish (although this is less common in specialty arthouse films). It is vital for the producer to mediate between these forces and to try to retain the overall vision of the project, especially in the face of pressure from financiers who may demand changes before they commit to financing, possibly to make it more commercial or generic, or pressure from a director who may want their own favoured writer to do a last polish. However, the final rewrites can also be a period of intense creativity and collaboration between the writer and the director, and screenwriter Olivia Hetreed explains that it is her favourite part of the whole development process, because: 'you're now working with the person who is actually going to make the film and is focusing intently on making the film work'.[6]

The shoot is the stage when the largest number of people are working on the project and the director is temporarily in the position of greatest power, because what he says on set is usually law. Scenes get added, dropped, rewritten or improvised on the spot, according to the demands of the schedule, the ideas of the actors and the vision of the director. The financiers are largely not as influential (unless they don't like the daily rushes they are being sent), and the producer is concerned with cost control and line production issues. So for the writer, being close to the director means having more influence over the final product. Some directors choose to involve the writer during rehearsals and on set during the shoot for last-minute rewrites (this is discussed in the case interviews at the end of the chapter), but it is more usual that the writer is allowed just a few polite visits to the set and the wrap party, and is mainly back in his room, writing another script for another company.

Stage 5: Post-production

The rough cut and first assembly are largely in the control of the director and editor, but as the edits continue the power of the financiers and distributors who pre-bought the film are in the ascendancy. The director has now shifted to being subject to the kind of control the writer was previously under: he is under contract (*resource power exchange transaction*), his opinion is now one of many, and he can be removed or overruled (although this is more common in studio films). Often he uses *personal power* and persuasion to try to bring financiers to accept his point of view, or reach an acceptable compromise.

The writer is not usually involved during the edit and post-production. The battle over the final cut is often between director and financiers and producer, and this rarely involves the writer – unless the director wants to include the writer's support as part of the lobbying for his edit, in which case the writer's views must be able to be aligned with the director's. This point also sees the rise of the creative influence of the film editor and the sound editor; and the input of special effects and music. Some producers and directors advocate bringing the writer in to see the first rough cut or early edits, because the writer knows the story well and may spot things which have been left out during the editing that are genuinely needed for character or plot development.

Stage 6: Marketing and release

The writer is never involved during marketing unless it is for press interviews if he or she is famous or has a newsworthy angle. At this point the distributor/ financiers are at their most powerful, because they control the marketing and release campaigns (as opposed to the equity financiers and broadcaster financiers, who do not have influence at this stage, but whose return on investment is often bound up in the success of the cinema marketing and release campaign). Note that the people who carry out the marketing campaigns are invariably employees of the distribution company or a sub-contracted marketing company, so are subject to *position power* (being told what to do by the chief executive of the distribution company), and limited by the resources made available (the size of the distributor's prints and advertising budget); but they are subject to virtually no power from the producer. It is often politically useful and helpful to involve the producer and director in feedback on marketing materials, but there is no real power relationship other than say the refusal of the director to do interviews to help market the film (*negative power*), which may damage long-term trust with the distributor. In fact, producers often express frustration at the release campaigns of their films, and after all the years they have spent developing and making a film it seems remarkable that its fate can often be decided by the efficacy of someone else's campaign and the film's performance over a single opening weekend.

Stage 7: The next film

The producer now has to return to the writer to discuss new projects, possibly at the moment when (if it has all gone wrong) the writer is feeling most dissatisfied with the final edit and how his own vision of the screenplay has been realized/transformed/mutilated. Having gone through an arc from high control to none whatsoever, it is now time for the writer to go back to high control and influence, because his next idea is the producer's next film. This is where the producer's careful handling of the writer talent within the team pays dividends (or not). Either the writer is prepared to collaborate again with the producer (even if not with the same director) or the producer loses that writer and source of new writing material to another producer; who may have more money, charisma, contacts, and above all be without the baggage of the last two to ten years of development hell and production tension. The boot is on the other foot. As shown in Chapter 2, the most successful film producers often form lasting bonds with writers and directors that go beyond individual projects and enable them to build up slates of work and development deals with financiers.

Proposing a typology of changing power dynamics and creative influence in independent film development and production

With the proviso that every film and every team is different, Box 5.2 is a summary of the changing power of the writer from development to distribution, and following that is a proposed graphic representation of the typical interplay of power relationships over the same period (Fig. 5.3).

Box 5.2 Summary of the changing power of the writer during the independent development and production process

Stage 1: Original idea and treatment

The team is only the writer and producer and sometimes a development executive.

Stage 2: First major draft, with feedback starting

The writer is probably at his most powerful and influential.

Stage 3: Feedback and redrafting: project attracting interest

Directors and financiers arrive. Writer now losing power. His opinion is one of many.

Stage 4: Final rewrites and shoot

Writer has less or no power. He can be replaced. Could gain influence on the shoot if involved by the director.

Stage 5: Post-production

The writer not usually involved.

Stage 6: Marketing and release

Writer never involved, unless occasionally for press interviews.

Stage 7: The next film

The producer has to return to the writer to discuss new projects. The writer now goes back to a position of high control and influence.

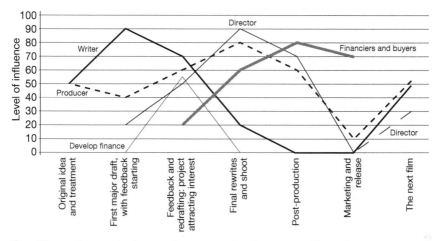

Note: The producer and writer are shown as starting the process with equal power, as an averaging out of the discrepancies of power at the outset that have already been discussed.

Figure 5.3 A typology of changing power and approximate creative influence of various players in independent film, from development to distribution[7]

Figure 5.3 represents a typical independent film, where multiple finance sources are external (rather than internal, as in the studio model); where the director is selected after the project is initially developed by the independent producer; and where the director does not have a major on-set role for the writer. In reality, every film would have a different graph, especially if a new writer were to come, the director to change, or a lead actor to come in with new script notes.

The graph is designed to show the relative creative power relationship, *not* the flow of money or earnings. That is why the last section represents the next film, and the financiers disappear from the graph at that point. If the figure instead represented business on this individual film then the distributors would stay in a position of high power, and the last section of exploitation by the distributors would potentially be very long to reflect the different exploitation windows and the long tail. The distributor retains control throughout this period until the licence expires and has to be renegotiated (which is the only time the producer and financiers regain temporary power, as discussed in the value chain section in Chapter 2).

Note that the development financier is shown as a separate line, influencing the drafts but dropping out as the shoot starts (when the financier is paid back on the first day of photography). However, the development financier is often also one of the production financiers, especially in the case of broadcasters, in which case the development financier's line would join with the other production financiers' line instead of dying out.

Analysing the changing power of the producer and the strength of the team

Note that the producer is the first person on board at the start of a film and the last off. Contrary to popular opinion, once his production fee is spread across the whole period he is unlikely to be the best off financially. The producer is also rarely in the most powerful position: his strength really comes from playing off the other power holders against one another.

The director often comes on late, gains a lot of power very fast (potentially alienating the writer), and then loses it again during post-production. The line ends up being dotted on the far right, in the *next film* section, which shows that perhaps the director wants to work again with the producer and writer, or he disappears off to other projects. By retaining a director for the next film the producer can start with a more coherent team, and probably operate on a more equal power basis between the producer, writer and director. For example, by having the director on board from the outset the producer reduces the potential negative impact of the arrival of an unknown director on the writer. In addition, powerful producers with name directors are able to resist the power of the financiers when they arrive because they can 'shop' the project more in the marketplace to different financiers and select the better deal. They can also use multiple funding sources to their advantage, controlling financiers by the principle of divide and rule. In short, the more powerful the producer and director are, the more they can reduce the strength of the financiers.

Figure 5.3 shows clearly that it is in the interests of the producer, writer and director to form a close team, so that they can iron out their own peaks and troughs, each person thereby gaining more power throughout the project arc. By having more trust, and accepting one another's involvement at more stages, they reduce the see-sawing of power between group members. This is of particular importance for the writer, in terms of safeguarding his vision during production, where he currently has little influence.

Note that the more experienced and bankable the writer and director are, the more power they would have at the start of the figure (on the left). The figure could be continued on the right to show that writers and directors start their next film with more power, but that depends on the critical success of this film. Indeed, this is usually how they raise their fees – not on the profit share on the successful film but on the fee charged for the next one. However, the producer can start the next film with more influence even without critical success, simply on the basis of having developed and delivered a substantial film on time and budget (the lack of critical success can be blamed on the script or the actors). The producer will also hopefully have developed contacts with financiers, which will aid the funding of the next film. It is generally hoped that the more films are made, the higher all team members start on the next film, as they gain in reputation.

The crucial thing for the producer to notice is that the writer is out of the creative loop by the time the shoot starts, and may be feeling emotionally flat and unwanted (the *creative drop*). The moment that the producer and director are busiest on the shoot is the moment when the producer could be paying attention to the lost writer, otherwise he may take his new ideas to another producer who has more time to invest in them. This is the time for the development executive to develop new ideas with the writer to line up the next project, and there is more on how to work with the writer during this creative drop in Chapter 10.

One last point on the power of the writer: during development his power line would in reality sometimes show little spikes of control, in favour of the writer or source material writer, every time the option comes up for renewal when the writer has the right of refusal to renew. This is often the case when there is a powerful underlying property and the writer has a break clause or approval clause; or else when the option and automatic renewals period expires and the producer has to go back to the agent and the source writer to ask for a new longer option (this happens more often). Until the producer completes the renegotiation the writer can temporarily demand better terms or more control (under threat of the right to walk away and take it to another producer: a rare example of the writer having *force power*).

The power of different types of financiers from development to distribution

In Fig. 5.3 the role of multiple financiers and buyers was simplified into a single line. The reality is more complex, with different financiers having different degrees of control, so in Fig. 5.4 the director and writer have been stripped out to show in more detail the relative power of the financiers over creative decisions. Note that this chapter has only looked at development within the independent sector. Chapter 12 compares this typology with the Hollywood studio system, where there is one key financier (Fig. 12.1).

Figure 5.4 assumes the distributor and broadcaster are a pre-buy or licence rather than a large equity position, and that the equity investors are looking to recoup much of their investment from ongoing sales. For the sake of simplicity, this figure just shows the local broadcaster and distributor, and not those in other countries who may also be pre-buying or investing. The larger the number of financiers, the more complex the picture. For example, if there are a large number of international pre-sales in the funding plan then another line would have to be introduced for the sales agent, who has to deliver the film to the pre-sales territories, and therefore can wield some limited power over the edit (in order to guarantee foreign distributors accept delivery of the completed film).

As Fig. 5.4 shows, traditionally the local broadcasters tend to be involved earlier and with more power in the development process than equity or pre-buying distributors, in part because broadcasters have development funds

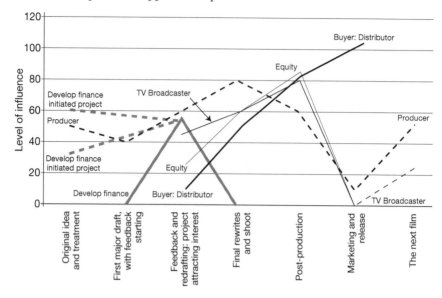

Figure 5.4 A typology of changing power and approximate creative influence of
different types of financiers in independent film, from development to
distribution (the writer and director are excluded for clarity)

and in part because without the confidence of a sale to a local broadcaster
it is harder to interest pre-sales and equity against unsold territories. During
the cinema release the distributors have all the power over the marketing
campaign, which is why their power line continues to rise, whereas local
broadcasters and equity investors in production funding are unlikely to
have any. A more complex graph could show multiple *different* financiers
with different levels of influence as a result of their levels of investment,
which would be more representative of the typical independent film. The
distributor ends in the most powerful position because they are controlling
the investment in prints and advertising and DVD release.

Development funding has also been shown in more detail: the dotted
lines to the left show the power of the development financier if they are on
board from the start of the project, either by funding development on a
producer-owned option (where they are less powerful than the producer)
or by initiating the project by buying the option themselves (where they are
more powerful than the producer).

Financiers like Film4 and BBC Films also like to develop lasting bonds
with writers and directors, so the broadcaster financier's line is shown
dotted and rising again on the far right to show the start of the next film,
perhaps backing the choice and development of the producer and director's
next project. As Film4's Head of Development Sam Lavender explained:
'The priority is to be able to partner up with the producer, writer, and

director. It's about our future relationships, not just about this film. It's not just a one-off, it's about developing hopefully a longer timeline.'[8]

The public funds are also contained within the lines for development funding and equity funding (although they request softer recoupment terms than pure equity). Sometimes public subsidy funding also comes with a challenge of control for the producer and writer. For example, one producer said during an interview for this book that the UK Film Council's development department, at the height of its power in the mid-2000s, would only release funding for the next draft of script development if the writer and producer were prepared to take on board the development department's script notes. This producer questioned whether 'soft' public subsidy money should really be attended by demands for this level of control. The danger of this level of intervention is two-fold: first, contingent *if-then* funding can decrease creativity, and second, if the gatekeeper becomes too powerful then the result can be a quasi-auteur film fund executive – where their desire to have *their* vision of the project realized can come into conflict with the vision of the writer and producer. This was an accusation also levelled by some producers at the UK Film Council's precursor British Screen. When the individual executive has the power of withholding funding then they have power to get their own way, but only through *reward transaction* power, which was shown earlier to cause potential resentment, de-motivation and reduced creativity.

The commitment matrix: analysing financier and stakeholder commitment to a project greenlight

Many development issues revolve around the power of financiers and their notes, which raises the whole issue of the commitment of financiers to the project and the role of the producer in closing that deal. However, the financier executive that the producer is dealing with may not have full greenlighting power and may then have to champion the film within his own organization. This is true for a Hollywood studio, a public fund or a broadcaster; indeed, wherever there are several individuals who participate in greenlighting a film. Figure 5.5 proposes the *commitment matrix*, which attempts to analyse different individuals' responses to a single film project. It can also be used to analyse an organization's response. The key job of the producer is to try to persuade all the potential financiers to move from a situation of *contingency, compliance* or *conflict* into one of *commitment*. He then has to try and keep them there whilst the deal gets signed, without losing the window of availability on key talent or the momentum on the project as a whole. This is why some producers choose the risky option of pushing films into pre-production in order to force financiers to commit to the project (it is risky because if they do not commit, the producer may be left with some of the expenses of the start of pre-production, not to mention the reputational damage).

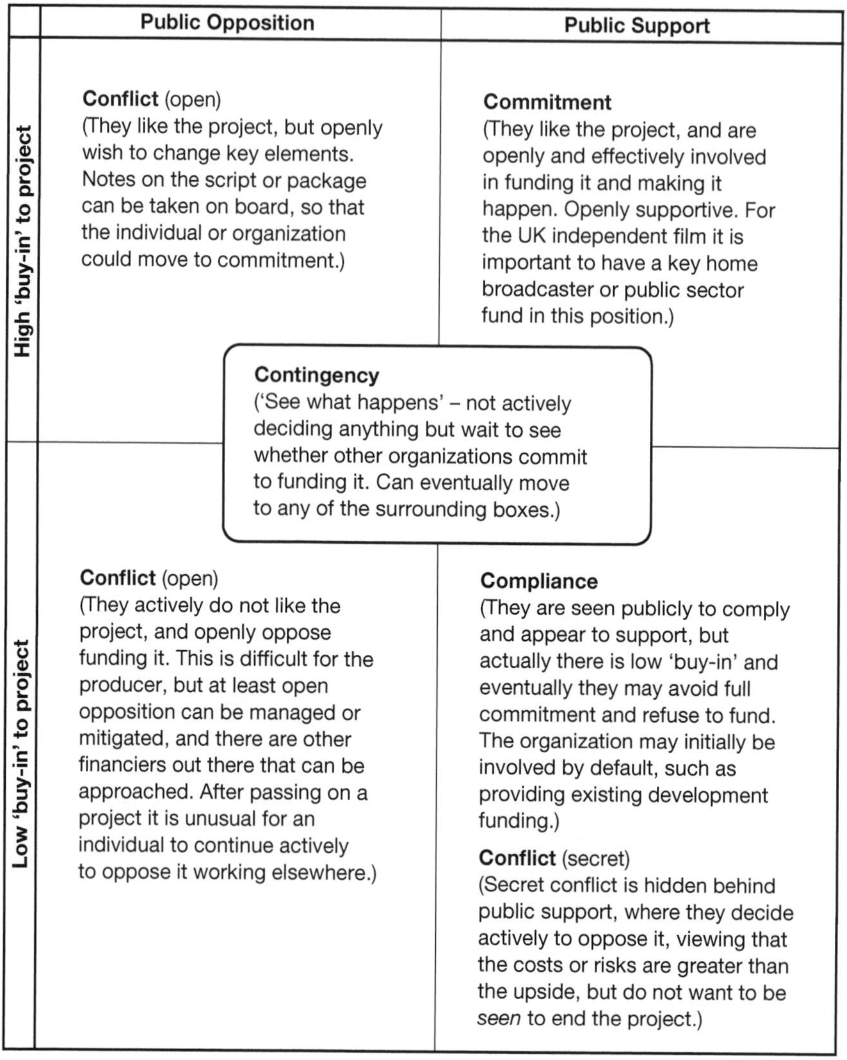

	Public Opposition	Public Support
High 'buy-in' to project	**Conflict** (open) (They like the project, but openly wish to change key elements. Notes on the script or package can be taken on board, so that the individual or organization could move to commitment.)	**Commitment** (They like the project, and are openly and effectively involved in funding it and making it happen. Openly supportive. For the UK independent film it is important to have a key home broadcaster or public sector fund in this position.)
Low 'buy-in' to project	**Conflict** (open) (They actively do not like the project, and openly oppose funding it. This is difficult for the producer, but at least open opposition can be managed or mitigated, and there are other financiers out there that can be approached. After passing on a project it is unusual for an individual to continue actively to oppose it working elsewhere.)	**Compliance** (They are seen publicly to comply and appear to support, but actually there is low 'buy-in' and eventually they may avoid full commitment and refuse to fund. The organization may initially be involved by default, such as providing existing development funding.) **Conflict** (secret) (Secret conflict is hidden behind public support, where they decide actively to oppose it, viewing that the costs or risks are greater than the upside, but do not want to be *seen* to end the project.)

Contingency
('See what happens' – not actively deciding anything but wait to see whether other organizations commit to funding it. Can eventually move to any of the surrounding boxes.)

Figure 5.5 The project commitment matrix: analysing stakeholder support or opposition to a project greenlight[9]

Note that in the commitment matrix there is a key distinction between open conflict and opposition (top-left box) and secret conflict and opposition (bottom-right box). Secret conflict may include sabotaging funding from the organization, either by openly opposing it in internal meetings or through passive resistance, such as encouraging negative comments and risk analyses. This section is of most concern to producers and internal company champions, because the external appearance of support does not match the true intent of the executive, which may be disguised or ambivalent.

Conventional business matrix analyses imply clear-cut decisions and motivations; however, this matrix has introduced an element of ambivalence with the internal *contingency* box, summing up the 'wait and see' mindset. Many individuals have different levels of ambiguity or ambivalence towards any action or strategy, and can hold opposing viewpoints simultaneously. Ambivalence can also be true of organizations or teams – sometimes the buy-in of a leader or key executive is not matched by all the staff or team, so different people in a team may be in different places within the matrix. People are also not static in their views but can often be gradually persuaded to embrace a project, so they may move from box to box in the matrix over time, as they become happier with the project (perhaps because of new drafts of the script, which have adopted their suggestions), or as the talent package changes, or as they become convinced of the potential advantages for their organization, possibly through brand association with other partners who are coming on board.

Having looked at the general pattern of power relationships and control during the development process, it is now time to look in more detail at the roles and influence of the development executive and the script editor, and consider how they can influence and support this process. As he is a potential fourth member of the creative triangle, the relationship between the development executive, the producer and the writer has to be very carefully managed. The right development executive is also vital for nurturing the long-term creative talent relationships that can grow a larger company and establish a vibrant slate of projects.

Case interview with screenwriter Tony Grisoni: Point of view – the creative triangle and the advantages of keeping the writer on board throughout

One area of dispute in the industry is whether it is good practice to have the writer on the set, or at least available throughout the shoot, and this depends in part on whether the director is used to working closely with writers and trusts them, and in part on whether the writer is professional enough to keep his distance and not interfere too often.

Writer Tony Grisoni believes there are many advantages to having the writer present. He is one of Britain's most experienced and respected screenwriters, working regularly in the UK and Hollywood, and he has collaborated with directors including Michael Winterbottom, John Boorman and Terry Gilliam. Tony started as a runner and third assistant director and worked his way up to production manager before becoming a writer. He has therefore had more on-set experience than many writers and this may affect his view of the potential involvement of the writer throughout the shoot process.

What I've found is that me staying in the picture is a very useful thing for a director or a producer. Instead of me delivering my various drafts of the screenplay up to the shooting script, and then them sailing off and leaving me on the quay, I'm there during the shoot. I know what's going on, I watch rushes along with the director, I'm aware of what's worked and what hasn't worked, or what's worked in a different way. Suddenly the script is coming up against reality, and it is also being developed because of the creative relationship going on between the director and the actors. ... The director's being asked a million questions every day, all of which he has to pretend to know the answers to. He has an ally, someone with ammunition, someone who can go away and rework a scene, drop a scene out, write a new scene, come back and say – how about this? Maybe a clearer head, who's not under such pressure. That can only be in the producer's interest. And I would argue that a film that I love and I'm part of – I never feel that I'm done with it until there's the final cut. ... You may have a situation where there is voiceover or voiceover is needed and therefore I obviously play a part there. But I think in less obvious ways I can, because I was there at the beginning with the script, so I think I still have something to offer. But as I say that works on two levels, on one level I absolutely believe I have something to offer to the film all the way through, and on another one I *want* to be part of the film all the way through because, because it satisfies me creatively, I need to be totally involved.

The usual objection proposed by directors and producers is that the writer may undermine the director on set or cause a creative power struggle at the heart of the film. However, this could be overcome if writers were accustomed to being on set and knowing what is and is not acceptable.

I've worked as a runner, as a third assistant, second assistant, first assistant director, and a production manager. I've done those jobs, so I'm aware of how things work on the floor. I'm not going to pop up in the middle of a director directing a scene and say: 'Oh I've had a great idea.' I mean that would be just *stupid*. So I know about how those things work, you have to be sensitive to how films are made. In the same way, the editing room is a little space for the director and editor to sit in as they work towards a first draft of their cut. And no-one in their right mind is going to walk into that and start having brilliant ideas, until they are ready to show something. So you choose your moment, and you have to be aware of the dynamic between people. I mean film-making seems to me to be all about the glue between people, it's all about the dynamic, you know. And then I come in on the rough cut, see the rough cut, and can be involved in discussions about where to go from there.

Grisoni also emphasizes that it makes the writer feel part of the whole social and creative adventure, which also creatively motivates him to do more:

What's going to get good work out of me is to feel that what I do *counts* for something and to feel that I'm part of a group making a film; that I'm part of the *social* act that is film-making all the way through. And if I feel that, then I'll do anything, of course I will.

Case interview: Opening up the debate – should the writer be on board throughout the shoot and edit, or not?

A series of interview extracts from different development executives and producers. Note that these interviews were carried out separately.

If Tony Grisoni's advice is followed it could become standard industry practice for the writer to be available during cast rehearsals (to discuss character and motivation), the shoot and the latter stages of post-production. This would require an extra line in the budget for travel and accommodation and *per diems* (daily expenses) for the writer during the shoot. This has the advantage of helping the writer to fine-tune their craft by seeing how the shooting and editing process works. However, some directors resist keeping the writer involved, and not all writers *want* to be. The following excerpts from interviews with other industry figures show a range of opinions, and there could be more discussion in the industry about actively encouraging directors and producers to keep the writer involved:

Sarah Golding (script editor): Some directors like the writer to be on set ... well, why wouldn't you, if you could have them there, just in case there's something that they can do for you, to get you out of a hole at some point. ... But I think that it's in the cutting room that the writer's presence can be fantastically productive. It can be so valuable for writers to have the experience of seeing how a story may be reconstructed by the film editor. ... Once they've got over the initial shock – 'Oh my god it's not the film I saw in my mind's eye' – and you get past that and you've seen the footage then you begin to look at it as something separate from your imagined film. I know writers who are brilliantly pragmatic in the cutting room. They put aside everything that was in the script and invent new ways of dealing with issues that have arisen. ... But it's just not custom and practice to automatically involve the writer in this way, and sometimes it's 'not allowed'. A lot of that comes down to the confidence of the director and their openness. And if the writer's prepared to participate in the edit then it's another opportunity to engage imaginatively with the film and it might help connect them strongly to the director or producer for future projects.

Andy Paterson (producer): When we were making *Hilary and Jackie*, we shot it in Liverpool, which is where the screenwriter Frank Cottrell Boyce lives. And he would come to set, and after about twenty minutes I'd glance up and see him wandering off, partly because his kid had a fiddle lesson or something, but mainly because he knew he'd done his job. We'd cast some amazing people, the director was in complete control of the process, and the director and writer were incredibly close, so he just didn't need to be there. And if we needed him to write something or whatever then of course he was available to us. He was totally welcome in the cutting room. I absolutely think the writers should be welcome at every part of that process, to be drawn on, because there's always stuff you need. But there's a responsibility on the writer's part to only be *useful* in that process – as soon as the writer wants to be co-directing the movie, then they're out of there ...

Screenwriter Simon Beaufoy comes down against the idea of the writer making changes at too late a stage, arguing that last-minute rewrites during the advanced stages of prep and shooting are not the right way to think through all the different possibilities. Beaufoy spends little time on set because he argues that his best work is done in a quiet, reflective state and not under the pressure of a shoot:

Simon Beaufoy (writer): The script should be right before the film starts, it should be like a lodestone. Daily changes on the film set are always a disaster.

Sam Lavender, Head of Development at Film4, says that there is no active policy at the broadcaster to encourage the writer to be on set or in the cutting room, and that the decision is in the hands of the director.

> **Sam Lavender**: Should it be policy for the writer to be involved on set? It's a really interesting argument, but again it's about how best that set operates, and how those egos come together. There is an argument for having writers in edits, but then again there's something quite painful about seeing what's happened to your stuff. Anand Tucker (director) talked about the process of directing and saying you have this amazing painting in your head, it's done on glass, then you smash it on the ground, and you throw away a third of the pieces, and then the edit is putting that back together as close to the picture as you had in the first place. ... But at the same time the original editor of a piece is the writer, so a writer might have some very useful input into that editing process. There's no set way, but there is a dominant way, which is – 'I'm the director and this is my film.'

> **Tracey Josephs** (Head of Production, Film4): We have helped to financially pay for writers to be able to go on set and would see it as a reasonable line item in the budget. We've certainly encouraged it, because we want the writer to feel invested and involved, but ultimately it has to be the director and producer's decision.

The question is whether the culture of the auteur director is being allowed to override the collaborative nature of the medium:

> **Christine Langan** (Head of BBC Films): It depends on the director to a large degree, and how confident and open they are. I mean (director) Stephen Frears is incensed if the writers think they're going to be doing anything anywhere else. He wants them there 24/7. I've had the situation of them saying to me 'I need to go home,' you know. And other directors will make it fairly uncomfortable for the writer to be around. They sort of think, you've had your time, this is my time. There's a sliding scale of hostility and friendliness.

> **Stephen Woolley**: [For us] the writer becomes part of the *family*, the family that make the film. You know, I've never banned a writer from the set, other than Toby Young (novelist: *How to Lose Friends and Alienate People*), who banned himself. But he wasn't the writer

who wrote the script, the (screen)writer was Peter Straughn. We've *always* had an open-door policy towards writers and never ever would I imagine that the writer couldn't happily come and learn about the process. And generally that's worked.

Christine Langan: I don't think the set is a great place for your average writer. ... I think the director is responsible for the mood and tenor (of the shoot), a deeply confident director will make it feel like everybody's opinions are valid, without being crowded and having too much disruption, and some are much more controlling than that, in a more overt way. But it is the role to have control, so they'll either do it charmingly or defensively or whatever. ...The edit is a different story. I think some writers are very talented in the edit. The script is being rewritten to some extent in the edit. But again it's a question of how much should they be there, or how regularly? And this is why it's such a fascinating business, because it's different every time.

6 The development executive and the script editor

'How many screenwriters does it take to change a light bulb?'
'What do you mean, it needs changing?'

(Film industry joke)

What is the difference between a development executive and a script editor, and where do they fit into the creative triangle?

There are a few key differences between the job of the script editor and the job of the development executive. Both of them work with writers and producers to make scripts as good as possible, and are important parts of managing the development process.

Script editors are usually freelancers who are paid a daily rate to provide personalized script feedback on how to make the script better. They may work on every new draft, or they may be called in just for a few days. They are not really editors in the 'cutting things out' sense of the word, but *dramaturgists*, which means they are advising and questioning issues around dramatic composition, story structure and character development. This is why in the US they are sometimes known as *script doctors* rather than editors. They are a bit like film editors, in that they have to understand narrative and characterization, plus have the judgement to see what works; but unlike film editors they do not then carry out the work of reassembly themselves: they have to empower the writer to do it.

Script editors will not usually be part of the packaging and marketing of the film (although they may provide advice and the better ones understand the film finance market very well, in part because some are ex-development executives). Usually their total work will add up to only a few weeks on the project, although their influence on new drafts can be immense. They are invisible to the public and do not usually get a formal onscreen credit, but may be mentioned in the 'thanks to' section. The script editor may be employed by the producer (usually) or by the writer, but the crucial difference is that they are self-employed, focused purely on that script (not permanently employed to work across the whole slate), and specialize in dramaturgy rather than management or production financing. The producer controls them through the *exchange power transaction* of contracting them for a specified period, like the writer. They do *not* usually want to become producers, and some of them are ex-development executives, who decided they wanted to concentrate on dramaturgy rather than development management. Therefore in the creative triangle diagram they would be shown outside, helping the writer but not breaking the lines between the producer and the writer and director, as shown in Fig. 6.1.

Development executives also provide the dramaturgical function, but unlike script editors the executives are permanently employed (full-time or part-time) by the producer or production company or broadcaster in order to help source and manage a whole slate of projects and writers working on them. The development executive will be permanently involved in the ongoing development (which provides creative continuity), and may be part of packaging discussions around the director and the cast. Often they are involved in the director's work with the writer on the last stages of the script during pre-production. Because of their involvement with packaging and financing, some development executives *do* end up becoming producers (partly because there is no easy career progression upwards from being development executive, other than moving sideways to a different, larger company). They are salaried, so the producer controls them through what is known as *position power* or *legitimate power* (the power that comes as a result of a role in that organization).[1]

The other big difference is that script editors are *reactive*, because they do not choose projects – it is the producer or writer or financier who brings them the script with a problem; whereas development executives are *proactive*, in that they are assembling slates and hunting out talent to work with. The personal taste of a powerful executive can heavily influence the slate at a company, and the first contact between a writer and a company may be the executive and not the producer. Script editor Kate Leys sums up the difference:

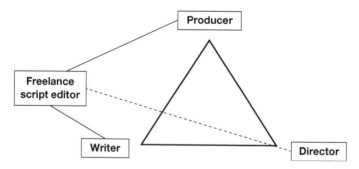

Figure 6.1 The script editor, a temporary freelancer, shown outside the creative triangle

As a development executive you're out there looking for stories, looking to put people together or put a manuscript together with a producer or a director and make a project. As a story editor you're round the other way: you're waiting for people with a project to come to you. Will you work on this? Can you help us with that? So it's a more passive relationship.

In their search for new talent development executives are therefore obliged to network and cultivate a social and professional system of relationships with agents, book authors, publishers, theatre companies, other development executives, and script readers whose taste they can trust.[2]

Another sub-section of development executives works for broadcasters or financiers, instead of producers. As such they have more power, because they can often allocate the financier's funding to development (as opposed to having to find funding), and the projects they put into development will have been seen by the head of film at the financier and been approved as a potential project to receive production funding, if the development works out well. However, the money comes with potential strings: the broadcast development executive is influenced by the company brand and commissioning policy of the broadcaster, so they are looking for projects that might fit the brand and may consciously or unconsciously be adapting the project to the needs of the company. The job itself also comes with strings, including the demands of internal meetings and corporate life, not to mention the workload, as Kate Leys remembers from her time as head of development at Film4:

> It is a 24/7 job. You're expected to travel at the drop of a hat. You're expected to attend everything, see every short film and play, and read every book. You know that your weekend reading pile is going to be ten scripts. ... And I think that's great, but there comes a point in your life where another 6.30 p.m. screening and a free glass of wine is no longer your idea of a good time.

However experienced they may end up becoming, most script editors and development executives come into the industry (usually from university) either as assistants to the producer, or else as poorly paid freelance script readers: producing coverage on speculative scripts to help sift out the good from the bad projects that have been submitted to production companies or broadcasters. There can be a large element of luck or nepotism involved in getting these work opportunities. They tend to learn their trade on the job rather than through formal training, working in the office until they are trusted to work directly with writers. This lack of training is sometimes identified by producers as a problem in the UK development sector.

Does the development executive come between the writer and the producer?

Within the concept of the creative triangle it could be said that the development executive can sometimes break the lines between the producer and the writer and director, as shown in Fig. 6.2. Interviews for this book showed that there is a perception amongst many writers that the development executive is 'in the way' between them and the producer, and that given the choice they would rather deal directly with the producer. There was a fear that the development executive may be misrepresenting the producer's notes and thoughts. As the writer-director Asif Kapadia succinctly put it: 'Try and deal with the top person. The people in the middle can really mash things up. They just tell you what they think their boss wants.'[3]

One anonymized writer was quite specific that he would prefer not to work with executives:

> I think the [creative triangle] model works best when there is no development executive, when the producer is the development executive and the producer has script sense and is fully invested in the material. That's not to say they can't have a development team to field new submissions and to get stuff to a certain stage.

Interestingly, many producers and development executives who were interviewed did *not* perceive this to be an issue, whereas the writers did; so producers may need to mediate this relationship and writers' perceptions of it more carefully. By contrast, the script editor (when they are used) is generally perceived by writers to have solely the interests of the project at heart, regardless of who is paying for their services, because they are working for the script and not for the producer or their own corporate career trajectory.

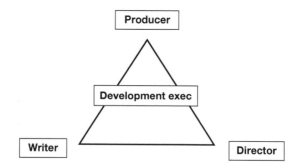

Figure 6.2 The position of the development executive, potentially interrupting the lines of the creative triangle

Another potential risk is that a project may have been selected and championed by the development executive but the producer is less passionate about it, so may not work so hard at financing it as other projects on the slate, or may subconsciously find excuses to keep it in development; and the reverse can also be true, where the producer selects and champions a project, but the development executive doesn't share the vision and tries to transform it into something else. Development executives potentially also have latent *negative power* through their role as gatekeepers to the producer; controlling access and the flow of information, and consciously or unconsciously filtering, distorting or rejecting information as they see fit.

Many of these issues revolve around trust, so a key issue is how much the producer allows the development executive to interrupt the paths of communication, and how much the producer enables the executive to be part of a more complex parallelogram of equal creative relationships (see Fig. 6.3). Above all, this is down to the character of the individual executive, and the trust and openness built up between all four parties.

Most writers say they always want the producer to be in the script meeting too, so they know that the executive has the producer's support and is not misrepresenting them, but they are aware that this is not always practical. Different views about how to manage this relationship are expressed in the case study interviews at the end of this chapter, but one approach is that the producer is present in the first meetings with the new writer, and then allows the development executive more space to work alone with the writer. Either way, it is important that the development executive or editor creates with the writer a neutral *safe space* of development, so that whilst throwing around different ideas and possibilities the writer does not have to feel afraid to fail. This can make the writer more forthcoming with wild ideas that they might not want to voice in front of the producer. There should be an element of confidentiality between the writer and the editor or executive, so if some ideas are discussed and rejected then the writer is secure in the knowledge that the failures disappear from the record, which in turn

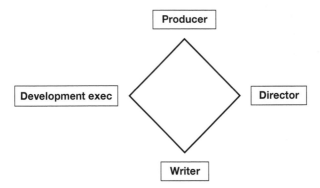

Figure 6.3 The development executive shown as an intrinsic part of the creative triangle, or parallelogram

encourages risk-taking. This is potentially easier for the freelance script editor than the development executive, who may have a conflict of loyalties and feel they should report everything back to the producer company or broadcaster, where their primary obligation lies. However, the writer and executive should also be able to develop a trusting relationship where the more creative discussions are still kept confidential.

Where do script editors and development executives fit into the power typology?

To go back to the Belbin team roles cited in Chapter 4, script editors and development executives tend to be: *resource investigators* (extroverted and enthusiastic, like the producer and director) and *monitor evaluators* (strategic and discerning, judging accurately). This places them as closer in character type to the producer than the writer, who is more of a creative *plant*, and yet they have to spend most of their professional lives managing writers. So where do they fit into the power typology (see Fig. 6.4)?

The development executive is shown having influence throughout the development period, whereas the freelance script editor only rises in influence each time he works on the script. Although they are both shown in this figure, in fact it would be unusual for a film to have *both* a development executive and a freelance script editor, because the executive would be doing the script work with the writer.

During the closing financing stage, before final rewrites, both the development executive and the producer are potentially more powerful than the writer, because this is the stage when the writer is most likely to be replaced by them; and also the stage where they are mediating the feedback from the financiers and therefore in a controlling position. However, at final rewrites stage the development executive is being superseded by the financiers and the director.

At their best, development executives and script editors are a crucial part of the development process. They provide a vital sounding-board for the writer and help to protect and develop his vision; they help shape the script and guide it through the maze of conflicting feedback from third parties; and finally they can build the long-term creative relationships and networks that are vital for a successful development business. Where their taste and sensibility is closely allied to the taste of the producer, development executives can be crucial in developing a large enough slate of projects to ensure a constant supply of new projects for the producer to sell into the financing marketplace.

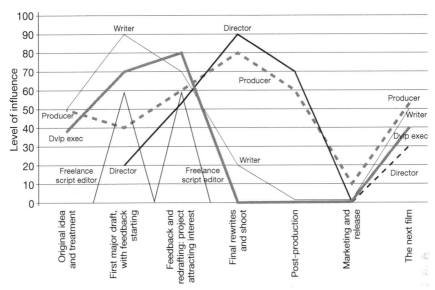

Note: This shows the in-house development executive at the production company, not the development executive at the financiers' company.

Figure 6.4 A typology of changing power and approximate creative influence of various players in independent film, from development to distribution, showing the roles of the in-house development executive and script editor

Case interview 1: The pros and cons of development executives and how you manage them (or survive being one)

The advantages and disadvantages of development executives

Tony Grisoni (writer): The script editor will read a script and tell you what you've done, and what you didn't see, which is actually very good because that's an indication that somehow the story's being told beyond you, you're doing things which you aren't conscious of, and there are things that you don't want to quite know consciously when you're in the middle of writing a screenplay, or else you become very self-conscious and you start destroying it somehow. But when you get to the end of your first draft, to have someone who is sensitive enough to see what you've done, to show you, and say: 'Look how this character behaves in this way, look for example how this young man constantly comes up against father figures, constantly seeks them out, even ending up killing them ...' Then you can see that pattern and you could strengthen that pattern or change that pattern. You can run counter to that pattern, or you could choose not to make it a pattern, but you suddenly have this tool which has been given you by someone from the outside.

Rob Sprackling (writer): I've worked a lot in a writing partnership, so I get feedback all the time. I already have another person's opinions to bounce off, so development executives have perhaps been less useful for me than for people who work on their own. That's not to say I haven't worked with some very good development people down the years – who have helped to throw a new light on a script and really take it forward. However, if they aren't so good, or if they have a fundamentally different creative view to the writer, this can result in a creative impasse which rarely helps the script. In my experience the best development executives work alongside the writers, making creative suggestions and helping to find solutions. This gets much better results than someone who simply hands over a typed list of changes.

Anonymized screenwriter: Development execs are just the luck of the draw. You might get one who instinctively understands your script and who is a joy to work with. Or you may get one who just happens to be working for the producer at the time and has no connection with your script whatsoever. In these cases it's a disaster. They normally want to change it into the kind of film that they want to see, rather than the kind of film that you wanted to make. ... Sometimes what happens is they have the power – and somebody who's maybe 28, who's never written a thing in their life, but maybe done a course or something and read some books, can come in and have the say-so over a script which has been created by someone who's invented every single scene and character. ... The bottom line is: who is the creative voice? If the writer can overrule the development guy, then no problem. If the development guy gets to dictate what happens in the script, or even gets the writer sacked, then the tail is wagging the dog and you end up with a mess.

The development executive as protector of the boss

Tom Williams (writer and ex-development executive): I think that my job when I was working as a development executive at FineLine was – I don't know the American football term but – the blocker, the line backer, to protect the quarterback who is the producer. So you'd be there to answer the phone to needy writers, or to take pitches from people who weren't quite at the level of the head of the company. And I think that is part of the process, in the way that an agent is part of the walls of Jericho around the film industry, so that the cream filters upwards. But I suppose as a writer you have to trust that the development executive will be invested in *your* script to the extent that if you develop a good screenplay it reflects well on both of you.

Some perceived issues around the development executive

Anonymized screenwriter: Development executives ... don't care about you. They are more concerned with protecting their jobs, their positions in the company and their relationship with the producer.

Anonymized scriptwriter: I haven't had a good experience as a writer or as a producer with script editors. ... I wouldn't want them personally. They have the potential to muddy the waters. You know the more voices that are involved the more chance there is of bad decision-making creatively. There's a difference between collaboration and a committee. As a producer your main job at every stage is to manage those creative collaborations.

Peter Ettedgui (writer): There's a kind of development exec. who are maybe second-guessing their bosses, rather than actually handing down their words. And I've certainly been in a situation as a writer when I've seen that happen, where there is a middle person between myself and the producer. And previously I had a very good relationship with the producer, and I felt very undermined by that, and had to ring up the producer and say, 'Look, is that really what you think too, because it doesn't seem to chime with what we'd said previously?' I think the really critical thing is that the *producer* manages the process.

Anonymized screenwriter: The nightmare of development is that feeling that you're with someone who is trying to be a wall between you and getting the film made. And that's either about feeling that they're not really empowered to make any sort of decisions or choices, so everything is 'Oh how interesting, I'll go and refer it back upstairs and come back down to you.' ... Or that they're so desperate to have a creative input that they're running away with it and saying 'Why don't we do this and that?' and then when you come back to the producers they say 'Where did all this stuff come from?'

Great script notes and execs can really help

Andy Paterson (producer and writer): I was on the phone to Screen Australia a few weeks ago about *The Railway Man*, which I'm co-writing, and people are coming up with comments, but suddenly there's this executive who's also a writer and he said something that I just knew how to go away and work with. And that's water in the desert for writers, when you get a note that actually makes you excited about going off and fixing something. It was recognizing something that you knew you were evading; looking right inside your soul and saying, in very polite and different terms: 'I don't think you knew what to do here. I think you evaded this problem, and actually you could do this.' So it's that level of insight into what you're doing, and being able to spot where you were struggling and throw you a lifeline. That's what you dream of.

Do you have script meetings with the producer and the executive both in the room? The complexity of authority versus safe space

There are many different answers to this, and it varies from team to team. However, one regular approach is that the producer and development executive discuss their notes together first, but they both do the meeting with the writer. This ensures that they are speaking with a consistent voice. The producer doesn't necessarily have to say much in the meeting with the writer, but the fact that they're there shows that the development executive is trusted and supported.

Kate Leys: Certainly my first meeting on a project I would like the writer and the producer to be there. ... It's a lovely way of a producer showing how much they support what the development executive is doing. It's a way of saying you all bring something different to the table: the writer is bringing one thing, the producer is bringing something and the development executive is bringing something else. ... And then I would quite like it if the producer then said, you know: 'I now hand over to you two – let me know when you need me to be involved next.' Because that gives you the space to get on and open things up. ... It's difficult for a writer to disagree with the producer; but it's possible for the writer to get something really thorny thrashed out with the development executive. It's possible for a writer to say, 'I've got no idea what to do with this act' to a development executive, in a way that they might never admit in front of a producer. So, it's often quite helpful to have some space on your own, and have some dialogue on your own and I would almost always try and do that. It's about being confidential. Technically my notes are always available to producers, but I think a good producer would always agree that it was quite a good idea for the writer to feel that they can try stuff out, and they can be a bit radical with the material without necessarily feeling it's going to be put under scrutiny in formal discussions. One of the great things I can say – as the story editor – is say to the writer, 'Have a look at changing the story around, in a page of bullet points, as rough as you please, and send it over for me to look at, and it's not for anybody to see.' And then you can really try stuff out, really push some boundaries. And quite often it's to discover that they *don't* work, but that's an invaluable process to go through. Because you've scratched that itch, you've established therefore what does work, and months later, when someone, you know, say a distribution financier, comes on board and then sends through a set of notes saying 'What you should do is this,' you know you've already done that and it doesn't work, so you've already got an answer. It's another way of getting more confident about your material.

Peter Ettedgui: In the first instance I don't think there should be more than one person [from the production company]. I think that the writing of the screenplay, in getting it to a first draft that is readable and submitable, should be to do with the writer, the director (if the director is around at that stage) and the producer. I don't think there should be anyone else in that bit of the process. The writer submits first of all to the producer, and that core team then has a pass on the script together. ... I don't think there should be anyone else involved in that process. You *can* have too many voices in the process at that stage and you have to let the writer write. You brought that writer in because you believed that writer could do that job.

Kate Leys: Writers often talk about not having the space to fail. Well in development you ought to have the space to fail, because nothing is sacred in development, you've got to be able to push it all and see if it's strong. If it's not strong enough then development is the place to figure that out. And if it is strong enough then it can withstand a good kicking. But a good kicking is sometimes something you need to do quietly. You can't necessarily do a good kicking and put all of that before a committee of financiers to discuss. God knows, that would be a nightmare.

Case interview 2: Script editor and development executive Sarah Golding on introducing the director to a project

Development executives don't work exclusively with the writer – another role might be to work with a newly attached director. This can be at an early stage of attachment or as part of a director's polish during pre-production. Not all directors are strong on script: the director may have been chosen for his visual brilliance, or his ability to create suspense or powerful action sequences, rather than because of a feel for the subtleties of characterization, structure or period detail. The director may even be working in a language that's not his mother tongue. Some directors are open to talking through the script in detail with the development executive or producer; others can feel uncomfortable asking for clarification on the sub-text of a scene. As ever, it is the discussion that helps to bring out these issues.

Sarah Golding: If a director has a problem with something then you really can't try to brush it aside and assume it'll be okay on the day ... you *excavate* the problem to find out where it stems from. Quite often, the writer knows that the scene works, and the producer knows that the scene works, but the director can be unhappy with it for some reason. Often when you dig it out it's not that there's anything wrong with the emotions, characterization or action of the scene, it's that the director may have a very valid difficulty working out how they're going to put it there visually. And sometimes that can be solved quite easily, without changing the content of the scene, but by altering the choreography of it.

The arrival of the director is the arrival of the visualization. A script is a literary artefact, but in his mind's eye the director is trying to convert it to an artwork. Scriptwriters are usually encouraged to keep visual descriptions and stage directions to a minimum, so that the director can bring his vision to it, but this can mean that the director's problem with a scene is not a verbal one (a need to change what the characters are saying), but a visual one (a need to change what they are doing or where they are). So if the producer or development executive can find the real problem, then the team can find a way to make the scene work, perhaps by changing the location or the number of people in the scene. Crucially this avoids a destructive wholesale rewriting of a scene that may in fact already work.

> **Sarah Golding**: The best way to pin down the problem is by asking questions. If the director cannot immediately define the problem, then I'd try throwing out some suggestions – is it this, or is it that? Or if such and such happened would that solve it? If you lay out a number of reasons why the scene might not be working for them then between you both you stand a good chance of sorting it out. You feel your way.

Sometimes the executive ends up becoming the mediator between the writer and director. They may be appearing to disagree with one another, but are actually just expressing themselves differently.

> **Sarah Golding**: Very often people think they're not agreeing about things because they have a different way of expressing an issue or a different emphasis, and there's a job of translation to go on in that case. How often have you sat in a room and somebody says, 'Well, it's this ...' and somebody else says, 'No, it's that ...'and in fact they're a hair's breadth away from one another. Maybe one person has an analytical approach, while the other is kinetic or emotional. The language they're using makes them *feel* further apart than they really are. So a mediator can come at it with 'What he's saying is this. ... She's not disagreeing with you. ... What we have in common is ...'

Sometimes the producer can do this work, but the value of employing the development executive or script editor at this last polish stage is that the producer is often trying to close the financing of the film. Creative disagreements that could damage a working relationship can be prevented through quick and sensible interventions by a semi-outsider like a script editor. This kind of mediation can have a positive impact on future potential collaborations, as well as on the outcome of the individual film.

Part II

Managing creative people in film development: control versus freedom

Part I of this book examined how the film industry works during development and financing, including the complexity of film financing systems and business models. It proposed that at the core of successful development is the powerful creative triangle of the producer, writer and director, bound together by trust and communication and in some cases supported and co-managed by the development executive. It also showed that film development teams are made up of different people with very different psychological types and roles, and with conflicting agendas and allegiances, working in an insecure and high-anxiety environment, where power and control are not static but shift within the team over time.

Part II looks in more detail at how the producer or development executive can best control that development process, and use creativity theories to manage and champion the work of creative people, especially writers. Above all, it tackles the question: *How can the creative team of the writer, producer, director and development executive work together most effectively? And how can the process be managed to make it work?*

The subtitle of this book includes *managing creativity*, and to do that it is vital to understand what creativity is, and who creative people are, so that they can be managed and encouraged most effectively. Theories about managing creative people in the workplace were developed in the 1990s;[1] however, these techniques are usually applied to managing creative people in conventional businesses (for example, research and development departments in manufacturing companies) and have rarely been applied to the creative industries, including film. This is a potential goldmine of techniques and theories. Some of these existing creativity theories are now explored and applied to current practice in the field of film development, focusing on producers, development executives and writers. These theories have not been studied, applied and published in this way before, and this book is a contribution to the existing body of literature on managing creative people, and provides the film industry with some new ideas to consider and test.

Chapter 7 looks more closely at what we *mean* by creativity, especially in the movies, and proposes some new models for analysing and considering creativity and originality in film. Chapter 8 looks at the personality traits that are usually associated with creative people, including writers and directors, and will examine the crucial issue as to what motivates creative people. Some parts of these two chapters may seem quite academic and complex, but they are vital preparation for chapters 9 to 11, which then apply these concepts more closely to film.

Chapter 9 looks at how to use this knowledge to manage and champion creative people, both during the development process and in larger media organizations. Chapter 10 applies this to the detail of the day-to-day development process, incorporating theories about managing creative people into specific industry advice on how to give script notes and how to be receptive to innovative new ideas.

Chapter 11 then looks at business theories about teams and how they might be applied to film development. It also explores the vital concepts of team culture and organizational culture, and sees how these can benefit both individual film project development and the long-term building of a sustainable film company. Successful companies often end up working in collaboration with the Hollywood studios, so Chapter 12 considers in more detail the difference between the independent and the Hollywood studio system.

Chapter 13 looks at the whole process from the point of view of the screenwriter, and proposes some techniques for the professional writer to thrive and survive in the competitive world of film development. Finally, Chapter 14 draws together all the themes of this book, and proposes some ideas about the future direction of the film industry and development.

7   Defining creativity in the movie business

> I don't want somebody trying to second-guess the market. I want someone
> telling me to be brave.
>
> (Screenwriter Tony Grisoni)

What is creativity? New, surprising and valuable

The word *creativity* has different values and associations in different cultures
and periods of history. There are already many reviews of creativity research,
and almost as many different definitions of what creativity is, so this chapter
will take just one useful definition of creativity and look at specific ways that
different levels of creativity and originality can be applied to film. Creativity
is a hugely complex field, and there is more information and a wider
reading list in the notes.[2] In 1990 creativity expert Margaret Boden of the
University of Sussex suggested the following definition:

> Creativity is the ability to come up with ideas or artefacts that are new,
> surprising and valuable.[3]

Margaret Boden's definition seems both elegant and compelling, and she
goes on to explain:

> Ideas here include concepts, poems, musical compositions, scientific
> theories, cookery recipes, choreography, jokes – and so on. 'Artefacts'
> include paintings, sculptures, steam engines, vacuum cleaners, pottery,
> origami, penny whistles – and many other things you can name.[4]

Margaret Boden includes the word *surprise*, which takes us away from simple
craftsmanship or beauty. It also requires the audience to respond
emotionally or intellectually, since surprise could be defined as an emotional
response to an unexpected significant event. Newness is also important
because creativity is meant to be a departure from the norm, but things can
be new without being creative and the word *novelty* is often used today in a
loaded and negative way (novelty for its own sake is not always highly socially

or artistically valued). So as well as *new,* Boden also uses the word *valuable.* Value or applicability is a crucial concept in modern creativity definitions, because something that is new is not necessarily creative or innovative unless it can be *applied* to something (now or in the future). However, 'value' as a term is also highly elusive, depending on social expectations and culture, and raising issues of context, frames of reference, timing, convention, intention and reception (both social and economic reception). There is not space here to explore this in detail, but in the world of film we have already seen that this is in part an interchange between producers, peers, markets, critics, audiences and the wider cultural world, as suggested by Fig. 7.1.

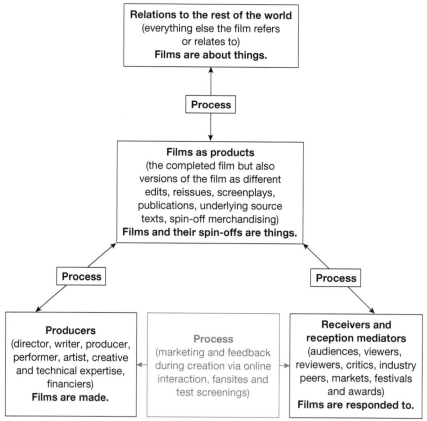

Note: This chart has been adapted by the author to represent film, and the grey section has been added to show how new technology and marketing enables the producer to be in direct contact with receiver/consumer during the creative process, which may affect the completed film. The growth of user-generated content also sometimes blurs the distinction between producer and receiver.[5]

Figure 7.1 The reception of creative ideas: where and when and by whom is value assessed? Abrams (1953)/Pope (2002)/Bloore (2011)

Box 7.1 New technology and user feedback in assessing creative value

New technology has given rise to user-criticism (online reviews from members of the public) and multiple levels of online community, blogs and bulletin boards. This potentially transforms the way that creative value is measured. Direct contact between the artist and the receiver/consumer is an interaction which has only recently become possible through online media such as websites, fanzines and social media. This is potentially *business-transformational* in that it allows the audience to influence the creation of the film before they see it. However, whether that is a good thing or not is another issue, and many writers and directors would resist the introduction of yet another feedback voice to interfere with their vision. Excessive market research may actually stifle creativity and innovation: cinema-goers in focus groups or online surveys may be inclined to ask for what they have already seen and enjoyed, because they are unlikely to imagine something they have not already seen. Therefore they may favour sequels and films packaging existing stars above new ideas or unfamiliar combinations.

The issue of reception within a social system led to an influential 1988 paper by the Professor of Psychology Mihály Csíkszentmihályi, where he applied a systems thinking approach to creativity and proposed that the creative individual is always operating within an existing disciplinary domain (such as literature, music, maths, various technologies, etc.), and that creativity can only occur when the individual's novel contribution to the domain is also accepted and endorsed by what he calls 'the field': the social system of gatekeepers and experts who control the domain and decide what should be 'recognised, preserved and remembered'.[6] For example, in the visual arts the field of gatekeepers includes art teachers, museum curators, collectors, critics and the administrators of government agencies dealing with culture. He points out that some domains, fields and organizations are more receptive to change and creativity than others.

Csíkszentmihályi suggests that creativity can be shown as three separate interacting boxes (see Fig. 7.2). He uses the example of the Renaissance in Florence, which came about because of the genetic background and upbringing of several key artists *combined* with the active attention and encouragement of wealthy patrons (the field and resources); intense competition with rivals (the field again); and the previous rapid expansion of the domain due to the rediscovery of classical art in Italy. Therefore creativity is part of a wider system and not solely dependant on the individual's creative ability.

Csíkszentmihályi's emphasis on the adoption of the idea by the field was influenced by the systems concepts of *interdependance* and the *feedback loop*. This is particularly relevant for development because of the role of gatekeepers and script notes. In the world of film, the creative evaluation

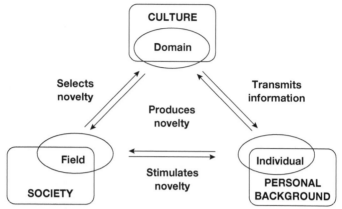

Note: 'For creativity to occur a set of rules and practices must be transmitted from the domain to the individual. The individual must then produce a novel variation in the content of the domain. The variation must then be selected by the field for inclusion in the domain.'[7]

Figure 7.2 The systems view of creativity (Csíkszentmihályi, 1988)

and feedback is first at the script development and financing stage, where the film idea needs endorsement by public and commercial financiers; and second at the cinema release stage, when the film is evaluated by distributors and exhibitors (who choose if and how to expose the product), industry peers, film festival programmers, award juries, government agencies that fund film, formal and informal film critics, academic writers (long-term reputation) and the audience itself, via box office figures and word of mouth (reception studies is a whole academic sub-section of film studies).

Csíkszentmihályi suggests that 'in the domains of movies or popular music, which are much more accessible to the general public, the specialized field is notoriously unable to enforce a decision as to which works will be creative'.[8] By this he means that the evaluation of the level of creativity of a project is more in the hands of the public than the professional field. However, in the case of film he may be thinking more of the Hollywood studio model, and may be missing the fact that before the film has been completed the work has *already* been controlled by some of the gatekeepers (for example, altered by feedback during the development or production process), because the people responsible for greenlighting are also influencing creativity (sometimes reducing it if they are averse to risk). It could also be said that film is over-regulated against creativity by its field of gatekeepers, and they can even come between the creative and his ability to practise within the domain because the barriers to entry are so high (especially the cost and high levels of competition for available funds).

Different levels of creativity

We need to move on from Margaret Boden's basic definition of creativity to an understanding of different *levels* of creativity. Boden points out that every one of us is creative to a degree, but that there are different levels of creativity and creative acts. She makes a distinction between a creative idea that is new to ourselves, but not new to others (although it is still psychologically a creative thought); and an idea that is also new to society and history. Boden calls the first of these ideas psychological creativity (*P-creative*), and the second historical creativity (*H-creative*). For the purposes of analysing how the brain works both are equally important, but for the study of society and culture the historical is more important.[9] Beyond that we need to distinguish between three different levels of creativity, including the level of creativity that only explores existing conceptual spaces compared to the level of creativity that transforms and redefines them (see Box 7.2).

Box 7.2 Boden's three forms of creativity (Boden, 2004)[10]

1. **Combinatorial:** Unfamiliar combinations of familiar ideas (like the cartoonist who chose to show Ken Livingstone as a newt, or Donne's poetic image of two lovers being like a pair of dividers). Something we all regularly do as we talk – creating analogies/images/metaphors.

2. **Exploratory:** (*E-creativity*) The exploration of existing conceptual spaces (a conceptual space is a convention, a cultural expectation, an artistic style or a genre. Conventions do not originate in one individual mind, but are built up by groups over time). Most art forms have a convention or genre. Exploring *within* the conceptual space is providing new ideas that hadn't been done before, but sticking to the 'road map' of the convention. For example, a new romantic comedy film can be creative without leaving the generic expectations of the romantic comedy.

3. **Transformational:** (*T-creativity*) Transforming the conceptual space (thinking the unthinkable; changing the way we think; redefining the road map; impossible surprise). Examples could include Darwin's theory of evolution and Einstein's theory of relativity. Within film and television this could mean changing the future expectations of a genre, or creating a new genre entirely. 'The deepest cases of creativity involve someone thinking something which, with respect to the conceptual spaces in their minds, they *couldn't* have thought of before. ... Thus the combination of old elements is only one part of creativity, some creativity can re-set the road map of the mind, so that the whole framework by which we view the world or a particular genre is reorganised.'

Margaret Boden's distinctions between these levels of creativity are similar to those of other creativity writers, as shown in Table 7.1;[11] and, like them, Boden's definition is taking account of scientific breakthroughs and creative problem-solving as well as the creative arts. These labels can be used to categorize the product, the person or the process. Other academics have also tried to explore different levels of change or transformation achieved by creative breakthroughs, for example Yale Professor Robert Sternberg who has worked on propulsion, intent and paradigm rejection (see Appendix A for an analysis of his work and a possible application of it to film genre).

Table 7.1 Different academic authors analyse exploratory and transformative creativity

Author	Exploring within convention	Breaking out/changing the way we think
Boden (1990, 2004)	Exploratory	Transformational
Guilford (1950, 1967)[12]	Convergent	Divergent
Gardner (1993)[13]	Little c creativity	Big C creativity
Bilton (2006)[14]	Convergent	Divergent
Csíkszentmihályi (1996)[15]	Novelty	Changes an existing domain
Ekvall (1997)[16]	Adaptive and confirmatory	Radical and revolutionary
Kirton (1987)[17]	Adaptors	Innovators
Sternberg (2006)[18]	Accept paradigms	Reject paradigms

Note: Creative people who are adaptors/explorers may even resist the innovators/transformers, who are threatening the conventions that they are operating within, as explained in Chapter 9.

Box 7.3 The difference between arts and crafts

Some films are said to be well crafted or workmanlike, but others seem to qualify as high art; so what exactly is the distinction between *art* and *craft* (even though there is sometimes an overlap)? Some will disagree but it is possible to argue that a craft is the skilful creation of a practical and decorative object, but it stays within the *exploratory* form of creativity. Consider, for example, a clay vase, taking shape under the potter's hands on a wheel. The vase is made according to existing conventions, using a mixture of personal talent and taught skills; it will serve its purpose (holding flowers) and it may perhaps be a thing of aesthetic beauty. In crafts the domestic utility of the artefact is important and a person may be inspired by its appearance and functionality to handle it and use it (it has been suggested that this may have its origins in our evolutionary biology and the manufacture of tools as both practical aids and as value objects). Without doubt something has been 'created', because the raw clay has been worked into a pot; but however skilful the craft, it is not necessarily art and *transformationally creative* unless it communicates a deeper message or is a new departure from existing forms and conventions.

By contrast, art may question, stimulate and challenge us and our preconceptions of the world, but it *does not have to be* practical or aesthetically pleasing. For example, a pot with a hole in the bottom of it may have an artistic message, but it would be useless as a practical container of water. In 2003 the ceramic pots of artist Grayson Perry won the British *Turner Prize* – the prestigious award organized by London's Tate Gallery to recognize an artist who has achieved new developments in contemporary art. Grayson Perry produced carefully crafted vases, but they were also art, representing the transvestite artist's own personal view of the world and his/her own identity. Society views Perry's work differently from similar clay pots found in a typical country craft fair, because of the message, vision and identity of the artist.

To complicate the issue, some artists are not the craftsmen who create their works. Artists such as Damien Hirst and Andy Warhol employed workshops of craftspeople to realize their ideas – it is the having of the idea that creates the art, not the craftsmanship of the act of manufacture. So if an artist does not need to be a craftsman, likewise a craftsman is not automatically an artist.

In film the technical skills of camerawork and sound are usually referred to as *crafts*. Rightly or wrongly they are perceived to be serving the vision of the auteur director/artist, rather than serving their own vision. They are employed as freelancers and are dependent on the next commission to set their creative direction. However, masters of their craft (such as key cinematographers) are viewed as akin to artists; they build a consistent body of work, work regularly with the same directors, and are powerful enough to select work that is in keeping with their personal style and vision.

The seven levels of creativity in film

Most film-making operates within craft and the exploratory creative field, because it is restricted to the generic expectations of the market and the audience and is therefore fulfilling the definition that creativity is 'a new combination of old elements'.[19] This is partly because the production investment costs are so large that risky transformational work is discouraged, or kept in low-budget or specialist/arthouse film-making. The creative emphasis is instead usually placed on the originality of the film-maker's *vision*, which means that he is still within a genre, but that the world he creates onscreen across several films reveals consistent preoccupations and visual styles (for example, Wes Anderson and Terry Gilliam). A film can be new, surprising and valuable (to use Boden's definition) and be a departure from expected norms, but still not change all the films that come after it in the way that a scientific breakthrough might. Even the greatest names in film-making cannot often claim to have *transformed* the conceptual space or created new genres. Recent directors as varied as the Coen Brothers, Tim Burton, Ang Lee and Martin Scorcese have produced bodies of highly identifiable and original work, but the genres they worked in could be said to have remained much the same as they were when they started, regardless of the success of their individual films. It could be argued that film-makers, like many other artists and storytellers, are more interested in representing the human condition than in the formal innovation of the language of film-making or its conventions.

In fact, the very principle of *cinematic genre* mitigates against creative innovation, because it categorizes itself by identifying similarity and continuity with other films, and is to a degree intentionally predictable, cumulative, nostalgic, functional, symbolic, repetitive and ritualistic.[20] Genre labels are elements or tools in a discursive process, used by film-makers, marketeers, critics and audiences to control expectation and influence discourse, even though they often apply, interpret and manipulate these labels differently from one another (for example, some marketing campaigns are different from the film-maker's intention or the audience's perception of the actual film).

However, many films can be creative in one way (such as in the use of new technology), and not in another way (for example, the same film may be very conventional in terms of genre). Therefore, to make these definitions work better for film we need to look harder at the grey area between the exploratory and transformational categories, and try to break down further the levels and types of change. Table 7.2 sets out a new series of definitions that may be more effective for analysing creativity and originality in these fields, putting particular emphasis on the boundary-playing mentioned by Professor Sternberg and others,[21] and the different ways that exploratory creativity can become transformational.

The assumption is that creativity needs to include a challenge to expected norms, involving risk and often causing change to the existing paradigm. Most of the transformational sub-categories are self-evident, but a few need further explanation.

Technology-transformational creativity

In film you can often distinguish between innovation in technology (SFX, 3D) and innovation in the type of story or its genre. For example, *Avatar* is not innovative as a story (imperial industrial force exploits indigenous peoples and their world, until they fight back using their own ways and traditions), but it *is* innovative in the way that it shows this onscreen, and it has demonstrated how creatively and financially effective 3D film technology can be. Sometimes film-makers like Lucas, Cameron and Lasseter (at Pixar) have to develop the new technology themselves, just to be able to make their films as they want them, and that trail blazing opens the technology to other film-makers. These technological advances sometimes also cause changes in cinematic form, making new methods of storytelling possible or acceptable.

Table 7.2 The seven levels of creativity and originality in creative industry products (such as film, TV programming, computer gaming and magazine publishing)

Boden heading	Proposed heading		Description
Exploratory	Exploratory		Conventional. Combinatorial. Operating within the genre, probably with a new storyline or situation, but not really challenging the genre
	Challenging		Testing or challenging the boundary of the convention/genre. It is challenging, but it does not *change* the ongoing convention, or it does so in a small incremental step
Transforming	Transformational	Genre/cross-genre, convention	High levels of originality. A radical challenge, achieving a *permanent change* in the industry or in audience expectation. Often identifiable in retrospect (after adoption by the industry), and not necessarily intentional. A film may be transformational in one sector and not in others (see left)
		Form (cinematic language, narrative form, non-linear, montage, film style, etc.)	
		Technological (e.g. 3D or computer animation), and production technique	
		Business (e.g. changing what is commercial)	
		Taste/social acceptability	

Business-transformational creativity

This involves films which have changed what the business and the audience think are acceptable and successful, even if they are in themselves not highly creative. For example, the first Rambo film, *First Blood* (1982), was not highly creative in itself, but it hit the zeitgeist and sparked three sequels and many 'hard-bodied' action imitators (such as *Die Hard* (x4), *Commando* (x2), *Double Impact* (x2), *Universal Soldier* (x2); and merged genres with sci-fi on *Predator*, *Terminator* (x4), *RoboCop* (x2), and *TimeCop*).[22] Therefore *First Blood* was business-transformational, even if the film itself was not inherently radical.

Some highly influential films can reignite Hollywood's interest in genres that had been thought to be dead, re-inventing them and achieving financial and critical success. Examples include: *The Godfather, Star Wars, Jaws, The Unforgiven* and *Pirates of the Caribbean*. Others take niche genres and make them mainstream: for example, the box office and Oscar success *Silence of the Lambs* (1991). Some films succeed because of the way they combine previously separate genres, for example in the way that *Alien* (1979) merged science fiction with the horror-slasher movie. Generically these films often spawn multiple further spin-offs within the exploratory space, rather than being wholly transformational, but they are indubitably business-transformational, triggering new trends.

The release campaigns of some films transform the business of marketing, but this is different because the creativity usually resides with the distributor or advertising agency rather than intrinsically with the film and the film-maker. However, sometimes the film-maker is involved from the outset on spin-off merchandising or cross-platform exploitation, especially where there is an intentional element of transmedia storytelling (an example is the *Matrix* computer games and comic books, as overseen by the Wachowski Brothers).[23]

Taste-transformational creativity

There is a separate sub-section of films which are not cinematically innovative, but which do push the boundaries of what is socially acceptable on film, and which are therefore creative and boundary-breaking in terms of the social and moral conditions of the time (for example, around sexuality and violence, such as the low-budget exploitation genres of the 1960s and 1970s. However some of these films are no longer as shocking as they were, since taste and acceptability has changed). Some films can even influence government and social policy, like Ken Loach's *Cathy Come Home* (1966) on homelessness and poverty.

Multiple-creativity

A film can have creative impact in several sectors at once, and at different levels. For example, *Star Wars* was *challenging-creative* in genre (combining science fiction with the western, with a dash of aerial warfare); and *transformationally creative* in technology (special effects and prosthetics) and business (resuscitating the science fiction genre, and powerfully consolidating the sequel/prequel model, the summer blockbuster, and merchandising spin-offs – a business model started by the original *Planet of the Apes* franchise).

Film-maker Stanley Kubrick operated creatively throughout his life by challenging or transforming convention, including genre (*Dr Strangelove*, *The Shining*); taste/acceptability (*A Clockwork Orange* caused outrage by its stylized portrayal of extreme violence); and form and technology (for example, he won an Oscar for the special effects in the innovative film *2001: A Space Odyssey*, which also challenged norms of storytelling; he used new NASA technology to film interiors in the period film *Barry Lyndon* by candlelight; and he influentially deployed the newly invented steadicam camera mounting for the hand-held sequences in *The Shining*).

It should be noted that television is perhaps more prone to major shifts in convention or genre combinations, because of the greater volume of output (and therefore commissioning); cheaper and faster production rates; returning rewards from a successful innovative format; wider use of prototyping; and the need for originality in a crowded marketplace.

The role of the writer in transformational creativity

The writer of the script during development can usually only be creatively challenging or transformational in certain fields, mainly genre/convention and taste, since the other fields are in the control of the director. However, the script can establish the possibility of formal or technological innovation for the right director, and a small number of writers are sufficiently distinctive for their vision to be consistent regardless of who is directing (an example is Charlie Kaufman, the writer of *Being John Malkovich* (1999), *Adaptation* (2002), *Eternal Sunshine of the Spotless Mind* (2004) and *Synecdoche, New York* (2008)).

This means that it is hard to be sure during development if a project will end up being highly creative, and there is a danger that the creativity can be undermined before the director gets to it. In fact, many innovative films are based on underlying novels, where the challenging endings or worldviews cannot be changed by the financiers during development because of audience and critical support for the original work. Perhaps the more innovative directors are attracted to novels simply because they can be more innovative than screenplays developed for the studio film sensibility. Stanley Kubrick based his films (other than his first two) on novels and short stories, often actively choosing scandalous or satirical books such as *Lolita*, *Red Alert* (which became *Dr Strangelove*) and *A Clockwork Orange* (which he shot on a comparatively low budget and without a script, following the original novel almost page by page on the set[24]). Kubrick's *The Killing* followed Lionel White's noir thriller *Clean Break* by telling the story out of sequence in a non-linear narrative, to illustrate different observers' perspectives of an event. As ever, challenge means risk, which means downward pressure on the budget to reduce the risk for the financier (for instance, George Lucas had to find innovative ways to reduce the budget for the first *Star Wars* film).

So why *do* some people (like Kubrick) insist on always pushing the boundaries of what is acceptable, and fighting against the status quo? Perhaps the answer lies inside the wiring of their brains and the make-up of their characters, as the next chapter will consider.

8   Who creative people are and how to motivate them

Psychology and insight

> A poet is a light and winged thing, and holy, and never able to compose until he has become inspired, and is beside himself and reason is no longer in him ... for not by art do they utter these, but by power divine.
>
> (Socrates, quoted in Plato's *Ion*, 533d–536d)[1]

Creative people: their heads in the clouds?

Screenwriters and directors are classic examples of creative people. We are all creative, to a degree, but, to paraphrase George Orwell, some of us are more creative than others. Creativity is present across most levels of human ability, but many researchers believe that high levels of creativity are more likely when various personality traits are present, combined with a suitable environment and motivation.

This chapter explores the bundle of underlying personality traits that over the years have typically been identified to characterize creative people: their aptitudes, behaviour, competencies, interests, attitudes and temperament.[2] And the next chapter asks how the producer can best manage them, especially in the case of the screenwriter and director during development.

There is a wider debate amongst some creativity writers about the tension between the post-Romantic image of the tortured creative genius and the reality of workplace and team-based creativity, but that is for a different book than this one (for a few thoughts and further reading see the chapter notes).[3] Suffice to say that film development usually involves an active mixture of individual work and team collaboration.

Summaries of the research into creativity character traits are shown in boxes 8.1 to 8.3. In a brief survey of creativity, psychologist Professor Raymond Nickerson produced a list of common personal characteristics of creative people (Box 8.1); Professor Simon Majaro of Cranfield approached it from analysing people working in marketing (Box 8.2); and Professor John Adair's widely read book *The Challenge of Innovation* suggested a few more traits (Box 8.3). Some researchers believe that creativity is more likely in people with higher levels of intelligence, but only when associated with the other personality traits.[4]

Box 8.1 Raymond Nickerson (1999): personal characteristics necessary for creativity[5]

General intelligence, domain-specific knowledge, curiosity and inquisitiveness, motivation, self-confidence, willingness to take risks, mastery orientation, self-competition, beliefs, choice and the opportunity to discover, self-management skills, tolerance for ambiguity and unconventionality, the ability to think analogically and to make remote associations, flexibility of thought, facility with visualization and the manipulation of mental images, and other factors.

'People are creative in different ways, to different degrees, and for different reasons ... Desire, internal motivation, and commitment are more important, in my view, than either domain-specific knowledge or specific creativity-enhancing techniques or heuristics.'

Box 8.2 Simon Majaro (1992): creative types[6]

- **Conceptual fluency:** able to produce many ideas
- **Mental flexibility:** adept at lateral thinking
- **Originality:** produce atypical results to problems
- **Suspension of judgement:** do not analyse too quickly
- **Impulsive:** act impulsively on an idea, expressing their 'gut-feel'
- **Anti-authority:** always willing to challenge authority
- **Tolerance:** high tolerance threshold towards the ideas of others.

Box 8.3 John Adair (1990): characteristics of creative people[7]

- **Superior general intelligence**: Ability to analyse and to recall information
- **Non-conformist** and adventurous. They value individuality
- **Independence of judgement**: Resilient to group pressures towards conformity of thinking
- **High degree of autonomy**, self-motivation and self-sufficiency
- **Relatively little talkativeness or gregariousness:** They can sometimes be rather solitary/need own space. Ambiverts (mixture of introvert and extrovert, tending towards introversion, but needing contacts with stimulating people)
- **Broad range of interests**
- **Sustained curiosity** and powers of observation
- **Enjoy problem-solving**
- **Intuitive/dreaming:** He or she listens to the truth from within, in the form of intuitions. They inhabit more the world of imagination, reverie and fantasy
- **Suspension of immediate judgement:** They are able to hold many ideas – often apparently contradictory ones – together in creative tension, without reaching for premature resolution of ambiguity.

Perhaps the most important trait in both Simon Majaro's and John Adair's analyses is the *suspension of immediate judgement,* which potentially allows for what Einstein called *combinatory play.* Carl Jung shared the view that creativity involved playfulness: 'The creation of something new is not accomplished by the intellect but by the play instinct, acting from inner necessity. The creative mind plays with the objects it loves.'[8]

The creative person is able rationally to absorb a problem and the information or domain skills around it (the *preparation*), but suspends judgement and does not rush to an immediate conclusion. Then he consciously and subconsciously 'plays' with the problem, seeking out unlikely solutions (the *incubation*) and therefore allowing the opportunity for lateral thinking. This requires what is called *de-focused attention,* which in turn encourages analogous thinking and combinatorial leaps. By contrast, less creative people seem to have more narrowly focused attention than creative people.[9]

This is linked by some researchers to the Freudian concept of *primary process thought* (unconscious, dreaming, free-associative, analogical, de-focused attention) and *secondary process thought* (conscious, logical, reality-oriented thought, focused attention). They argue that creative people have more access to the analogical primary process thought or are able to switch between the two more effectively than 'normal' people.[10] It has been suggested that this correlates with the two hemispheres of the brain, where the right hemisphere is the home of primary thought (unconscious and de-focused) and the left is the home of rational secondary thought. However, this idea is now widely thought to be an over-simplification, complicated by the fact that it is now known that if a specific region of the brain is injured then its functions can sometimes be assumed by a neighbouring region (implying a greater degree of adaptation and flexibility within the brain). Research has also found that both hemispheres of the brain are involved in creativity, implying the brain is using rational as well as intuitive processes, so the reality may be more complex than a mechanistic left/right split.[11]

The frontal lobes of the brain are involved in cognitive and emotional inhibition and disinhibition, so differences in that part of the brain may also be part of the make-up of the creative mind. Brain scans of creative people doing creative tasks seem to display less frontal lobe activity, perhaps reflecting cognitive disinhibition (in other words the creative mind is intellectually disinhibited and therefore more permissive of weird ideas and connections).[12] Lateral thinking is one of the areas of creativity which may also have a neurological basis, because some people's brains seem more inclined to *cross-talk* between parts of the brain that are not usually connected (whether they are left or right hemisphere or not), which is also shown in conditions like the genetically transmitted condition *synaesthesia.*[13] Very creative people are also over-represented among the relatives of schizophrenics.[14]

Either way, some major creative breakthroughs have been made when the conscious linear mind is at rest and the unconscious mind takes over, resulting in a moment of insight or illumination. One of the most cited examples is that of the German scientist August Kekulé, who in the 1860s was working on the molecular structure of petrochemical hydrocarbons, and had been struggling with the unusual behaviour of the benzene molecule. According to his own account, he fell asleep in front of the fire whilst watching the sparks in the fireplace making spinning circles in the air, and when he was dozing he dreamt of a serpent, eating its own tail (an ancient mythical symbol, dating back to Egyptian times). When he woke, he had the breakthrough idea that the benzene molecule might be shaped like a ring, where the carbon molecules are linked with one another, which indeed turned out to be correct (see Fig. 8.1). His unconscious mind worked to figure out the solution whilst his conscious mind was semi-dormant.[15]

Other examples of illumination include the writing of Coleridge's poem 'Kubla Khan' during an opium-induced dream, and of course the original Eureka moment. According to the Roman writer Vitruvius, the ancient Greek physicist Archimedes had been set the task by King Hiero II of figuring out how much gold was in a crown, without damaging it or melting it down. Archimedes had given up consciously struggling with the task and was relaxing in the bath when he suddenly realized the solution: you should put the crown in the bath too. The volume of an irregular object placed in a vessel of water would be equal to the volume of water displaced by it. He is meant to have shouted out 'Eureka' (which is Greek for 'I have found it'), and in his excitement ran down the street naked. From this he later developed Archimedes' principle, which explains how an immersed object displaces its own weight of fluid: a key principle in the study of buoyancy to this day.

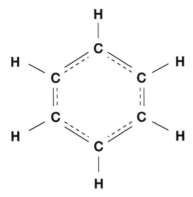

Figure 8.1 The benzene molecule

The mystery of this sudden dramatic illumination used to be credited to divine inspiration, since it seemed to come magically and apparently from outside the artist. It still is a mystery because opinions in cognitive science and psychology are divided about exactly what is going on in the brain at these moments,[16] but it is now apparent that the ability to do this is one of several factors that distinguish the highly creative mind from the minds of the rest of us. Colin Martindale of the University of Maine has studied the biological bases of creativity and explains:

> The creative act involves the discovery of an analogy between two or more ideas or images previously thought to be unrelated. This discovery does not arise from logical reasoning but, rather, emerges as a sudden insight. All of the theories of creativity reviewed say essentially the same thing – that creative inspiration occurs in a mental state where attention is defocused, thought is associative, and a large number of mental representations are simultaneously activated. Such a state can arise in three ways: low levels of cortical activation, comparatively more right-than left-hemisphere activation, and low levels of frontal lobe activation. Creative people do not exhibit all of these traits in general but only while engaged in creative activity.[17]

Furthermore in all the breakthrough cases described above, the person also had the domain skills and experience to make the breakthrough – without that immersion in the domain another person with a similarly creative mind would not be able to have had the breakthrough idea. Anyone can fall asleep in front of the fire and dream of snakes, but only someone thoroughly immersed in studying petrochemical hydrocarbons can also make the connection with the benzene molecule.

The creative process and film development

A number of writers have analysed the whole creative process in detail, from the nineteenth-century physicist Herman Von Helmholtz, to the 1920s scientist Henri Poincaré, to the 1950s Madison Avenue advertising executive James Webb Young. Their views are combined and summarized in Box 8.4.

The same creative stages were also invoked by film director Alexander Mackendrick in his book *On Filmmaking*,[18] and within the *preparation* stage both Mackendrick and Young emphasize the importance of gathering the raw materials of the creative task, both the ones that directly relate to the task (or film story); and also the lifelong quest of curiosity. Young emphasizes the importance of browsing, almost fifty years before the web made it simple; and also the need to store the information in scrapbooks and filing cabinets so that it can be found easily (he would have loved databases and iPads). This is what Young calls 'the inquisitive store of general knowledge

---

Box 8.4 The creative process: the five steps of the creative mind[19]

1. **Preparation:** Gather raw material (*perspiration*):
    (a) The materials of your immediate problem (like an advertising commission, or a new series – know your product and know your audience or market).
    (b) General materials – a life-long job (the inquisitive store of general knowledge and ideas, constantly being developed and grown by creative people). The vital importance of browsing. To store information it is important to use file index/scrapbooks (like Sherlock Holmes)/databases.

2. **Conscious work:** Work over these raw materials consciously in your mind (*perspiration*), working on rationally solving the problem (saturation).

3. **Incubation:** The subconscious mind continues the synthesis (example: Sherlock Holmes at a concert). (Note that time-pressured brainstorm processes often do not allow for this. It is only the suspension of immediate judgement that allows for incubation.)

4. **Illumination:** The sudden birth of the idea – Eureka! (*inspiration*). Sometimes in a state of sleepiness or distraction from the problem. The subconscious and the conscious come together to provide the solution. (Kekulé–sleep–benzene molecule.) (Poincaré: 'unconscious work is possible, and ... only fruitful, if it is on the one hand preceded and on the other hand followed by a period of conscious work.')

5. **Verification** (or evaluation or implementation): The shaping and development of the idea to practical usefulness (*perspiration leading to application/innovation*). This is sometimes where other members of a creative team bring their analytical and completer/finisher skills to work the idea through to application (innovation is the mixture of idea and implementation). Many creatives are not so good at the completer/finisher stage, and lose interest, moving on to the next problem, or gathering more general raw material. The true value of the team and the creative business occurs here, in exploiting the idea.

Note: A quote attributed to Edison says that creativity is 1 per cent inspiration and 99 per cent perspiration. This is referred to above in italics.

---

and ideas', and he argues that inquisitiveness is the most important character trait of creative people:

> Every really good person in advertising whom I have ever known has always had two noticeable characteristics. First, there was no subject under the sun in which he could not get easily interested – from, say, Egyptian burial customs to modern art. Every facet of life had fascination

for him. Second, he was an extensive browser in all fields of information. For it is with the advertising man as with the cow: no browsing, no milk.[20]

For the film scriptwriter there are also other important raw materials that James Webb Young leaves out of his analysis. These are the personal experiences of powerful emotions like grief, love, fear, hatred and so on. They cannot be put into a file index or database, but they are the writer's stock-in-trade: those experiences are the basis for understanding human nature and for triggering those vital empathetic mirror neurons in the viewer's or reader's mind. To include this, Young's wording could be redrafted as: 'the inquisitive store of general knowledge, ideas, *and emotional experiences*'. Unlike other creative people, writers also require empathy and emotional intelligence, because they are playing with stories and characters, rather than just with intellectual ideas and concepts.

Like Young's emphasis on inquisitiveness, other academics refer to *curiosity* as a key starting point for the creative mind.[21] This can be encouraged by the right work environment, and Raymond Nickerson suggests that curiosity is contagious, so fostering a need to enquire within a group can prompt a greater degree of creativity.[22] This can also apply to larger companies: if the company culture or team leader constantly encourages research, questioning, and exploration of new areas, then this may lead to future creativity. Some companies encourage time for development people to explore personal projects and sideways thinking, famous examples including 3M, Lockheed ('Skunk Works'), Genentech and Bell Labs (AT&T). Google's development staff spend one day a week or 20 per cent of their time on their own start-up ideas, called Googlettes, one of which became GoogleMaps.[23] The animation film company Pixar even has a free in-house department running courses, known as the Pixar University, which encourages all staff to have a wider breadth of knowledge and skills, and allows more contact with colleagues outside their immediate team. This policy seems counter-intuitive in normal business terms, because these creative members of staff are taking 'time out' and are not being immediately productive for the company; but on the plus side it encourages intrinsic motivation, curiosity, lateral thinking and innovation from sideways ideas, and above all keeps these highly intellectual individuals motivated and hopefully loyal to the company.

Time and time again writers and creative people point to the fact that you need to study your field and practise your craft, so that you are ready for those breakthrough moments when they occur. The head may be in the clouds some of the time, but it is working very hard most of the time.

Looking again at the five stages of the creative mind in Box 8.4, in film development the script feedback notes from the producer and financiers would occur during stage 5: which is the *verification* or *evaluation* phase. The writer then returns to stage 2 to try to solve the problems by writing the next draft or polish. However, if potential solutions to the problems have been proposed by executives or producers in their script notes, then that may mitigate against the writer having the stage 4 *illumination* moment – the use of the unconscious mind to provide the breakthrough of another idea which is perhaps more creative than the ones already on the table. This is a key reason why the writer needs to have the time and flexibility to explore different options, rather than being expected to enact solutions proposed by the executives that he does not fully buy into (which is both de-motivating and less creative).

Allowing for time ... and the problem of bad brainstorming

This chapter began by pointing out that the suspension of immediate judgement is an important character trait of creative people, but it can be actively encouraged in the workplace and the development process. For example, there may be no need for a solution to be found by the end of a script meeting. Time and reflection may enable the writer to find a more creative solution, by allowing de-focused attention and divergent thought patterns the time to operate. In other words, more time is allowed for stage 3 of the creative process: *incubation*, leading to *illumination*. Recent research from Harvard Business School's Professor Teresa Amabile has clearly shown that unreasonable or too rapid deadlines can be detrimental to creativity because they remove the time necessary for the creative brain consciously and subconsciously to muse on the problem. However, Amabile explains that it is different if the creative person buys into the deadline and considers it to be *meaningful urgency*:

> People understood why solving a problem or completing a job was crucial, and they bought into that urgency, feeling as though they were on *a mission*. They were involved in their work and felt positively challenged by it. The sense of urgency and the ability to focus are probably related, for two reasons. If people believe that their work is vitally important, they may be more willing and able to ignore a variety of distractions in their workdays. Meanwhile, managers who share this sense of urgency may free people from less-essential tasks.[24]

Another problem in the creative industries is the reliance on *brainstorming*, especially in marketing and design companies and in television idea generation. Brainstorming was originally developed by the 1940s American advertising executive Alex Osborn, specifically to address the problem of premature judgement of creative ideas. He proposed that brainstorming was a way of generating ideas, but judgement and evaluation should be done later at a *separate* meeting.[25] However, nowadays the pressure of work means that this often does not happen and new ideas are instantly evaluated in the brainstorm meeting. Ironically, a system designed to reduce hasty judgement has ended up encouraging it, and more and more writers are starting to highlight the problems with brainstorming.[26]

One recent MBA dissertation carried out by a senior broadcast executive showed that one reason for that is that the people who chair brainstorming sessions (for example, in television companies or advertising agencies) are often very busy people and feel they do not have time to entertain ideas that they immediately think are wrong, so they close them down. Busy executives may disrupt the flow of meetings by taking phone calls or being called out to other meetings. There is also a gap between how managers *think* they are behaving and what is actually happening. The dissertation examined theories of managing creative people and then observed a leading independent television production company in action, and there was a clear difference between what the interviewed creative director and chief executive *said* was important to encourage creativity and how they actually behaved in two observed brainstorming sessions; and 'it appeared that negative manageral behaviour, such as closing down ideas without explaining why, had a far more detrimental affect on creativity than whether the session was extrinsically or intrinsically driven'.[27] Dismissals of ideas and interruptions of the process caused the creative energy in the room noticeably to drop, whereas praise and affirmative behaviour had a strong observed effect in raising energy levels and engagement in the room.[28]

It is important to allow time properly to consider and prototype ideas before ruling them out. The overall prevalent practice of brainstorming and creative group work is currently coming under increasing criticism, especially when it is used to work on an inappropriate problem or when it is wrongly managed. Research shows that many creatives would rather work with one or two peers in an informal way, rather than in a large team; and that the act of listening to other people in a brainstorm may even *stifle* creativity.[29] Furthermore, group activity causes increased cortical arousal in the brain and encourages secondary process thought, rather than reduced cortical arousal which encourages primary process and lateral thought.[30] This may seem to be at odds with the views of those producers who talk about developing an initial treatment in close dialogue and discussion with the writer. However, this is a close creative relationship between two people, where trust and understanding can be developed, as opposed to larger brainstorming groups, where there is a more performative element and time is often limited to a couple of hours.

To conclude, what the producer needs to consider is how to ensure that ideas are given enough time to develop and grow, without dispensing with the suitable deadline necessary to focus attention.

The downsides of creative people

John Adair and some other writers can be a bit relentlessly upbeat about the attributes of creative people, who are also a rather awkward bunch, as shown in Box 8.5. They can be impulsive, make up rules as they go along, and tend not to know their own limitations. They are unlikely to be practical, dependable, responsible, logical or even sincere.[31] Furthermore they have a firm sense of themselves as creative,[32] which may increase the likelihood of copy-cat prima donna-type behaviour.

Box 8.5 A few downsides of creative people

- **Self-obsession:** The emphasis on the importance of personal vision can lead to what seems like a sense of self-importance or arrogance. They can react strongly and personally to criticism and praise. Therefore giving feedback or notes has to be handled with care.
- **They need to be heard:** It is vital to have the vision seen, the book published, the idea valued. Recognition and praise, especially by peers, is more important than money. This is important knowledge for managers.
- **Feeling 'hard done by':** Many creative people are capable of complaining that others have unfairly had more luck/money/recognition than they have. Note that creatives will often *complain* about lack of money when what they actually *want* is to be valued. They usually don't go into it for the money.
- **Awkward and rebellious:** They instinctively resist conformity and the status quo – and they question things, especially authority.
- **The irresistible urge to create** (to the exclusion of all else)
- **Unreliable/bad at deadlines/prone to procrastination**
- **Do all of the above reflect personal insecurity?** The tricky question is whether insecurity is an intrinsic character trait of creatives, or a learned behaviour as a result of being creative and working in very reputation-based industries like film and the art world.

At what point does the valuable act of 'keeping ideas in creative suspension' suddenly become procrastination? And when is non-conformity just being downright awkward? The very things that make people creative can also make them difficult to live with. Or indeed difficult to manage, as Rob Goffee and Gareth Jones of the London Business School explained in their article 'Leading Clever People' in the *Harvard Business Review* (see Box 8.6).

Box 8.6 Managing creative people – like herding cats (Goffee and Jones, 2007)[33]

> 'Most clever people don't like to be led. This creates a problem for leaders.'

1. They know their worth. They have tacit skills – knowledge that can't be transferred independent of its holder – rather than skills that can be easily codified.
2. They're organizationally savvy and will seek the company context in which their interests are most generously funded.
3. They ignore corporate hierarchy. They care about intellectual status, not job titles, so you can't lure them with promotions.
4. They expect instant access to top management and if they don't get it they may think that their work isn't being taken seriously.
5. They are well connected and are usually plugged into highly developed knowledge networks – who they know is often as important as what they know. This increases their value to the organization but also makes them more of a flight risk.
6. They have a low boredom threshold and will leave if you don't inspire them with your organization's purpose.
7. They won't thank you even when you lead them well. *They don't like to feel that they're being led.*

The last item on Goffee and Jones' list says that creative people don't like to feel that they are being led, and here is the crux of the problem for the producer. The rebelliousness against authority and desire for independence will make the giving of notes and management of writers and directors even harder. And that is not all. Research literature on the difference between artists and non-artists, and the difference between creative and less creative scientists, continually throws up expressions and words that should ring alarm bells for the manager; such as emotional sensitivity, lack of conscientiousness, aloofness, lack of warmth, arrogance, and even hostility (see Table 8.1).

Considering that a large part of the development process is giving feedback notes on a script, the sensitivity and protectiveness of the creative person can also be a problem, as producer and Head of BBC Films Christine Langan explains:

> You're not going to get the best out of a creative person by being too tough with them. I mean they can be very insecure and (as a writer) you make yourself very vulnerable. Often people who become writers are *least* well disposed to *be* writers, that's the great paradox of them: to have that great intelligence and sensitivity and perspicacity maybe is not going to give you the thick skin and resilience you need.

Table 8.1 Consistent personality findings of creative people, found from the academic literature comparing artists and non-artists, and creative and less creative scientists (Feist, 1998)[34]

Consistent personality findings of creative people, found from the academic literature comparing artists and non-artists

Trait category	Trait
Non-social	Openness to experience Fantasy-oriented Imagination Impulsivity Lack of conscientiousness Anxiety Affective illness Emotional sensitivity Drive Ambition
Social	Norm doubting Non-conformity Independence Hostility Aloofness Unfriendliness Lack of warmth

Consistent personality findings of creative people, found from the academic literature comparing creative and less creative scientists

Trait category	Trait
Non-social	Openness to experience Flexibility of thought Drive Ambition Achievement
Social	Dominance Arrogance Hostility Self-confidence Autonomy Introversion Independence

Creative sensation-seekers and risk-takers

As part of the informal research for this book some groups of screenwriters were asked to sum up their failings as creative people. They included (only half in jest) such activities as heavy drinking, drug abusing, womanizing and enjoying extreme sexual practices.[35] That is sometimes the popular archetype of the dissolute writer: drinking green absinthe in the bars of *fin-de-siècle* Paris or strung out on LSD in Greenwich Village in the 1960s, but is there any real basis for it? According to Professor Marvin Zuckerman of the University of Delaware there is a clear link between creative people and an identifiable personality type called *sensation-seekers*.[36] This is especially true in the category known as *experience sensation- seekers*, who are seeking intense experience through the stimulation of the mind and the senses, and who can indeed find expression through the time-honoured combination of 'sex and drugs and rock 'n' roll'. This is by contrast to physically adventurous sensation-seekers, who might be attracted to mountain climbing or other dangerous sports, and are less likely to be creatives.

Professor Zuckerman has spent over forty years researching the sensation-seeking personality trait, including its role in risk-taking behaviours and its basis in neurology and biochemistry. He believes that high-experience sensation-seekers are more likely to indulge in divergent thinking; and because creativity could be defined as the ability to think in an original way, it is therefore a part of novelty-seeking and experience-seeking. In his research Zuckerman has shown that people identified as high sensation-seekers are also more prone to sexual experimentation and substance abuse, including smoking, drinking and taking illegal drugs (especially when sensation-seeking is combined with high testosterone levels).[37] There may also be a connection between the genetically influenced differences in dopamine levels in the brains of sensation-seekers, their aroused response to risk-taking and novelty, and the fact that orgasms release a dopamine-oxytocin high.[38]

Professor Richard Ebstein has identified relatively high heritability for the sensation-seeking personality trait and even a specific gene linked to it,[39] and a possible extension of this is that there may also be a genetic link to creativity or some of its elements. However, not all creative people are sensation-seekers, and vice versa, so again this is part of a bundle of occasional character traits of creative people and not a direct correlation. For example, the famously innovative film director Stanley Kubrick was scared of physical risks in real life, and was 'absolutely terrified' when his lead actor Malcolm McDowell took him for a fast drive in his sports car whilst filming *Clockwork Orange*.[40]

On the issue of sexuality and gender there has also been research that indicates that some creative people have androgynous inclinations, in that they also show traits associated with the opposite sex or express the traits of their own sex less strongly than average men or women.[41] In other words creative men are able to embrace their feminine side and creative women can be more at ease with their masculine side. This may be a reflection of the flexibility of their creative mindsets, or it may also be a conscious or subconscious expression of their desire to be non-conformist.

Intrinsic motivation: 'needing to want to solve the problem'

Professor Teresa Amabile argues that cognitive skills and personality traits are not sufficient on their own for creativity to flourish; the person also needs to be *intrinsically motivated*: doing what they are inspired by and *really* want to do. The idea of intrinsic motivation first emerged when the animal psychologist Harry F. Harlow used the expression to describe how monkeys showed immersive concentration and pleasure when solving puzzles. The moneys enjoyed doing it for the fun of it and not for any basic survival need, like getting food.[42] This idea was developed and tested by various psychologists interested in creativity,[43] and then became the cornerstone of Amabile's seminal 1983 book *The Social Psychology of Creativity*, in which she stated: 'An inner passion to solve the problem at hand leads to solutions far more creative than external rewards, such as money.'[44]

If they are passionate about their work then creative people can become completely absorbed to the level of what creativity theorist Professor Mihály Csíkszentmihályi calls *creative flow*, where the external world disappears and they are totally immersed in the problem or the creative act (see Box 8.7).[45]

Box 8.7 The nine aspects of the enjoyment of creative flow (Csíkszentmihályi, 1996)[46]

- Clear goals every step of the way: we know what needs to be done
- Immediate feedback to one's actions: successes and failures are immediately apparent
- Balance between challenges and personal skills: if challenges are too high we become anxious, too low and we are bored
- Merging of action and awareness
- Distractions are excluded from consciousness: focused concentration
- No worry of failure: sense of control
- Self-consciousness disappears
- Sense of time becomes distorted: clock time no longer reflects experienced time
- The activity becomes *autotelic* (Greek for something that is an end in itself): self-rewarding.

  'It is only after we get out of flow, at the end of a session or in moments of distraction within it, that we might indulge in feeling happy. And then there is a rush of well-being, of satisfaction that comes when the poem is completed or the theorem proved.'

However Teresa Amabile went further than just recommending intrisic motivation; she argued that extrinsic motivation (like payment or promotion) may actually *inhibit* creativity. Her research found that: 'the intrinsically motivated state is conducive to creativity; whereas the extrinsically motivated state is detrimental'.[47]

In short, a creative person is *intrinsically* motivated if he perceives himself as engaging in an activity primarily out of his own interest in it, but he is *extrinsically* motivated if he perceives himself as engaging in the activity because he has to, or in order to obtain some extrinsic goal (like payment or promotion). Whilst it is common sense that we work harder at something we enjoy, it is more counter-intuitive that extrinsic encouragement will actively put us off, and may even reduce what intrinsic motivation we originally had. This is known as *over-justification*, and research in children and adults has shown that financial rewards that are contingent on the completion of a task are seen as controlling and coercive, and reduce the person's feeling of self-determination and self-motivation.[48]

This of course doesn't mean that film producers shouldn't pay writers, it just means that money does not motivate them to do their best work. For example, surveys have shown that many artists' commissioned work is significantly *less* creative than their non-commissioned work, because of the degree of constraint they felt about how the work was to be done.[49] Csíkszentmihályi's own research interviews also upheld this concept, and convinced him that creative flow was *autotelic*, a Greek word meaning something that is *an end in itself*. The vital concept is that creative people don't want to feel bought – they want to feel *valued*. Recognition for the idea is much more important to them than cash.[50] For the producer it is sensible to make the writer *feel* valued, maybe through involving him more closely in other areas and decisions, taking him on research trips, and staying in regular contact through dinners and drinks. This can continue after the film is completed, for example by making sure that the writer is invited to premieres and film festival events. Sure enough, creativity research has shown that praise or unexpected rewards after the successful completion of the job are *not* seen as controlling extrinsic motivation, but instead encourage a feeling of competence, and may enhance the writer's intrinsic motivation to continue working on the project, or make the script better. In other words the spontaneous reward for success is better than the dangling carrot.

More motivation theories

Valuing the vision and self-reliance of a creative person will encourage them, but excessive use of preset financial rewards, imposed deadlines, evaluation or powerful command structures are likely to instead reduce creativity.[51] This could be in part because creative people tend to be more motivated by self-actualizsation, personal fulfilment and peer reputation.

In the 1950s the motivation expert Abraham Maslow produced a system to categorize motivation and called it the *Hierarchy of Needs* (see Fig. 8.2). According to Maslow, people usually need to achieve and master the basic deficiency needs (biological, physiological, safety, love) in order to move up to self-actualization needs and become *meta-motivated* and reach their full potential.[52] This influential idea was also adopted and developed by the business theorist D.M. McGregor in the late 1950s.[53] However, many artists are motivated directly by self-actualization, reputation and personal growth, and will put up with physical discomfort and lack of food in order to pursue their art, so they are *meta-motivated*, without having fully satisfied the basic needs. Frequently belongingness and family love needs come below their

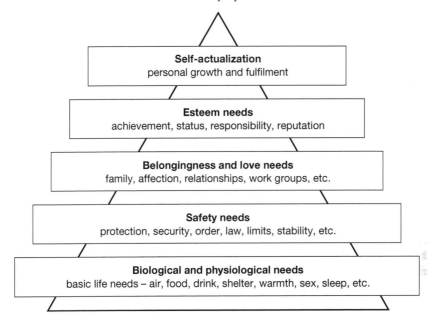

Figure 8.2 Maslow's Hierarchy of Needs (1954)[54]

need for personal artistic fulfilment, as summed up by the quote from the English author Cyril Connolly, who famously wrote: 'there is no more sombre enemy of good art than the pram in the hall'.[55] And since some creative people are also boundary-pushing sensation-seekers they might even choose to rebel *against* 'safety needs' like security, moral limits and stability; and instead pursue risk and excitement.

In 1969 the psychologist Clayton Alderfer adapted Maslow's Hierarchy of Needs to his own similar ERG theory: *Existence* (the basic survival needs), *Relatedness* (social relationships) and *Growth* (intellectual curiosity and achievement). Alderfer agreed that the existence needs needed to be satisfied before moving up the scale, but he then proposed the concept of *frustration regression*, which is where the failure to satisfy the higher goals causes people to focus back onto the lower order needs. In the case of some creative people a dissatisfaction with creative life or lack of success could lead to excessive sensation-seeking, for example in the form of drink and drugs, self-indulgence and pursuit of financial reward instead of creative stimulation.[56]

Recent research by David Hesmondhalgh (at the University of Leeds) and Sarah Baker (at Griffith University in Australia) has confirmed that many people in the creative industries want to work in them because of their desire for creative self-realization and autonomy (again high up on the hierarchy of needs); and also to be part of the social and intellectual 'buzz' that goes with those industries, including teamwork, socializing and esteem (social needs).[57] In keeping with Maslow and Amabile's research on intrinsic motivation, these people are prepared to work for long and antisocial hours and initially on low pay (or even unpaid, as work experience) in order to be part of that creative world. Some employers in those cultural industries take advantage of that willingness to exploit their workforces, or employ young people from affluent middle-class backgrounds (who can afford to subsidize themselves) rather than people from poorer working-class backgrounds, thus potentially depriving themselves of a more diverse workforce.[58]

To conclude: by being more fixated on personal growth and achievement, creative people are motivated a bit differently from conventional people, and knowledge of these motivation factors is important in order to manage and inspire them; however, there is also a moral responsibility not to exploit them through unreasonable demands or low pay.

Synergistic extrinsic motivation: external support vs. control

However, extrinsic motivation proved to be more complex than was first thought; and after further research and feedback from other academics Amabile revised the theory in 1996, to add this qualifier about extrinsic motivation: 'Intrinsic motivation is conducive to creativity; *controlling* extrinsic motivation is detrimental to creativity, but *informational or enabling* extrinsic motivation can be conducive, particularly if initial levels of intrinsic motivation are high.'[59]

So there is a distinction between the negative effect of the *controlling* type of extrinsic motivation or external pressure (for example, being paid to do a task not of your own choosing, losing control over the process or the outcomes because of the payment, fear of evaluation or replacement), and the positive effect of *informational, enabling* or *synergistic* extrinsic motivation and support (for example, the addition of resources, extra training, access to information, and supporting the autonomy or control of the creative).

These different types of external motivation (or support) also have positive or negative effects at different *stages* in the process, as Fig. 8.3 shows. Intrinsic motivation is most important at the beginning of the project (problem definition, or in the film case the synopsis stage of development), and the response generation stage (solving the problem/screenplay drafting). Supportive external motivation/investment (*synergistic motivation*) is valuable at the right stages in the process, especially during research (stage 2: preparation) and then selling and packaging the film (stage 4: validation). In other words, external investment at the right moments is felt to *support* the work of the creative, rather than detract from it or become too influential upon it.

Evaluation is also a particularly complex area for extrinsic motivation. It is likely to have a negative and demotivating effect, because success is felt to be in the hands of external parties and their feedback may not support the creative person's vision; but it can have positive effects on creativity when it is work-focused and constructive (just like script feedback notes).[60]

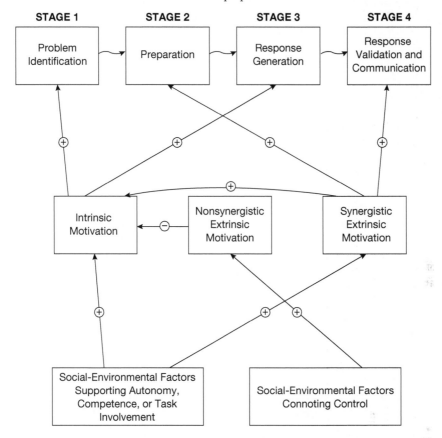

Figure 8.3 The componential model of creativity: mechanisms of social-environmental influence on creativity (Amabile, 1996)[61]

Applying intrinsic motivation theories to film development: writers vs. hacks

In the case of film development these ideas about intrinsic rather than extrinsic motivation mean choosing a writer according to his genuine passion and interest in the subject, and then investing in supporting his research and championing his vision. Paying a large amount of money to get a disinterested writer to work on a project is unlikely to secure a good creative outcome. This is bad news for the Hollywood system, where the producer usually selects the stories and then hires and fires the writers who work on them. Writers are given feedback notes from lots of different sources (evaluation and supervision); they are constantly aware that they might get dismissed; and if another writer does replace them they know that they are unlikely even to get an onscreen credit, regardless of how long they worked on the project (in the US under current WGA arbitration practice the first and last writers on the project are most likely to get that credit, especially on adaptations). On other occasions the writer may be hired to do a dialogue polish and know from the outset that they will be uncredited, and that if the film is successful some other writer will lift the gold statue for best writer on awards night.

To compensate for this lack of control and credit, Hollywood writers are often paid dizzying amounts of money (much better than their intrinsically motivated arthouse colleagues), but if Amabile's research is to be believed then ironically the large sums may actually make them feel less motivated. They have been 'bought' rather than valued; and this may explain why some Hollywood writers dismissively refer to themselves as *hacks*, the old pejorative term for an employed writer working on a newspaper or writing pulp fiction who is being paid by the word and sent on assignments that are chosen by the boss.[62] The symbolic distinction is between the creative novelist/poet (possibly starving in a garret, but at least writing from personal inspiration) and the paid hack (who has sold out and is prostituting his talent). The hack is replacing intrinsic personal motivation with extrinsic financial motivation; and divine inspiration with the lure of filthy lucre. Despite the financial rewards these self-styled hacks feel cheated, perhaps more so because of them. Marlon Brando could have been speaking on behalf of all embittered writers when he spoke these famous words from *On the Waterfront*: 'I could've had class. I could've been a contender. I could've been somebody, instead of a bum, which is what I am, let's face it.'[63]

Fittingly, Brando's character is complaining about having ruined his career by selling out (after being paid to take a dive in a prize fight). As long ago as the 1950s Hortense Powdermaker summed up the demotivating power of money in Hollywood as follows:

> For writers, artists and scientists, the satisfactions inherent in their work have always been primary. It is questionable whether money ever can be the only satisfaction for any of them. The essence of a writer's drive is his interest and curiosity about his fellow men and a desire to communicate the results of his observations to an audience. ... In Hollywood the situation is reversed. The financial rewards come first, in weekly pay checks. The script on which he works is apt to be a confused jumble of many people's ideas and unrelated notions. The occupational satisfactions, traditionally part of the writer's craft, are lacking. ... Even though the scriptwriter's name may be among the list of credits for a movie it is rare ... for him honestly to feel that he communicated anything of his own to an audience.[64]

Skills plus environment plus motivation

To emphasize the importance of motivation, Amabile produced a diagram (Fig. 8.4) showing the overlapping of personal skills (domain or craft skills and creativity skills) plus motivation to produce an intersection where

Domain-relevant skills

Include:
- Knowledge about the domain
- Entire intellectual education
- Technical skills required
- Special domain-relevant talent
  (e.g. in the case of art: drawing skills)

Depend on:
- Innate cognitive abilities
- Innate perceptual and motor skills
- Formal and informal education

The creativity intersection

People are most likely to be highly creative here, where their skills and motivation overlap. Individuals and their mentors need to identify where their strongest interests lie.

What they 'can' do is covered by domain skills and creativity skills, what they 'will do well' is covered by intrinsic motivation. All three must be in place for high levels of creativity.

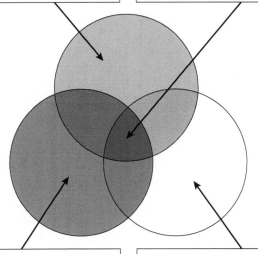

Creativity-relevant skills

Include:
- Appropriate cognitive style (including breaking the perceptual and cognitive set, keeping responses open, suspending judgement, using wide categories, memory, etc.)
- Implicit or explicit knowledge of heuristics or rules for generating novel ideas
- Conducive work style, including concentration, persistence, high energy and productivity

Depend on:
- Training/general education
- Experience in idea generation
- Personality characteristics

Task motivation

Includes:
- Baseline personal attitude towards the task
- Perceptions of own motivation for undertaking the task (dependent on external social and work factors)
- Sense of personal freedom

Depends on:
- Initial level of intrinsic motivation towards the task
- Presence or absence of salient extrinsic constraints
- Individual ability to cognitively minimize extrinsic constraints

Figure 8.4 Components of creative performance and the creativity intersection (Amabile, 1996)[65]

deeper creativity is likely to occur. Take intrinsic motivation off the map and creative solutions will decline. It may be possible to teach domain skills (crafts) and perhaps enhance some creativity skills, but motivation is more variable and situation-dependent.

In the early 1990s Professor Robert Sternberg and his colleagues at Yale concurred with Amabile's emphasis on motivational and social influences as well as cognitive and personality traits. They developed a similar model to Amabile's *componential* one, arguing that creativity needs the *confluence* of six distinct resources, namely: intellectual abilities, knowledge, styles of thinking (preferred ways of using one's skills), personality (not implicit character traits but behaviours that the individual can choose to adopt), motivation and environment.[66]

To conclude: this chapter has concentrated on identifying the character traits of creative people so that the producer or executive knows more about the writers and directors they are working with. Furthermore, if creatives don't intrinsically want to solve the problem or carry out the creative work, then money will only partially encourage them and it may put them off, because they feel bought. So the crucial decision for the producer is to find the right writer for the material, and then trust them, motivate them and commit to them, so that they feel part of the enterprise rather than a 'gun for hire'.

The academic research of Amabile, Sternberg and Csíkszentmihályi emphasizes the idea that for creativity to occur the multiple cognitive and intellectual attributes of the creative person need to be matched with a suitable environment and intellectual domain for the encouragement and reception of creativity. The work environment at least can be managed by the film producer or executive, so the next chapter will look at how to do that and get the best out of creative people – a tricky proposition when they hate being managed and want to be in control themselves.

Insight: the parable of the two seeds

Since this is a book about stories this seems like a good opportunity to tell one.

One day a traveller was walking along a road through the desert, on his way home from exploring the lands beyond the sea. All of a sudden a genie appeared out of thin air in front of him, and stood blocking his path. The traveller fell to his knees in fear and astonishment.

'You have been travelling through my lands without my permission,' said the genie. 'The penalty for that is death.'

'I beg your pardon, oh wondrous one,' said the traveller. 'But I didn't know these were your lands, or I would have asked your permission. But I beg you to spare my life, for I have a wife and children who depend on me, and without me they will surely starve.' The genie thought about this for a moment.

'Very well,' said the genie. 'I am feeling a little bit merciful today. If you can answer this one question correctly, then I will spare your life.' And with that he held out both of his large and magical hands. In the palm of each hand was a tiny little seed.

'One of these seeds will produce an evil and pernicious weed, that will swamp all the other plants in its path,' said the genie. 'But the other will produce a very beautiful orchid, prized in the court of the Sultan for having beneficial healing qualities. You must decide which is which.'

In horror, the traveller looked at the two seeds. As close as he looked, he could see no difference whatsoever between them.

'But, oh great one, they look exactly the same. How can I decide?'

'That is *your* problem,' said the genie. 'Decide which is the flower and I will reward you with untold riches; the respect of your peers; and your wife and children will live in comfort for the rest of their days. But choose the weed and I will strike you dead on the spot. You will be hidden under the endlessly drifting sands and your family will not even have a carcass to bury. So, my friend, how do you choose?'

So what did the traveller do?

He looked long and hard at the two seeds in the genie's hands. He picked them up and held them to the light, but there was nothing at all to tell them apart.

Then the traveller had a wonderful idea. He took the two seeds and planted them side by side in the soil by the road. And then he waited ...

By night he slept by the side of the road, wrapped in his blanket, and by day he watered them, fed them, and tended them. Eventually up came two little green shoots, but they too looked exactly the same; so he kept on watering them and feeding them, until eventually it was quite obvious that the one on the right had a beautiful white flower, but the one on the left was a sour and spiky thistle. So the traveller pointed to the flower and said to the genie:

'On the right is the beautiful flower, oh glorious one, and on the left is the evil and pernicious weed.'

'You are quite right,' said the genie. 'So I will spare your life, and all that I have promised will come to pass. Farewell.' And with that he disappeared, back into thin air.

And the moral of the story is that ideas need time and careful nurturing before you can tell if they are good ideas or bad ideas. So never be too quick to make up your mind ...

9 Managing creative people and film development

Too much discipline hobbles the imagination; too much freedom leads to indulgence.

(David Puttnam, producer)[1]

Chapter 8 showed that there are certain character traits associated with creative people and that they are motivated in different ways from other people so a different set of tools is needed to work with them. This chapter now looks at the idea of creative leadership and managing creative people, with some emphasis on larger media and film organizations.

Creative leadership

Professor Teresa Amabile has researched and written widely about encouraging creativity in the workplace, and her conclusions are summarized in boxes 9.1 and 9.2. In keeping with her work on intrinsic motivation, Amabile places a lot of emphasis on choosing the right people for the job, according to their personal interests and skill sets, and setting the right task so that they feel fully challenged. She also describes the importance of work teams that combine diverse backgrounds and skills. However, there is a very careful balance to be struck between giving clear guidelines about what is needed, and granting sufficient autonomy and freedom for the creatives to find their own solution. Managing creativity is all about finding where to operate on a continuum between freedom and control, as shown by the quotation from David Puttnam at the opening of this chapter.

The *Tannenbaum and Schmidt leadership continuum* is often used in MBA business education to illustrate different types of leadership style, from highly controlling on the one side to delegating a lot on the other (see Fig. 9.1). As we have seen, creatives generally don't want to be followers, resist micro-management and need maximum freedom within stated constraints, so they will require a leadership style to the right of the scale; but some other company staff may respond better to closer control and clearer targets, and for them the leader may move to the left of the scale. In most independent film development situations the screenwriter is given a lot of

Box 9.1 Summary of how to support creativity in organizations (Amabile, 1996)[2]

Leadership

- Maintain a balance between clear motivating direction in the work and individual autonomy in conducting the work.
- Present a clear strategic direction for projects and for the organization, but encourage autonomy in the day-to-day carrying out of their projects.
- Clearly communicate a vision of the organization as creative and innovative.

Rewards

- Avoid using rewards as bribes or controlling factors.
- Recognize and reward good creative efforts, even when the ultimate result may not have been profitable.
- Use rewards that confirm skills and the value of the individual's (or the team's) work.
- Use rewards that enable individuals to pursue work that they are interested in or challenged by.

Reception of ideas

- Encourage frequent work-focused feedback (as opposed to person-focused criticism) among peers as well as from supervisors.
- Discourage excessively critical evaluations of new ideas.
- Avoid emphasis on maintaining the status quo.
- Embrace risk.

Teams and organizational support

- Match people to projects and teams according to their interests and so that their skills are optimally challenged.
- Form work teams that combine diverse backgrounds and skills.
- Ensure open, supportive interaction between groups to avoid competition and infighting.
- Provide logistical and tangible support by reducing red tape and approval layers and by committing sufficient resources.
- Encourage positive tension for creativity by emphasizing the importance and urgency of projects, but avoiding extreme time pressures.
- Facilitate communication, collaboration and idea support among and between work teams as well as constructive challenging of new ideas.
- Demonstrate that creativity and innovation are valued by focusing communications within the organization on the excitement and potential of the ideas being generated.

Box 9.2 Accept failure and risk in order to support creativity (Amabile et al., 2008)[3]

Accept the inevitability and utility of failure

- Provide sufficient time and resources for exploration, and accept that some things will not work.
- Experiment constantly, fail early and often. Test with prototypes.
- Create psychological safety to maximize learning from failure.
- Decrease fear of failure.
- Recognize different kinds of failure and how they can be useful.
- Create good mechanisms for filtering ideas and stopping dead-end projects.

Motivate with intellectual challenge

- Protect from commercial pressure too early in the process.
- Clear paths through the bureaucracy for creative ideas.
- Let people do 'good work' (where the work is seen as noble/technically excellent/meaningful/engaging to the worker/ethical).
- Show the higher purpose of projects wherever possible – make them into a mission to achieve something great.
- Grant as much independence as possible.

Diversity works

- Get people with different backgrounds and expertise to work together.
- Encourage individuals to gain diverse experiences that will increase their creativity.

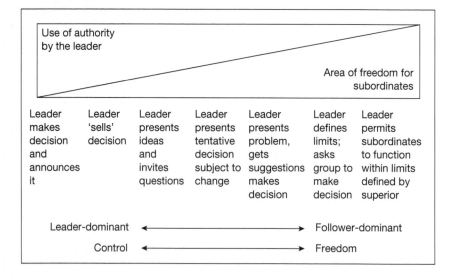

Figure 9.1 Tannenbaum and Schmidt's leadership continuum (1958)[4]

freedom, at least over the first few drafts, and the producer is more a collaborator than an employer. However, in the studio system the executive/ studio producer is more dominant and controlling.

Creative leadership becomes more complex in bigger companies with many employees. In media terms this could be a film distribution company, TV broadcaster, or a large production company with TV and film outputs. As shown in Fig. 9.2, these larger media companies are often made up of a mixture of *creatives* (originators) and *transformers* (support staff and finance). These are potentially different types of people, with different expectations and motivations, and therefore different types of management styles along the leadership continuum are required to get the best from them. Because of the expectations of the media business, most people working in those companies want some degree of freedom, and the more people share in decisions, the more they are motivated to carry them out well. Although it is not always possible to share decisions over ends (i.e. goals, objectives, aims or purposes) it is usually possible for the manager to involve others more or less fully in the means (i.e. methods, techniques, conditions and plans).

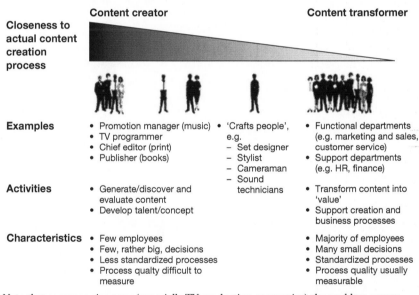

	Content creator		Content transformer
Closeness to actual content creation process			
Examples	• Promotion manager (music) • TV programmer • Chief editor (print) • Publisher (books)	• 'Crafts people', e.g. – Set designer – Stylist – Cameraman – Sound technicians	• Functional departments (e.g. marketing and sales, customer service) • Support departments (e.g. HR, finance)
Activities	• Generate/discover and evaluate content • Develop talent/concept		• Transform content into 'value' • Support creation and business processes
Characteristics	• Few employees • Few, rather big, decisions • Less standardized processes • Process qualty difficult to measure		• Majority of employees • Many small decisions • Standardized processes • Process quality usually measurable

Note that as companies grow (especially TV production companies) the problem comes when there are more transformers and support staff than creators in a company, especially when the managerial roles are better paid or have higher internal status.

Figure 9.2 Content creators and content transformers in large media organizations, and how they differ in activities and characteristics (Aris and Bughin, 2006)[5]

Box 9.3 Amabile's environmental components for creativity (Amabile, 1988)[6]

1. **Active encouragement of creativity:** Information and support for new ideas, communicated openly between all levels in the organization. Championing of ideas and rewarding of creative people
2. **Autonomy:** Individual freedom and control must be an integral part of day-to-day work
3. **Resources:** Basic materials and information for the work must be available. This includes time for uninterrupted thought[7]
4. **Pressures:** Positive challenges must be communicated, deadlines agreed together, and negative perceptions of workloads/false deadlines avoided
5. **Reduce organizational impediments to creativity** (influences of conservatism and internal strife)

Creative leadership and abandoning control

The following quote from Teresa Amabile highlights the potential conflict between the corporate manager's need to control and the creative person's need for flexibility to come up with creative solutions:

> Creativity is undermined unintentionally every day in work environments that were established – for entirely good reasons – to maximise business imperatives such as coordination, productivity and control.[8]

A lot of creative leadership is therefore about abandoning control (delegation is really about accepting the power and autonomy of others). Instead, the leader has to create an environment where other people's creativity can thrive and where they can be confident that the leader will champion and support their work. As Amabile puts it: 'One doesn't manage creativity. One manages *for* creativity.'[9]

This loss of direct control can be especially difficult for those leaders who may have started in the industry as creatives, because they instinctively want to control and be part of the creative process. This is why a lot of producers are good at running their own small companies but bad at running studios or the film divisions of broadcasters or public bodies. Creativity expert Mihály Csíkszentmihályi explains:

> Each of us is born with two contradictory sets of instructions: a conservative tendency, made up of instincts for self-preservation, self-aggrandizement, and saving energy, and an expansive tendency made up of instincts for exploring, for enjoying novelty and risk – the curiosity that leads to creativity belongs to this set. We need both of these programs. But whereas the first tendency requires little encouragement

or support from outside to motivate behaviour, the second can wilt if it is not cultivated. If too few opportunities for curiosity are available, if too many obstacles are placed in the way of risk and exploration, the motivation to engage in creative behaviour is easily extinguished.[10]

This is especially difficult in TV and film, where producers or studios may incline towards the conservative simply because the medium is genre-oriented and project financing is already risky without introducing extra novelty and risk into the screenplay. The role of the development executive or producer is very similar to the role of the boss in a company who is looking after creative thinkers, as Rob Goffee and Gareth Jones of the London Business School explain:

> As many leaders of extremely smart and highly creative people have learned, you need to be a benevolent guardian rather than a traditional boss. You need to create a safe environment for your clever employees; encourage them to experiment and even fail; and quietly demonstrate your expertise and authority all the while. You may sometimes begrudge the time you have to devote to managing them, but if you learn how to protect them while giving them space to be productive, the reward of watching your clever people flourish and your organization accomplish its mission will make the effort worthwhile.[11]

This is coupled with handling deadlines, appraisal and feedback of drafts, and the management of incoming powerful stakeholders. This mixture of achieving support, control and freedom for the writer is the biggest challenge facing people managing development.

Adaptors vs. innovators

But reality is yet more complex, because it is possible to divide creative people into *adaptors* and *innovators*, two different types who may resist one another even within the same team or organization (see Table 9.1). Adaptors tend to work within or stretch existing agreed definitions and seek likely solutions to *do things better*, whereas innovators work separately from the paradigm or customary viewpoint, and are less concerned with doing things better and more with doing things *differently*. Adaptors are therefore more allied to the convention (Margaret Boden's exploratory creativity), whereas innovators are more radical (transformative creativity). This has an impact on how teams are assembled, because adaptors will sometimes cooperate well in a team with innovators, but may sometimes close down the innovator's radical ideas and ways of working, especially if convention is being challenged. Conversely innovators may become frustrated with the adaptor's allegiance to the genre or status quo.[12]

Table 9.1 Summary of research into behaviour descriptors of creative adaptors and innovators, showing why they come into conflict (Kirton, 1976)[13]

Adaptor	Innovator
Characterized by precision, reliability, efficiency, methodicalness, prudence, discipline, conformity	Seen as undisciplined, thinking tangentially, approaching tasks from unsuspected angles
Concerned with resolving problems rather than finding them	Could be said to discover problems and discover avenues of solutions
Seeks solutions to problems in tried and understood ways	Queries problems' concomitant assumptions; manipulates problems
Reduces problems by improvement and greater efficiency, with maximum of continuity and stability	Is catalyst to settled groups, irreverent of their consensual views; seen as abrasive, creating dissonance
Seen as sound, conforming, safe, dependable	Seen as unsound, impractical; often shocks his opposite
Liable to make goals of means	In pursuit of goals treats accepted means with little regard
Seems impervious to boredom, seems able to maintain high accuracy in long spells of detailed work	Capable of detailed routine (system maintenance) work for only short bursts; quick to delegate routine tasks
Is in authority within given structures	Tends to take control in unstructured situations
Challenges rules rarely, cautiously, when assured of strong support	Often challenges rules, has little respect for past custom
Tends to high self-doubt. Reacts to criticism by closer outward conformity. Vulnerable to social pressures and authority; compliant	Appears to have low self-doubt when generating ideas, not needing consensus to maintain certitude in face of opposition
Is essential to the functioning of the institution all the time, but occasionally needs to be 'dug out' of his or her systems	In the institution is ideal in unscheduled crises, or better still to help to avoid them, if he or she can be controlled
When collaborating with innovators: • Supplies stability, order and continuity to the partnership • Sensitive to people, maintains group cohesion and cooperation • Provides a safe base for the innovator's riskier operations	**When collaborating with adaptors:** • Supplies the task orientations, the break with the past and accepted theory • Appears insensitive to people, often threatens group cohesion and cooperation • Provides the dynamics to bring about periodic radical change, without which institutions tend to ossify

Many business organizations will culturally favour *either* people who are adaptors *or* innovators, depending on the leadership and internal organizational culture. Most large organizations move away from innovation and towards the adaptive model because of the restrictive effect of conventional organizational management, time pressures, cost, risk reduction and product conventions (in the case of film and TV, the generic expectations of the sales market and the audience). To counter this, some large organizations have separate research departments, one for new product generation and 'blue sky' development (staffed with innovators), and one for the continuing development and adaptation of existing products (staffed with adaptors).[14]

Within small media companies the key for a good leader is to understand the strategic needs of the organization and the emotional and motivational needs of individual staff and regular freelancers, and adapt the leadership style accordingly. The leader has to decide overall whether to favour adaptors or innovators, and where to operate on the leadership continuum with each individual.

Conclusions

To return to the motivation issue, as discussed in the last chapter, the executive must remember that the social environment (particularly the presence or absence of external pressures) can influence creativity by influencing the person's passion for their work. External pressures (or external motivation) in the work environment can decrease intrinsic motivation and therefore creativity. External pressures with a proven negative effect on intrinsic motivation include the expectation of external evaluation or monitoring, contracted-for-reward procedures, competition with peers, and constrained choice in how to do one's work.[15] All of which are present in film development, especially in the studios. But people who have the appropriate support and autonomy to do challenging creative work tend to be more satisfied and therefore may stay longer with their organizations, which is in itself a key part of building a sustainable long-term creative business.[16]

The next chapter continues to develop these themes of intrinsic motivation and creative management, by looking in detail at working with the writer and providing effective script feedback notes. It examines techniques for drawing out ideas from a writer or director, and looks at issues around how to listen responsively. How do you give concepts the time and space to develop, and how do you make sure that you are not closing down good ideas too quickly?

Box 9.4 Summary points: managing creative people[17]

- Your key decision is who you put into the team. The tasks being assigned must match the interest of the person. Otherwise the creative person will not engage properly via intrinsic motivation (Amabile 1996).
- Make the team diverse in its background and expertise (Amabile 1983).
- Administrative machinery is a distraction from their desire to be creative. They need to be protected from organizational rain: the rules and politics. Exempt them from some admin tasks and meetings (Goffee and Jones 2007; Amabile 1988).
- You need to be a benevolent guardian rather than a traditional boss ... encourage them to experiment and play and even fail; and quietly demonstrate your expertise and authority all the while (Goffee and Jones 2007).
- In the organization ensure open information sharing, idea sharing and idea rewarding. Otherwise the information-gathering side of the creative process is not being fed with up-to-date information (Amabile 1998).
- Allow constructive conflict and encourage dissent (West and Sacramento 2006; Boynton and Fischer 2005).
- Give ideas time and space – don't close down discussion too fast – remember the parable of the two seeds.

Case interview: Killing other people's babies

Ivana MacKinnon (development executive and producer):

The Scouting Book for Boys (2009) was a very easy film to develop when it was just us [Jack Thorne, the writer, and Ivana as producer]; and we had a first draft that everyone loved. But then it was a very difficult film to develop for about a year, because the minute more voices got involved the film went totally off the rails, and we almost lost it. And the only way it got back on the rails actually was by us going to Jack and saying – you need to sit down and you need to write the script that you want to write because you've tried to write the script that everyone else wants you to write and it's gone wrong. Not because everyone else was wrong about what they were saying, but because it was a very delicate, very personal script that it was almost impossible to give notes on. So we would either get very vague notes, or more direct ones that took the project in very uncomfortable directions.

Eventually, the only way we could resolve it was to go back to Jack and say – write the script that you want to write, and use all this experience of taking it in the wrong direction. Because the fact is that the year of everything going wrong, and the year of taking it in directions that didn't work, were actually very valuable ones to take back to the script. But Jack said something really interesting, which was that people always tell you that you have to kill your babies to be a scriptwriter, and he said – that's not always true, you have to kill other people's babies, because people are always telling me the bits that they love in my script, and if someone powerful tells you what they love, you desperately want to keep that in, because – this is the bit they love. But actually those are often the bits that aren't working. So you've got to be confident enough about yourself to kill the bits of your script that [the executive] loves, if you know that those aren't the bits that are going to make it a great script. And that's just about confidence, but also really understanding about the story that you want to tell.

Case interview: The confessions of an anonymous script reader

(See Appendix B for some sample Reader's Report forms.)

I spent five years script reading, often for Working Title, because they had so much work that I didn't really need to go anywhere else. But also I was reading for New Line and others. And this is when I was starting out on my career as a screenwriter and I would try and read a script and do a script report in the morning and write my own scripts in the afternoon. Sometimes I don't think that's the most healthy way to be a writer, but you have to make a living. So I'd go into the office once a week, pick up a sack of scripts, often books in fact, and then dive into them. I think my process as a reader was first and foremost to read through it as a putative audience member – irrespective of whether I like this kind of movie or not – does it do what it sets out to do? And at what level of quality – brilliantly or averagely or terribly? And then whoever your client is you have a sort of commercial brief which is – we're looking for X, Y and Z. And at Working Title, for example, that might change from year to year: 'This year we're looking for $100 million dollar movies.' Then they'd make a couple, like *Thunderbirds* for example, and then they would say: 'Now we're looking for $20m movies, and we're looking for some Working Title 2 stuff' (lower budget and experimental).

So I read the script from both creative and commercial levels. I would then do the report, and tick boxes – you know, structure good, premise good, story bad, all that sort of thing. Which aren't really distinctions you make as you're reading it, it's more when you sit down and think about it afterwards. So then you'd have the writer recommendation and script recommendation. So the writer recommendation could be ... 'Good script but not for you, but maybe meet the writer.' Or you could have: 'Writer recommendation – pass; but script recommendation – yes, consider it,' which means there is bad writing but a really good idea, so take a look at it because actually there's something in there and it might be something you want to buy and then jettison the writer and develop it with someone else.

So I was kind of second-guessing market forces ... but it's always very presumptuous of a reader, who nine times out of ten would be a wannabe writer themselves. So I just tried to be as objective as possible, as I still am, reading scripts. You read a great script, you're overwhelmed with admiration, and a bit of envy; but you don't just sit there picking holes in it.

There were some scripts I would read and just think 'Go and make that tomorrow, because it's beautiful.' And nobody would make it. Or somebody would buy it and then develop it for a couple of years and take away all that was good about it. All those sort of horror tales. And then other times you'd read something and think 'This is really turgid, but I can see it has commercial value ...'

The idea that because a story works well as a novel or on stage it will work by default on the screen, as a film or as a TV adaptation, is myopic and naive. Unfortunately it is an all-too-common form of arse-covering among the producers, development community and subsidy funds, who are then able to point to the sales achieved by the book so that when the film bombs they will still have a job. It breaks my heart to see great, original screenplay ideas, many of them modestly budgeted, consistently overlooked as producers throw their money into the fifth, tenth, twentieth drafts of 'big' novels which, in many cases, will never make a satisfying movie. I read countless drafts of *Foucault's Pendulum*, which was in development for years at Fine Line, when an 8-year-old could have told you it would never be a movie.

I would say (my skill as a writer) definitely improved whilst being a reader. ... If I've read a thousand scripts, which is probably a conservative estimate, I've learnt *something* from every one. And particularly when you apply your analytical energy to it after having read it. If it's a bad script, why is it bad, what makes it bad, and how could it be made good? Or could it never be made good? If this is a good script, why is it good? What are the decisions the writer has made, consciously or otherwise, and what can I learn from that and apply to my own material?

10 The script meeting
Listening and feeding back

Note giving is an art and a craft. It must happen in an atmosphere of earned trust and approval if it is to avoid defensive resistance. It must be specific and concrete. 'Make it funnier' will not do. Nor will half understood jargon from a weekend screenwriters' course. Talk of 'narrative arcs' and 'epiphanies' and the writer will politely nod and go home to look longingly at the gas oven.

(Tony Garnett, producer)[1]

The above quotation from veteran producer Tony Garnett highlights the frustration that some writers and producers feel when they get script notes that have not been properly thought through, or where the notes are trying to impose unsuitable solutions. How to give effective script notes and feedback is one of the most complex skills of managing development.[2] It varies massively between different producers and executives, and also depends on the nature of their relationship with the writer. The case interview section of this chapter describes the suggestions of some development executives on note giving, but below is a summary of key points that have been consistently raised by interviewees. For simplicity, the word *producer* will be used throughout this chapter, but the advice applies equally to anyone who is managing the writer during this process, including development executives and script editors.

Most feedback is through a combination of discussion and written notes, but it is worth distinguishing between the start of the process and the end. At the beginning of a project there are major notes that require face-to-face discussions and the building of group trust and a unified vision. These notes will be around key issues like genre, character arcs and story structure beats. However, later drafts may well have a lot of notes around smaller issues of detail, like feedback on dialogue drafting or stage directions on specific pages. These could be dealt with more by email, especially where there is already a good relationship.

How to give notes: a summary

- Be consistent – keep returning to the vision of the type of film you are all trying to make, and refer everything back to that.
- Try to ask questions rather than provide answers. It is the writer's job to find the answers.
- Respond as quickly as possible to the newly delivered draft, because it shows you value the writer's work. Or at least explain that you will read it immediately, but you need to gather other people's feedback before a larger meeting.
- Don't expect solutions to be found within that one meeting. The writer needs time to go away and muse on the problems.
- Be positive as well as finding problems – writers need to know what works as well as what doesn't. Otherwise they may cut the bits you thought worked.
- Be concise – this means reading the draft through several times and thinking the notes through, not just coming up with vague generalizations.
- Be coherent. The producer and development executive should agree their notes in advance and provide a single coherent set of notes to the writer. It is not the writer's job to try to resolve your disagreements. If passing on notes from third parties, such as financiers, make sure that you have fully understood them (it is hard to champion what you don't believe or understand), and filter out what you do not agree with. It is also the producer's job to resolve any big contradictions between the views of different third parties before passing them on to the writer, unless it is a very major issue.
- Use the first person to introduce your notes, such as: 'I felt that ...' or 'It seemed to me that ...'. This makes your view personal and one of many, and is therefore less combatative than saying 'This bit doesn't work'.
- Don't confuse symptoms and causes. If you identify the bit that isn't working for you, then the writer can work out how that has been caused.
- Don't just read the marked up changes since the last draft – it is important to get the flow of the new version. For example, the writer may have resolved a problem in a scene by changing the lead up to it in previous scenes, rather than changing the scene itself.
- Opinions vary on how many notes should be provided in writing before the meeting. Many producers and executives would rather talk it through, and then provide the written notes at the end. Another technique is to prepare for the script meeting with a very general email or enthusiastic phone call, to give the writer time to think around key issues before the meeting.
- It is vital for the producer or writer to follow up the meeting with written notes, to make sure everything is clearly agreed and understood.

Sometimes people take away different impressions from the same meeting. This also protects the writer if the producer later changes his mind.

- Encourage risk-taking – make sure the writer knows they can try difficult solutions and ideas, and that you trust them to do that.
- Encourage freedom – don't be too prescriptive. Creativity is about play and fun and exploration.
- Keep positive energy and momentum throughout the meeting, and especially end it on a high note. Remember that the writer has to *want* to go and write the next draft, not be despondent.
- Whoever is being paid by whoever, remember that you are really partners on the journey to tell this story.

To conclude: be consistent, questioning, positive, concise, coherent, use the first person, encourage risk-taking, don't expect instant solutions, and keep up the momentum.

But what about talking about the marketplace? It has already been shown that creative people are often not motivated by money or financial concerns (even if they do want paying), but there is no right or wrong answer about how much the producer talks to the writer and director about the market and marketability of the film. It is up to the producer's relationship with them and his individual personality. Some writers and directors like to imagine at the start what a poster for the film could look like, and what the tag line could be; and some don't want to think about that sort of thing and want to discover it for themselves on the journey of making the film.

It is also worth remembering that each delivery of a new draft is the continuation of a discussion. For example, the French writer-director Radu Mihaileanu (*Train de vie, Vis et Deviens*) sees the delivery of the draft of the script to the producer as part of the collaboration, not as something that should be evaluated solely in terms of good or bad. The main thing the creative producer has to do is to give that draft a very careful reading, and then use it as a springboard for further discussion and collaboration:

> It is hard work to be a creative producer. You have to do a very attentive reading of the script. .... We [the writer] have been working for months with the details, with the doubts. ... We finally deliver. We don't want to hear just if it is good, or bad. Instead we want discussion. Ask us questions. We have worked for such a long time on our own, now we want guidance.[3]

Box 10.1 Working with writers: script discussions and steps towards successful rewrites (Travis, 2002)[4]

- Express enthusiasm!
- Find the genesis of the story and discover the writer's underlying vision or motivation: what is compelling him to write it?
- Find *points of agreement*. Go back to them when you need to, if you are disagreeing over something, and then work forward again.
- Go *from the general to the specific* (start with overall themes and premise, then major events, then characters, then sequences, scenes and specific moments).
- Identify *black holes* in motivation or plot, and then correct them, or cover them up or be explicit that they are there and carry the audience with you.
- Explore different *what ifs*.
- Make an effort to understand a writer's reluctance to make a particular change; you may gain greater insight into the script or the writer's motivation.
- Be devil's advocate to your own suggestions, especially if the writer accepts them too easily.
- Let the writer rewrite – then re-read the result several times (it may be surprising because it is different to what you had in your own mind's eye, but it may be better).
- Be aware of *the ripple effect*: where an apparently small change in one place can cause other details to unravel.

Replacing a writer: If it is really not working and the rewrites are not delivering, then work with the existing writer to identify and try to resolve problems; identify and agree when an impasse is reached; agree that a new writer may need to be brought in (ideally to work with the team, rather than completely replace the writer) and try to keep the existing writer involved and collaborating if possible – they still have a lot of experience and value to bring. This may work for example if there is the need for a dialogue polish or comedy pass.

Where to give notes

The other issue is *where* to do the note giving. Several people said that lunches or dinners are important for getting to know one another, or for throwing around ideas at an early stage, but are not the right place for script notes. Some people use their own office, others use industry venues like members' clubs, and others recommend doing them at their home, to make it more informal. One idea is sometimes to travel to the writer's home, so that the producer is going to them, rather than the writer always having to go to the producer, especially if the writer lives out of London. Travelling to the writer implies that the producer's time is no more valuable or important than the writer's time, and it helps reduce the employer and employee effect of calling the writer into the producer's office. Sometimes it also works to invite the writer to the producer's home for the weekend, as a bond-building exercise (especially if the producer lives in the countryside somewhere).

Internalization, rather than compliance

It is important to remember that even the most experienced and professional writer will respond emotionally to criticism, however well they hide it. The internalization of the scriptwriting process and the character traits of the creative person always makes it personal. Chapter 5 also showed how the writer progresses from a situation of high power and control at the start to being subject to many different influences and notes, and the need for careful management as a result. So in what ways does the writer actually *respond* to these notes and feedback from powerful newcomers?

The writer could actively reject or passively ignore the notes, although this is risky because he has probably assigned his rights to the producer and can be replaced if he does not cooperate, and he has a vested financial interest in getting the film financed (remember: his largest fee is on the first day of shooting). Many writers ignore some of the notes, in the hope that this will not be noticed in the new draft. If the writer *does* accept the notes he may need subconsciously to reduce the dissonance between what he is now doing and what he would be doing if he was uninfluenced. One of the ways to think about this is to look at the three psychological mechanisms for adjusting to powerful leadership influence, as identified by social theorist Herbert Kelman[5] and developed by Charles Handy.[6] These are known as *compliance, identification* and *internalization*:

- **Compliance:** The recipient agrees to the influence attempt because it is worth his while to do so. Compliance usually results from the use of certain types of power and influence as discussed in Chapter 5, specifically the use of force, rules, procedure and some power exchange methods. The implication of compliance is that the individual is doing what he is doing because he *has* to do it, and it may therefore be accepted grudgingly. Compliance implies that he has to *comply* with a command. The onus for seeing that he does what he is supposed to do thus remains with the leader – the initiator of influence (here the producer). This is very much *extrinsic motivation*, and therefore a hindrance to creativity (see Chapter 8).
- **Identification:** The recipient adopts the idea of a proposal because he admires or identifies with the source: the initiator of influence/the charismatic leader (say, a film producer or director). He wants to establish or maintain a satisfying self-defining relationship with a person or group; however, the recipient becomes dependent on the leader

and is more inclined to obey than initiate. Identification is *conforming*, it does not maintain itself indefinitely, and any initial enthusiasm for a project can evaporate without constant contact with the leader's vision. Again this is more *extrinsic* than *intrinsic motivation* (this is the way that most film shoots work, with close control from a respected and inspirational director, over a relatively short and high-pressure period, thus preventing the danger of the leader losing influence).

- **Internalization:** The recipient adopts the idea or proposal from the leader *as his own*; he internalizes it so that it becomes one of his possessions, aligned with his own values and ideas. Therefore he has to have the freedom to reject it and discuss it openly with the leader *before* accepting it. The change will be self-maintaining because the recipient believes in it and has internalized it (like a therapist or business consultant who persuades a patient or company that the solution is their own and not his). This is potentially *intrinsic motivation*, especially if it is aligned to other aspects of the writer's vision.

These ideas were developed through studying attitudes to change from social influence and policy messages, and analysing workers and leaders in companies; but they cast light on the responses of writers receiving notes from directors or financiers, and also chime with Amabile's concepts of motivation. Charles Handy explains further:

> Compliance and trust do not go together. Internalization and identification imply choice on the part of the recipient, the right to reject as well as accept. Compliance carries no such implication. Often a manager will start off using persuasion or some form of magnetism in an attempt to influence and hope for a free and accepting response. When his attempt is rejected he will fall back on position or resource power and ensure that his views are adopted. The result will be compliance, meaning lowered commitment and no guarantee that what he wants to happen will continue to happen unless he enforces it.[7]

The aim of the producer or development executive should be to avoid compliance and instead encourage internalization and intrinsic motivation, as the stronger route to higher levels of creativity. Internalization is easiest when the script notes identify a problem with the script and it is left up to the writer to find his own solution to the problem, which he then buys into. This is harder when notes are too prescriptive (for example, Why doesn't the hero do this or that? Why don't we move it to Los Angeles?) and the writer feels forced into doing something he does not believe in (by the use of resource power or the implicit threat of dismissal).

Responding to new ideas

It is important for a production company to develop long-term relationships with talent, and a crucial part of that is learning how to respond to ideas that are being brought to you by writers and directors (or for that matter members of staff or other industry figures). This ability to respond to new ideas is especially important during late development. After finishing any intensive project, many creative people are left feeling flat and directionless, sometimes even depressed and unwell, and this is known as the *creative drop*. In the case of the director this could be the end of the edit, or for the writer the start of the shoot, when they have completed their work and lost power (so there is a risk that if the producer is focused on making the current film they may fail to respond to the writer's new ideas for the next one). Therefore, if the director or writer does find a new idea and is excited by it then it's important that they should be encouraged, partly because it avoids losing them to another producer, and partly because it may be their way out of the post-project depression or writer's block – even if they do not end up writing that particular film. As writer-director Radu Mihaileanu explained:

> There is a delicate period in between two movies. We are in a 'no man's land'. It is like we have finished a love story and we are waiting for the next love story to start. Often when the (last) film works, people think we want to do the same story again. I don't want to reproduce the same. I want something new. The producer must help us to find our own story – to find what we want to do next. Often we are lost in that period. It is a difficult to choose a new adventure.[8]

Imagine a scenario where a writer or director is pitching a new idea to a time-pressured producer, possibly at the end of a meeting or on a brief phone call. There is always a danger that the producer may assess and close down an idea too quickly, and as a result may miss the next big hit. Assuming that this is a writer with whom the producer wants to develop a relationship, what are the guidelines for exploring the pitch and responding carefully?

First, it is vital to allow the writer time to explain his ideas, and for the producer to try to find out what is really at the heart of them, by asking questions to draw the idea out. It is all too easy to close down an idea by going into rational analysis too quickly (see Box 10.2 for some examples of how to kill an idea). Take a case where a writer has just read a novel and is trying to persuade the producer to option it. The producer has just scan-read it, but on first glance he cannot see the appeal. The producer could use the following lines to try to draw out the writer's motivations and passion for the project:

- 'I've read it and I really enjoyed it. Which was your favourite bit? Yes I loved the bit where ...' (This shows the producer has read it and fully understands it, and implies empathy with the writer's taste.)
- 'Why are you so excited about the idea? What was it that really drew you into it?' (Maybe there is something about the characters that really attracts the writer – say, the father/son relationship at the heart of the story – and the story is peripheral to why he wants to do it. This kind of question may help draw it out.)
- 'What do you think you could do to improve it? What's your take on it? What's your vision?'
- 'Do you know the novelist and his work? What do you like about the rest of his work?'
- 'That's really interesting – listen why don't we have dinner in Soho on Thursday and we'll talk it over some more ...'

The last line may seem like a classic delaying tactic, but actually it is more useful than that. The producer has gained time to reflect and to read (or re-read) the book properly, which is only polite if the talent is that enthusiastic. Re-reading shows the producer trusts the writer's opinion and will take it seriously; and after asking the above questions he will now be able to read it with an eye to what the writer sees in it. He may have missed something on the first reading. It also means, crucially, that the producer has managed to suspend immediate judgement, and is allowing the idea time to grow and germinate: classic creative person activity. But gaining time has another advantage – it also gives the writer time to reconsider and maybe *he* will have changed his mind by the time he meets the producer, and will have gone off the story and replaced it with a new and better idea. The proposed dinner must be soon, because if it is a month off then the writer will feel that the producer does not care, and will feel deflated. A meal also provides an opportunity to ask more questions in an informal setting, to draw out more about the writer's taste and to help build trust. The producer might be able to re-channel that enthusiasm into an original screenplay around similar themes that are not dependent on an underlying book (if there is no marketing value in the book then it may be a waste of funding for him to buy the rights to it – better to pay the writer to do something original that he and the writer will both own).

At the first pitch of an idea it is also important to avoid arguing about marketability or costs, because these are extrinsic issues that the writer may treat lightly or get irritated by (note that three of the ways to kill an idea in Box 10.2 are about money). Of course there are occasions when an idea really is not right for the company, and there is no point in stringing the writer along; however, it can be argued that if the aim is to build a long-term relationship then it is worth discussing the idea, if only to build trust and understanding. Eventually the writer will know the producer's taste and business direction well enough to *know* which projects to bring him, and that only develops after spending time together.

Box 10.2 The ten best phrases to kill an idea (Rudkin and Murrin, 2002)[9]

1. 'Yes, but ...'
2. 'We've tried it before ...'
3. 'That won't work because ...'
4. 'Have you really thought about the implications ...'
5. 'We don't have time for this right now ...'
6. 'Put it down on paper ...'
7. 'Exactly how much is this idea of yours worth ...'
8. 'Please do a cost-benefit analysis and then we'll talk about it ...'
9. 'OK, I hear you, but we've just invested millions in doing it another way ...'
10. 'That's fine in theory, but it doesn't work like that ...'

To conclude: by making quality time to talk with the writer, the producer is showing his ideas respect, avoiding taking the wind out of his sails at the first meeting (the writer may have psyched himself up to talk to the producer about the new idea), and may be able to get beyond the superficial pitch (what happens) to the heart of the story (what it is really about, or why he is passionate about it). Above all, the producer should not drop the project on the phone, which would be disrespectful, but instead give the idea time.

Listening to creativity

Box 10.3 The ten ways to understand and develop an idea (greenhousing ideas) (Rudkin and Murrin, 2002)[10]

1. 'Tell me more ...'
2. 'Why are you so excited about the idea?'
3. 'How's it different to the way the world is now?'
4. 'How did you get the idea/where did it come from?'
5. 'What would the positive consequences be?'
6. What would it look like?'
7. Let's go for it anyway!'
8. 'What I like in the idea is ...'
9. 'How can we make this better?'
10. Let's push this further ...'

Asking questions is usually a good way to draw out the writer, either in script meetings or when talking about a new script idea, and a few simple examples are shown in Box 10.3. However, there are also a useful series of techniques known as *motivational interviewing*, which are used by doctors and psychiatrists to resolve patient ambivalence towards a medical problem, for example when the doctor needs to effect a change in the patient's behaviour, such as stopping heavy drinking or substance abuse. To do that the doctor needs to encourage the patient's motivation for change, so that the patient is part of the solution and not part of the problem. In other words, for the treatment to work in the long term the patient has got to *want* to change.

Motivational interviewing was developed by the clinical psychologists Professor Stephen Rollnick and Professor William Miller,[11] and is designed to be non-judgemental, non-confrontational and non-adversarial – exactly the kind of approach that may work well in questioning and empowering writers. They give examples of doctors using open questions to encourage speech and empower the other person (such as 'How are you feeling today?' or 'How can I help you?'), instead of simple closed questions with single-word answers (such as 'Where does it hurt?' or 'How long has it been happening?'). If doctors are working with people with particular problems they may also ask questions which open up the prospect of the future, and where something is leading (such as: 'What would be a first step for you?', 'How would you like to take this forward?'), or they may use hypothetical questions (such as 'If you did decide to go ahead, how do you think you would you go about it in order to succeed?', 'If we carry on as we are how do you see things in five years' time?' or 'What currently impossible thing, if it were possible, might change everything?'). All these examples are designed to make the person being questioned feel in control and valued as part of the decision and the process.

Rollnick and Miller also advocate using a system of *listening by reflecting*, which is when the doctor repeats or sums up what the patient has just said, perhaps highlighting the bit he is interested in. It shows he is taking the person seriously, and proves he is listening and agreeing with him. The other person then either confirms or denies the reflection, helping him to refine his own thoughts further. For instance, what the producer *thinks* the writer is saying may not be what he means, so listening by reflecting is a good way of drawing out the truth or helping the writer to elaborate. Here is a simple example of a script meeting where the producer (or development executive) is listening by reflecting:

Writer: Well, I think the lead character is quite clear about his goals in the script. He says at the start of the second act that he wants to sail across the ocean single-handedly, and that nothing will stand in his way.

Producer: So, his main goal in the film is to sail across the ocean single-handedly.

Writer: Well, I guess his *main* goal is to win the love and respect of his family; but he's going to do that by sailing across the ocean on his own.

Producer: And he's sure that he'll win his family's respect by doing it.

Writer: Well, he thinks he will, but in fact I suppose he *really* needs to spend more time with his son and his daughter, because they hardly ever see him. And he thinks his wife doesn't love him any more, whereas she's really just overworked. So it's more complex than just the journey in the boat. I guess that isn't really clear yet. Perhaps we need to look more closely at the setup in act one.

Producer: That's possible. I love the idea that he thinks he has to leave them and be all alone to make them respect him, and yet really he needs to spend more time with them.

Writer: That's right. That's right. Maybe we need to make that clearer, at the end of act three, when he gets back from the journey. So that's his moment of realization. He's travelled all that way and gone through all those risks and dangers, but really the problem was back at home all the time ...

In this rather simplistic example the producer is not *telling* the writer that there is anything wrong with the script, he is just repeating back to the writer the things that he is saying, and encouraging him to explain in more detail. Only the last sentence from the producer is not a precise reflection, because it is adding a value judgement about how much he personally likes that aspect of the story. This would probably not be the way a psychiatrist would use reflective listening, but it is suitable for a producer who needs to reassure the writer that he loves and supports the story. As in the above example, some reflections can be quite simple and stay close to what the other person has said, just to stabilize them and show interest; but other reflections can be more complex and, by reframing or exaggerating what has been said, and maybe using different words, can cognitively alter and develop the material and affect the meaning.[12]

Of course, if over-used this reflectivity could become very irritating indeed and the writer may feel that the producer is parroting him, but it may be a useful technique, especially if it is interspersed with other types of question. Rollnick and Miller advocate that you should try and ask two reflective questions for every one direct question (see Box 10.4). They also suggest that the voice inflection should go down at the end of the reflective statement, instead of up. This is because going up at the end of the sentence could sound like a challenge and a question, instead of an agreement (unless you are Australian and it happens to be your speech pattern).

Box 10.4 Show that you are listening and reflecting (Rollnick, Miller and Butler, 2006)[13]

- **Listening by reflecting:** Instead of posing another question, give a short summary of what has just been said by the other person. You are agreeing with them but also drawing them out and making them develop their ideas further.
- **Spend more time listening than talking:** Try not to ask two questions in a row. Try to offer at least two reflections for every question.
- **Make notes and write things down** (it shows you are taking them seriously), but not to the extent that they think you are not listening or are avoiding eye contact.
- **Use body language** to re-affirm your receptiveness and agreement. Nodding approval. Open stance. Relaxed. Matching and mirroring non-verbal behaviour and body movements.
- **Acknowledge the value** of what you have heard: use affirmative responses and encouragement.
- **Consider complexity:** Remember that many people can be *ambivalent* or undecided about things. People can hold two possible options in suspension, and not decide between them. And what they are saying may not be what they *mean* to say.
- **Listen – don't interrupt:** First, they probably know more about the subject than you do, and second, they need time and space to explain their feelings and ideas.

This listening by reflecting technique is used by some of the better chat show hosts; and is also used in social science research, where it is referred to as *active listening, verbal mirroring* or using *interpreting questions,*[14] as social science researcher Janet Ruane explains:

> The verbal mirror shows the respondent that the researcher is indeed listening to everything. It also gives the respondent a chance to correct any misunderstandings by the interviewer. Most importantly, though, the verbal mirror provides the respondent with an opportunity to say more – to continue the dialogue and delve deeper into the topic.[15]

Similar to the technique of listening by reflecting is the technique of *summarizing.* Summary statements link together and reinforce material that has been discussed, but they don't just have to occur at the end of the meeting: summaries can be done at various stages within it, according to when the producer feels that progress has been made and needs reinforcing.[16] Again it shows that you have been listening carefully and the writer has the chance to disagree with the summary statement or refine it, so it reinforces the sense of agreement and consensus around how the script is going to proceed.

Rollnick and Miller identify three types of summary. There is the *collecting summary*, which is mid-conversation and possibly contains just a few sentences, maybe starting with 'so if I am following this right ...' or 'let me get this clear ...', and ending with a question like '... what else?' or '... is there anything I've missed?' Then there is the *linking summary*, which may be drawing together different sequences or areas of discussion to try to find a linking theme or conflict. It may use words like 'and' to combine themes, or 'but' to identify a discrepancy, or use the linking phrase 'on the one hand ... and on the other'. And finally there is the *transitional summary*, which is at the end of the meeting, and is preparing for the next step: such as the new draft or the next meeting. The transitional summary confirms who is going to do what, and how the team is going to progress things (for example, who is going to write up the formal summary, or who is going to carry out the research). Ideally, this should build momentum and enthusiasm, so that people leave the meeting on a positive note. The reason it is not called a *concluding* summary is that it is setting the agenda for going *forward*, rather than closing the discussion. Like psychotherapy, the process of script development is a series of incremental steps forward, not something that is solved or resolved in just one session.

The sound of silence

Another key issue for producers is to be able to *listen* carefully to the answers, and not be afraid of silence. This seems obvious but is harder than it sounds: just try having a conversation with someone for five minutes without one of you speaking or making any affirmative sounds at all and it rapidly becomes very difficult for both people. The reason is that we are socially programmed to encourage communication with verbal approval, even with small sounds; and if the person talking does not receive that encouragement they quickly feel abandoned.

However, in the course of conversation we are sometimes in fact *interrupting* the other person. We think we are keeping the conversation going, by showing approval or encouragement, but sometimes that stops or changes the train of thought of the other person, as researcher Janet Ruane explains:

> Rather early on in our training as social beings, we learn the value of friendly banter that can keep awkward silences at a minimum. (Think about your own awkwardness when you hear a deafening silence on the other end of a phone conversation – if you're like most people you will rush in to fill the void.) The researcher, however, must put this convention aside during a qualitative interview. Moments of silence in an interview should be appreciated as instances of thoughtful punctuation. Frequently there is something to be learned from the silence. If the researcher rushes in and prematurely breaks the silence,

important data may be lost forever – the respondent may feel embarrassed and never return again to the issue that prompted the silence. A good researcher will learn to respect silences. In doing so, the researcher is apt to discover how silences can be springboards into important topics of discussion.[17]

Silence gives people space to think. Sometimes even another question is a potential block to an ongoing train of thought. Rollnick and Miller go further and say that asking and listening are not the same thing at all, and many questions are in fact *roadblocks,* that stop the speaker's flow: 'Roadblocks to listening include agreeing, disagreeing, instructing, questioning, warning, reasoning, sympathising, arguing, suggesting, analysing, persuading, approving, shaming, reassuring, and interpreting.'[18]

However, as mentioned, too much silence feels threatening so there is a fine line between drawing somebody out and causing them to dry up completely. These types of skill can be taught and practised, and it is possible that many producers and executives may benefit from learning to listen.

These concepts about questioning and listening apply not just to scriptwriting but also to creative ideas in general. Leaders of larger organizations need to take care to give attention to employees who are bringing them ideas, as the American business writers Davenport, Prusack and Wilson explain:

> Idea practitioners (creatives) are primarily motivated not by money or power but by intellectual stimulation and the excitement of seeing ideas transformed into action. ... Whatever you do with regard to cash and perks, don't fail to reward idea practitioners with *attention.* Your willingness to hear them out, and to get visibly behind an idea, is a powerful motivator – and your disregard counts as a penalty.[19]

Box 10.5 What do writers say they want?

The following points came from several different writers during interviews for this book:

- Direct contact with the producer instead of development executives (or as well).
- 'Get back quick with notes – otherwise the self-confidence dies ...'
- Notes: deal with *big* issues – not the minutiae. It is the writer's job to do minutiae. Don't micro-manage. If you want to be a writer, go and be a writer.
- 'Twenty pages of notes are really really offputting.'
- 'People work better when they feel you have confidence in them.'

- Prefer face-to-face meetings and discussions to email notes.
- Feedback as questions. 'If someone says "do it like this" then as a writer you won't write your best. Don't do the writer's work for them. Better to ask a question and let the writer find their own solution.'
- Producers should not control – they should enable.
- 'Something we write, as a first draft, is a proposal for dialogue.'
- Please say *something* positive …

This chapter has summarized the feedback of many of the interviewees, including screenwriters (see Box 10.5); and has also drawn from other disciplines and research to find new techniques for questioning and listening. The case interviews will now explore the detailed advice on script note giving from a selection of experienced film industry practitioners, including a larger case interview with the script editor Kate Leys. Chapter 11 will then look at other ways of strengthening the development team, using theories about the successful teams and concepts of team culture and organizational culture.

Case interviews: Giving notes and running script meetings

Most producers and development executives think they handle the giving of notes very well, and yet writers are full of horror stories about meetings where they have left feeling demotivated by criticism and confused by conflicting notes. Writers' agent Julian Friedmann explains:

> Many producers can't read anyway. They just aren't particularly good at it. … I think a significant proportion of them are bad at working with writers. They don't know how to give notes. Equally, most writers are bad at taking notes, they don't know how to listen or respond to them. So it's not as if I've just got a big downer on producers, I think a lot of writers are their own worst enemies.

Whilst there is no ideal way to give notes, and it varies based on personal relationships and trust, this section will now try to assemble some examples of good practice, based on interviews and general feedback.

Written notes in advance of the meeting? Or all notes face-to-face?

Ivana MacKinnon (development executive/producer): I tend to give written notes because I find you can be very clear and it takes away some of the emotional response. I think the writer can read the notes, have the emotional response to it which a writer is always going to have, and then you sit down and talk about them, at a point where what you wanted to say has been put out there. I know there are other developers who would never give written notes, and think it's a completely inhuman way of going about things, and you should only give notes in person. But I often find that when we give notes in person you go and cop out, and actually there's lots of things that you wanted to say but you never did. But it really depends on the person you're working with. There are other writers who I wouldn't give notes to and I would sit down and talk to.

Kate Lawrence (development executive): Just doing it over the phone and sending written notes doesn't work. You've got to get in a room and discuss things, and not have time constraints. And when things are written down in note form it seems a lot harsher and more prescriptive, and that's not what you mean. It's got to be a process of give and take, and you get quite a lot out of talking around subjects, which happens more in a meeting. People are more relaxed and you can have a general conversation first, discussing wider things before you get down to specifics. When you're on the phone you've only got an hour's conference call or something, and people are talking across each other, so it's more difficult.

Be specific

Sam Lavender is Head of Development at Film4, and admits that development meetings with a financier can be stressful for the writer, because there may be only an hour or so in which to receive and process all that important information. Therefore it is vital for the executive to be very well prepared:

Sam Lavender: The important thing is to be as specific as you can possibly be, as clear as you possibly can be. And make sure that as early as possible in the process you have as clear an understanding between you, the producer, and the writer, or director if he's involved, exactly what you want to achieve – what the ambition of the project is. Not necessarily the scale of budget, although that might come into it ... but really an understanding about what the story's about. Not necessarily how you're going to get there or what the details of the story are going to be, because that's figured out in the process;

but why you all love it and why you love the potential of it. And then the note-giving process ... I say, be specific about the script, read it very, very closely, read it in one sitting, then read it again, and prep a meeting as much as you possibly can. Never give a note that you don't feel. And if there are other people who will feed into the notes who've read it, introduce them into the process as early as possible so that they can build the relationship with the writer as well. ... So – don't rush, be thorough and be *specific*. Vagueness can be a big problem.

BBC development editor Ed Wethered agrees that re-reading a script four to five times is vital, so that the feedback can be well informed and very detailed. However, first drafts often share some specific problems:

Ed Wethered: It's a cliché but there's something you can almost always say about almost every first draft ... the first act should be shorter, ending on say page 28 rather than page 38; and you can almost always say that the central character needs to be more active.

The producer and development executive need to agree the notes together first

Kate Lawrence (development executive): You don't want to get into development by committee, which I know a lot of writers feel sometimes. ... Before we ever give notes or have a meeting on something we make sure that we are all on the same page ... It's very frustrating for writers if you give contradictory notes and they don't know who they should be listening to ... so we try and work that out ourselves in-house before we ever talk to the writer.

Tom Williams (screenwriter): I've got more confident about pushing back on notes. I've recently received notes from two producers on a project when they would do Producer A's notes followed by Producer B's notes, and I've gone back to say: 'This is not working for me. I need to get notes with a consensus view.' It's that awful thing where you get notes from three or four different people and you have to make sense of the madness.

Filtering and mediating other people's notes

Sam Lavender: The important thing is to present a unified set of notes, because otherwise you're going to put the script into a holding pattern of people writing to order to different briefs. So have that conversation with the co-financiers, and be as clear as you can possibly be about what kind of film you intend to make.

Ivana MacKinnon: A producer can be very useful, because if he has been involved from the start he can almost interpret notes, because writers sometimes just hear the negatives, the horrible things. And I think often a writer will come out of a meeting, especially a financier's meeting, feeling just pummelled and battered and broken and bruised, and only hearing things that are negative. And then the producer's role is to say: 'No, okay that was really positive and I think this is how we can interpret what they're saying in a positive way, and we need to do it to make the script better.' So I think that's when they can be very valuable, as a filter, an interpreter, and actually someone who says, 'No, you don't have to listen to all of these things.'

Remember to be positive

Many writers complained that they don't get enough praise and positive feedback, and maybe the execs forget that for the writer it is often personal:

Anonymized scriptwriter: Every good producer knows that when you deliver a new draft their first response should be 'That's brilliant!'

Sam Lavender: The most important thing is that you love the writing, and you think there's something special there. I don't think you can say that clearly enough, in that first meeting and for meetings to come. If someone starts feeling like they don't own this thing, they won't do their best work.

Olivia Hetreed (writer): It makes an awfully big difference if someone is able to present the notes in a positive light rather than a negative light and there are producers who I would work with again because it's a pleasure to get notes from them, and the notes are always coherent. I always feel they're moving in the right direction. They manage to offer possibilities and suggestions without becoming prescriptive.

Respond quickly to the new draft

Ivana MacKinnon: The writers spend weeks, months, sitting in a room, desperately pounding their heads against a desk trying to figure something out, and then they deliver it, and then they're thinking, 'They're going to call me tomorrow, they're going to call me tomorrow and tell me what it's like, they're going to call me on Monday and tell me what it's like.' And then weeks and weeks pass, and by the time they actually get a phone call or an email they're just jaded. ... So getting back to people quickly, just to show them basic human respect, is sometimes lacking in the big machine that can be the film industry. It makes the difference between a writer having a good experience, even if a film doesn't get made, and having an experience where they feel like they're doing all the creative work and not getting respected for it.

And if you cannot respond quickly, because the producer is on a shoot or the financiers are responding slowly, then at least give some initial feedback quickly so the writer knows he has not been forgotten.

Kate Lawrence: I sometimes have discussions with writers over the phone, initial discussion, where perhaps we haven't got our written notes ready on a draft, but I want to tell them what we're feeling in very broad brushstrokes. ... I don't like the idea of a writer being on tenterhooks with no communication. I wouldn't like that if it was me. But sometimes I might have read it and one of the producers, but the other producer is on set so hasn't had a chance to read it, or it's been sent to the development financier but we haven't heard from them yet. I think as long as you just keep telling the writer where it is, then, okay it might be frustrating but it's better than silence.

Then again, sometimes it is the writers who do not deliver on time, but still expect the producer to respond quickly.

Anonymized producer: Sometimes you wait and wait for the writer to deliver. Invariably they are late and then they give you their work like it's a Christmas present, and expect you to read it and get back to them within 48 hours. ... And I can understand it, because they are sitting there waiting, desperately hoping that you are going to love what they have written.

Case interview: Script editor Kate Leys

Kate Leys is one of the most respected script editors in the business. She has also been head of development at several companies, including Capitol Films and Film4, where she was part of the small team commissioning and developing films like Four Weddings and A Funeral, Trainspotting *and* The Full Monty. *She developed* Orphans *and brought in* East is East *and* Girl with a Pearl Earring.

Giving notes: Be truthful, confidential, constructive ... and do it in the first person

What do I consider the best way of giving notes? Absolutely truthfully, and in absolute confidence. There is no compromising on either of those. ... If you tell a writer the truth about their story, then it's valuable and the writer will trust you. It's clear that you know the story and have thought about it, and you have something to say that they recognize. It's really important that those notes and that conversation are never going to be discussed with anybody else.

I don't believe it's ever necessary to say anything that isn't constructive. There's no point in saying, 'This bit is rubbish.' You can say, 'This bit isn't working yet.' But I don't think there's ever a need to be dismissive. ... There's no point because an under-confident writer can't tell you a story.

I also think it's really important to frame notes in the first person. ... There might be lots of things that *I'm* not understanding, and that's useful for the writer. Hearing somebody say, 'I find that bit a bit flat' is identifying the problem and owning the response to it; that leaves the writer free to solve the problem. And mostly what goes wrong with notes is people don't do that; instead they identify and decide what the solution must be. And then the note then comes out with the word 'you' at the beginning of it. So if I'm working with a group of writers and I want them to give notes to each other, I make it a rule that you must begin every sentence with the word 'I', and they always find it a bit uncomfortable for about ten seconds, and then they relax and actually everybody gets it. It works and it's incredibly effective.

Questioning: a technique to draw the other side out

I'm the audience. I'm just the *first* audience and so I'm asking: 'Why are they doing this?' Often a writer has decided in advance what it is they're going to write, but then when they write it, it doesn't come out like that. And so it's hard for a writer to see what has come out: the gap between what they think they've written and what I'm reading. And so asking questions really is about: 'I don't understand this. You keep saying that they're looking for the treasure but they keep stopping. They're not really looking for the treasure, in fact they're falling in love with each other here for twenty pages. So, it might be useful to think about how they could they be falling in love *while* they're looking for the treasure; or is the treasure actually, after this bit, not going to be so important?' It's a question all the time because my feeling is that it's the writer's job to solve this. It's the writer's story, it's never my story. So it's about saying: 'What do *you* want here? You could do this and you could do that; or you say you want this, but actually you've written that; so you choose, what do *you* want?' I don't usually have a plan in my head. ... I'm not good at strategic planning and manoeuvering. So the idea that I would ask questions in order to draw something out ... ? Well if I'm asking a question usually it's just because I want to know the answer.

Try and find the core of the story

I love, love, love stories. Really, it's the thing I couldn't live without. ... Somebody asked me the other day, 'Is there such a thing as a story that can't be made to work?' And I realized that – no, I don't think there is a story that can't be made to work. Because it isn't about making something work, it's about finding what it is that is really happening in that story, and finding what is driving that storyteller to tell that story, and then going from there. Sometimes you have to dismantle an awful lot of things before you get to that, and you end up telling a different sort of story. Sometimes you have to go quite far back, but yes, I think there is always something there. What motivates the writer and what is driving the story are often very closely connected. What's driving the story is often not looking for treasure, or falling in love; what's really driving it is often something much simpler and often quite dark – like fear of being on your own. It's often to do with fear, there's a million kinds of fear, and feeling your way towards that is often what a writer is doing. Writers are extraordinary people.

What is 'bad development'?

I think the problem with development is that we are a very narrative literate world, and the reality is that all of us can tell you when a story's no good. A room full of 5-year-olds can tell you when a story's no good. You could take ten manuscripts, one good one and nine really bad ones, and you could take them to the nearest bus queue and every single person would tell you which was the good one. It isn't difficult. ... The business of identifying *why* it isn't any good and then what it is that you actually need to *do* to get it working is a whole other skill. ... Producers who would not dream of trying to do the film editor's job, they all think that they *can* do the story editor's job, because they know how to read a story and they got a nice grade for their A-level English.

So most bad development stems from people being fantastically over-confident about their ability to discuss a story and identify its problems ... an awful lot of people trying to run meetings, trying to solve problems and in all the wrong ways. But you know, if you solve the problem in a story it's going to be *your* solution to somebody else's story, and it's never going to quite fit.

Plus, the issue of where something's really going wrong and where it *seems* to be going wrong is massive. Because where a story goes wrong is, I would say, 90 per cent of the time not where it needs solving. That's the symptom – that's where it emerges as a problem. You know the old cliché about *if the ending isn't working, it's the really the beginning that isn't working*? Well that's true. Quite often that scene here at the end that's a bit flat, is flat because you didn't really sort out this scene here on page 20, that set it up. The problem is almost always a symptom, rather than a cause, and you've got to get up close to know that.

Secret script editing: why we pretend that script development doesn't really happen

One of the things that's quite interesting is that sometimes I get hired in secret, by two sorts of people. I get hired by producers, who're working with writers who won't work with script editors or won't do formal development in that way; and they are writers who are usually very successful, they're successful enough to throw their weight around. And it's that classic thing about success, you get surrounded by people who won't say 'no' to you, and so it's easy to develop a belief of yourself as absolutely marvellous in every respect. And what they want to do is they don't want to sit with a story editor, what they want to do is lunch with a producer. So the producer will hire me, essentially to do notes for them to talk through at lunch with the writer.

The other way I get hired in secret is the other way round. I sometimes get hired by writers, out of their fee, because they're working with producers who believe that they can do development by doing lunch with their writer. And then what happens is I get hired by the writer. They do the lunch with the producer, try and make sense of the lunch discussion in a set of notes and then bring them to me and say: 'What does this mean? And what do I actually need to do with the script?'

So I get hired in secret by producers and I get hired in secret by writers. And I have to admit, I'm a bit uncomfortable about it sometimes because although the work is very intriguing, I am aware that I am colluding in something that finally denies the value of development. There is something in there about the way that people are quite wary of story development. And it's quite a British thing. I think there is an expectation, a kind of latent, hidden, tacit belief, that a writer is born either talented or not talented. You've either been touched by the lightning or the hand of God, or you haven't. And that what you do as a creative person is you go along on your own, and you struggle and you come back with something that's finished and we look at it and we either go – 'Fabulous!', or we go – 'Crap!' There is no way else. ... Compare that to the approach to creative writing, for instance, in the States, and there is a completely unproblematic view that it's an area that you can discuss and consider, and that yes, of course you need to be talented ... but actually there are other parts of creative writing that you *can* teach, and that you can train people in the building blocks, and then teach them some craft and technical skills. Look at successful novelists and screenwriters in America and many of them are associated closely with universities, or teaching on creative writing programmes or film-making programmes. It's not even worthy of comment, whereas here the schism between the teaching and working reveals the suspicion we have of anything that might *'interfere'* with the creative process.

I think there is a sort of core belief that a screenplay ought to emerge fully formed, and that this leaves people wary of development. I think it's beginning to shift, but it's still out there: collaboration is still a dirty word in screenwriting. It's not in the rest of the film industry. It's the myth of the creative, isolated, struggling genius, whose talent must be protected and if necessary fought for. It's the big thing people coming into the industry always worry about: 'How will I fight off people's notes?' Well, why would you? Writers worry overmuch about interference. If you're working on a story and you're really clear in your mind about what it is and what you're doing with it … then going in to have a conversation with somebody who's read your story and knows about it and cares about it and wants to make some suggestions for it ought to be a fantastic experience.

11 Strengthening the development team culture and building a sustainable creative company

> Choose people who are better than you and then let them get on with it.
> (Alex Graham, producer)

This chapter examines two key MBA business concepts, which are rarely applied to development and small production companies: team theories and organizational culture. They are both important to understand, and can be used to strengthen the development team and help build a sustainable film company based on retaining talent.

Introduction to teams and culture

The last quarter of the twentieth century showed a rise in popularity of business theories about the productivity of teams of people, including books like *The Wisdom of Teams* by the McKinsey consultants Katzenbach and Smith, and *Management Teams* by Meredith Belbin.[1] Teams were thought to be more effective and more creative than people working on their own, especially if the team was assembled with the right mix of people with diverse and complementary attributes. The sum of the parts was considered greater than the individual. Some of these ideas can be applied successfully to film development if we consider that the film development process is really a team activity, where the group shifts and changes during the process.

People are instinctive social creatures, experienced at reading and mimicking the behavioural signals of others (those mirror neurons again). They learn from one another and copy one another, and never more so than in the workplace. The way that people regularly behave in a team or a company (which is after all only a permanent and salaried team) is known as *organizational culture*. This is sometimes summed up as: *the way we do things around here*.[2] It is the identity or personality that the team or company takes on, as a result of the behaviour of all the people in it, including its attitudes, shared experiences, beliefs, norms and underlying values. This has to be more than just a published company mission statement or a marketing slogan, and at its strongest the culture can reflect a series of jointly held values and assumptions that underpin all decisions and behaviour.

There are two ways that this concept of group culture is vital for the producer: first, the individual project's development team culture (which may ensure consistent creative decision-making and prevent vision drift), and second, the production company's overall culture (which may encourage investors to support it and creative talent to work for it). This chapter will examine both of these in turn, and then look at how this can be vital in attracting and retaining talent.

Box 11.1 Definitions of organizational culture[3]

There are many different definitions of organizational culture …

> Organizational culture could be defined as the identity or personality the organization takes on.
>
> (Robbins and Bardwell 2002)

> The culture of a group is a pattern of shared basic assumptions that the group learned as it solved problems of external adaptation and internal integration, that has worked well enough to be considered valid, and, therefore, to be taught to new members as the correct way to perceive, think, and feel in relation to those problems.
>
> (Schein 1985)

> The company's own way of doing things … a richly developed and deeply rooted system of values and beliefs that distinguishes a particular organization from all others.
>
> (Mintzberg 1989, defining ideology, a particularly strong form of culture)

Small team culture, as applied to film development: anxiety, sharing experience and bonding

One of the leading researchers into the internal culture of small teams and organizations is Professor Edgar Schein from the MIT Sloan School of Management. In his definition of organizational culture (see Box 11.1) Schein emphasizes that it emerges as a result of the group learning from shared experiences, and that behaviour is then passed on to new arrivals. Schein carried out extensive research that studied the early stages of small task-defined groups, and showed that the process of a team assembling, setting goals and working together quickly created an internal culture of shared understanding. Initially, there is a moment of anxiety, as people meet for the first time, and Schein suggests that overcoming that anxiety and power vacuum is so important that it becomes the first of what he calls *marker events*: the key moments in the evolution of the team and its journey that all the people in the team will recognize, consciously or unconsciously.

There is sometimes a moment of silence, and then as members of the group start to talk, and share their experience and ideas, the group dynamic quickly starts to form and the anxiety relaxes. Perhaps one person may make a suggestion, and whether it is accepted or rejected by the rest of the group then helps to build the group identity and culture. The group is taking on its own separate identity:

> If person A makes a suggestion, and person B disagrees, it may appear to be just two members of the group arguing, but the emotional reality is that the other members are witnesses and make their own collective choice on whether to enter the conversation or not. Only two people have spoken, but *the group* has acted and is *aware* of having acted as a group.[4]

The team is beginning to 'learn' its identity, and a sense of mission and identity is formed as the members decide on a course of action, form goals and procedures, and start working towards solving problems. Each successful step forward becomes another *marker event*, as the group starts to gain confidence and roles are adopted.

In normal corporate life these anxiety moments of group formation are reduced by the existence of a series of organizational 'crutches', such as a predistributed formal agenda; an existing leadership or power structure through the company hierarchy (for example, a meeting is often called by someone with power over the rest of the group); an awareness of a shared company culture (how we do things around here); social behavioural norms (a wider societal culture or industry-specific culture); and formal procedural rules on running meetings (sometimes part of company culture, sometimes not). These 'crutches' usually help people overcome the anxiety moment of the formation of a group.

But in the case of drama development many of these 'crutches' are absent. There is probably no formal agenda or procedure (although the screenplay or treatment is often discussed chronologically), and the main players are not members of a joint company culture (unless they have worked together before, and have shared experiences). Sometimes in early development meetings there is the added complication that there is no funding and the writer is working 'on spec' until after a formal application to a development source or commissioning editor. This breeds extra suspicion about the commitment of the producer and the writer to one another and to the project. Therefore drama development teams from their very formation are prone to extra anxiety, which cannot be mitigated by the 'crutches' employed by ordinary companies with teams.

The way the film industry conventionally gets around this anxiety moment is to assemble the team in a social environment rather than a meeting room, for example over lunch or dinner. Breaking the ice starts with general conversation and getting to know one another, maybe swapping stories about other people in the industry or other films that have been worked on, so that discussing the task itself (working on a new screenplay) can be put off until the initial anxiety has relaxed (maybe it is raised at the end of the dinner). In other words, the film industry's acceptable 'crutch' is not a formal agenda but social interaction, alcohol and eating together.

More anxiety for the members of the development team

At the same time as the group is starting to form, the individual members of the group are trying to figure out whether or not they will fit into it, and whether being part of it is the right thing for them, as Schein explains:

> When the group first comes together, the most fundamental issue facing it as a whole is 'What are we really here for? What is our task?' At the same time each individual in the group is facing basic social survival issues such as 'Will I be included in this group?' 'Will I have a role to play?' 'Will my need to influence others be met?' 'Will we reach a level of intimacy that meets my needs?' As the group gathers in its appointed space, various participants, coming to terms with the new situation, will display their own coping style. Some will silently await events; some will form immediate alliances with others; and some will begin to assert themselves by telling anyone who cares to listen that they know how to deal with this kind of situation.[5]

It could be said that in film development teams other survival issues also come to the fore, especially for the writer. These survival issues are hitting higher on Maslow's *Hierarchy of Needs* towards *self-actualization* (see Chapter 8): 'Will my creative vision survive the input of other people in the group?' 'Will this group be powerful enough to enable the film to get made?' 'Is this a worthwhile and valuable process?' Furthermore, since writers often work on their own, the mere inclusion of themselves in a team which is questioning or influencing their creative output is simultaneously anxiety-inducing (a perceived threat to the integrity of their vision and fear of change) and stimulating (because creatives like the company of other stimulating people, and because this is a step towards getting their film made). But there is also an even deeper issue: that of survival itself. As shown, writers and directors are prone to being removed by the producer and may have already experienced this in their careers, perhaps for selling purposes rather than deep creative differences or failure (such as the needs of packaging, or attaching a director's favoured writer). Therefore 'Will I *survive* as part of this group, or part of this project?' will also be a key question, especially since the producer usually controls the rights and therefore has the power to change the development team at will. So at the heart of the internal questions is: 'Do I *trust* these people and want to work with them?'

Resisting newcomers to the team

Edgar Schein places emphasis on the creation of culture and identity as a moment of shared emotional reaction *between* those people in the team, and therefore this is not shared by outsiders. If you did not witness what has happened then you are not a proper member of the group. Therefore it is quite logical that the arrival of new members creates conflict, even if they arrive only an hour after the initial moments of the group forming, and this is exactly what Schein's research proved:

> This act of being in or out of the group is quite concrete, in that any person who did not attend and witness the event cannot know what happened or how people reacted. A new member who arrives one hour late will already feel the presence of a group and will want to know 'what has gone on so far.' And the group will already feel that the newcomer is a 'stranger' who 'has to be brought on board.'[6]

Schein believes that company culture is formed in a similar way to this small group culture, with new incomers (or members of staff) needing to be inducted formally or informally into the organizational culture so that they 'belong', and this will be examined later in the chapter.

This problem of new arrivals could be said to be even more prevalent in film development, where the group is very small and sometimes very fluid, with new members (such as a script editor and eventually the director) arriving, or the team regularly receiving input from temporary group members (like financiers) who do not buy into the culture of the group, and probably *want* to remain temporarily outside it (their own emotional and sometimes financial commitment to a project is still in question), as seen in Chapter 5. The development group is prone to anxiety and disruption at each of these points of arrival, and to provide good leadership, the producer needs to be aware of this dynamic and be able to take steps to minimize it.

More reasons for the weakness of film development teams

If this was not enough, there are broadly four *more* reasons why the film development process can create weaker teams than other creative groups or conventional work groups.

1. Lack of regular meetings or consistency of effort

Development groups do not meet as regularly as working groups in a company, where there may be catch-up meetings once a week, or informal meetings at the water cooler or at one another's desks. Film meetings are more likely to be further apart, even maybe several months apart. Meetings may only be triggered by a new draft being produced and circulated by the writer or director, who has therefore remained more closely and emotionally involved than the other members of the team and therefore feels he is putting in a disproportionate amount of effort.

2. Long project timescale and uncertainty of outcome

It is well understood from the start that script development will take a long time and that a successful outcome is very uncertain (even if the film is produced the writer may feel it does not reflect his vision). This means that at the moment of formation of the team, all group members may be wary of total commitment to the group because of the possibility of failure or personal removal from the group. Within an ordinary company a working group's outcomes and targets are usually much shorter term, and capable of regular, objective and SMART evaluation (like sales targets)[7] to achieve *quick wins* and rewards, which then help to bond the group with shared success. Within film development there are few quick wins and there is no high likelihood of long-term wins. However, this is offset by the value of continuing relationships; the previous successful completion of a film may provide the memory of reward and positive outcome. Again the importance of continuing relationships in forming new groups comes to the fore. Without it the group is in danger of early disintegration and lack of motivation.

3. Uncertainty of payment

Sometimes there are low levels of early development funding, if any. The majority of payment is on production, not development, and, as mentioned, production is uncertain. The difference in ordinary companies is that people are usually salaried, so the outcome of the project and the team's success or failure is not going to impact as heavily on whether or not they will be paid.

These issues are less prevalent in TV development where scripts are often produced as part of a semi-commission after a verbal pitch, or a confirmed commission based on a treatment, or recommission (for example on a series or serial). The turnaround and outcome is relatively quick, with often one greenlighting agency (as opposed to the many possible finance sources and greenlights in independent film) sometimes providing swift and clear feedback. The development period may be within a year and meetings will be more regular, sometimes around a pre-existing group (headed by a series producer) or a team with an existing culture and shared assumptions of behaviour. Characters may already be set, storylines follow existing generic expectations, and the format and expectations of the audience are clear.

All three of the above factors mean that in film team members are liable to remain individuals and not become fully integrated into the group. As a result they may pull out. For example, a writer may choose to offer the script to another producer when the option expires; the producer may choose to drop the project from his slate or attach a different writer; or the director may choose to attach himself to another project; and so on. For a team to function properly there should be an overlap between the needs of the individual, the team identity and the task objective, and without that overlap there is a tendency for the team to remain underdeveloped, the individual to dominate, and the task to fail (see Fig. 11.1).

4. Unable to learn as a team

A vital ingredient of working in teams is that you should learn together from your mistakes. Business schools teach that at the end of the team activity or project management the team must make time to reflect on what has gone wrong and right, and try to build on that for the future. However development teams often cannot do this because the screenplay is completed before the film is made, the writer is often not involved during the shoot and is no longer with the rest of the team, and at the end of the project there is no other retrospective learning process moment because the team has split up (the producer is exploiting and releasing the film, the director is going on to the next film, and the writer finished work on it many months earlier). The learning process is also complicated by the critical reception and box office performance of the finished film, which can provide a short-term colouring of the perceived creative value of the project which may not be matched by its long-term reputation.

Figure 11.1 The interaction of needs in team performance (Adair 1990)[8]

Techniques for *overcoming* weak film development teams

Given all these problems for development teams, it could be asked how film development ever happens at all. Perhaps the characters and motivations of creative people come into play, since we have seen that they are often highly self-motivated (even compulsive), intrinsically motivated in their particular field, and driven by a search for self-fulfilment and ego needs. Their desire to be recognized, to belong to the film culture and to see their vision told on the big screen can be enough to overcome all the obstacles and compel them to work together with other people, in pursuit of their vision.

There are also perhaps some ways that careful producers can try to overcome these potential team weaknesses.

1. Mitigating lack of regular meetings or consistency of effort

This could be overcome by encouraging regular social meetings and informal progress reports that will enable the writer to bounce ideas off the rest of the team, and therefore tie the writer and his creative process into the team, and the team into the work of the writer.

2. Mitigating long project timescale and uncertainty of outcome

If they are experienced then all the people in the team know that this is what the film industry is like and so their expectations are altered. Just as organizations and teams have a culture, so do professions and industry sectors, and people who work in the film development sector adjust to that culture.[9] The producer needs to ensure that if someone is a newcomer to the industry (perhaps a writer or director who is transferring from theatre or television) then they should be fully prepared for the timescale and other risks.

A strong communication strategy may also help mitigate the team worrying about failure. If the producer keeps communication open between all members of the team then the writer, director and their agents are aware that he is actively working on financing or packaging and that momentum is continuing: a big fear of a writer can be that the busy producer is financing a different project and theirs is languishing on the shelf. This could be done formally by doing a monthly team email updating on progress. This type of team practice is characteristic of companies and could be perceived as a bit corporate, so it is important to get the tone right. If the email is copied to everyone in the team, then it keeps everyone engaged, gives the impression of openness, and gives the producer a chance to communicate good news as well as bad – otherwise members of the team only hear about the rejections and not about a good chance meeting or opportunity.

However, regular emails mustn't take the place of face-to-face meetings and socials, and it is vital to celebrate small wins together. For example, if a producer has secured a meeting with a key finance source, it is an idea to not just communicate that by email, but to call an evening drink meeting to announce the meeting, and then the producer, writer and development people can celebrate together, while also planning how to approach the meeting. They can bond over the positive news and drown sorrows together if necessary further down the line (the writer will have felt involved in the preparation for the meeting). Depending on the writer and the trust relationship it is *maybe* worth taking the writer to those key meetings, because it shows the writer that the producer trusts him and is prepared to involve him in the process – even if he is asked beforehand not to contribute too much during the meeting. If the meeting is a success then both the writer and producer feel they have succeeded *together*, and if it fails, at least the writer can see that the producer did his best and the writer had a chance to contribute. Furthermore, the producer and writer can then do the post mortem and deal with disappointment together, since even experiencing failure can be a bonding exercise. On the other hand, this joint meeting approach is potentially a high-risk strategy: it may not work with all writers and financiers, and it reduces the producer's ability to filter and mediate script notes from the financiers.

As part of the face-to-face meetings and social catch-ups, the producer could also ask about the writer's other projects and ideas so that the door is open to further collaboration in the future. This emphasizes that the relationship is a long-term one and not just based on the success or failure of this one project, thus reducing fear of failure and increasing trust and engagement. It is always important to talk to the writer about the next project, but at the heart of it is the fact that both parties enjoy working together, as producer Stephen Woolley explains:

> We make the (development) process as much fun and as painless as we can, but at the same time we work very hard. So we worked hard with [writer] Peter Straughan on *How to Lose Friends*, and during that process we talked a lot about what he wanted to do next, and things that we liked, and he came up with an idea for us which we optioned. So that's how I think it works. I mean I've made over twelve films with [director] Neil Jordan, but we've never signed a piece of paper saying – you *have* to work with me. Through that process of making those movies, I made films with other film-makers. ... We came back to each other all the time because we *enjoyed* working with each other, not because we had to.

3. Mitigating uncertainty of payment

As shown in Chapter 8, research has demonstrated that financial remuneration is not an important motivator of behaviour for most creative people; however it may be for their agent, whose job it is to protect and remunerate the writer. So the question might be not how to keep the writer involved on the remuneration issue but how to keep the agent involved. One strategy is to involve the agent in some of the social meetings described above, or in creative meetings with the producer to get the agent's feedback on the new draft (some agents get more creatively involved than others). Agents are also very well connected and networked, so it may be possible to enlist their help in getting the project to certain finance sources or pieces of talent like directors and actors (some of the larger US agencies have a policy of packaging projects with their own clients). If the agent feels involved in the development and financing and can see momentum on the project then he may be more likely not to discourage the writer from doing one more rewrite beyond his contractual obligation.

A better option for the producer is to try to find some new development money, since even a small payment is better than no payment at all (as long as it is not demeaning or demotivating for the writer). Alternatively, the producer could suggest to the agent an improvement for the writer in the back-end deal or an associate producer credit in return for extra unpaid work on the project.

4. Mitigating being unable to learn as a team

One way to do this is to involve the writer during the shoot and post, which helps encourage learning from mistakes and more discussions as a group. Another way is to work regularly with the same team to build a consistent culture, as happens at companies like Sixteen Films (see the case study at the end of this chapter). That way the next script is being planned and written while the previous one is still in post, encouraging a more seamless learning and reflection process. Staying together and looking forward to the next project encourages learning from mistakes and building knowledge and trust, whereas separating the team (and working with other people) may imply blame or failure. Ken Loach's producer Rebecca O'Brien explains:

> One of the great advantages of working regularly with the same people is that you get more opportunity to make mistakes, which you can then learn from; and I do think that people can get better at doing their crafts by doing more, and that's something which is quite difficult for many film-makers to get their teeth into, because there aren't enough opportunities to work.

If maintaining the team for the next project is impossible because of other commitments, then there could be some form of learning moment built into the end of the development or production process. For successful films this can be when the team is reunited at a film festival or premiere (although these are moments when the publicizing of the film is uppermost), or there could be some informal gathering, possibly during the shoot or perhaps over a meeting followed by a celebratory social event, where the development process can be properly discussed and built upon. This then leads smoothly into discussion of the next project.

One company that is committed to formal reflective post mortems is the Hollywood animation company Pixar. It has the advantage that most of its creative and technical staff are permanently employed in the organization, so unlike most film companies it is not always assembling new freelance teams for each project. This makes it easier to have reflective post mortems, and yet there are still techniques used by Pixar that may be applicable elsewhere, as its president Ed Catmull explained in a 2008 article for the *Harvard Business Review:*

> Although people learn from the postmortems, they don't like to do them. Leaders naturally want to use the occasion to give kudos to their team members. People in general would rather talk about what went right than what went wrong. And after spending years on a film, everybody just wants to move on. Left to their own devices, people will game the system to avoid confronting the unpleasant. There are some simple techniques for overcoming these problems. One is to try to vary the way you do the postmortems. By definition, they're supposed to be about lessons learned, so if you repeat the same format, you tend to find the same lessons, which isn't productive. Another is to ask each group to list the top five things they would do again and the top five things they wouldn't do. The balance between the positive and the negative helps make it a safer environment.[10]

Pixar is rightly famous for its ability to manage creativity and champion innovation, and it emphasizes creative teamwork and peer review as an intrinsic part of its culture, from the origination of the idea onwards.

> Unlike most other studios, we have never bought scripts or movie ideas from the outside. All of our stories, worlds, and characters were created internally by our community of artists. ... After *Toy Story 2* we changed the mission of our development department. Instead of coming up with new ideas for movies (its role at most studios), the department's job is to assemble small incubation teams to help directors refine their own ideas to a point where they can convince John [Lassetter] and our other senior filmmakers that those ideas have the potential to be great films. Each team typically consists of a director, a writer, some artists, and some storyboard people. The development department's goal is to find individuals who will work effectively together. During this incubation stage, you can't judge teams by the material they're producing because it's so rough – there are many problems and open questions. But you can assess whether the teams' social dynamics are

healthy and whether the teams are solving problems and making progress.[11]

Again the emphasis is on the power of the team above the power of the individual idea. The formation and effectiveness of teams is the subject of the next part of the chapter.

Development teams: forming, norming and storming

Chapter 5 showed that most development teams are not static – they develop, change and evolve. For some of the reasons already outlined, film teams can be more unstable than conventional business teams; however, there is also a good body of literature about the phases that most teams go through. One of the most influential thinkers in this field is Bruce Tuckman, who examined fifty different research studies of group development and proposed a unifying model, which identified the stages of *forming, storming, norming* and *performing*, before the group either disbands or goes back to some form of re-forming. This is summarized and adapted in Table 11.1.

In order to get to a high level of performance the group has to go through the disruptive process of *storming*, which involves conflict, disagreement, and even hostility. Some groups never perform properly, because the conflict between different people (leading to a lack of trust) or lack of agreement on a shared mission means that the storming phase never moves to *norming* and then *performing* (perhaps this is what the film industry would call 'creative differences'). It could be argued that the film development process means that the team changes so often and is subject to so many newcomers that it is frequently forced back into forming and storming. Maybe this is why some creative projects stay in the period of storming (for example, combative development meetings that do not reach proper trust and cooperation), and do not progress to effective team working.

There is a further propensity to revert to storming because of the unequal nature of the team: initially the writer is doing most of the work and is being critiqued by the others, which can lead to resentment from the writer and drives the group back into storming rather than performance mode. It could also be suggested that all creatives make these stages harder, because they resist being led, instinctively rebel from teams, and often want intellectually to challenge the status quo (maintaining storming). Add in the power of individual egos and a desire to protect personal vision, and it is amazing that film development teams ever succeed at all.

However, the leader (or producer) needs to note that norming must not be allowed to stifle dissent or argument – otherwise it prevents creativity. Too much group hegemony and agreement might create a team culture that resists challenge or change. It may be suggested that to be at its most creative, or endlessly re-creative and challenging, a group needs to be kept closer to storming, and not allowed to become *too* cohesive (this is in

Table 11.1 Stages of group development and performance, summarized from Tuckman, and adapted also to show leadership and culture[12]

	Interpersonal relationships and behaviour (the way members act and relate to one another)	Group task activity (interaction as related to the task itself)	The role of the leader/manager/culture
Forming: (testing and dependence)	Testing and dependence. Establishment of dependency relationships with leaders, other group members, or pre-existing standards. Orientation, testing and dependence. High anxiety levels as members attempt to create an impression and influence one another. But possibly externally polite.	Orientation to the task. Unclear objectives, uninvolvement, uncommitted members, confusion, low morale, hidden feelings, competition, poor listening, politeness.	The supervisor of the team tends to be directive during this phase. Clear leadership. Orientation accomplished through testing, to identify the boundaries of interpersonal and task behaviours; establishment of dependency relationships with leaders and other group members. Key moment for culture: the first anxiety moment.
Storming: (resistance to group influence and task needs)	Intra-group conflict and polarization around interpersonal issues. These behaviours serve as resistance to group influence and task requirements. Symptoms: lack of cohesion, hidden agendas, confrontation, volatility, resentment, anger, inconsistency, and maybe even failure. Some relationships in the group may be damaged in this period, and may never recover.	Internal resistance to group influence and task requirements. Team members put views forcefully – conflict, hostility, disagreement. Emotional response to task demands and inter-group rivalry, which illustrate a struggle for status and control in the group. If storming is successful there may be agreement on more structures and procedures.	Supervisors of the team during this phase may be more accessible, but still need to be directive in their guidance of decision-making, especially to prevent too much conflict. Balance between control and freedom necessary. Culture is already forming as group members watch and listen to one another.
Norming: (openness to other group members)	The beginning of cooperation. Team members adjust their behaviour to each other as they develop work habits – begin to trust each other. In-group feeling and cohesiveness develop; new standards evolve and new roles are adopted. Resistance is overcome, more listening, identifying strengths and weaknesses.	Open exchange of relevant interpretations; intimate, personal opinions are able to be expressed. Questioning performance, review/clarify objectives, change or confirm roles. 'Small wins' and progress may confirm success of approach.	Supervisors of the team tend to be more participative than in earlier stages. The team has to function. Team members can be expected to take more responsibility for making decisions and for their professional behaviour. Group culture, the way we do things round here, is now starting to be embedded.

	Interpersonal relationships and behaviour (the way members act and relate to one another)	Group task activity (interaction as related to the task itself)	The role of the leader/manager/culture
Performing: (constructive action)	Roles become flexible and functional, structural issues have been resolved, high levels of task performance. Behaviour is supportive of task performance. Group coherence, pride, concern for people in the team.	Group energy is channelled into the task. The team members are competent, autonomous and able to handle the decision-making process. Interpersonal structure becomes the tool of task activities; group energy is channelled into the task; solutions can emerge. Confidence, high morale, success.	The leader of the team is very participative: the team can run itself. If the team is successful the culture becomes strong – learnt from successful activity. (Note: Teams in this phase may lose their creativity if the norming/performing behaviours become too strong and stifle dissent, and the team begins to exhibit groupthink/homogeneity.)
EITHER: Return to Storming or Re-forming	Disagreement about the way forward (possibly due to failures or mistakes or drift) sparks internal rivalry, resistance, lack of commitment, and a return to storming. Some relationships break down and people leave or are replaced.	Reassessment of tasks and strategy. Many long-standing teams will go through these cycles many times as they react to changing circumstances and new members; or the return to storming may cause the group to split up.	The supervisor/leader may decide to replace members of the team, or there may be a change in leadership. Either may cause the team to revert to storming as the new people challenge the existing norms and dynamics of the team, and affect the new culture of the team.
OR: Adjourning (breaking up the team)	The team breaks up, either due to disagreement, or on purpose because the task is finished. Anxiety about separation and termination, sadness, range of feelings towards leader and group members. Disengagement.	Completing the task and breaking up the team. Evaluation and self-evaluation. Success or failure?	The supervisor is again a leader: directive and evaluatory. It may be the supervisor who triggers the closure of the team.

keeping with the research of Boynton and Fischer in their 2005 book on *Virtuoso Teams*, where they show that controlled conflict and competitiveness encourage high performance[13]). As a result you need a form of perpetual but controlled *re*-storming.

The same applies to new members of the team. The danger is that teams are likely to choose new people in their own image, where sometimes they may *need* more challenge and disruption. When correctly handled, the arrival of new people can stimulate and re-energize a group, rather than destabilize it. A good example is the animation director Brad Bird (*The Incredibles*), who was employed at Pixar specifically to shake up the company culture and introduce new, exciting elements to their work:

> When [Steve] Jobs, [John] Lasseter, and [Ed] Catmull approached Bird they said, 'The only thing we're afraid of is getting complacent. We need to bring in outside people so we keep throwing ourselves off balance,' recalls Bird. 'So I was brought here to cause a certain amount of disruption. I've been *fired* for being disruptive several times, but this is first time I've been *hired* for it.'[14]

Furthermore, a team that is too homogeneous and not diverse enough may not reach the creative storming period. They will go for the easy solution rather than confront the problem of bigger solutions. This comes back to the importance of choosing the right members for the team in the first place (as argued by Meredith Belbin in Chapter 4 and Teresa Amabile in Chapter 9).

To conclude: an effective team is one that has shared aims and objectives, open expression of feeling and clear communication, a balanced range of diverse skills, the power and resources to operate autonomously, strong commitment to the group (but also trust and loyalty between the people in it), and overall a shared belief in the group's values and culture.[15] Note that in a company that is dominated by a strong and controlling leader (for example, an entrepreneur prone to micro-management) the existing hierarchy or management culture may prevent the constructive chaos of storming within a work team, and thus stop the team gaining enough internal autonomy and performing at a proper level (coming up with anything original). The same type of problem can be seen in brainstorming sessions that are over-managed or where ideas are closed down too quickly. Again the issue of control vs. freedom comes to the forefront of creative management.

There have been several mentions of the importance of team culture and company culture, so the next half of the chapter will examine this in more detail, and explain why it is so vital to understand it at a company level as well as at a team level. Many of these issues are also vital to building sales companies and distribution companies, since they too are highly dependent on people and contacts, and like producers their reputation is based on their track record and the next projects coming down the supply chain.

Why is organization culture so important for a production company?

More than most companies, media and film organizations rely on creativity and intellectual property to generate income because they constantly have to create new product and reinvent themselves. The company only has a history of past successes, contacts, experience, reputation and 'heat'. They have lots of potential, but few valuable assets, other than people, and this makes it difficult to raise significant equity investment for operating capital for media organizations. They are difficult to value and therefore difficult to sell and provide a return to the investor (especially those without large libraries or successful returning TV format commissions or exclusive access to key onscreen talent). The only thing to sell as an indicator of future potential is the people, the internal culture (which ties the people together) and the past track record. Such organizations are therefore highly dependent on those creative people – who could easily leave and work elsewhere. Therefore it is vital for a media business to figure out how to get hold of the best creatives, such as writers and directors, get the best out of them, and keep hold of them. Loyalty and high creative performance are more likely if the individual feels 'at home' in the company, as well as valued and supported. It is the existing culture that helps them to feel these things, and therefore helps to attract and then retain them.

Box 11.2 Why culture matters to a producer/entrepreneur[16]

- As a producer, a strong *organizational culture* is your single best chance of being able to sell your business as *a going concern*, because the company will keep going, even without you or your star director, because of the culture.
- It changes you from a one-man band (maybe with an assistant and an address book) to an organization (that is sellable). A key reason that many entrepreneurs fail to grow and sell their organizations is that they micro-manage and do not allow employee or team autonomy.
- It makes the organization *unique*, the team strong and the product reliable. Culture works on film sets, development teams, even marketing. It encourages consistency. Alignment between employee values and company values/business strategy encourages conviction and loyalty.
- A strong culture does not just include permanent staff – it could include regular freelancers, collaborators, creatives (writers and directors and shooting crews). But they must all 'buy in' to the culture.

- Culture also affects the way the public perceive your company and product, especially with larger companies. The public's contact with employees on phone lines or through reading interviews in the media helps build trust in the company and an understanding of *what you stand for*. Internal culture and externally perceived philosophy may be a large part of the created brand awareness. The extra element of *philosophy* in the *marketing mix* is represented by culture.
- Above all, culture enables you and your company to *replicate*. Like DNA. It reduces reliance on single talent (like one film director or piece of creative or business talent), encourages mentorship, bringing on new talent, and loyalty.

Professor Edgar Schein argues that levels of organizational culture can be classified into three broad categories: first, the things that you can sense about the behaviour of people and the appearance of the workplace; second, the publicly espoused values of the organization (like the mottoes or mission statements); and finally, the underlying beliefs and unconscious assumptions about what works and what does not work. These are sometimes in sync with one another, but also sometimes at odds (for example when a re-branding or a new slogan does not really reflect the way people behave or what the organization really stands for. What people say and what people do are often very different). This is explored in detail in Fig. 11.2.

If a prospective writer is visiting the company office, and wondering whether to work with this producer or financier, all these conscious and unconscious cultural signals are subliminally or overtly influencing the answers to his questions: 'Do I like these people?' 'How do they treat the people who work with them?' 'Do people seem happy?' 'Do I fit in here?' 'What do they stand for?' 'Will they protect my story?' and finally 'Do I trust and want to be with these people for at least the next three years?' But this doesn't just affect the writer-for-hire. If the visiting prospective writer is still deciding on the company to option his idea or hot literary property, then the answers to these questions will decide whether or not the producer gets the rights, or whether it goes to another company that *feels* more suitable for the writer.

So how does this work in reality? One instance is the husband-and-wife producer team Stephen Woolley and Elizabeth Karlsen at Number 9 Films. When talking to people who have worked for them, the words 'family' and 'friendly' regularly crop up; the office is staffed with people who have been associated with them for many years. In the case interview in Chapter 5 Stephen Woolley mentioned that 'the writer becomes part of the *family*, the family that make the film', and that the writer would not be refused on set and in the cutting room. They invite writers to do script meetings at their family home in the country over weekends, so that they feel trusted and part of their lives. These are cultural behavioural decisions that send out clear messages, and they may encourage writers to return and work with them again.

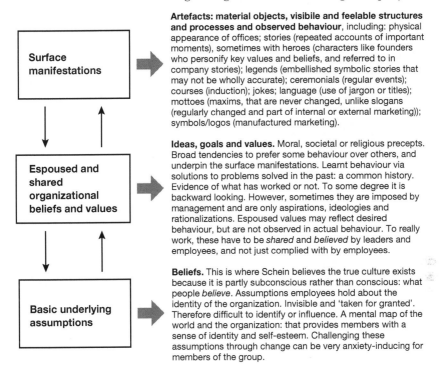

Surface manifestations

→ **Artefacts: material objects, visibile and feelable structures and processes and observed behaviour,** including: physical appearance of offices; stories (repeated accounts of important moments), sometimes with heroes (characters like founders who personify key values and beliefs, and referred to in company stories); legends (embellished symbolic stories that may not be wholly accurate); ceremonials (regular events); courses (induction); jokes; language (use of jargon or titles); mottoes (maxims, that are never changed, unlike slogans (regularly changed and part of internal or external marketing)); symbols/logos (manufactured marketing).

Espoused and shared organizational beliefs and values

→ **Ideas, goals and values.** Moral, societal or religious precepts. Broad tendencies to prefer some behaviour over others, and underpin the surface manifestations. Learnt behaviour via solutions to problems solved in the past: a common history. Evidence of what has worked or not. To some degree it is backward looking. However, sometimes they are imposed by management and are only aspirations, ideologies and rationalizations. Espoused values may reflect desired behaviour, but are not observed in actual behaviour. To really work, these have to be *shared* and *believed* by leaders and employees, and not just complied with by employees.

Basic underlying assumptions

→ **Beliefs.** This is where Schein believes the true culture exists because it is partly subconscious rather than conscious: what people *believe*. Assumptions employees hold about the identity of the organization. Invisible and 'taken for granted'. Therefore difficult to identify or influence. A mental map of the world and the organization: that provides members with a sense of identity and self-esteem. Challenging these assumptions through change can be very anxiety-inducing for members of the group.

Figure 11.2 Organizational culture: Schein's levels (1985, 2004, 2010)[17]

In short, the way the producer and development executive behave and deal with writers will reflect the culture of the company, and will tell prospective financiers and collaborators a lot about the producer's intent and whether to work with them going forward. It is also reflected in many other decisions, from the appearance of the office to the choice of projects on the development slate. In terms of building a good reputation and a distinctive identity, the power of organizational culture in establishing a creative company cannot be underestimated.

How leaders create and change organizational culture

Organizational culture is usually established by the founders or leaders, and the way that they behave influences the way everyone else behaves (see Box 11.3 on how leaders establish organizational culture). In the initial anxiety and vacuum at the moment of formation of a group or company, a great deal of influence can be wielded by a charismatic leader figure with a clear plan and vision. What once were only the founder's assumptions and beliefs eventually become the group's shared assumptions; once they have been proved right and successful.

Box 11.3 How do leaders create and embed culture?[18]

Primary (embedding)

- Personal charisma and communication skills (including personal behaviour, such as fairness, consistency, passion, emotional outbursts)
- What leaders pay attention to, measure and control on a regular basis
- How leaders react to critical incidents and crises
- How leaders allocate resources
- Deliberate role modelling, teaching and coaching
- How leaders allocate rewards and status
- How leaders recruit, select, promote and excommunicate.

Secondary (reinforcement)

- Organization design and structure, systems, and procedures
- Rites and rituals of the organization
- Design of physical space, environment and buildings
- Stories about important people and events (shared history, some controlled, some uncontrollable)
- Formal statements of organizational philosophy, mission, creeds and charters.

Edgar Schein argues that culture develops first from the beliefs, values and assumptions of founders (communicated to the rest of the group by personal charisma or day-to-day management behaviour); second, the learning experience of the group as the organization evolves (success helps reinforce the vision of the leader, and helps embed the group's experience as valuable and therefore to be repeated); and third, the beliefs, values and assumptions brought in by new members, once they are accepted by the group (although there may be a delay before this new influence is shown to be successful and is accepted).[19]

However as companies grow larger the situation becomes more complex. The company could shift from an entrepreneurial ad hoc structure and operational style to a more bureaucratic one, where the leader has less day-to-day contact with staff and a layer of middle managers starts to develop. Most production companies are founded and led by producers who started as creatives, and they might not really *want* to be managers and administrators (or might not be very good at it), and may be bad at delegating creative decisions. As the company grows, new employees bring their own beliefs and assumptions, which can threaten the existing company ones (large numbers of new arrivals as the result of rapid growth or merger can be a major threat to the culture). The leader may be unable to try to influence newcomers in a larger organization in the way he was able to influence the smaller start-up group, and indeed some people work better with smaller groups, rather than by mass communication.

As a result of growth, the *dominant culture* often splits into sub-groups or *subcultures*, in part because human beings are social creatures who like to 'belong' to small teams rather than huge ones, so they instinctively form smaller groupings (in the same way that groups form social cliques and friendships within even quite small offices). Larger organizations can develop subcultures around many different areas of activity (for example, there can be subcultures around departments or job functions or geographical locations or products, each with their own leader and reflecting their own preoccupations or systems or geographical region), and there can even be *counter-cultures* where the subcultures adopt a position that is consciously or subconsciously opposed to the dominant culture. In addition, company governance sometimes shifts from the founder to a chief executive and board of directors, which can result in strategy drift and, more importantly, culture drift (and increased short-termism due to limited terms of office and demands of shareholders for profits), all of which has an impact on the culture.

These larger company issues do not usually affect film companies, which tend to stay small (although integration can result in larger companies, often with strong subcultures around their subsidiaries such as distribution, production and sales). However, these are very relevant issues for larger television production companies that diversify into lots of different programmes and production units. The larger the company, inevitably the greater the turnover of staff and therefore the infusion of outsiders (including radically introduced outsiders such as a new CEO or senior manager). The result can be a large organization which does not have a uniform culture, and is less capable of being controlled by the leader.

The problem with corporate cultures and subcultures is that they instinctively resist change and disruption, because culture is intrinsically conservative, based as it is on what has happened in the past and what has been proved to work before. This means that companies may recruit similar people who fit safely into the existing culture, rather than recruiting riskier individuals who may be challenging; and over time this can cause a company to drift from being creative and innovative to being predictable and unresponsive. It also means that the culture can be very resistant if a new leader comes in with new ideas, or if corporate strategy or internal processes have to change due to external competition or changing business imperatives – much as most individuals are naturally resistant and anxious about change. The 'way we do things round here' can become suffocating, inflexible and counter-creative, and it is vital for any leader undertaking managed change fully to understand cultural resistance and how to overcome and transform it over time, including the use of small wins, achieving the support of middle management, challenging and unlearning existing behaviour, and embedding new norms and values.[20] On the plus side, once and if the changes have been shown to be successful or profitable they will quickly become absorbed into the new culture.

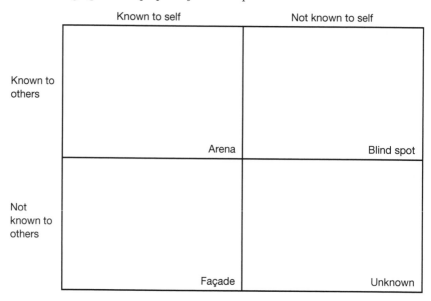

	Known to self	Not known to self
Known to others	Arena	Blind spot
Not known to others	Façade	Unknown

Figure 11.3 Johari window: identifying different perceptions of behaviour[22]

The complexity of studying culture

Into this complexity comes another problem for the leader: it is actually rather difficult to study and analyse culture, especially in your own organization, particularly if it includes your own behaviour and other people's responses to it. Similarly, the way that a group perceives itself may be different from the way in which it is perceived by others, as shown in Fig. 11.3 (this mismatch is at the heart of some of the comedy in Ricky Gervais' TV series *The Office*). This is why psychotherapists are never able to analyse themselves – they have to get a colleague to do it for them – and why *know thyself* is one of the hardest aphorisms to live up to. Culture is an abstract and shifting concept and varies according to the subjective viewpoint of the observer. Many different authors have written about the complexity of observing and identifying organizational culture, and the importance of culture in understanding resistance to corporate change or reform, and a selection of further reading is in the notes at the end of the chapter.[21]

Note: Figure 11.4 shows the impact of different cultures: showing the complexity of commissioning adapted screenplays (and the distance of the screenwriter from the final market); the interaction of wider societal culture, organizational cultures, and the culture of the development team; the basic power transactions of finance; audience reception; and likely market research into projected audience response. The line linking the development team culture with the financiers shows the advantage of raising finance from sources that match the vision and culture of the team. Sometimes one of the financiers can be on board the project and part of the development team from the start, and therefore be within the development team dotted box.

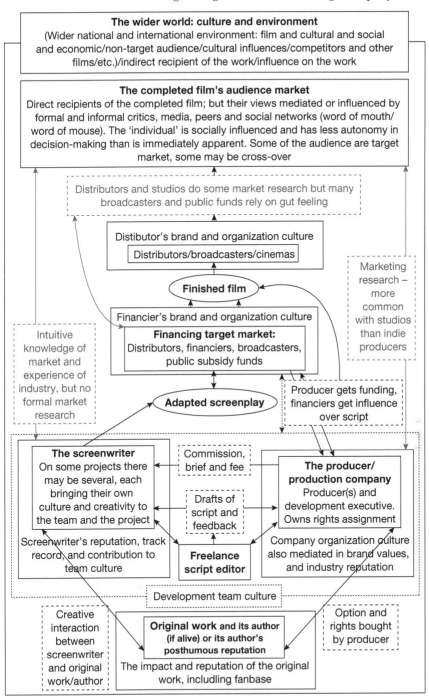

Figure 11.4 Representation of the screenplay commissioning and distribution process

The complexity of culture across the entire commissioning and development process

To conclude: Chapter 2 (about the value chain) has already shown that the producer's relationships with writers and directors can create a team that provides some form of continuity in a business that otherwise has to cope with a fragmented and multi-player value chain. This enables the producer to build a company with a track record and future potential, rather than a series of separate individual films; and the culture of the company is vital in helping to achieve this, despite the complexity of understanding and controlling it. This chapter has shown the importance of understanding culture, since a strong creative culture can help attract the right talent, and the following case interviews will show how it can also help retain talent.

At its core, culture is all about values and identity: the values of the leader and the composite values of the people as they behave when they are in the team. However there is a further complexity if you consider that the entire process of financing, distribution and audience reception is in fact a series of interactions between lots of different organizational cultures and value systems, many of which are not directly connected, as well as the complication of macro-national cultures (as represented in Fig. 11.4). This cuts to the heart of issues around value and the reception of creative ideas, which are central returning themes in this book.

Case interviews: Retaining and developing talent

Stephen Woolley (producer): We often work with the same people again, because the process has been rewarding in terms of what they've brought to the table and what we've brought to the table. For instance, Mark O'Rowe wrote *Intermission*, which was a big success in Ireland and a big hit for John Crowley, the director, who subsequently is on everyone's list of A list directors. And then Mark wrote a script for us called *Perrier's Bounty*, which wasn't so successful; but Mark is now writing *End of Sleep* for us, so the fact that *Perrier's Bounty* wasn't successful doesn't deter us from wanting to work with Mark because we didn't perceive it to be his fault. We have a great loyalty to the people that we work with, given that the experience has been good. So Peter Straughan, who wrote *How to Lose Friends and Alienate People*, is writing a time travel film for us at the moment. David Nicholls wrote *When Did You Last See Your Father*, and is now writing *Great Expectations*. There's a much more loyal appreciation of writers here (in the UK) than I think you'll find in Hollywood.

Julie Baines (producer): It's about getting writers and directors at an early stage and supporting them, nurturing them and helping them make their first film. Being very supportive, but also allowing their creativity to come through. I'm a team player, and I really believe that the team makes the film, and that collaboration is healthy creatively for a project.

Stephen Woolley: I'm talking to Billy [Ivory, writer of *Made in Dagenham*], because *Made in Dagenham* won the Variety Club of Great Britain Best British Film of the Year. I've invited Billy to the ceremony. He's part of the team that made the movie, and I think that's really important. Every year we have a Christmas party where we invite all of our writers and directors and people to come and chat and exchange ideas. We don't want them to be paranoid, nor are we paranoid, so I think it's an important factor of what we are like (as a company).

Kate Lawrence (development executive): I suppose we're very collaborative and from the off you would know that Elizabeth [Karlsen] and Stephen [Woolley] are going to be hands on through the development process. ... They're very supportive, they really do back their writers, directors and cast, and will fight for people's corners if they believe in it. We think a lot about who we attach to write and direct things, and we want those relationships to continue. So there is no financial reward for them to stay with us (like a retainer fee), but I guess it's just because they like the way we work, or they like our aesthetic and get what our taste is.

Rebecca O'Brien (producer): The people who are best at producing get the hang of the fact that you need to be developing your next project before you finish shooting the one before. I think we first crossed that bridge when we did *My Name Is Joe*. That gave us enough income to develop the next one.

Sam Lavender (head of development, Film4): The one thing you have to do as a producer is have good ongoing relationships with talent. I could talk for ages about quite how hard it is being a producer. You've got to have the skills to be able to play off financiers, put a deal together, time it right, take it to market at the right time, all of that stuff; but if you do all that, and during the process you haven't maintained your relationship with the people who, let's face it, the financiers are *really* interested in – the screenwriters and the directors – then you've got to start all over again.

Case study: The power of the team and the creative triangle in action – Sixteen Films: a formula for critical acclaim and good business[23]

Sixteen Films is a good example of the creative triangle in action, plus a strong company culture. Producer Rebecca O'Brien and director Ken Loach have worked together since she co-produced his comeback film *Hidden Agenda* in 1990. Paul Laverty has been Loach's main screenwriter since *Carla's Song* in 1996. Together the three of them have worked on films including *My Name is Joe* (1998), *Sweet Sixteen* (2002), *A Fond Kiss* (2004) and the Palme d'Or-winning *The Wind that Shakes the Barley* (2006). More recently they all worked on *It's a Free World* (2007), *Looking for Eric* (2009), *Route Irish* (2010) and *The Angels' Share* (2012).

The basic idea for the next Loach film usually emerges through conversations first between Paul Laverty and Ken Loach and then with Rebecca O'Brien, often based around key political or social issues more than individual stories. One idea becomes favoured as the next possible project, and Laverty goes off and does about six months of research into the basic concept or setting, often while Loach and O'Brien are financing or prepping the previous film (a good example of project overlap, so that there is a supply of new material for the slate). Through that research process one or two specific characters 'bubble up' as the key focus for the story, and plot points and story arcs emerge. The story develops through interviewing people and researching background, as though it was a documentary rather than pure invention (this is similar to the way that Simon Beaufoy sometimes works).

The next stage is that Laverty delivers a document of character and plot notes, but not yet a formal treatment. That is then talked through with Loach and O'Brien, and then Laverty will sit down and write the first draft, over a month or two. At this stage producer O'Brien usually avoids applying for development funding from production financiers, like the BBC or Film4; she prefers to retain control and freedom by relying on company income from the exploitation of other films and a couple of successful MEDIA slate applications (European subsidy money). This allows them to decide with whom to make the film once the script is already well developed. It also means that treatments are not sent out at an early stage – the first thing financiers will see is a completed and well-honed script.

After that first draft is delivered, Loach and Laverty and their long-standing script editor Roger Smith get together for a thorough script meeting lasting a day or two. Smith is an equally trusted member of the team and another long-term collaborator: he and Loach first worked together at the BBC in the 1960s, including working on the BBC's *Wednesday Play* (Smith was the story editor of the first series and wrote the script for the film *Catherine*, which was Loach's first production for the BBC). Smith was also the scriptwriter on Loach's *Up the Junction*, and they have worked together on every Loach film since *Land and Freedom* (1995).

Loach, Laverty and Smith (with perhaps a few general notes from O'Brien) go through the first draft methodically scene by scene and talk about any issues and problems. The approach is simple: they start on page 1 and work through to the end, talking over all the notes and working out what's needed to make the story work, as producer Rebecca O'Brien explains:

> Unless you take that process in a very practical, pragmatic way, you never get through it, and you need to just sit down and do it in a sort of solid way, and that's always seemed to me to be the best way to work on a script – just doggedly plodding through it. The magic comes as a result of the correct chemicals going in; it's an alchemical process. It's always simply about what makes the drama work best, and putting things in a good order and working out where the surprises should come.

Then Laverty goes off with the notes and comes back a few weeks later with another draft, and the script conference and redrafting process starts over again. Since the four of them have worked together across many projects there is a lot of trust and understanding about what is expected, so it often only takes two or three drafts before there is a script that is ready to go out to finance. Meanwhile, O'Brien will have been talking to the usual distributors and financiers who tend to back Loach's films, so by the time they receive the working draft they are ready for what the project may be like.

Whilst O'Brien is assembling the production finance, they go into the start of soft pre-production: a six-month period where Loach goes to the locations with Laverty and the location manager, starts working with a casting director to find key cast, and begins doing his own research for the story. What Loach discovers in his location and casting research will continue to inform the script. O'Brien suggests that there is an advantage to starting soft pre-production during development in order to keep the momentum up on the project:

> You so often have to kick start a film into production, you might as well be preparing it. In the modern film financing world, so many financiers insist on knowing who the cast is, where the locations are … so many of the basic production bits of information need to be found out for their purposes before they will give you any money. And in most cases that's the most difficult thing to do because you don't normally have the development money, to finance that process. … Ideally we do the research and dovetail nicely into production … for instance usually we've got most of the locations and most of the cast before we even start official pre-production.

This is where a development slate with a public subsidy fund like the European Commission's MEDIA scheme enables the producer to fund soft prep as well as script writing, and keep up the momentum on the project. The script is revised during the recces, until a final shooting script is agreed before the production starts.

Screenwriter Paul Laverty is also involved during actors' rehearsals in the last couple of weeks before the shoot: the actors are finding out who their characters are and Laverty helps them fill in their back story and the set-up for the story:

> For instance if we've got an army in the film, we'll send the cast off to an improvised boot camp. Or if we have a teacher we'll send them to a school. If we have a family we send the members out for a day or two together, so that they can bond. So that's what we'd be doing with the cast before we shoot. And Paul will invent things for them to do with Ken's help or vice versa. And Ken might stage a sort of prequel scene which he would get the actors to improvise in that period.

Once the finance is closed and the shoot starts Laverty is not regularly on set because most of the shoot is carefully planned, in part because Loach and O'Brien shoot the film 'in sequence', starting at the beginning and going through the story so that the actors are themselves carried on the journey. Furthermore, Loach gives them the script pages only a day or so before the scene is shot, and sometimes gives only some of the actors the script, so that the others have to respond to what is being said without being prepared for it. At the start of the film even the lead actors do not know how the film ends, or indeed whether their character will live or die. For example, in the filming of *Land and Freedom*, which was set during the Spanish Civil War, one character was wired up with explosive effects to simulate being shot, and until the sequence was filmed the other actors did not know that that character was going to die. Capturing the responses of the other actors is an important part of the technique, as Loach is on record explaining: 'Acting is about reacting, isn't it? The first time you hear something, you respond to it in a way that you never would if you were to hear it again.'[24]

This means that sometimes Laverty is called upon to alter the script to accommodate one of these spontaneous reaction moments that is changing the characters' relationships, as O'Brien explained:

> As we shoot, what sometimes takes place is that things happen that we didn't expect to happen. So, a character who's been surprised by something may react in a different way to the script, which is a perfectly legitimate way to react, but then we might need to change the next scene. For instance, when we did *Bread and Roses*, when the main woman was told by her sister in the film about her previous life, and the fact that she had prostituted herself for money and that was the money that paid for her sister to come up to LA, we really thought that the reaction would be that she would run away and that she would be upset. But what happened was that made them closer, so we needed Paul to come and rejig everything. ... We might decide to fill a gap with a new scene, in which case Paul will do the new scene but he's not around all the time.

The difference between Ken Loach and Mike Leigh (to whom he is often compared) is that Loach fully scripts the film but only gradually gives it to the actors as they shoot (so that they improvise reactions on set); whereas Leigh develops the script with the actors *before* writing the script, and whilst the actors may improvise some dialogue on set, they always know the outcome of the story.

Script editor Roger Smith and Laverty are also involved again after the first rough cut of the film, advising on how to shape the next cuts (usually working with Loach's editor Jonathan Morris, another member of the regular team). Since Smith is not involved during the shoot he brings an extra distance when viewing the rough cut, and is said to be quite ruthless at removing anything that does not drive the story.

A further indication of the closeness of the team is that when in 2002 Loach and O'Brien decided to set up their own company, they also asked Laverty to become an associate director:

He needed to be part of the company simply because he's the third part of the tripod that holds the whole thing together. And although he's not involved in the running of the company, it makes sense that he's part of it ... we needed to do something which said that he was part of Sixteen Films.

Not only does it send a signal to Laverty that he is an intrinsic and trusted part of what they do, but it also sends that signal to the outside world. Furthermore, projects are developed without formal writer's agreements in place until a few months before pre-production, because the trust relationship between them is so strong. Even the production fees are very similar, which removes the need for complex negotiations, as O'Brien explained:

Paul and I have a tacit agreement that we should be paid equally, so Ken gets a fee and then Paul and I get a bit less, but not much less and we get the same, because it reflects the equality of our roles.

This approach to sharing similar fees to encourage parity and sense of a team was also characteristic of the low-budget thriller *Shallow Grave* (the feature film that launched Danny Boyle's film career). Producer Andrew MacDonald, writer John Hodge and director Danny Boyle all worked for the same fee and the same potential profit share (the three went on to work together on *Trainspotting* and *The Beach*).[25]

To conclude: Paul Laverty is involved in an ongoing creative interaction with Loach and the story and the actors from the genesis of the idea, through recces and rehearsals to rewrites on the shoot and work with the editor on the edit – a creative collaborator who is there from beginning to end. This explains why Loach, Laverty and O'Brien are regarded in the industry as a creative triumvirate, rather than just people working together. In a way development never really starts and stops – it is a central part of making the film; and starting the next one. For a company that has made seven Loach films in only nine years, plus three shorts and two feature films with other directors, something seems to be working well.

12 Working with the Hollywood studio system

Being independent in a world of prefabricated daydreams

> The Hollywood producer changes the director because the film's not working. He changes the writer because it's Tuesday.
>
> (Film industry joke)

The last chapter was about using culture and teamwork to build a production company with a strong track record based on creative value. However, there often comes a point during a successful company's growth when the lure of Hollywood beckons, especially if one film is very successful. The producer may be offered a development output deal, and the writer and director may be approached to work on studio projects. The purpose of this chapter is to consider some of the key issues that may arise and highlight the differences between independent and studio development; with emphasis on how some smaller companies making independent specialist films manage to survive and play the Hollywood system. There are already other books that cover development in Hollywood in detail, and a selection of these are mentioned in the notes section at the end of the book.[1]

Studio development and the distribution machine

As shown in Chapter 2, Hollywood and its film studios operate in a very different world from independent film-making, because the film is often developed, produced and distributed internationally within a single integrated company. It is important to emphasize that studios are not really production companies at all. They are distribution companies that gain control of content by bankrolling production and then controlling the global distribution channels to market.[2] Studios spend more money releasing a film than they do making it. The internet threatens to challenge their control because it is a way of marketing that they do not control, but cannot afford not to exploit, especially due to the decline of the DVD.

Therefore the studios only develop what they foresee producing and distributing. Their ownership of distribution means that marketing knowledge can feed into early development decisions, in a way that is impossible in the indie sector (where the producer does not control distribution). The downside of this is that studios are prone to invest heavily in things that have done well before, leading to franchises, remakes and predictable mainstream product. This mitigates against creativity but reduces the corporate risk and enables studio executives to protect themselves against responsibility for box office failure. Screenwriter Olivia Hetreed has worked in the UK and the US, and she confirms that it is the awareness and focus on the market that is the key in the US:

> I think the difference is more to do with their confidence and knowledge of the market and of the kind of film they're trying to make and so on. There's a clarity about what it is they want ... the bigger players look at the back end as well as the front end of the process.

For the producer the advantage of being in development with the US studios and other national studios or larger broadcasters is that they have the ability to finance production and distribution, and therefore it is a 'one-stop-shop' where you are embarking on a process that could lead seamlessly to the cinema screen (since some of them own those screens too). However, a recent survey estimated that every year about 2000 new project ideas or scripts are added to the Hollywood development rosta; and that at any one moment there are a total of roughly 5000 projects in various stages of development, which is of course more than will actually get made.[3] So getting into development is only the start of a very long and competitive process, subject to wider corporate influences that do not affect independent development in the same way, such as the influence of the corporate parent and its brand (all the major studios are part of larger media conglomerates); changes of key personnel (if the development executive who optioned your project leaves for another studio, for example); and changes of internal politics and corporate strategic direction (such as a switch in taste towards other genres of film or the purchase of the studio by another conglomerate).

Sometimes studios acquire projects that they do *not* intend actually to produce. First, there is the *vanity acquisition*, where they want to develop a relationship with the writer or director, even if they do not like the particular script they are putting into development. Second, if they already have a similar project in development, they may acquire a script simply to remove the competition; as Hollywood lawyer John Cones explains:

> The effect of putting a film project into development at a major studio/distributor is, in most cases, simply to take it off the market. Some in the industry actually accuse the studios from time to time of intentionally acquiring rights to certain projects, just to eliminate the competition of a project that is similar to one already in development, without, of course, informing those tied to the doomed project.[4]

In the past the US studios have only had to pay close attention to the home market and overseas income has been the icing on the cake. However, the international market is becoming increasingly valuable and flops in the home market can still be huge financial successes once they have played internationally. Conversely, foreign films produced for the right budget for a foreign market can also play in other territories, and even in a niche way in the US, all providing profitable activity for the existing distribution infrastructure. Over time this may cause a shift in which projects are being developed and where their key distribution markets may lie. US film studios and television networks are increasingly targeting the emerging BRICS nations (Brazil, Russia, India, China and South Africa), which represent around 40 per cent of the world's population and are projected to dominate the world's economic growth in the coming decades.[5] This may also result in a rise in studio output deals with local production companies, especially those with commercial product in the specialist budget range; and already Universal, Fox, Sony and Disney support local language production and/or acquisition programmes. However, the studios also sometimes set up acquisitions departments to pursue this strategy, only to close them down a few years later when the need for cost-cutting arises. For example, in 2011 Warner Bros closed down its international acquisitions group in Los Angeles, and Paramount Pictures closed its worldwide acquisitions group which covered international and domestic acquisitions and local language production.[6]

The studio output deal and first look deal

The alternative between outright studio development and independent development is the producer with the *output deal* or *multi-picture deal*, where there is a formal or informal arrangement with a studio or broadcaster that all the projects he develops will be offered first to the studio for production financing (the *first look*), and in return his development costs and overheads are picked up by the studio. This option on exclusivity is how most US studio projects get developed. For the studio it ensures access to that producer and his talent social network; and for the producer it increases the odds of production finance via the studio one-stop-shop, but still enables the producer to shop the project around if the studio rejects it (although if the package changes substantially after the studio's rejection, for example by the addition of name cast or director, then the producer may have to re-offer it to the first look studio). Since producers making mainstream films in the US have to work through the studios anyway (to access production finance and the distribution network, and to get legitimacy with talent agents to get offers to stars), it makes sense also to offset their development risk with them. However, the studio overhead deal does not remove the risk of reputational damage for the producer, as Hollywood journalist Edward Epstein explains:

232 Managing creative people in film development

Each negotiation over changes in the script with writers, agents, studio executives, co-producers, potential directors, and stars risks further depleting the goodwill they need for other projects. And if these negotiations end up alienating writers (and/or their agents), as is often the case, it can complicate the task of getting other writers for future projects. On the other hand, if scripts do not conform to the expectations of the studio, producers risk losing their deal, and the status and credibility they gained from it.[7]

For the executive in charge of a fund there is also a reputational risk in turning down a first look project, as author and ex-Lucasfilm executive Jeffrey Ulin explains:

How much do I subjectively like the project, and what are the chances that if I pass on it my competitor will produce it and make me look like a fool? The second question is made more difficult because you are likely dealing with someone either famous, or if not outright famous than likely highly regarded and well connected; if that were not the case, there would be no first look relationship to begin with. The threat of taking a project across the street to a bitter rival and having the ability to actually produce it with them is very real. Hollywood is littered with the lore of so-and-so passed on that project or he had the courage/vision to get behind X. Careers are literally made and broken on these decisions.[8]

Even once a film is accepted by the studio first look deal and the studio is apparently intending to make it, the project still has to go through a further and rather nebulous financing stage, where a final draft is created, cast and director are attached, budgets approved, and the package finalized – all of which requires more funding and creative input from the studio before the final greenlight. So the project is not yet out of development hell, even if the first look has been activated. In addition, once it is accepted for production the producer cannot offer it to other studios, so sometimes a studio may activate their first look just to remove a rival project from the development market.

The other problem of dealing with the studios is that key executives can suddenly go to a different job, either inside or outside the organization, leaving projects behind them which the incoming executive may be reluctant to pick up, as writer Rob Sprackling explains:

Loads of wonderful scripts and wonderful films that really should have got made were all missed out on and never got made, because someone moved on, and a new executive came in and canned the whole thing. That's one of the reasons you have to be terribly lucky to get a movie made, because you have to happen to have an executive stay in place long enough (because it takes five, seven years for a film to just get through all the hoops it's got to get through to get made, and if it's animation it takes even longer). You've got to get enough things in place and get over the line in time; because if the executive goes before that point, it doesn't matter how close you were, it's dead, because the new guy isn't going to carry it on.

A typology of the five types of film distributed in the US

In Chapter 3 we defined the different types of British film being produced; Table 12.1 gives a definition of the different types of US film being produced, or acquired and distributed. This accentuates the distinction between Hollywood films, indie films (short for independent films and in the case of the US usually referring to films made with a New York sensibility, outside the Hollywood financing system and/or culture), and imported foreign-language films. The word 'Hollywood' is being used here to encompass the US-based major studios, mini-studios and studio-supported producers that are feeding the integrated distribution system. It is worth remembering that in the 1930s and 1940s each studio had its own brand and associated type or genre of film (such as the western or the musical), often with associated stars under exclusive contract to the studio. Today that brand distinction has largely disappeared (with the exception of animation companies like Pixar/Disney and Dreamworks) and the studios are all competing with one another across all genres.

The culture of hiring and firing writers, and a typology of power in the film studio development process

Chapter 5 proposed a typology of power in independent development. As mentioned, the big difference with the studio system is that instead of multiple external finance stakeholders, there is a single internal finance source from development to distribution, which means the power of the producer and/or studio executive is very strong from the outset and therefore there is less see-sawing of power between the players. The writer never gains the same level of initial power as he does in the first drafts of an independent film. The culture of film development in Hollywood has always accepted the regular hiring and firing of writers, but this is compensated for by higher fee payments (see the section 'Writers vs. hacks' in Chapter 8), as film journalist Mike Goodridge of Screen International explains:

> Writers are basically treated in a different way in Los Angeles. They're paid lots of money, and they rewrite and rewrite other people's material. That's how they survive and make a living. They have to develop a really tough thick skin. But if they're being paid fifty grand to write a new version of a script or rewrite somebody else's, they will just do it; and

Table 12.1 Five types of film distributed in the US

Blockbuster Hollywood	Mainstream Hollywood	Specialist Hollywood	Specialist indie	Foreign acquisitions
Tent-pole release films based on major release dates, increasingly dominated by repackaging existing properties such as remakes, sequels and spin-offs from television (either recent successes or older popular programmes like *Mission: Impossible*) or video games and other toys (*Transformers*), where audience recognition of the title or concept is predictable. Action-thriller and superhero movies dominate. The bigger returning animations also fall into this category, because of their use of star names (real or animated or both) and big campaigns based on key holiday dates (the *Shrek* franchise, *Kung Fu Panda*, all Pixar movies, etc.).	High concepts and recognizable genres, like rom-coms, thrillers, non-blockbuster science fiction, dramas, etc. This is the bulk of Hollywood output, but is now suffering from downward pressure on budgets unless big stars attached. This is where mainstream Anglo-Hollywood films are targeted, such the Brit-coms (see Chapter 3, Table 3.1). Sometimes a studio will open a mainstream romantic comedy with an actress star name on the same dates as a rival studio's action blockbuster, to try to draw the non-action audience to the relationship movie.	Arthouse films with Oscar aspirations, funded primarily out of the studio's desire to gain reputation within the Hollywood creative community, and not expected to make large profits, but may cross over to mainstream. Split between the higher budget directors (Scorcese, the Coen brothers, Lee, Eastwood, Fincher, Jackson, Burton, etc.) and the lower budget directors (Wes Anderson, Paul Anderson, Woody Allen, and international directors like Jean-Pierre Jeunet and Guillermo del Toro). This is where Anglo-Hollywood specialist films are targeted, such as *Atonement* and *The English Patient* (see Chapter 3, Table 3.1).	Arthouse American indie films, often made on very low budgets by production companies from New York or the smaller LA companies, often with a quirky feel or a dark European aesthetic. Some are picked up and break out, like *Little Miss Sunshine, Juno, Sideways* and *The Kids Are Alright.*	Foreign-language films and British films that are not made by Hollywood companies for the US market. Low budget by Hollywood standards, often quite well funded by public subsidy and broadcasters in home territories.

Blockbuster Hollywood	Mainstream Hollywood	Specialist Hollywood	Specialist indie	Foreign acquisitions
Major stars and/or special effects and/or high concept and/or franchise. Increasingly 3-D. Director sometimes has a track record in the blockbuster field ('from the director of . . .'), or may be unknown outside industry.	Major stars. Director sometimes unknown outside industry, because the film is being sold on the stars and concept, and not on the director's name. Not auteur-based.	Arthouse stars, 'serious' actors, marketed on the presence of a name director. Relatively auteur-based.	Unknown actors or niche character actors (or anything with Julianne Moore). Director may have specialist audience following (Tod Haynes, etc.). Sometimes very auteur-based.	Unknown foreign actors (speaking a different language). Directors unknown in the US, or occasionally an auteur director with specialist audience following.
Distributed internationally by US studio system or fixed output deals, with major marketing campaign.	Distributed internationally by US studio system or fixed output deals, with big marketing campaign.	Distributed internationally by US studio system or fixed output deals, with specialist marketing campaign targeted at key audience.	Acquired by local distributors, or occasionally the specialist arms of US studios (as an acquisition), with very specialist marketing campaign targeted at key cities.	Acquired by specialist arthouse local distributors, and often opened initially only in New York and LA or a few other cinemas in key cities.
Festivals: No, apart from occasionally an opening or closing gala screening.	Festivals: No.	Festivals: Yes. High profile. But not dependent on them for funding or distribution.	Dependent on festivals like Sundance and Cannes to be spotted by critics and acquisition execs and picked up for distribution.	Dependent on festivals like Cannes and Berlin and Toronto to be spotted by critics and acquisition execs and picked up for distribution.
Audience type: Mainstream, Mainstream plus, Aficionado. See Chapter 3, Table 3.2.	Audience type: Mainstream, Mainstream plus. See Chapter 3, Table 3.2.	Audience type: Mainstream plus, Aficionado, Avids/'film buffs'. See Chapter 3, Table 3.2.	Audience type: Aficionado, Avids/'film buffs'. See Chapter 3, Table 3.2.	Audience type: Avids/'film buffs'. See Chapter 3, Table 3.2.
Developed by studios or mini-studios or major producers with studio output deals or overhead deals.	Developed by studios or mini-studios or major producers with studio output deals or overhead deals.	Developed by studios or mini-studios who wish to develop their relationships with key talent (vanity projects) or wish for awards profile and art reputation for the company. Occasionally developed by an independent producer and sold to (or co-produced with) the studio.	Developed by the production company, often with little studio support, unless a name director or actor involved. Unlike in the UK, in US there is no public subsidy for this.	Developed and produced by the foreign territory. No US development or production investment likely.

Blockbuster Hollywood	Mainstream Hollywood	Specialist Hollywood	Specialist indie	Foreign acquisitions
Increasingly returning franchises and remakes. This trend shows a return to the movie business' fairground origins and the importance of spectacle and effects above content.	Usually original screenplays, and a few adaptations, especially thriller novels and mainstream novels.	High-profile literary novels; stage play adaptations, including musicals; and auteur-backed original screenplays. Often epic and cinematic in scale and conception.	Some original screenplays, and adaptations of books or plays.	Original screenplays, often by a writer-director, or adaptations of foreign novels or plays with no audience recognition.
Success or failure in this sector can make or break a studio, due to the huge investments involved.	Reliable, mainstream, heavily test screened, often predictable and sometimes totally forgettable.	Always a strong niche, but downward pressure on budgets. Companies like The Weinstein Company are increasingly co-producing with the bigger European countries and broadcasters to bring down the cost of production (for example, Oscar-nominated *My Week With Marilyn*, co-produced with BBC Films and Trademark Films).	Recently in trouble due to Hollywood studios closing or cutting back on their specialist acquisition and distribution arms, which some of these films relied on for effective distribution.	Increasingly in trouble due to Hollywood studios closing or cutting back on their specialist acquisition and distribution arms.
Level of likely creativity (see Chapter 7, Table 7.2): Rarely creative in storytelling, but can sometimes be business transformational (because of high marketing exposure) or technology transformational (because of high effects budgets).	Level of creativity: Rarely creative or transformational, unless sparking a run of a particular type of rom-com or buddy movie.	Level of creativity: Likely to be creative, challenging, sometimes transformational.	Level of creativity: Likely to be creative, challenging, but rarely transformational.	Level of creativity: Likely to be creative, challenging and original, partly because of the input of other non-American cultures and traditions; but not likely to be business transformational because the audience is very limited.

often they will hand in their version and bits of their version will be taken out and put into the next version. But they've got fifty grand in their bank account and that's how they can pay their bills. Certainly in the studio system it's a much more pragmatic approach, whereas in the UK film is art. There are writers in the UK, for example, who *refuse* to rewrite other people's work. This is the difference between those two cultures.

Screenwriter Tony Grisoni agrees, but adds that such writing work also ends up with complicated arrangements for who gets the onscreen credit:

> I did a lot of rewrite work (in Hollywood), so a screenplay that had already been through two or three hands would then come to me. The deal was you get very handsomely paid, but you wouldn't even dream of getting a credit, and your work goes into this pot and then gets picked up. And it probably goes on to another three writers after me. And often nothing would happen to the project anyway – it would just die. But there's a whole system of agreements with the Writers Guild of America where if it's an adaptation the first writer can lay claim to everything that the novelist had, from characters to plot. There was that nonsense when Terry (Gilliam) and I worked on *Fear and Loathing*, because that was a novel and there had already been another screenplay by other writers, and although we were starting from the beginning they wanted a credit on it.

One anonymized writer who has worked a lot in America explained the typical difference between the European approach and the Hollywood approach as follows:

> In the UK and in Europe writers are more respected, considered, listened to and worked with. In America they're more sacked, moved around and dispensed with. The films are higher budget and there's obviously a lot more power and control within the studio system, because they're not just buyers in the movie: they own the whole thing. I guess there's a lot of pressure on executives and producers over there, and the writers tend to be the fall guys. If something's going wrong then the writers are sacked and moved on. It's very, very rare that you'll have a Hollywood movie where one writer has just stayed on it throughout the whole thing and no-one else has been brought on. I've worked in Hollywood, and in a number of cases I've sold original scripts there, and I've also come in and rewritten other people's work. All the things I've sold, I've been sacked off, every single one. And everyone I know who's ever sold a script, they've been sacked off that as well. And I've gone in and replaced people that I know have been sacked off their own scripts, and those same people come in and replace me on mine. So it's a kind of merry-go-round. It seems to cost an awful lot of money to constantly hire these new writers and then move them on. I don't

know how sensible it is, either creatively or financially, but that's the way they work it. In the UK, the writers are more treasured, like you get in theatre, where the writers are normally retained, or at least their opinions are valued, and it's rare you're completely shunted off your own script. We have a literary tradition here, we've got Shakespeare, we kind of value writers more. In France, where I've worked as well, the writer and the auteur is very highly valued, and the producers are very much second fiddle to the auteur.

The further problem with high development costs in Hollywood is that when projects that are developed at one studio go into *turnaround* (see Chapter 1), they are often not picked up by another studio because the cumulative development costs have become too high for them to be recoupable on the eventual production budget. This escalation of the development budget is probably a direct result of the repeated hiring and firing of writers.

Figure 12.1 proposes a simplified typology of power within studio development, showing that on the average film, instead of one writer there could be three or four. The director is usually selected after development, but does not need to have the power to attract external financing and foreign distribution sales, as long as he is approved by the studio and can attract cast. The director is employed on a *transaction reward* model and as a result is more prone to being replaced than directors on independent films, especially on mainstream and blockbuster Hollywood films. The director's influence is shown to drop during the final edit, because of the power of the studio executives at that stage, and the fact that the studios regularly use public test screenings of edits and other forms of market feedback. It should be pointed out that by showing the studio exec. as a single line the figure also does not fully reflect the internal complexity of studio greenlighting and multiple executives controlling the deployment of resources (see the commitment matrix in Chapter 5 for more on this).

The Hollywood social network

The studios are sometimes accused of being money machines, driven solely by the profit motive; however, that is to miss an important part of the context. Edward Epstein's book *The Big Picture* repeatedly makes the point that decisions at Hollywood are also made to satisfy the complex and interlocking social network in which all the players operate:

> In addition to their desire to offer a product that will appeal to financiers, merchandisers, and licensees, studio executives need to preserve and nourish their relationship with stars, directors, producers, and agents who define the Hollywood community – a community in which studio executives both work and play. If studio executives made

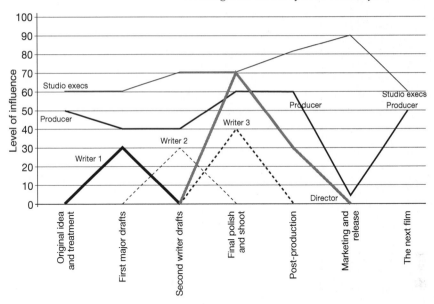

Figure 12.1 A typology of changing power and approximate creative influence of various players in studio film development and production

only films that maximized the amount of money in their clearinghouses they would do so at the serious risk of losing their standing in that community and, with it, their connection to the people, events, honors, and opportunities that brought them to Hollywood in the first place. ... Kept constantly aware of these wheels within wheels at dinner parties, sporting events, award ceremonies, and other social functions – as well as media interviews – studio executives seek, along with strictly commercial projects, projects that will help them maintain both their standing in the community and their own morale.[9]

Therefore the need to make profit is balanced against the need to be *seen* to be sometimes making art. This tradition of wanting to be seen as an art form can be traced back to the arrival in Hollywood of European artists and film-makers fleeing the Second World War, such as Billy Wilder, Michael Curtiz, Fritz Lang, Anatole Litvak and Otto Preminger.

Some decisions are also made in the interest of starting long-term relationships rather than for profit. So-called *vanity projects* are a way of keeping a piece of star talent working for a studio, so that they do not start working elsewhere. The profit is in the future of working with that actor or director, not on the current project. For example when James Schamus' Focus Pictures picked up the US distribution rights to director Peter Cattaneo's commercially under-performing film *Opal Dream*, they did so not because of the film, but because they apparently wanted to develop a relationship with Cattaneo and get his next film into development at their own company.

This is also true in the independent sector: many decisions in film are not what they appear on the surface, but may be driven by the need for peer recognition, personal aspiration and a desire to build relationships in what is a very people-based industry. What sometimes appears on paper to be a financial mistake can still be a good reputational move in the longer term.

The spec. script: development without a commission

During the 1990s and early 2000s Hollywood would pay large advances for *speculative scripts* (or *spec. scripts*), with the prices driven up by powerful agents and bidding wars, as described in Thom Taylor's 1999 book *The Big Deal: Hollywood's Million-Dollar Spec Script Market*. However this was slowed down by the strikes by the Writers Guild of America in 2007 to 2008, and the big payouts were further reduced by the global recession and studio retrenchment, which left them less willing to compete with one another for large advances on risky spec. scripts and increased their reliance on adaptations, franchises and sequels/prequels. At the time of writing there were signs of renewed activity in both spec. script acquisition and the amounts paid by distributors for acquisition of completed independent films at the 2011 Sundance Festival, both trends reflecting the rise in award nominations and box office appetite for more specialist and original films during the 2010 and 2011 awards seasons. The majority of spec. script acquisitions are reported to be relatively low-cost new writers, but it maybe shows increased willingness to take risks and look for new voices.[10]

Anecdotal and trade press accounts suggest that Hollywood is increasingly concentrating on either low-budget specialized films with a clear niche market and possible awards profile (via acquisition or produced with name auteurs) or else much higher budget *tent-pole films* (the blockbusters that support their other films and around which their annual release schedules are built).[11] It is the medium-budget films that are being squeezed out, and all specialized films are having their budgets reduced (even those by name auteurs like the Coen brothers).

The other trend is that the franchise concept has sometimes moved on from being based on a one-hit film followed by a series of self-contained sequels or prequels (which was the *Indiana Jones* and *Batman* model). Instead, some franchises are now being developed to be more like a television serial, where the story is intentionally told across several films, each film ends with a cliff-hanger, and audiences come back year after year to find out how it will all end. This trend goes back to the *Star Wars* sequence (especially the ending of *The Empire Strikes Back* in 1980), but recent examples include the *Bourne* trilogy; *Harry Potter and the Deathly Hallows – Parts 1 and 2* (2010 and 2011); *The Lord of the Rings* (*The Fellowship of the Ring* (2001), *The Two Towers* (2002) and *The Return of the King* (2003)); and the

James Bond films *Casino Royale* (2006) and *Quantum of Solace* (2008). Then again, some fail to get past the first instalment of the franchise, such as *The Golden Compass* (2007) which was meant to be the first of three films based on Philip Pullman's *His Dark Materials* trilogy. Whilst many of these examples of rolling franchises are based on an underlying book series, this is nevertheless a possible ongoing trend in development and production.

Case interview: Rob Sprackling – a British writer on working in Hollywood

Rob Sprackling has been a screenwriter for the last twenty years, working with long-term writing partner John Smith. They conceived and wrote the original screenplay for the animation movie Gnomeo & Juliet *(2011) which has taken around $200m worldwide. They also wrote the screenplay for British film* Mike Bassett: England Manager *(2001).*

Rob has written (or rewritten) for most major studios in the US including 20th Century Fox, Dreamworks, Disney, Buena Vista, Paramount and New Line. In the UK he has worked for Working Title, BBC Films, Aardman, Pathe and Miramax.

Why do films get made?

The reason films get made in Hollywood is sometimes very little to do with the script. They get made because – hang on a minute – Robert De Niro has suddenly become free, he was going to do another film, that film dropped through, he's now available, the money's come in, the planets are in alignment and if we just say 'Yes let's make this movie!' it will now get made. And the script might be crap, the script might be beautiful, who knows. It's got nothing to do with the script, it's got to do with the fact that Bobby was free and Alan had the money and all those things fell into place at the right time. And so the notion that this whole thing is carefully calibrated, and everyone would say 'Oh no, this script isn't quite ready just yet, I think just another two months and this'll be perfect and then we'll make that film.' No, it's nothing to do with that. Some films get made which haven't even got a script, it's just because Tony's had an idea which someone quite liked and they were all available, and we've got this window. And wonderful, beautifully crafted scripts which are perfect and should have been made, never got made, because those planets didn't align.

The importance of the writer in comedy

There are different types of film. If you're doing an action blockbuster the screenplay isn't that important. You might need a bit more excitement in the third act, so the producer will hire in some guys and say – can you write three more action sequences over there – and it all goes in and works fine. However, I work in comedy and I believe that the funniest movies have the writer as the main controlling influence. Either the writer is also the star, the director or the producer, whether it be a Woody Allen movie, Charlie Chaplin, Laurel and Hardy, the Marx Brothers, *Withnail and I*, *Life of Brian*, *Spinal Tap*, *Airplane*, *Team America* – every comedy that I've ever loved, the writers were the people who had the most creative control. When a comedy gets made by a Hollywood studio – writers normally get hired and fired and consequently you end up with a more generic comic voice – as opposed to something that's authentic, original and genuinely funny.

Case interview: Stephen Woolley – a British producer on working in Hollywood

Stephen Woolley's many films as a producer or executive producer include Made in Dagenham *(2010),* How to Lose Friends & Alienate People *(2008),* The End of the Affair *(1999),* Little Voice *(1998),* Twenty Four Seven *(1997),* Michael Collins *(1996),* Interview with the Vampire *(1994),* The Crying Game *(1992),* Scandal *(1989),* Mona Lisa *(1986) and* The Company of Wolves *(1984). He also produced and directed the film* Stoned *(2005).*

The dominance of franchises

If you're making films in studios then there definitely is a more conscious decision to repeat success and that comes in two forms. Firstly, the studios always want a franchise (that's always been the case, ever since Hollywood began). ... And then there's something that suddenly clicks like 3D, and obviously the development of scripts that are very 3D friendly is what's happening at the moment.

Certain subject matters will be in vogue and very easy to develop at certain stages, and then they fall out of fashion. For instance, there was a time in the 1970s and 1980s when people wanted to make sword and sorcery movies. So you had John Boorman making *Excalibur*, for instance, and *Dungeons and Dragons* and *Krull*, and all these movies with cloaks and big swords. ... But after the *Conan the Barbarian* sequel these movies just suddenly dried up, and it was like a dry well. So you get swept along in this frenzy of trying to second-guess the audience.

Hollywood is inclined to invest more in post than the script

Of course, 3D and spectacular action pictures cost a lot of money; so on *Spiderman* and *Batman* you're into 100 millions and 200 millions. You're basically setting yourself a very high bar, which makes life at the studios precarious, because any one of those can bring you down quite a bit. And then you're thinking about how much you spend to *release* that film. So if you're investing in something which is half a billion worldwide, then a potential flop is unacceptable. So for *Avatar* to have been unsuccessful would have been unacceptable. Jim Cameron [the director] and the studio would have put that film into post-production for a decade if they didn't get it right. We were doing ... *Interview with the Vampire*, and *Titanic* was going to be the big summer release, and the rumours on *Titanic* were that it was a terrible, terrible flop. It was going to be the turkey of the year, in the way that *Godzilla* was for the studios. Unreleasable, was the term used. And so they took it off the summer release, worked at post-production, and moved it to a Christmas release. Whatever they had to do, they did. And obviously it turned into one of the biggest grossing films ever. So there is a tendency in Hollywood and the studios to grab on to a particular star or a particular trend and then rush something into production and sort it out in post-production.

What happens in development is that if you have a set of very powerful people involved, let's say you have Jim Cameron for instance, or Robert Zemeckis [*Back to the Future*, *Forrest Gump*] or Steven Spielberg, then there's a tendency that no-one's going to argue with Stephen Spielberg. So often Spielberg is wrong, and the script isn't quite up to muster – like all of us he's only human. But no-one's going to blow the whistle on that, because what studios always think is – okay, we've got Tom Cruise, we've got Steven Spielberg, we've got a high concept, we've got a potential huge market for this, we'll sort it out in post. Then they'll have re-shoots and re-shooting and re-ending and new endings and alternative endings and the all-important previews. They might preview a film three, four, five times; they might preview a film fifty times. They might have one alternative ending, they might have ten alternative endings. That's where the money is spent.

Money isn't spent on the screenplay. It's spent on acquiring rights, intellectual property, getting the right brand, like Marvel comics or a bestselling novel. ... But often there are forces at play that are out of their control, such as ... is 3D going to last? Or Tom Cruise/Brad Pitt/Johnny Depp/whoever the star is has got another movie to move on to. Or there's a window at Christmas or Thanksgiving that we have to hit ... all those factors will crowd in, so the development is under such stress.

Firing writers and the problem of credits

I think the big difference [between the US and Europe] is that because of the limited resources people have in Europe, the tendency is not to hire and fire writers so much, but to stick with the same writers through thick and thin, in order to get the script into the condition that you want it to be. Rather than what they tend to do in America, which is they'll go with the first draft, and they'll say this is good but we need it to be better and instead of going back to the writer again they'll go to another set of writers. That was my experience on developing *Raging Harlem*, one of the movies that I developed in America, where we had four writers. In fact it was five writers, but there were three individual writers and a couple – writing partners. And ironically with that film, the scripts that were the most significant were the second writer's scripts, which really pushed the film along. Because the first draft was bad, the third draft pulled the film back again, but then the two writers we used at the end actually created the script that we could then finance. And ironically the Writers Guild [of America] awarded the first writer a credit, and the third writer a credit, but really it was the second and the fourth that did all the work.

Interview with the Vampire had been around for a very long time. The novel was written in the mid-1970s, and everyone had written scripts for *Interview with the Vampire*. And Neil [Jordan]'s trick was to literally not worry about the inherent problems involved in the book, because everybody was obsessed with – oh it's a child vampire, oh you can't have the child falling in love with the older vampire, oh there's a gay vampire, and the audience doesn't like that. It was all the questions of sexuality, which of course were the essential ingredients that made the book so successful. Anne Rice was sexualizing the vampires, so Neil just rolled with it, and did an absolutely true version of the book. And when it came to the credits, Anne Rice got the credit for the script, even though Neil had never read her copy of the script. We didn't even know she'd written one. But because she *had* written the first script, she went in and claimed the WGA credit. I don't think Neil even got a shared credit for that, I think it was just Anne. And yet everyone involved in that movie knew that it was Neil's script that had made everyone excited again and brought David Geffen and Warner Bros back to the table and said: 'Great, we're going to make this now, it's a fantastic script!'

Often first writers are quite happy to be fired, because once you've done your first set of drafts, you're guaranteed the credit. ... I think it influences the process hugely because I think the writer who writes the first draft is imagining that he's *not* going to be writing the next draft. The two ends of the game that are most lucrative is – be the first guy on the block to write the draft, and then be the guy who does the polish. The polish is where you get the real money, because they put you on a daily basis, so you get X amount per day and everybody imagines you'll only be working for three or four days. And six months later you're still doing that, and you're making a lot of money. It's a whole different way of thinking ...

13 The writer

Surviving development and negotiating success

> You should make alliances. Alone you are weak and vulnerable. Stay in touch with your peers – exchange information and enthuse about the latest film, or a contact made. Be generous.
>
> (Tony Grisoni, scriptwriter)[1]

The best writers in the industry are simultaneously able to defend their vision and also collaborate with other people. They respect the world of film finance but know when the tipping point comes, beyond which a project may be irrevocably damaged. They seem to be able to hold in creative synergy the needs of the market and the needs of their vision. How do they achieve that balance and what does the new writer need to know when starting out in the industry?

A writer has only two resources to make money: his talent and his time. Talent could be divided into craft, which can be taught and practised; and creativity, which is probably innate and dependent on intrinsic motivation, but which can be encouraged (by a suitable environment, collaborators, resources and browsing). The amount of time spent on a project is important: making sure that not too much time is spent on a project that is going nowhere, and that the time is being spent in a structured and effective way. Most professional writers work to a strict daily timetable, around their most effective creative times; and spend the rest of their day on meetings, correspondence and browsing (films, art galleries, internet, and occasionally daytime television).

The amount the writer can charge for his time is based on reputation, which includes things like: what he's like to work with; how many films he's had produced in the past (which is usually down to the producers involved and the actors attached); and above all the success of those films, either artistically (dependent on word of mouth within the creative community, plus critics and awards) or financially (especially box office figures, because video figures are hard to find). However, financial success is *also* reliant on the circumstances of the release, including a willing distributor who invests effectively in the right type of release for the film, the effect of the weather and the competition on the opening weekend, and the reaction of the critics and the public. Even awards can be influenced by heavy distributor investment in lobbying and marketing.

What all this goes to show is that many of these reputational values are actually out of the direct control of the writer, so good luck is a large contribution to professional success. The one reputational aspect that *can* be influenced by the writer himself is the first one: personal behaviour and relationships. As one film writer succinctly put it: 'Your success as a film scriptwriter probably depends less on your skill with words than it does on your ability to deal with people.'[2]

One such example is screenwriter Simon Beaufoy. He has had box office flops as well as huge successes, but people are willing to work with him again and again because of his amiable and professional manner, as well as his innate skill as a writer (see case interview below). So it is important to remain professional and positive. Each project is not just about that individual project – it is about future projects, either with that same producer or with others in the wider film business social network who will be influenced by word of mouth. Development executives and producers talk amongst themselves about their latest projects, and word can get around if a writer is difficult to work with. It is vital for the new writer to build positive relationships – they could be important for years, since most people in the industry will be there for the rest of their working lives. Therefore the writer should be careful whom he decides to trust and work with.

It is also important for the writer to avoid being too defensive or afraid of collaboration, and always to be open to new ideas. For example, in script meetings there is no need to respond to notes immediately; instead, allow time to reflect and consider them carefully (see the case interviews below). Dwight Swain is one of the few American scriptwriters who has written about how to survive script meetings, and he advises writers to try to relax, listen, and give every idea careful consideration; to keep animated and enthusiastic, rather than surly and resentful; to stay properly respectful (no matter how stupid an idea initially appears to be); and above all to capture the executive's imagination by talking scenes rather than the whole story (emphasizing confrontations, colour incidents, conflicts and big, exciting moments). And he advises that writers learn how to draw meetings to a close:

> Cultivate a sense of timing; a feel for the moment when all that's pertinent has been said. When that moment arrives don't hesitate to beam, straighten up your papers, and say, 'Well that shapes things up, right? At least so far as I am concerned ...' Then, if anyone else sees fit to halt the exodus, that's up to him.[3]

Agents are vital in helping to guide the new writer through the process of networking, choosing who to work with, and developing a career. But writers can also make good use of their agents for script feedback, especially those who are interested in the ongoing creative process (some prefer to remain more focused on the business aspects). Whilst they should not be part of the creative triangle as such, agents are often very experienced: they see many scripts at different levels, and they are very *au fait* with the financing process. The agent's feedback also provides another independent piece of feedback to help the writer triangulate where the problem in a script might be (or ammunition to defend a script against notes that he feels are potentially damaging).

Receiving and clarifying the brief

The impression given by some screenwriting books is that usually the writer comes up with the idea and then develops and protects it. However, the professional writer knows that more often than not they are working on someone else's idea or book. Therefore it is vital to get a really clear brief from the producer about what *they* want from the source material and what kind of film they envisage emerging from it (which other films are like it, what cast and market it is aimed at, and so on). Many writers are initially afraid to ask these questions, perhaps because they want to have freedom to explore, and many producers can be evasive when asked these questions, perhaps because they do not yet have the answers themselves, but as usual it is vital to ensure that the same project is being made by all concerned. One way of doing this is to agree an imaginary poster tag line, or choose an image or two that sums up what the story is all about. If it is an adaptation the screenwriter needs to pin down the producer and development executive to what *exactly* has attracted them to the property, and also which bits they think are *not* working. While the writer needs to come to their own conclusions on some of these issues, it is helpful to start knowing what the producer thinks, otherwise the writer could accidentally remove the parts that the producer most liked, or spend ages developing the parts the producer wanted taken out.

If there is no development executive on board then there is sometimes an argument for employing a script editor at that early stage to help thrash out a possible structure and beat treatment with the writer, and get the producer's approval *before* moving on. The script editor can even be used to ask the producer those awkward questions that the writer does not want to be seen to ask. It is also good practice for the writer to go away and write up his notes on the brief and send them to the producer to have them confirmed – clarity is required at every step of the process. Screenwriter and ex-development executive Tom Williams definitely argues for a clear initial brief, which may hark back to his days as an advertising copywriter. He also prefers contact with the producer as well as the development team to be sure that the brief is shared by everyone, and thinks it is reasonable always to refer the drafts he delivers back to that initial vision:

> My job is to execute a brief. I'm providing a service for the producer, and the development team are intermediaries between the writer and the producer. ... I'd want a kick-off meeting where you have all parties involved in a room or on a conference call together and we agree the brief. ... Such as: this is what we like about the book we've optioned, this is what we're not so crazy about with the book. ... Give me the poster that you see for this movie, and the one-liner ... one image and one line, you can call it the theme or whatever. Something to stick above my desk just to remind me: this is what I'm working on. That's what I really look for in a development team, and in the notes as well: a real sense of direction. Let's all remember this poster, and this one-liner and this very succinct delineation of what this project should be. Is this script delivering against that – yes or no? ... If there isn't that definition of the project at the start I think it's impossible to tell right from wrong.

Again, it is important to write up that brief and make sure that the agent is aware of it. This gives the writer more protection in the longer term against any suggestions that he hasn't delivered.

Changing writers

However hard the producer works at trying to keep the creative triangle together, there are occasions when a writer gets as far as he can in drafting a script, and a new writer needs to come in to provide another take on the project, especially if he has extra skills in a particular area (for example, a dialogue polish or comedy polish). Sometimes the writer hired to do the job is just not delivering what is necessary, as script editor Kate Leys explains:

> My job, when I'm working on a story, is the script. My job is not the writer. The producer's job is the writer, my job is the script. I work to the producer. I work with the writer, but I work *for* the script. ... If I think the writer is not the right writer I will say so, and I will be the first to say so, and I will keep to that. If I think the writer can't do it, or doesn't get it or is obstructing it for reasons of their own, or is hostile, then I'll say so. But if the writer's hostile to me, then I should go; because the point here isn't me, the point is the script.

In light of this, the professional writer has to accept that sometimes it is inevitable that someone else will be brought in to work on the script, and it is then their unenviable task to try to deal with the handover as efficiently as possible, so as not to cause bad word in the industry, or else to try to retain some control over the project by staying close to the producer and the executives. Box 13.1 suggests some of the ways that the writer may try to handle this process. On the other hand, it is also important for the producer and development executive to handle the process of replacement carefully. Kate Leys admits that sometimes this is a very difficult moment:

> Sometimes it goes wrong and people take things very personally. Sometimes people's fear overwhelms them. People who have issues about leaving things or being left. Their fear will come out and they'll be hostile, because that's just a manifestation of being frightened, and usually they calm down later.

Depending on how much the departing writer has done, the producer could sweeten the pill by choosing to retain or increase the onscreen credit for the replaced writer, possibly as a joint credit with the new writer, or as a separate 'story by' credit (some of this will be predetermined by the writer's contract, and in the US in particular some of this may be determined by external arbitration).

Box 13.1 The producer wants to bring on a new writer

A few ideas as to how the writer could handle it

You, the writer, could walk off the project and never talk to them all again, but if you do decide you want to maintain the relationship and accept the need for a new writer, how do you proceed?

Try to find out as much as possible about the producer's reasons for doing it. Is it a simple dialogue polish, for example, to add some comic lines, or is it a substantial character rewrite or story change?

Does it really damage your vision or might it help make a better project? Is this a make or break in your relationship with the project? If not, how do you manage it?

- Be part of the decision as to who the new writer is (attend the meetings and the interviews if possible).
- What is the level of seniority and experience of the new writer? Can they bring a lot to it that will ultimately benefit your reputation and the project? Are they good enough for their reputation to help get it funded by the BFI, BBC, Film4?
- Establish that you remain the lead writer, both emotionally (in the triangle) and in the credit.
- Stay as close as possible to the producer and director. For them, this may be a business decision, not a personal one. Don't assume it is personal.

Sometimes a writer is secretly relieved to come off a project, especially if both the producer and writer have been aware that it has not quite been working out, as Christine Langan of BBC Films explains:

> We had a situation recently on an adaptation where we felt that the novel was going to throw stuff up quite easily, and certainly it's rich; but actually technically it's more challenging than any of us had taken account of. And the writer loved the material, but struggled with different elements of it, and the drafts were not moving forwards. They were almost getting worse, and it had crossed my mind that this writer might not be the right person, as much as I had respect for him. But I hadn't really gone so far as to think: 'We'll get rid of him, we'll replace him.' I was more frustrated at how he wasn't getting it better from one draft to the next, despite lengthy conversations and notes and so on. So then we had a meeting. We were the BBC end of things, and we were all very candid about what we saw as the problems in the script, and we had a very frank conversation about the underlying material and the process of adapting it and so on, and subsequently he decided to come off the project, because he gauged, from what was being said, how much work it was going to entail.

Kate Leys also gave an example in which the writer admitted to her that he was relieved to be leaving the project because it was an adaptation that he had been commissioned to write and that he had never really wanted to do. And his wasn't the only case:

> There was another one that happened recently where it just became clear to everybody, including the writer, that this just wasn't working. It was something that had been originated by the director, and the director and producer had commissioned the writer to write it. So it was appropriate that he left. ... I mean he was disappointed, but I don't think he was disappointed to leave. I think he was disappointed that he couldn't do it, which is a different thing.

Like some marriages perhaps there are some creative relationships that are meant to end, and the important thing is just to try to end them as amicably as possible.

There are also occasions when the writer does not know the rewrites are happening. Even name writers like Tom Stoppard sometimes get their scripts polished without their knowledge, as director John Madden explained in an interview with Linda Seeger:

> Somewhere between Tom [Stoppard] finishing his second draft of the film [*Shakespeare in Love*], and it going into production ... I think it had undergone a 'polish' and it had happened without any of us knowing

it, including Miramax [the production company] when they bought the script [from Universal]. Though still unmistakably Tom's, it had become slightly romanticized and been made more polite. Some things that might have been thought questionable for an American audience, such as the fact the whole movie concerned an affair while this man was married and had children was sort of swept under the carpet in the script. So Tom said 'Okay, if I'm to do some work – which I'm very happy to do – I'd rather start with the script I wrote.'[4]

Tom Stoppard was not himself the first writer on *Shakespeare in Love*: that was Marc Norman, and it was based on an idea by his son. Marc Norman developed it for about five years before Stoppard got the script. (It was originally intended to be made by Universal, with Julia Roberts as the star, but was eventually picked up from turnaround by Miramax, and won six Oscars, including best screenplay for Norman and Stoppard. That was ten years after the first idea for the film was developed.)

Case interviews: Receiving notes – script meetings from the writer's perspective

It is interesting how much of the advice for writers is about seeking clarity and communicating openly. The case interviews below will explore this further, and the chapter concludes with an interview with Simon Beaufoy about how a professional writer also has to be a diplomat, a negotiator, and even a bit of a psychiatrist.

Bite your tongue and give yourself time to think

One piece of advice that emerged from many interviews was that the writer should not feel they have to respond quickly to notes or ideas.

> **Julian Friedmann** (writers' agent): Never react negatively to bad notes. Always be respectful and say: 'That's interesting, can I have time to think about it?' Even if you're planning to ignore it. Then come back saying: 'I'm so grateful that you raised that issue because it made me look at a certain part of the script again, and I now think I've found a better solution.' And hopefully the producer's ego is such that they look at your solution, they like it, and they don't notice that you've actually ignored them.

> **Tom Williams** (screenwriter and ex-development executive): Don't say the first thing that comes to the top of your head, and don't get

defensive about your position. The old adage is: 'Don't listen to their solutions, listen to their problems.' These are intelligent people, who do this all the time and it's their job. So if they do have a problem, try and understand it. Try and figure out whether it's a creative thing or a commercial pressure that's being laid on them. And then interpret that and go back with your suggestions.

Anonymized scriptwriter: I'm terrible at getting notes. I hate being told what to do, which is why I ended up being a kind of freelance bloke who doesn't have a regular job. So whenever I get notes, it's very rare that I'll ever go: 'Whoo, great, notes, you know, fantastic! I can't wait to hear what somebody else's opinion is about what I should do.' However, obviously sometimes you get notes and go: 'What genius, they're brilliant, of course that solves the problem, wonderful!' When I first read notes, I can barely even bring myself to read them. It almost feels like someone defacing your work. ... The best way you can react is to read the notes and then put them down and don't say anything to anyone. Certainly don't call anyone and say 'I can't bear these notes.' Go away, have a biscuit, go and get drunk, come back the next day, read the notes again. And inevitably when you come back and you read them again, (a) they never seem quite as dramatic or as wrong as when you read them first time and (b) you can often start to see the good in the notes, and you can start to find solutions. Oh yeah, it's not exactly what they're saying, but I think the broader point that they're saying is this, and I can see how we can evolve to that, and so you can come back to the notes with other notes, suggesting: 'Well we could do it that way, we could do it this way.'

One writer said that he *never* tries actually to propose the solutions in the first meeting, however much the producer or executive tries to encourage it, but tends to try and absorb the feedback and then go away and think about it, rather than be backed into a corner. Olivia Hetreed agrees:

Olivia Hetreed (screenwriter): You should feel free not to come up with a solution in the meeting. For most writers your brain doesn't work like that or you wouldn't be a writer. If you came up with the answer in the room, you'd be a stand-up comedian or something. What writers do is go away and think about it, and eventually puzzle it out rather slowly.

However, writers are *supposed* to be passionate about their work, so it is acceptable sometimes to fight your corner and stand up for what you believe in. It is just wise to decide when and how to do it:

> **Kate Lawrence** (development executive): Sometimes you are the first person that the writer is going to react to, and they can be cross and frustrated and all those things, but that's fine. I wouldn't want to meet a writer who didn't want to defend what they had written.

The writer should take notes and summarize the conversation

Some writers like to get the notes from the development executive, and others like to make their own notes during the meeting (in fact the process of note taking can be a good way to avoid responding to a newly pitched idea). Either way it is vital that written notes form the basis of the next draft, in case there is any disagreement about the way the script has developed as a result of the notes.

> **Olivia Hetreed:** I always take notes in meetings as well. I will then compare my notes with the notes I've been given or the notes that they send afterwards. And if they don't send notes afterwards, then I will send notes, of my recollection and saying: 'I think this is what I'm doing, is this what you think I'm doing?' Then you don't waste time and effort doing the wrong thing, or having misunderstood something. ... What you don't want when you deliver the new draft is for people to sit down and read something, and feel disappointed because it's not what they expected. You want them to be thrilled that it's better than they expected.

> **Julian Friedmann** (writer's agent): Get the notes in writing, and make sure that everybody is clear. ... If there's a meeting and no written notes, then I want my client to make notes and email the producer saying: 'Thanks for the meeting, this is what we agreed,' and copy it to me. I can't tell you how often I get an email or a call from a producer saying: 'Very efficient of your client but points 4 and 5 were not agreed, he or she's misunderstood it.' So it clarifies that. It also means we avoid a very common problem, which is this: the writer delivers a draft, the producer or the script editor meets the writer and says it's not working and tells them what they want. The writer doesn't believe what they want will work, but has very little

choice. So he does it, delivers, and the producer says – it doesn't work, you're fired. One way of avoiding this is to make it perfectly clear that the writer *doesn't* think it'll work, has given it some thought and has got maybe some alternative suggestions. So you go on testing the ideas, *before* committing to the draft. And then if the producer says, 'It doesn't work', then I can go in as the agent and say, 'Well you're going to have to pay that delivery payment because we warned you it wasn't going to work, we've done what you wanted us to, you pay for it.'

Vision drift

Screenwriter and ex-development executive Tom Williams argues that there is a common myth that development will always improve a project, whereas sometimes scripts can be strangled by over-development and rewriting. He argues that within a few drafts it is important to draw a temporary line under the project and get a potential director on board before the next draft, because 'the director is the lynchpin of the golden triangle ... the lynchpin of all decisions really, from the minute he or she comes onto the script'. This may prevent the kind of vision drift that can occur when a project goes through several rewrites, with feedback from many different people but with no director on board to control the vision. The problem for producers is that they resist sending a script out to directors too early, to prevent bad industry word of mouth if it is not fully developed; and second, many directors' agents resist sending a screenplay to their clients until there is money on board (which is why it is valuable if the producer has the contacts to get a script straight to a director).

> **Anonymized scriptwriter:** I've certainly worked on a project where I felt the notes were driving it further away from where it needed to be. I got more and more despairing. ... The development person did understand what the story was about, but the producer didn't like the source material and didn't trust it at all, and tried to make it into something completely different from how it started out. Ten years later, I think now that I should have walked away from it. At the time I didn't, I just carried on doing it, until it disappeared into the sand.

> **Julie Baines** (producer): I think a project can be over-developed. This usually happens when there are too many opinions being

> expressed. It's the producer's job to keep this under control. I siphon the comments and decide what to take note of and pass on for discussion with the writer or director, and what to dismiss and not mention. You cannot please everyone and your project will definitely suffer if you try to. So I act as a filter.

However vision drift can also occur *because* the director has come on board, and is taking the project in the wrong direction.

> **Julian Friedmann** (agent): I can look after my clients better in the development stage by rolling up my sleeves and getting involved. ... I know nothing about the production period, I wouldn't dream of offering an opinion on whether you should use this camera or that. But there's a lot that we have in the past left to producers, only to discover that they've effectively killed it. At the moment I'm a bit upset because there's a very good production company where on a small horror film they became very invested in a young director and it transpired that the director insists on doing a rewrite which was a complete dog's breakfast. I mean it was horrible, and my client was completely sidelined, and my client is an A list writer. We now don't think with this director attached it'll ever get made. Why? Because the producer got so invested in the director, who was the wrong person.

And on the other hand sometimes a script is taken *away* from the director for more rewrites:

> **Anonymized scriptwriter:** I've been involved in another project recently where I think it's been totally over-developed by a triumvirate of development executives who sort of developed it to death. ... They brought me in to solve some problems and we ended up sort of throttling it, collectively. I think the danger is that you squeeze the originality and the life out of it. ... They made a significant error, I think, by excluding the director, because the director had lots of good ideas and he could have been managed better. The triangle was sort of dysfunctional on pretty much every level.

Case interview: Simon Beaufoy – the screenwriter as a diplomat, negotiator and psychiatrist[5]

A screenwriter is a professional storyteller, but sometimes the screenwriter also has to be a diplomat and negotiator and psychiatrist, in order to protect the script and negotiate the choppy waters of development, as shown in this interview with Simon Beaufoy (The Full Monty, Slumdog Millionaire).

Simon Beaufoy shot to prominence in 1997 as the screenwriter of the Oscar-nominated and BAFTA-winning film *The Full Monty*. The film was an international success, Beaufoy himself became a hot property, and scripts he had already written were subject to industry bidding wars. One such project was a low-budget film about hairdressers, which was optioned by the US production and distribution company Miramax, which wanted to develop a relationship with this new writer. However, the relationship did not develop well: *Hairdressers* had a different comedic tone to *The Full Monty*, and in Beaufoy's opinion Miramax were trying to push it in the wrong direction:

> They tried to get totally inappropriate actors involved for that sort of low-budget, home-grown British film. It was a small-scale script that was being forced to be big budget.

As development continued he came under more pressure from Miramax to make changes that he did not want, until he was eventually told: either you do these script notes or we will give them to someone else. So Beaufoy left and the film ended up being rewritten several times with several writers. It was made in 2001 under the title of *Blow Dry*, but Beaufoy disliked the completed film so much that he fought to get his name removed from the credits. However, for Miramax there was good marketing value to putting his name on the publicity material, and Beaufoy eventually had to accept the onscreen credit 'based on a screenplay by', and the posters went ahead with the strapline: 'from the writer of *The Full Monty*'.

Beaufoy says that this is the only time to date that he has been forcibly removed from a film that he originated. He could have become embittered by that experience, but instead he took the lesson to heart and is now enthusiastic about the importance of working together with the right producers to make the script as good as possible, and not allowing that type of situation to happen again:

When everyone is walking down the path in the same direction, it is not a problem. It is only when different people have different ideas about where they should be going. Then it becomes a nightmare.

He suggests that it is actually part of the writer's job to keep everyone walking down that same path. In order to achieve that, the writer has to be a diplomat, a negotiator and maybe even a psychologist/psychiatrist. His key points could be summarized as follows.

Choose the producer team carefully

The first lesson is to choose the producer very carefully, so that the film the producer wants to make matches the film the writer wants to make (for more on how to select a producer see Box 13.2). Beaufoy says:

It's all in the choices you make very early on in the development process. Who you choose to work with and who owns the rights.

It's important to study the sorts of films that the producers have made, and to think about the team as a whole:

You have to have the right combination of people to get it made. Not *just* get it made, but also get it made in the way that will complete my vision.

Beaufoy is often approached by producers with an option over a book or play, and he has to ask himself whether he feels he is the right fit for the material, and whether he is intrinsically motivated by the story:

If it's not a story I like, however brilliant their idea may be, I don't do it. It might be the best film ever, but I might not be the right person to do it.

Beaufoy is also sometimes frustrated by the negotiation process at the start of development, especially the protracted negotiations between writers' agents and producers' lawyers. He complains that a lot of time and energy is wasted at this early stage, when they could be getting on with the job:

Why don't we agree not to make unreasonable demands of one another at the start? It would save a lot of time. Let's face it, there's hardly any money at stake anyway. The point is to enable it – make it start happening.

He argues that having selected your team you then have to trust them and try to make the relationship work. Most people in the industry are very bright, so it is worth giving even their strangest ideas time. Everyone has the same end in mind, which is to make the best movie possible:

You've got to try your best to make it work. It's like a relationship, a marriage, that has to be negotiated and compromised, not a full-on confrontation.

What happens when projects move home

Projects do not always stay with the same producer, or with the same finance source. When a project moves from place to place (on what he calls 'the funding circus') the project starts all over again, with a new development department and new creative opinions:

Different development people have different opinions, so there is always someone else giving different feedback to the last lot. ... Each executive or financier has their own taste and wants to make their own mark on the film.

This is also bound up with the organizational culture at the different companies. For example, Beaufoy noted that when one project went from Film4 in the UK to Fox Searchlight in the US the opinions and mindset of the executives came from an entirely different culture and series of assumptions and preconditions. Any organization has its own way of doing things and its own image of itself, and this is reflected in the notes you receive (see Chapter 11 on organizational culture).

The thing they like about the project may be different from what the previous company liked, and sometimes things removed by the notes of a previous company may even be reinstated in the new company. Beaufoy places great emphasis on the complexity of keeping the original vision whilst the project moves between different homes. At one level, scripts are very vulnerable to that process of being pushed about and shoved around; but at another level he has come to trust the innate strength of the script, and the fact that it can actually be very resilient to 'superficial change', as long as the writer is there to protect the underlying idea.

This becomes even more of an issue during the financing and packaging period, where different organizations may be thinking of an entirely different scale of budget. On one film, for example, Fox Searchlight wanted bigger actors, and their requests changed the nature of the project.

> These are not all bad decisions – you just have to steer them through, and try and avoid any big mistakes.

The danger is that the demand for bigger stars can push up the budget and that puts more pressure on the writer to make changes demanded by financiers or stars, since there is more riding on the project. In fact, on the above project that wasn't the case, but that was in part because of the support of the producer and the writer for the original vision. Simon summed it up as follows:

> You have to try and keep your vision intact as the script goes between all these organizations and all their internal cultures. It's like a child being passed from parent to parent, or even from care home to care home, trying to find a permanent family.

There are also issues of corporate branding. Each organization wants to associate itself with film projects that will augment and boost its own brand and present a coherent image to their audiences, subscribers or overseas partners. Beaufoy suggests that Miramax (for example) had a conscious policy of associating itself with arthouse festival hits and award winners, so films in development that may have a good chance in this niche were more likely to be picked up by that organization. This also meant that Miramax worked repeatedly with directors and actors attached to those types of projects and who had currency in the arthouse awards sector.

The screenwriter as diplomat and negotiator

Simon Beaufoy explains that receiving notes diplomatically can be as important as whether or not you actually take them on board. He says that however mad an idea may seem, it isn't helpful to lose your temper and walk off. The damage done to the relationship might be worse than the note itself. To start with, it might not be such a bad idea after all, and second, these are their creative ideas and you need to give them respect. Just as you don't want people to reject *your* ideas out of hand, they don't want their ideas to be rejected either.

Sometimes, he says, 'powerful people throw ideas at you off the top of their heads'. This is not intended to be an insult to you (although it may feel like it when you have laboured for months over a draft), it is simply that they are under time pressure and feel they need to have an opinion. Above all, he advises not contradicting people directly, but taking the heat out of it, keeping the conversation moving and then finding a third option that works for everyone:

> Just say, 'that's a very interesting idea' – and ask for time to work on it. Don't say it won't work. You have to let them retain their sense of power. And anyway, maybe when they get the next draft they've even forgotten what they said.

He suggests that you do not need to incorporate all notes given. As a rough guide, accepting maybe 60 per cent of notes will do; but it is vital to take them seriously before rejecting them. Even if you do eventually reject the ideas, you have to do it in a way that doesn't seem like you are. Sometimes you can talk them round to your point of view in a meeting, but sometimes it takes place over a much longer period. They might have correctly identified a problem but just provided the wrong solution, so if you can find the right solution, one that suits both of you, everyone will be happy. By the end of the meeting it's important that everyone in the room feels that they have been properly heard, and won their points – or at least some of them – and in part because they are paying for it.

> These guys with five million dollars *do* have a right to input on your script. You just have to handle it over time. The screenplay is actually more elastic than I ever thought. It can be twisted, bent, manipulated and still do what it was first meant to do when you started writing. I used to think changing elements of a script might ruin it. I don't think that now at all.

Beaufoy tries to strike a balance between accepting some input (and trusting the 'elasticity' of the script to absorb it), and having a free-for-all where the vision is lost under too many competing voices. However, there may come a point when you need to walk away, if you feel that the 'soul' or 'spirit' of the script is really being destroyed by the wrong notes or too many voices.

Unlike some writers, Beaufoy recommends asking for the script notes to be emailed in writing in advance. This gives the writer the time to be angry, and then overcome the anger and consider a response before the meeting itself. He also suggests that having to write down notes might reduce 'off the top of the head' suggestions from producers. Beaufoy insists that notes are written up and collated onto one page, especially notes from various different sources, because then the contradictions that often occur are argued over and ironed out before they reach him.

He believes, however, that it is up to both the writer and the producer to keep up the momentum on the project, not the producer alone. And this includes ending meetings on a positive and forward-looking note, even if that is not how you feel. In a way, Beaufoy is behaving both as a writer *and* as a producer (by keeping up the momentum and diplomatically handling the opinions of key financiers and stakeholders). Perhaps that is one of the reasons why he has been such a successful screenwriter, and is held in such regard in the industry.

Match the film and the budget: more money does not always bring more freedom

After *Blow Dry* Beaufoy deliberately chose to avoid higher budget projects and stick to the lower budgets, where he would have more creative freedom:

> It's a very simple sliding scale – the more expensive your film, the less control you get as the writer or the director. And as the money comes down, people take less and less interest because they've got less and less vested interest in terms of cash. So on a $15m film you can go out to Mumbai and nobody from America came to trouble us at all. It was way too far to fly. And it was only $15m. Who cares? *Benjamin Button* was $160m or whatever it was. They had much bigger worries, so they just let us get on with it.[6]

Beaufoy explains that when *Slumdog Millionaire* was originally budgeted at about $20m it was impossible to get funded, but once the budget had come down to $15m it was closer to what the market would bear:

> Look, the crazier your idea the lower the budget. It's really, really simple. Film-making is a business. And I think writers should always be aware of that. Like it or not it's a business. But you just have to bring your budget further and further down the more mad you are. And when you're in the insane asylum you fund it yourself. You shoot it on your camera and do it your way. And you've got complete control over your craziness but it has to cost almost nothing to anyone else. And that's the way brilliant films happen. ... If you want a big Leicester Square premiere of your film you're going to have to work in the traditional patterns. If you want to be a film-maker that tells stories you don't have to make them on film any more, you don't have to make them on celluloid. You can make films very cheaply now and do them in your way with absolute control and put them out on the web, get them out on YouTube.[7]

To conclude

Beaufoy's key points are to choose the people you are going to work with carefully and then trust them; keep up the momentum on the project and avoid becoming entrenched; and give new ideas time – there's got to be a willingness on both sides to accept new ideas and not to close them down immediately. All these points are in keeping with the creativity issues raised in chapters 8, 9 and 10. When asked what has made him become a better writer he answered:

> I'd say that over the years I haven't learnt how to write better. I've learnt how to incorporate other people's input and how to negotiate it. And that's actually made the scripts get better.

Box 13.2 What is the writer's single most important decision? Choosing the right producer

1. It is the producer who gets the film made. Is this one up to it?
2. Does he share your vision? Do you trust him to choose the right director and cast (and hopefully involve you in those discussions)?
3. Very few financiers read the same screenplay twice. Once rejected, it often stays rejected. Therefore choose the wrong producer to send it out (one whom financiers may not trust) and you can put your project back years, or kill it completely.
4. Does he have a large, well-funded slate of projects? On the plus side, slates indicate the producer's level of funding, ambition and influence. The current wisdom is the more projects a producer has, the more chance he has of getting one into production – but will it be yours? The larger the number of projects the less chance the producer has of personally managing the creatives, and the more reliant he will be on the development executive. Furthermore, the leadership of the producer has to be reduced if there are lots of projects requiring leadership. Eventually the momentum will drop – or when the 'stars align' on your project the producer may be busy working on something else.

Things to ask yourself about the producer and development executive: a checklist

- [ ] Do they share my taste in movies, books, plays?
- [ ] Why do they want my screenplay? Is it personal?
- [ ] What is their track record? Other feature films? High-status TV drama?
- [ ] Do they have a guaranteed way in with BFI, BBC and Film4?
- [ ] What are the other company employees like?
- [ ] Check up on them. … Can I talk to other writers with whom they have already worked? What is their reputation in the industry?
- [ ] Do I trust them to protect my vision? Check the following:
  - [ ] What kind of film is it? Ask them to name similar films.
  - [ ] Ask them what kind of director and cast they would imagine – a wish list. Do they match my choices?
  - [ ] Ask them if I can work closely with the director and perhaps even be on set (although this is eventually the director's decision). This is a good test of their openness to the concept.
- [ ] Do I want to spend five to eight years with this person or this team?
- [ ] What does my agent think of them? Have other clients worked for them?
- [ ] Above all: can I trust them?

14 Into the future

A creative way to develop better films

> Sometimes I've believed as many as six impossible things before breakfast.
> (Lewis Carroll, *Through the Looking Glass*)[1]

This last chapter is divided into three sections. The first asks the crucial question: in an ideal world what could we do to improve development? It uses answers from interviewees to suggest different possibilities. The second looks at recent developments and future trends in the film industry and new technology, and asks: what does the future hold? The final section draws together some overall recommendations for good practice in development and highlights a few of the emerging themes of the book.

1. In an ideal world, what could be done to improve the process of film development?

This book would not have been possible without the generous time and honesty of all the interviewees. Some have been quoted in detail in the book, and others have informed the overall research and narrative. At the end of their interviews they were all asked the same blue sky question: what could the industry do to improve the independent film development process? The fact that there was a whole range of different answers to that question implies that there is no silver bullet that will magically cure all the problems of development; however, many of the answers provide food for thought. Some concepts have already been mentioned in the book, like retaining the writer on set, but others are more radical and may require a cultural change in the industry, possibly encouraged by a change in the policies and behaviour of broadcasters and public funders.

Develop a very detailed treatment, and get the director involved in development

Time after time interviewees emphasized the importance of the writer and producer (or director) initially working out the story *together*. And the more they had worked together, on film after film, the more this practice seemed to be rooted in their work, as though the trust and joint understanding built up through developing the story together lasted not just into the first film, but into the next one too.

Another part of this recommendation is to encourage directors to be involved from an earlier stage in the development process, perhaps including them more in the selection and optioning of specific properties. This would also have the benefit of training directors to work more with writers (which was also identified as a problem, especially for more auteur directors). Could some public development funds target some money to help directors option and develop projects? The even more radical solution is to let some writers have a go at directing, instead of the other way around, as Rob Sprackling suggests:

> I would love to see a lot more writers end up being directors, like in France. We have an auteur voice, and the person who's created this thing gets to see it through. Obviously you have to have the talent to be able to direct, and to work with actors and have a visual eye, but you can bring in a director of photography who's responsible for a lot of the visual side, and really if it's comedy then the fabulous panorama vista shot isn't that important. ... So I'd like to see a lot more writers being trusted to go further with it.

The emphasis on developing the treatment properly is echoed by writers' agent Julian Friedmann. He argues that the usual fee structure and standard industry contracts push writers quickly into producing a first draft, rather than working for longer on the treatment (see case interview). He uses the example of successful TV writers who often spend up to 70 per cent of their time on various treatments *before* they start the script:

> For me, going too early to script drafting greatly increases the likelihood of failure. ... If you don't get the foundations right, it doesn't matter how much lavish care you put into the furnishings and the paint, the building is not going to stand up for very long. The foundations have got to be completely solid and you don't do that by rushing into the script.

Some producers don't like spending a lot of money on treatments, because they think it is money wasted, and want to get as quickly as possible to a first draft so that they can take it to the market and use it to raise development funding. However, Friedmann thinks the writer should be paid more to keep reworking the treatment until it is right.

Case interview: Julian Friedmann and the power of the treatment as the blueprint

Nine times out of ten, a film never gets made because the script is based on a wholly inadequate treatment, and therefore it doesn't work, so the writer gets fired. I did a little bit of anecdotal research and called about ten experienced and successful clients, and said: 'How much of the total time do you spend on the treatment, between the first time you're commissioned to write something, and the very last word you write … ?' And it varied between 50 per cent and 70 per cent of their time. These are writers who almost *always* got their scripts produced. So I tend to try and encourage a process where you start by doing a selling document in four sections:

1 **A half-page pitch/hype:** If you look at the back of ten bestselling paperback novels in Waterstones bookshop, it's very similar to what they do – they don't tell you the story, they tell you what *kind* of story it is.
2 **Character biographies.**
3 **Statement of artistic intent:** As an agent it's critically important that I know *why* a writer wants to write something. I need to know what their connection with the material is. … Why are you writing it, and why are *you* the right person for it?
4 **Synopsis:** Write it in the present tense, imagining you're describing what you see, so it's written very visually. It's a mirror image of the film, although a highly speculative one. You can get a sense of the pacing and the tone. And by writing in the present tense it also has immediacy; you feel you can see the film in your mind's eye.

That structure works well, because it enables readers to choose the order in which they want to take in that information. For example, I never read the character biographies until the end, but some people start with character biographies. So you make it easier for the person you're trying to persuade, by letting them have a little more choice in the order in which they read. Also, if you look at twenty treatments or proposals from writers, it's a mish-mash of all of those four things. It's a bit of pitch, it's a bit of back story, it's a bit of character biography, it's a bit of the plot, and it's very difficult to read a document like that.

   I think this type of document prevents a lot of the problems which later arise in development. It is a selling document, written as a team with the writer and the producer, absolutely done by both of them. They talk and then the writer goes away and does a draft, and then the producer responds to it. And I sell this to producers by pointing out that it is an incredibly useful document for them to go out and start raising money, looking for directors, looking for sales agents. It's very clear, and it short-cuts a lot of the potential problems that are going to arise.

Reduce the size of development slates

For several years many producers have been leaning towards building larger slates of development projects, and this trend was encouraged by public funding for slates from the UK Film Council and European MEDIA funding. However, some writers who were interviewed suggested that producers should instead reduce the size of their slates and select only a few to work on intensively. This perhaps reflects the commonly expressed view of writers that they want more access and attention from producers. It may also reduce the need of producers to employ full-time development executives, because the slates become more manageable for the producers themselves, perhaps with the help of a script editor or a part-time development person. The opposing argument from producers is that they need to develop lots of projects in order to improve their chances that at least one of them will get made. The ideal size of slate is a difficult balance between reducing risk of failure, achieving capacity to develop effectively, and avoiding spreading the producer too thinly across projects.

Partnership options

Some writers argue that if the producer is unable to raise a decent option and development fee then the writer should not be obliged to assign all rights, but should be able to enter into a more participative partnership in which rights could be shared rather than fully assigned to the producer. This would move the writer from a *submissive transactional exchange relationship* to a more balanced and persuasive power relationship, as well as strengthening the writer's ability to influence the latter stages of development. Some producers instinctively resist this, viewing it to be a reduction of their control, but on the other hand it may help build the trust and communication necessary to keep a project creatively on track, especially when there is not enough money upfront.

Workshopping and script readings could be a key part of the creative and development process

Another possibility is to raise and allocate funding for actors' read-throughs and workshops, so that the writer and director can explore more ideas and road-test a few concepts, especially with comedy, where the performance and perceived funniness of the script can be so important. The BBC's head of film, Christine Langan, explains:

> Table-reads are really valuable, maybe improvising material and putting actors and writers together. Anything that would inspire writers, and put the wind up this slightly formulaic notion of, 'Read a book, option a book, put all the pieces together, boom!' Which works, by the way, but it's maybe replicating something, rather than finding a whole new element.

This could be facilitated by more development funders actively encouraging it on a regular basis rather than simply permitting it as a line in the budget.

Use the writer during shoot and post

The decision of whether to continue to involve the writer is traditionally taken by the director, but should it be? As Tony Grisoni argues in Chapter 5, the director's need for control could be outweighed by the potential advantages of having the writer on set and in post-production (enabling rewrites to solve problems, using the writer's deep knowledge of the characters; strengthening the group vision of the film; tying that writer closer to the production company for future projects; and benefiting the training and experience of the writer by being part of the ongoing creative and professional process). The argument that a writer could be a disruptive influence on the set could be solved by the producer's power to remove him easily from the shoot. However, it may need a proactive change in culture, in which financiers and producers take it for granted that the writer may be a potential ongoing asset, and will not just accommodate it but encourage it. If it becomes standard to want the writer there (assuming the writer wants to be), then the decision will no longer be chiefly at the sole discretion of the director.

More training for everyone

Better training and pay for development executives and script editors

As mentioned in Chapter 6, most script editors and development executives start as runners, assistants or script readers, and they learn their trade on the job. Writers and producers sometimes identify this lack of formal training as a problem in the development sector. As well as training in script analysis and Socratic questioning, there are also other useful interrogative and developmental techniques that are rarely used in the industry, such as *motivational interviewing* and *neuro-linguistic programming*. This lack of formal training perhaps connects into the fact that it is hard to make much money as a script editor, and so people move on to become writers themselves, or producers. Julian Friedmann suggests: 'Script editors are not valued enough and not paid enough for it to be a career destination. As a result of which producers abdicate development to unqualified people.' Therefore more training and more support and respect for the role of script editors may improve their status in the industry.

Script training for producers

Several different interviewees said that producers are not good at reading scripts, and needed more training in analysing scripts and working with writers. Some even said that producers should try writing scripts themselves, so that they understand the emotional process and sense of ownership involved, and that some scriptwriting experience could be gained as a compulsory part of a wider producer training programme. Writer and producer Peter Ettedgui said that script training would give producers more strength in their own judgement, because they often have to make the final decision:

> Otherwise there's no way you will be able to negotiate the vagaries and the twists and turns of this process. You've got to know that sometimes as a producer you're going to be siding with your financiers, because what they are saying is right, and you're going to be arguing with your director; and sometimes the boot is on the other foot and you are defending the director, not because he is the hallowed creative, but because what he is saying is right and it is better for the film. And if the producer does not have that judgement then it is impossible.

Training for writers, including bringing in film editors

Training is necessary not just for new entrants, but also as interventions in writers' careers after some initial success, for example through mentorships, scriptwriters' retreats and group working. This may help writers develop beyond their first films and into a more professional and creative career. A large number of people interviewed suggested that another possibility for training writers might be to be mentored with film editors, so that each can learn more about what the other does. Initiatives like this that help to build collaboration as a positive, enjoyable and cross-disciplinary activity should help remove barriers to creativity and risk-taking. Another way to do this would be to encourage the writer to be more involved in the edit of a film that he has written, especially after the first assembly (although the director may feel threatened by this). Several people also suggested actively involving film editors in development because of the similarity of the roles of the film editor and writer. Getting feedback on the script by a film editor may be a way of ironing out structural and dramatic issues at an early stage: usually the film editor fixes some of these issues in the edit, but it may be cheaper, easier and more effective to fix them in the script.

The other identified training need is for writers to know more about producing, and some suggested they should follow their work through further into the financing period and activity. Both Peter Ettedgui and Kate Leys feel that writer/producers are one way forward (for the right people, who feel attracted to that work), and that is how the writer can best protect his script. However, producer Andy Paterson disagrees: 'You don't want writers to feel they have to become producers to protect their work.'[2]

More screenwriter training for writer-director auteurs

It has been pointed out that some writer-directors are better directors than they are writers, and are poor at collaborating with writers. Very few writer-directors go on screenwriting courses because they think of themselves as directors first, and their degrees or other training are often in film-making or fine art, rather than writing. One possibility is establishing mentorship schemes (where established writers work with first- or second-time directors). Training schemes specifically for writer-directors to learn about writing could help.

More money ... and making development more profitable

The last suggestions in this section are about money, rather than about the creativity that it funds. Extra funding for development was often the top request from interviewees, especially of course from producers. But where should it come from?

Plurality and diversity of development funding

As shown in the first three chapters, a lot of UK development money is often linked to production funds or constrained by the taste and brand association of the companies involved (BBC, Film4, BFI National Lottery Film Fund). As producer Julie Baines puts it: 'Film4 and BBC Films are very director-led. So unless you have one of their hot directors attached to your project, it is going to be difficult to develop a project with them.'

The major non-public development funder is Working Title Films, and they also are linked to production and certain types of film. It was therefore suggested by some interviewees that it was important that some public funding for development is used to encourage diversity and plurality of development funding, to enable the development of genre films and commercial films that would *not* usually be picked up by BBC Films and Film4. It could enable producers to option and develop projects without immediately tying themselves to production funds and losing rights, and could also be used for writers and directors to option underlying rights that they are passionate about. Some funding could have the specific remit to encourage the migration of writers from TV and theatre. There were also issues raised by some interviewees about the need to fund more original screenplays, as opposed to the recent dominance of funding for adaptations.

The 2012 UK Film Policy Review emphasized the importance of diversity and plurality of taste among gatekeepers of publicly funded development funds and wanted to encourage producer autonomy from gatekeeper influence. The review proposed that BFI development funds should be returned to companies that have put projects into production for reinvestment by the producer in future development activity – both rewarding them for success and giving them greater autonomy over development decisions (at the time of writing, the government and the BFI had not responded to the review's recommendations).[3]

One screenwriter (who chose to be anonymous) wanted more public development funding to be made available directly to the writers, thus breaking the 'portal' of the producer being the person who presents projects:

> Let's stop the producer being the only person who has a relationship with the development funding bodies. Why not have the writers go in with their ideas direct – and the funders pick the winners from that? They can then attach an appropriate producer to handle the business side of things. This happens all the time in television – the broadcasters trust the writers to head up their own work, both in America and the UK, resulting in a really high standard of programmes. You would see a switch in the balance of power from the business people to the creative people, because it's a creative industry … and then you will find all the new people who don't have the luxury of knowing a producer have a chance to come in directly. And then it's an even playing field, based on the quality of the work, not on the name of the producer.

More development funding as a result of broadcaster acquisition of films or a tax on exhibition income

Some producers call for broadcasters to acquire more UK product, rather than just showing their own film strand-developed films and US acquisitions. Whilst this would have a major effect on production, it might also kick-start better funded development from private equity investors (if there were more routes to the necessary UK broadcast sale). At the moment there is little encouragement for private investors to invest, because the projects in development that are most likely to get made are the ones already being developed with the broadcasters and/or lottery support. This could effectively exclude projects developed outside that system. Therefore the development of more projects would be boosted *if* the broadcasters funded the production of more films than they developed. Likewise independent development would be boosted if BSkyB and Channel 5 were to commit to a slate of production funding or acquiring more UK film product, because this would again separate the process of internal broadcaster development from production, and encourage private funding of development.[4]

Another way of paying for more development may be to look further along the value chain for money. For example, producer Rebecca O'Brien voices the views of some producers when she argues for a tax on exhibition:

> The main weakness in the industry is that exhibition doesn't fund production, and that flaw is the reason we need public subsidy in the first place. If we had a more direct relationship with exhibition, or a tax on exhibition that went to the production company, then we would be better placed to take projects to a further state of development without having to call on outside subsidy.

Private equity funding for development

So what about attracting more private investors, perhaps via the UK government's Enterprise Investment Scheme (EIS), where there is a tax advantage for high net worth individuals to invest? It has been seen that development funding is very high risk, tied up for a long time, receives only a small premium on production, and is a small part of the profit share of the completed film (about 5 per cent of producer's net, after the distributors have taken their fees and costs). Perhaps more private investors would put money into development (or buy shares in EIS-funded development slates) if it was standard for production agreements that were greenlit by the broadcasters, public subsidy funds and equity funds to include a better development premium and a better percentage point in profit share for development financiers (especially when that development financier is not also one of the production financiers). Concerted effort by the dominant broadcasters and film funds to change these standard rules of trade may have a significant benefit for everyone in development, as well as increasing the number of quality scripts on offer. During the early 2000s many film budgets expanded to accept the fees of many executive producers involved in the tax break finance schemes that were prevalent at that time – could a similar thing now be done to support a bigger development premium?

There is also the question of the *timing* of the investment. Producer Rebecca O'Brien suggests that more development funding is really needed when the project is already quite well advanced:

> It's the secondary stage of development, when you're packaging a project, that needs more financial support. You've got funders

interested in your project because of the subject, but then you need to do more to get them to sign on the dotted line. That's the tricky bit, and an awful lot of projects fall down at that stage. ... You need a second or third draft, which is expensive, you need a lawyer, a casting director, a budget, and spend possibly £50,000 to £100,000 to make it really viable. Once you've got momentum on a project, it's very much the producer's job to keep that going and what can be a real stumbling block is the fact that you run out of steam just at the point where you need the steam to keep going.

The logical continuation of this line of thought is to earmark some development funding for exactly this stage of advanced development. This may be a better moment for private investors to be encouraged to invest, because their money is tied up for a shorter period of time, and there is already a coherent script or talent package in place (reducing risk). This is also the approach of the European MEDIA Development Slate Funding scheme, where at least two of the three to five projects applying for funding must be well packaged, and have strong financing and distribution strategies already in place, before the development support is granted. It is possible that a production consortium may raise an EIS fund specifically for this late stage of development, as development gap funding.

More public funding for development in general, including for the producer

In 2007 to 2008 of all the public funding spent in the UK on film, only 2.7 per cent was spent on script development. This is compared to 56 per cent on production and 12.4 per cent on distribution and exhibition.[5] In the following year of 2009 to 2010 this rose a little to 3.5 per cent, but this was spread across a total of 150 grants,[6] so it is still not much for each producer and writer. And there lies the problem, because most of what little money there is goes to the writer, so how can the producer survive?

There is no doubt that more money spent on development buys writers the time to fine-tune their scripts, and producers the chance to survive without having to force projects into production in order to pay the bills. The UK Film Policy Review recommended that recouped BFI funding from film projects should be reinvested in future film-making and development activity by the successful producer (rather than being returned to and retained by the public fund), which if adopted may increase development investment and enable producers to survive financially during development.[7] The last word on this is left to producer Stephen Woolley, with a typically passionate plea for better recognition of the role of the creative producer in development:

I think that in an ideal world what would be great is if the role of the producer and development was respected by allowing there to be money to cover overhead, so that we're not on a conveyor belt of having to make a film, because if you don't make the film then you can't pay the rent, and if you can't pay the rent, you'll have nowhere to live and then you'd have to fire Joe and then you'd have to fire everyone; and so, you make a film. That's the process that leads to making bad films. ... Who pays for the rent? Who pays for the fax machine? Who pays for the telephone? The producers have to pay for everything, and it's not seen as part of the development process. Whereas they [development financiers and broadcasters] will pay for a writer to go to Morocco, or they'll pay for a writer to go to Cuba, but will they pay for you to get a bus to Stoke Newington? No. Because as a producer you're not respected in the same way as a writer is. So even though it's your project, you brought it to them, you developed it, you hired the writer, you've made the script – you can pay for your own bus to Stoke Newington. Oh, the writer wants to go to Acapulco to do some research? Fine, not a problem. I find that really outrageous. It's like we don't exist, we're invisible people. And yet we have to do everything.

2. Anticipating the future

The myth of digital democratization of content?

The early to mid-2000s saw a spate of books and blogs that were proselytizing the power of the internet to free up content and democratize film-making. These included books like Tapscott and Williams' *Wikinomics: How Mass Collaboration Changes Everything* (2006); Lasica's *Darknet: Hollywood's War Against the Digital Generation* (2005); and Anderson's two books *The Long Tail: How Endless Choice is Creating Unlimited Demand* (2006) and *Free: How Today's Smartest Businesses Profit by Giving Something for Nothing* (2010). The kickback is now underway, with questions being raised by books like Levine's *Free Ride: How the Internet is Destroying the Culture Business* (2011); Pariser's *The Filter Bubble: What the Internet is Hiding from You* (2011); Morozov's *The Net Delusion* (2011); Turkle's *Alone Together* (2011); and Vaidhynathan's *The Googlization of Everything: And Why We Should Worry* (2011). It has become apparent that some organizations working in journalism, publishing, television and film are struggling or closing down – not because they are bad at creating high-quality content, but because they are unable to make enough money to pay for the high cost of production of that content.[8]

So what about film? As the cost of high-quality video cameras fell, the call to arms was that the digital revolution would give voice to a brave new world of guerrilla auteurs, providing innovative and risky content. It doesn't seem to have happened to date, apart from more short films on YouTube and more short film festivals across the globe. Digital technology has made it easier for young film-makers to build a portfolio of early work and get it out onto the web, but not yet to get *paid* much for it. The choice of which film-makers then get selected to be developed into feature film-makers still comes back to the same old gatekeepers (in the UK these are the bigger film schools, BBC, Channel 4, and the BFI National Lottery Film Fund). In fact there is a danger that the BBC may need to spend less money on early training for new talent because the cheap technology has relieved them of the need to do it.

While more films have been made at micro-budget level in the last ten years, research three years ago for the UK Film Council showed that most of them do not find a sales agent to represent them in the industry marketplace, or decent distribution in the consumer marketplace.[9] The basic reason is two-fold – the lack of recognizable actors (which still influence the majority of cinema-goers and therefore the distributors), and the lack of marketing power compared to the studios. The few successful micro- or low-budget films that do get wider distribution (like the 2010 horror film *Monsters*) are often completed or post-produced with funding from a distributor or studio, and the completed film then has the soundtrack and special effects necessary to make an impact at the box office (however, they are no longer made as cheaply as the PR often makes out).

So who *have* benefited from the so-called digital revolution in TV and film content? In large part it is the distributors and the existing corporate players. When there is a successful new start-up digital company on the block they are eventually acquired by one of those players. While content creators in film and TV struggle to raise production funding (especially since the decline of DVD and Blu-Ray's lack of impact), elsewhere the video streaming websites, aggregators and distributors have all made money (they are closer to the consumer end of the value chain or are monetizing their product through advertising, from which the content creator does not usually get much income). The cynic's view is that all these content distributors have used the myth of democratization and free content quietly to make more and more money for themselves and their shareholders, without having to pay as much for the content. Likewise, some broadcasters have used the idea that independent TV producers could retain rights (and re-exploit the film via international sales) as an excuse to drive down the broadcaster commission fee, whereas in reality most small to medium independent TV producers lack the economies of scale and access to big international sales outfits necessary to really make up for the loss of that upfront commission fee.

So instead of causing a brave new world of democratization of content, arguably the new technology has increased the role of both old and new gatekeepers to the wide-reaching channels and subscriber bases; has increased digital piracy (which has reduced income from DVDs and therefore made it harder to fund film production); has increased the emphasis on celebrity presenters for television documentaries; and finally has increased the power of recognizable stars or long-running movie franchises in film production. In TV the digitally encouraged plethora of material and channels available has had the unintended consequence of placing more emphasis on trusted and identifiable channel brands, rather than less. Schedules may sometimes be making way for *iPlayer* streaming systems, but the old broadcaster is *still* the commissioning and marketing brand behind them. The more crusading pro-internet voices reply that at least the new digital film-makers can get their work 'out there', for example on portals like YouTube. Surely that is democratic? But who owns YouTube? In 2006 Google paid $1.65b in stock for YouTube. They use it to generate advertising revenues for themselves – little of which will be seen by the creator of the content. So who is going to make most money from the digital democratic revolution? It's probably not 'You'. It's 'Them'.

Convergence, divergence, fragmentation and the future of the film value chain

Convergence in telecommunications has brought together previously distinct media (such as TV, film, telephony and the internet) into a single household provider that bundles it all together; perhaps with the addition of a wifi/mobile network provider for accessing on the move. In the early 2000s it was expected that this convergence would be mirrored by the growth of a single device that would do everything too, but unexpectedly the consumer ensured that the opposite happened: *divergence* occurred and the content ended up going to lots of different new devices with a plethora of software interfaces. This cornucopia of competing platforms and formats may actually have slowed consumer uptake and impacted on video-on-demand (VOD). In effect there has been delivery convergence and device divergence.

As a result of digital technology a lot of potential changes affect the market for feature films and the value chain. First, as mentioned, there is the long-expected growth of internet downloads and VOD (something that is finally happening in the UK with the arrival of streaming services from Netflix and LoveFilm, despite problems with broadband speed, especially in rural areas); second, there is the reduction of production costs due to the digitization of the whole film-making process (especially in ultra-low-budget film-making); third, there is the digitization of cinema screens, which reduces physical distribution costs and increases the profitability of cinema releases of niche films and back catalogue (or will once the problematic *virtual print fee* system is finished or revised);[10] fourth is the short-circuiting of the value chain through producers potentially being able to market and distribute their films directly to the consumer (although few producers have done this to date); and finally, there is the suggested long-term growth of the niche market via Chris Anderson's *long tail theory* (as a result of web sales and the growth of internet-based retail aggregators such as Amazon and Play.com).[11] In these last two potential areas of impact (distribution and long tail exploitation) the grip of aggregators and established distributors with large advertising budgets has been resisting new entrants and ensuring that any niche profits benefit them rather than the content creators.

Integration has often been suggested as a way for producers to benefit at more stages of the value chain and thus transform the industry (see Chapter 2). However, many recent cases have not seen producers becoming distributors, but distributors becoming producers (like Revolver Entertainment), or distributors becoming producers and facilities owners (like Vertigo Films). One further effect of the recent move of distributors into production is that types of film are now being developed and made in Britain that were not previously favoured by the predominantly arthouse production community, for example youth culture films and family films, like *Streetdance 3D, St Trinian's, Shank* and *Horrid Henry*. Perhaps a further reduction in distribution costs and a growth in VOD may finally encourage more producers to become their own distributors. However, as journalist Mike Goodridge of Screen International points out, there is still the question of resources and time:

> Producers in Europe are spending so much time raising the funds to get the film made, and hopefully getting a production fee, that they don't have time to think about self-distribution. For the studios the whole point of making movies is to make money off distribution, so they're incentivized to make movies that hit an audience. Hence the scriptwriting process is much more doctored over there, because they literally are their own distributor. They can't just leave it to chance. For producers here (in Europe) it's just about getting the film made.

The Viacom chairman, Sumner M. Redstone, is famously credited with coining the expression that *content is king*; but it has since become an oft-quoted media truism that *distribution is queen*, and, on the chess board at least, the queen is much faster and more powerful than the king. In the last few years internet organizations like YouTube and RapidShare have made money without really owning all the content they distribute. With piracy still rampant, the real question is how content producers can share in more of the income generated by the distributors.

So what about film libraries and back catalogues, potentially such a source of income according to *long tail theory*? In the late 1990s and early 2000s the value of film libraries had risen dramatically, with investors spending billions of dollars purchasing them in the hope of profits from future digital exploitation. However, even then a Hollywood economist pointed out that 'more guesswork and ambiguity appear in the valuation of film library assets than in perhaps any area relating to the financial economics of the movie business'.[12] By 2012 those reservations had proved well founded and, contrary to the expectations of the long tail, the prices fetched for companies that owned movie and television libraries had actually dropped (for example, MGM, with an extensive film library including the James Bond franchise, sold for almost $5 billion in 2004 but drew bids of less than

$2 billion in 2010, resulting in a Federal Bankruptcy Court-approved reorganization plan).[13]

The harder question is how this change will impact in the longer term on the value chain and finance recoupment. Whilst people end up paying to view their films in different ways, it has been suggested by some that the basic economic product of feature film might not be substantially altered by these changes. For example, academic writers Graham Vickery and Richard Hawkins suggest:

> Although the sources and types of costs may be shifting, the overall ratio of investment to return would appear not to be changing ... it seems likely that overall production levels for feature films and television programming will continue to follow already established output patterns, with production increases likely to come in the form of entirely new types of content, aided by lower cost and higher quality digital content creation and distribution technologies.[14]

However, Angus Finney's book *The International Film Business* (2010) foresees a more radical shift, where players at the distribution and exhibition end of the chain may choose to spread back along it and become involved in production:

> Ultimately, internet marketing and its growth in sophistication and specific demographic reach, will encourage end-users such as cinema owners and chains, pay-TV operators and even video game operators to enter the production market themselves. A world where these players commission development and feature films which in turn help drive their respective platforms will cut out third party distribution completely. The cost of marketing will be borne by the production financier rather than carried over to the distributor.[15]

Certainly, new devices to play movies are proliferating, including cable set-top boxes, games consoles, mobile phones, portable DVD players, desk computers and laptops. New methods of transporting them from device to device include high-speed home broadband connections, wifi networks, chips, cards, ultra-portable hard drives and new high-capacity memory sticks.[16] If Angus Finney is right then providers of the technology could also become involved in generating and delivering content, thus operating at different points along the chain. This trend is increased by the pivotal role of the *electronic programme guide* (or EPG): the user-friendly interface between the device and the available content, either on the web or on a subscription or fee-based 'walled garden' section of the web (like iTunes). If the channel (TV/satellite/cable) or computer game console comes with an easy-to-use EPG that makes purchase simple, then that provider may end up controlling how the consumer selects and experiences content (and which content they are given the option to see).

Let us assume that this model is accurate and the future of digital TV is subscription, where people pay monthly (via the device provider or telecom company) to receive bundles of basic and premium services, where they will be able to download or stream film and TV content. In this case there will be wider consumer choice, but there will also be ways for the portals to influence that choice, like the selected films or albums that appear on the top page of Spotify or iTunes or Amazon. Presumably those companies that can pay most to get their mainstream products onto that top page will gradually annihilate the niche products. There may also be ample opportunity for the subscription-based distributors to amortize their marketing costs and 'lose' the profits from individual film successes within the larger pool of content, so that content creators find it hard to recoup. (Does this sound at all familiar to the current Hollywood model of accounting?) Certainly, it means less freedom of access to diverse and niche content than the web originally seemed to promise, and it could be argued that it is in the next few years that consumers need to be very vocal and active in their support for independent creative product in many of the web-based cultural industries – before the larger media organizations sew it up.

Changes in the TV production value chain: fragmentation and unbundling

It is worth looking briefly at the recent fragmentation of the value chain in other media sectors, in case there is a similar future for film. The advent of new business models and platforms in television has increased the complexity of its value chain, or even started to fragment it completely. This is the result of a media product or company having multiple suppliers, subsidiary spin-off products and delivery methods (boosted by the net, new mobile devices and multi-channel television). As an example, look at a conventional single-broadcast TV channel, like BBC1. It once generated all its own content in-house and delivered it to the audience via a single device: the TV set. Producers and writers were employed in-house, and star performers were on long-term contracts with the broadcaster. This was a simple corporate value chain. However, nowadays BBC1 may receive its content from a mixture of suppliers, including some in-house production; external commissions from independent production companies; co-productions with other broadcasters (where the cost of production is shared); acquired completed product (for example, buying in a series from the US); or a mixture of all of these. There may be a further blurring of these distinctions by bought-in content being enhanced by re-packaging and re-editing (for example, a documentary bought in from the US may have a new 'English' voiceover added and different music). This results in a far more complicated value chain.

Furthermore, the commission is no longer for a single product, like a TV programme to be watched on the box in the corner of the room, but may instead encompass multi-platform content including telephone mobisodes, interactive competitions, specialized website content like games, and other transmedia techniques (some of which may be designed and even provided by different companies). And the programme or additional content may be streamed on the web (via iPlayer) or downloaded to a portable device. The external supplier companies may have their own complex value chains of suppliers and different buyers (for example, selling the same programme to different networks around the world or selling DVDs direct to the consumer).

Therefore in the example of a TV channel there is now no single coherent value chain in one company creating a single product. This gives rise to the academic concept of the deconstruction or disintermediation or fragmentation or unbundling of the value chain.[17] This is perhaps less applicable to the film value chain than it is to the TV value chain, because film currently still relies on a single product, albeit distributed in a variety of ways and sometimes subject to lucrative spin-off merchandising products like computer games. In addition, certain types of film lend themselves to transmedia storytelling more than others (for example, thrillers, science fiction and horror films appear to have more opportunities than more arthouse or specialist films or romantic comedies; some target audience demographics are also more inclined towards transmedia).

With the film value chain under pressure from new technologies and the changing demands of international audiences, it is worth planning for the effect of value chain fragmentation in the future. But as screenwriter William Goldman once famously observed (although he is usually misquoted): 'Nobody knows anything ... it's a guess – and, if you're lucky, an educated one.'[18]

The same is of course equally true about the future in general and the future of the film business in particular. As the Master of Suspense Alfred Hitchcock once put it: 'There is no terror in the bang, only in the anticipation of it.'

3. Recommendations for good practice: a creative way to make better films and better business

Storytelling is an ancient cultural art, at the centre of what it means to be human. It has always used a mixture of language and performance, and is part of trying to make sense of ourselves and our place in the world. The playwright and screenwriter David Mamet has observed that a sense of story is integral to how we perceive reality, and perhaps we instinctively construct a story even where there isn't one: 'It is the nature of human perception to connect unrelated images into a story, because we need the world to make sense.'[19]

Stories help form and reinforce culture, and provide an insight into other people's lives and our shared humanity. Film is an example of a complex commodification and industrialization of the production and transmission of storytelling; and it has evolved into a hugely popular and entertaining art form that now travels effortlessly across international boundaries. Since its earliest days cinema has been driven by new technology, and recent developments in digital downloads and streaming are just the latest in a history of adaptations to new equipment and changing business models.

The process of exploiting creativity for entertainment and commercial gain causes tensions between various opposing concepts: such as between cultural value and financial value; between the roles of the visionary artist and the businessman; and between the conflicting urges of freedom and control. And yet many of these tensions actually fuel the art form rather than damage it. This book has cast light on the process of screenplay development and film finance, and drawn out some of the complex and symbiotic relationships at play, as well as looking deeply at issues around what we *mean* by creativity in film and what distinguishes creative people. In interviews for this book many people said that each team and project in development was so very different that it would be impossible to arrive at any generalizations or typologies. However, many themes and consistencies did emerge, and this brief and personal overview of particular themes will try to draw out a few of them.

One key theme was the power of creative collaboration, but where the individual still has autonomy and is not subsumed into the group: the old problem of control vs. freedom. Creative people need to have the freedom to explore ideas themselves, and find their own solutions to problems. It is amazing how often concepts of trust, communication and the value of long-term relationships were mentioned by interviewees. And yet these things are often taken for granted and difficult to plan for.

Research has shown that for creativity to flourish a person's creative character traits and domain skills (for example, the craft of scriptwriting) have to coincide with intrinsic motivation, and that means choosing the right people for a particular job or project. Time and again interviewees for this book mentioned the importance of choosing who to work with. It could be summed up as: *Choose who you trust and trust who you choose.* So producers have to choose the team carefully, but then trust and champion their creative people and try not to micro-manage them. And other members of the team have to trust one another and be aware of the valuable work they are each doing.

When assembling the team, it is not worth making higher and higher offers of money to try and buy a name person if they are not really inspired by the story. Research has shown that if a creative person ends up feeling bought it will actually decrease their motivation, because counter-intuitively they will feel less personally valued, rather than more.

All the team need to be aware that power and control is shifting and changing inexorably through the development and production process, and do what they can to keep everyone on board and engaged. There is also a responsibility on the writer to be proactive, professional and diplomatic, and to keep up the momentum on a project as much as the producer.

The key to building a successful film production company is *not* having good ideas for films. Instead, it is developing and nurturing relationships with creative talent like writers, directors and script editors, who can regularly and consistently turn good ideas into great movies. To encourage their loyalty it is important that the company is somewhere they feel at home: where their values and ambitions are matched by the producer's and everyone else's. This is all part of the vital concept of organizational culture and strong team identity, which in the long term may help build a truly sustainable company.

During and after script meetings it is vital to give ideas time and space – don't close suggestions down too fast. This is the key to finding creative solutions, which sometimes occur when you are least expecting them rather than in the heat of a script meeting. After all, many creative breakthroughs were initially rejected as impossible or unfeasible. It is up to the writer to explore lots of solutions to a problem and find a way through it, and that is a journey that he can be helped on but that ultimately he has to make himself. The same is true of the director.

Creativity comes in many shapes and sizes, and a film can be transformationally creative in one sphere (including business), whilst being very generic in other spheres. Creativity certainly includes the freedom to take risks, question expectations and challenge the status quo, even within a generic and industrial art form like film, as long as the budgets and the target audiences match the risks. Therefore the producer always needs to remember to ask: *are we making the film for what it is worth, when selling it in the international film marketplace for that genre; or has the cost of the cast, the director or the shoot pushed it beyond what we can sell it for?*

The question of how to encourage writers to take risks during development was asked of many of the executives interviewed for this book, but most of them put it down simply to the need for trust and an open relationship. Maybe it is the writer's job to take risks, and the producer's and development executive's job to encourage them, discuss them and evaluate them over time.

The other major theme has of course been money, and its relationship with creativity. In itself money does not inhibit creativity. For example David Lean, Stanley Kubrick and James Cameron were all very well funded at certain stages in their careers, and still their creativity flourished. It is the strings that are attached to the money that count. It is often said that money is the root of all evil, but actually the quote is: 'the *love* of money is a root of all kinds of evil'.[20] Money does not in itself ruin films: what counts is how you raise it, how much you raise, how you spend it, and what the effect of the money is on the project. Time and again producers have stated that the important thing is the match of the funding source (and its brand) to the type of film being made, from development funding all the way through to distribution. Choose the financing partners carefully at every step of the way and the film is less likely to be driven off course.

However, if the producer sells out and takes the money from unsuitable sources, then the financiers may turn it into a different kind of film – they are just remaking it in their own image and trying to make the kind of film *they* want to distribute. That doesn't make the finance source wrong, or 'evil', it is just that their values and target audience differ from the writer's. So getting a film made at all costs may result in the payment of a good fee on the first day of principal photography, but it is not good long-term business, for the writer or his creative partners. It is not just getting it made that counts, but getting it made in the right way. So the balance between money and creativity has to be carefully managed and considered, but not avoided.

Looking back a few thousand years, the Greek God Hermes was able to be the patron god of creativity, commerce *and* communication, all in one. The ancient Greeks did not share our modern preoccupation with the conflict between creativity and commerce. That was the distant past, but maybe it can also be the future, especially in this modern interconnected media world.

This is an academic book, based on research, reflection and the discussion of existing theories, as well as the proposal of some new ones. People in the film industry are sometimes suspicious of formal education, academia and business theory, possibly because many of them worked their way up through the industry and feel that on the job is the best way to learn. However, this book shows at least that academia and business theories can cast some light on the film process, and provide tools and techniques (especially around managing creative people, organizational culture and working in teams) that can help the practitioner understand and manage their work better, and build companies based on creative talent.

Above all, what is needed for successful script development is a strong creative team of producer, writer, director and development executive, with a coherent vision of the type of film that they are setting out to make, and a commitment to make it together. This will reduce many of the risks of creative drift or genre confusion that often result in a bad movie. Get that team right at the start, like a lodestone of vision and intent, and all the rest should follow. Only a strong vision can survive the inherent complexity of the fragmented multi-player value chain and the vacillating power relationships that are involved in getting a film developed, funded, made and distributed to multiple devices all over the world, in what is a highly diverse and rapidly changing marketplace. The stakes are high, but the potential rewards are enormous.

Appendix A

Sternberg's analysis of levels of creative contribution, as applied to the science fiction film genre

This appendix is relevant to Chapter 7, and analyses the borderline between exploratory and transformational creativity.

Robert Sternberg, Yale Professor of Psychology and Education, has tried to assess different levels of creative impact and change, and Table A.1 attempts to summarize his views. He is thinking chiefly about creativity and innovation in science and technology rather than the creative arts, but it is possible to adapt his thinking to film, and some possible examples of films in the science fiction and superhero genre have been put in the right-hand column of the diagram (science fiction is an excellent category to use because unlike some genres it crosses regularly between mainstream and specialist/cult; it is often driven by technological innovation in special effects; and the subject matter itself is operating in border areas of the imagination[1]).

Table A1.1 'All change': summary of Sternberg's categorization of creative contributions on the propulsion principle, as applied to film[2]

Effect on the paradigm of the creative contribution		Subdivision of creative contribution	Effect on crowd[3]	Possible movie examples from sci-fi and superhero films
Accept current paradigms	Paradigm preserving that leaves the field where it is	1 Replication: the field is in the right place. Re-affirming, static, stationary motion (as of a wheel turning), remaining within genre.	Not crowd-defying	Most mainstream films occur in this section. For example: conventional superhero franchise remakes that do not progress the genre, like Joel Schumacher's *Batman Forever* and *Batman & Robin*, starring Val Kilmer and George Clooney as Batman; *The Matrix Reloaded* and *The Matrix Revolutions* (both 2003); *Spider-Man 2* (2004) and *Spider-Man 3* (2007).
		2 Redefinition: an attempt to redefine where the field is, but not change it.	May be crowd-challenging	For example: a different *type* of superhero movie, but not challenging the underlying genre, such as the more radical action hero remakes, including Christopher Nolan's *Batman Begins* (2005) and *The Dark Knight* (2008), starring Christian Bale; Tim Burton's *Batman Returns* (1992); and James Cameron's *Aliens* (1986).
	Paradigm preserving that moves the field forward in the direction it is already going. (Note: Most cinematic innovation occurs here.)	3 Forward incrementation: motion: move the field forward in the direction it is already going.	Leads the crowd	Some of the better franchise films, which establish or reinvent a character or franchise, such as Tim Burton's *Batman* (1989) with Michael Keaton, which started the modern Batman film franchise; and Sam Raimi's *Spider-Man* (2002). Other sci-fi films could include George Pal's hugely influential and consolidatory *The War of The Worlds* (1953), which won the Oscar for SFX; *Invasion of the Body Snatchers* (1956); *Close Encounters of the Third Kind* (1977).
		4 Advance forward incrementation: an attempt to move the field forward in the direction it is already going but by moving beyond where others are ready for it to go. Propulsion leads to forward motion that is accelerated beyond the expected rate of forward progression.	Goes beyond normal and is maybe crowd-defying (may or may not be accepted by mainstream)	Sci-fi thrillers that redefine and revitalize what is possible, such as *Superman* (1978), which started the whole concept of the superhero movie as a mainstream phenomenon; and *X-Men* (2000), which revitalized it. Breakthroughs in technology include the advanced use of 3D in Cameron's *Avatar* (2009), which has triggered other 3D sci-fi films. Ten years before *Star Wars*, *Planet of the Apes* (1968) won an Oscar for make-up and set the trend for sequels and prequels (five in total), comics and a TV series. Some films inspire through their radical look and feel, such as Terry Gilliam's dystopian black comedy *Brazil* (1985) and Kubrick's stylized *A Clockwork Orange* (1971). Merging genres is another form of creativity, such as *Blade Runner* (1982), which merges film noir elements; and *Alien* (1979), which merges slasher elements (and spawned three sequels, two prequels, and a franchise of novels, comic

Effect on the paradigm of the creative contribution		Subdivision of creative contribution	Effect on crowd[3]	Possible movie examples from sci-fi and superhero films
Reject current paradigms and attempt to replace them	Paradigm rejecting contributions that move the field in a new direction from an existing starting point	5 Redirection: take the field from where it is to a different direction. The propulsion leads to motion in a direction that diverges from the way the field is currently moving.	Crowd-defying (may or may not be accepted by mainstream)	Sci-fi thrillers that invent a new sub-genre or movement, and redefine what sci-fi as a whole is capable of, such as *Metropolis* (1927); *The Day The Earth Stood Still* (1951); and *The Matrix* (1999), which incorporated martial arts choreography, Japanese animation influences, computer gaming and new SFX techniques.
		6 Reconstruction/redirection: an attempt to move the field back to where it once was so that it may move onward but in a different direction. Propulsion is backward and then redirective.		Rare examples of creative redirection are George Lucas' *Star Wars* (1977) and *The Empire Strikes Back* (1980) (moving sci-fi away from the previous serious and allegorical sci-fi films after 2001, like *The Andromeda Strain* (1971) and *Silent Running* (1972), and back to *Flash Gordon*-style blockbuster entertainment).
	Paradigm rejecting contributions that move the field in a new direction from a new starting point	7 Reinitiation: move the field to a different as yet unreached starting point and then move from that point. Propulsion is thus from a new starting point in a different direction.	Crowd-defying – unlikely to be mainstream audiences. Maybe specialist/cult	Some highly original films start from a wholly new place, play with narrative form, and evade generic expectation: Kubrick's *2001: A Space Odyssey* (1969); Tarkovsky's *Solaris* (1972) and *Stalker* (1979); and writer Charlie Kaufmann's *Being John Malkovich* (1999) and *Eternal Sunshine of the Spotless Mind* (2004). More obscure examples include the French films *Last Year at Marienbad* (1961) and *La Jetée* (1962) (a time travel romance, which inspired Terry Gilliam's *12 Monkeys* (1995). *2001* established sci-fi as a serious art form, beyond the previous limitations of the genre; however, other films in this category are often so challenging and idiosyncratic that they stand alone and do not necessarily move film-making in a 'different direction'.
Integrate multiple paradigms	Combine approaches	8 Two formerly diverse ways of thinking about phenomena into a single way of thinking. The propulsion has the effect of two different approaches linked together.	Crowd-defying – unlikely to be accepted by mainstream audiences. Maybe cult	This seems to be difficult to apply to the film industry, because as a category it is more based on scientific breakthroughs where previously unconnected fields are combined (for example Einstein's Theory of Relativity). In film genre combination occurs above under 5 or 7.

There are three problems with the Sternberg model when it comes to film, and other genre-based creative industry products (like TV and music). First, Sternberg insists that a creative contribution has to be an *intentional* attempt to propel a field or domain from wherever it is to where the creative thinks it should be.[4] This is less applicable to film (and elsewhere in the creative industries), in that intention is harder to gauge. Many directors are driven by 'the story they need to tell' (which inspires innovation only if existing cinematic forms or technology do not deliver); and some breakthroughs are identified only after they have been screened and accepted by the critics or the industry (vis-à-vis Csíkszentmihályi's fields).[5] Famous examples of artists that have substantially and *intentionally* changed their discipline include the Romantic poets, the French Impressionists and Expressionists, the Pre-Raphaelite Brotherhood, Cubism, Futurism, Abstraction, and modernist novelists like Joyce and Woolf. Film movement comparisons include the French new wave of the 1950s and 1960s, Italian neo-realism, and the rise of exploitation and horror films in the 1960s (which created whole sub-genres of niche film-making).

The second problem is that the Sternberg model also covers creativity in sciences, such as medicine, mathematics and technology. In the sciences, there is a clear and understood body of existing evidence and theory that makes up the domain, and new breakthroughs in research or thinking can be clearly seen in the context of that existing domain. In the humanities, research and creativity often add to and re-interpret the corpus, rather than diverging from it (this also ties into the problem of proving intention to diverge).

The third problem is a practical one and it can be seen in the attempt to fit film examples into the table, where it proved difficult to find clear examples of films that fitted categories 6, 7 and 8. Most films fit into 1 and 2, and most adopted innovation into 3 and 4. There are just too many films that fit partly into one category and partly into another category for the model to be successful when applied to film.

Sternberg's work is also cited in Chapter 8, and Table A1.2 gives a summary of his investment theory of creativity.

Table A1.2 The confluence of interrelated resources for creativity: Sternberg's investment theory of creativity[6]

Component	Component description	Confluence of components
Intellectual abilities	(a) Synthetic skill to see problems in new ways, escape conventional thinking. Upfront time to think in new ways: metacomponential planning[7]	*Confluence* (definition: a coming together of streams or ideas into a single place) *The components have to come together to result in creativity. But creativity is more than a sum of a person's level on each component. Strengths can counteract weaknesses, and interactions can occur between components.* Plus there is the decision to act: 'To be creative one must first *decide* to generate new ideas, analyze these ideas, and sell ideas to others ... The skill is not enough: one first needs to make the decision to use the skill.'
	(b) Analytic skill to recognize which ideas are worth pursuing	
	(c) Practical-contextual skill to persuade others of the value of one's ideas	
Knowledge	Enough knowledge of a field to think deeply and move it forward, but not so much as to become entrenched in current thinking	
Styles of thinking (preferred ways of using one's skills)	A preference for thinking in new ways, and a decision to do so	
	Think globally as well as locally	
Personality (note that as Sternberg defines them these are not implicit character traits but behaviours that the individual can choose to adopt)	Recognizing questions that are important and those that are not	
	Willingness to overcome obstacles	
	Willingness to take risks	
	Willingness to tolerate ambiguity	
	Belief in oneself (self-efficacy)	
	Willingness to defy the crowd and fight opposition	
Motivation	Intrinsic task-focused motivation (rather than extrinsic) (Amabile 1983), resulting in immersive 'flow' (Csíkszentmihályi 1996).[8] Sternberg argues that motivation is 'not something inherent in a person: one decides to be motivated by one thing or another'. Others might disagree. Being made to be motivated is likely to become extrinsic motivation	
Environment	Supportive and rewarding of creative ideas	
	Forum for proposing ideas and listening to them	
	However, creativity can still occur in an unresponsive environment: 'The creative individual must *decide* how to respond in the face of the nearly omnipresent environmental challenges that exist.'	

Appendix B

Examples of script reader report forms

1. Company with Hollywood links: script report

Title:
Author:
Format:
Length:
Genre:
Location:
Period:
Budget:
Submitted to:
Submitted by:
Submission date:
Reader:
Date:
Logline:

	Excellent	Good	Fair	Poor
Premise				
Plot				
Characters				
Dialogue				
Structure				
Visual				

Brief:
Script Recommendation:
Writer Recommendation:
Synopsis
Comment

2. Typical industry coverage report

Title:
Format:
Writer:
Genre:
Location:
Period:
Budget:
Audience:
Reader:
Date:
Logline:
Brief summary:
Comments:
Evaluation grid:

	Poor	*Fair*	*Good*	*Excellent*
Concept				
Structure				
Character				
Stakes				
Visuals				
Dialogue				
Marketability				

Recommendation: Pass? Meeting?

3. Government subsidy fund script reader feedback form

Title:
Format:
Writer:
Genre:
Location:
Period:
Analyst:
Date:
Logline:

Development Summary:

- Concept
- Structure and plot
- Characterization
- Dramatic stakes
- Genre and tone
- Dialogue
- Visual style
- Market potential

Recommendations:

In consideration of the above analysis of your project, here is a list of recommendations generated specifically for you to aid the development of your screenplay.

- Overall
- First act
- Second act
- Third act

Notes

Introduction

1   In 2010 worldwide box office for American films alone was worth $31.8 billion, before DVD and other income. Source: Motion Picture Association of America, MPAA (2011) *Theatrical Market Statistics*, MPAA, Washington, available at http://www.mpaa.org/Resources/93bbeb16-0e4d-4b7e-b085-3f41c459f9ac. pdf, accessed on 1.03.2012, p. 3.

2   Rizzolatti, Giacomo and Siniglalglia, Corrado (2008) *Mirrors in the Brain – How our Minds Share Actions and Emotions*, translated by Anderson, Frances, Oxford University Press, Oxford. Recent research monitoring the brain region of the superior temporal gyrus has shown that similar brainwave activity occurs when the subject either hears words or just *thinks* about them. A similar effect occurs with seeing images. This implies that the power of imagining or recalling is closer to actual experience than had previously been thought. Source: Pasley, B.N., David, S.V., Mesgarani, N., Flinker, A., Shamma, S.A. et al. (2012) 'Reconstructing Speech from Human Auditory Cortex', *PLoS Biol* 10(1), available at http://www.plosbiology.org/article/info:doi/10.1371/journal. pbio.1001251, last accessed 21.05.2012, and Nishimoto, S. et al. (2011) 'Reconstructing Visual Experiences from Brain Activity Evoked by Natural Movies', *Current Biology* 21(19): 1641–6.

3   The neuroscientist Professor Vilayanur Ramachandran argues that empathy and mirror neurones may be a vital part of how human beings create a sense of society, social understanding and culture: 'Mirror neurones also permit a sort of "virtual reality" simulation of other people's actions and intentions, which would explain why we humans are the "Machiavellian" primate – so good at constructing a "theory of other minds" in order to predict their behaviour. This is indispensable for sophisticated social interactions and some of our recent studies have shown that this system may be flawed in autistic children, which would explain their extreme social awkwardness.' Ramachandran, V. (2003) *The Emerging Mind: The Reith Lectures 2003*, BBC/Profile Books, London, p. 44. Researchers working with Professor Ramachandran have shown experimentally that a loss of mirror neurones may be the key deficit in autism that explains many symptoms of the disorder. Source: Oberman, L.M. et al. (2005) 'EEG Evidence for Mirror Neuron Dysfunction in Autism Spectrum Disorders', *Brain Res Cogn Brain Res* 24 (2): 190–8.

4   Rizzolatti and Siniglalglia (2008) op. cit., p. xii.

5   Girard proposed the theory of *mimetic desire*. People copy one another not only with language and gestures, but also with what or who they desire. Girard, René (1961) *Mensonge romantique et vérité romanesque*, Grasset, Paris; English translation: (1966) *Deceit, Desire and the Novel: Self and Other in Literary Structure*,

Johns Hopkins University Press, Baltimore. For an accessible introduction to Girard see Kirwan, Michael (2004) *Discovering Girard*, Darton, Longman & Todd, London.

6   Hume, David (1740) *A Treatise of Human Nature*.
7   'The famous director of theater and opera, Peter Brook, remarked on the recent discovery of mirror neurons as simply signifiers of artistic truth that seasoned theatrical performers have always known: when an actor probes and discovers the parts of his character that are most real, most human, "as one person enters something that is thought to be his deepest subjective experience, there can be an instant recognition, a shared understanding between everyone else who is watching".' Ben-Zvi, L. (2006) 'Staging the Other Israel: The Documentary Theatre of Nola Chilton', cited in *The Drama Review* 50(3): 42–55.
8   Alexander Mackendrick directed classic British films such as *Whisky Galore* (1949), *The Man in the White Suit* (1951) and *The Ladykillers* (1955). This quotation is from Cronin, Paul (2004) *Alexander Mackendrick on Film-making*, Faber and Faber, London, p. 3.
9   For further reading, the key recent book on mirror neurons is Rizzolatti and Siniglalglia (2008) op. cit. It is also dealt with (amongst a thousand other fascinating ideas about the brain) in Professor Ramachandran's accessible and enlightening books *The Emerging Mind* (2003) and *The Tell-Tale Brain: Unlocking the Mystery of Human Nature* (2011). However Raymond Tallis challenges the emphasis on mirror neurons and 'neuroaesthetics' as a way of approaching literature in his article 'The Neuroscience Delusion', *Times Literary Supplement*, 9 April 2008, and in more detail in his book (2011) *Aping Mankind: Neuromania, Darwinitis and the Misrepresentation of Humanity* (in which he complains about the increasingly over-reductive approach of what he calls 'neuromania').
10 For more discussion of the historical approach to concepts around creativity versus commerce, and the nature of cultural industries in general, see Hesmondhalgh, David (2007) *The Cultural Industries*, 2nd edn, Sage, London, pp. 1–26 and 51–76; and Negus, Keith and Pickering, Michael (2004) *Creativity, Communication and Cultural Value*, Sage Publications, London. The Graeco-Roman god Hermes/Mercury was patron god of creativity, commerce *and* communication, possibly because creativity was considered to be the result of inspiration from the gods, and Hermes was the messenger of the gods.

1 The bigger picture

1   Hunter, Evan (1997) *Me and Hitch,* Faber and Faber, London, p. 16.
2   The proposed definition of development: note that in the case of studios the definition would not end with the making of the film, but its subsequent distribution, so it would be redrafted: 'so that enough money can be raised to get the film made and then marketed and distributed to a suitable target audience.' However for the independent producer the raising of the distribution and marketing budget is the responsibility of the purchasing distributor and not the developing party.
3   The Hollywood 50 per cent adaptation figure is from Wasko, Janet (2008) 'Financing and Production', in McDonald, Paul and Wasko, Janet (2008) *The Contemporary Hollywood Film Industry*, Wiley-Blackwell, Oxford.
4   The UK 40 per cent adaptation estimate is from an interview for this book with Film 4's Sam Lavender (head of development) and Tracey Josephs (head of production), and the BBC estimate comes from an interview with Christine Langan (head of BBC Films).

5   For a good introduction to media law contracts see Appleton, Dina and Yankelvits, Daniel (2010) *Hollywood Dealmaking: Negotiating Talent Agreements for Film, TV and New Media*, Allworth Press, New York; or D'Agostino, G. (2010) *Copyright, Contracts, Creators: New Media, New Rules*, Edward Elgar, Cheltenham, UK. More specialized is Fosbrook, Deborah and Laing, Adrian (2009) *The Media Contracts Handbook; 4th Revised Edition*, Sweet & Maxwell, London, which is a compilation of standard contracts, aimed at media lawyers.

6   This is a paraphrase of Ulin's Rule of Distribution Value, in Ulin, J. (2010) *The Business of Media Distribution: Monetizing Film, TV, and Video Content*, Amsterdam, Boston, MA, Focal Press/Elsevier, p. 5. The advent of internet distribution initially cut across this model by threatening simultaneous non-exclusive flat-priced access, which is why in 2010–12 iTunes and other websites started to provide web 'walled gardens' of fee-paying window exclusivity. On p. 65 Ulin explains further: 'Complicating the challenge of segmenting rights into bits are the dual factors that licenses can be bound in multiple ways (e.g.: exclusive vs. non-exclusive, in perpetuity vs. limited periods of time, worldwide vs. in discrete territories) and that third parties often retain stakes in or approvals over the use of content being licensed. While at one level there is an owner (who may or may not be the creator) and a consumer, between the two is a labyrinth of rights, inputs, and approvals. Licensing content is fundamentally complicated.'

7   Source: Ulin (2010) op. cit., p. 65.

8   Powdermaker, Hortense (1950) *Hollywood, the Dream Factory: An Anthropologist Looks at the Movie-Makers*, Secker & Warburg, London, p. 151.

9   For an analysis of Puttnam's level of creative control over projects, see Adler, Tim (2004) *The Producers: Money, Movies and Who Really Call the Shots*, Methuen, London, pp. 8–10. Adler suggests that he made a habit of using relatively new directors in order to be able to better influence the shoot. The introduction to his book also provides an accessible analysis of the creative roles of veteran Hollywood producers Sam Spiegel and David Selznick.

10 Pardo, Alejandro (2010) 'The Film Producer as Creative Force', *Wide Screen* 2(2): 1–23, p. 12. Pardo goes on to point out that on some films directors also become producers, but their total control of the film's vision is apparent even when there is ostensibly a different director on the actual shoot: 'Movies like *Poltergeist* or *Young Sherlock Holmes*, for instance, though directed by competent craftsmen (Tobe Hooper and Barry Levinson respectively), are essentially Spielberg's films. Similarly, no-one thinks of *The Empire Strikes Back* and *The Return of the Jedi* (directed by Irvin Kershner and Richard Marquand respectively) as anyone's but George Lucas' films.'

11 Epstein, E.J. (2006) *The Big Picture: The New Logic of Money and Power in Hollywood*, Random House, New York, p. 281.

12 Finney, Angus (2010) *The International Film Business: A Market Analysis*, Routledge, Oxford, p. 28.

13 Ibid., p. 25. Finney cites the figures in Euros, and they were converted into pounds at the rate of 1.14 Euros.

14 UK Film Council/Skillset/Attentional (2007) *Study of Feature Film Development*, UK Film Council, London, p. 7.

15 UKFC et al. (2007) op. cit., pp. 4 and 19.

16 UK development statistics: the period surveyed is 2006–2007. Source: UKFC et al. (2007) op. cit., p. 4.

17 Finney (2010) op. cit., p. 27. $1,000,000,000.

18 Finney, Angus (1996) *The State of European Cinema: A New Dose of Reality*, Cassell, London, p. 18.

19 The US 10–20 per cent development conversion figure is from Ulin (2010) op. cit., p. 57. The 5 per cent US studio development conversion figure is from

Finney, Angus (2010) *The International Film Business: A Market Analysis*, Routledge, Oxford, p. 27.
20   Finney (2010) op. cit., p. 27.
21   National Film and TV School/Finney, in ibid., p. 24.

2 Show me the money

1   The first half of this chapter is a revised version of a paper published online by the UK Film Council in 2009. Bloore, Peter (2009) 'Re-defining the Independent Film Value Chain' (online) UK Film Council, London, available at http://industry.bfi.org.uk/media/pdf/h/b/Film_Value_Chain_Paper.pdf, accessed 22.05.2012. Also available at UEA Digital Repository.
2   'In no other business ...' Squire, J. E. (ed.) (2004) *The Movie Business Book*, 3rd edn, Simon & Schuster, New York, p. 4.
3   Michael Porter's value chain idea was developed from existing concepts of business systems being used by the consultants McKinsey, and writers like Gluck (1980), Bauron (1981) and Bower (1973), as cited in Porter (1985) op. cit., p. 36.
4   Porter, Michael E. (1985) *Competitive Advantage: Creating and Sustaining Superior Performance*, Free Press, Macmillan, New York, p. 37.
5   Adapted from ibid., p. 35.
6   For more on the value chain and its application to different industries see Lynch, Richard (2006) *Corporate Strategy*, 4th edn, Financial Times/Prentice Hall, London, pp. 203–6; and Lynch, Richard (2009) *Strategic Management*, 5th edn, Pearson Education, Harlow, pp. 130–44 for discussion of a value chain case study at Louis Vuitton and Gucci; and pp. 318–27 for discussion of integration, acquisition and growth at Rupert Murdoch's News Corporation.
7   Macnab, Geoffrey (2011) 'New European Studio', *Screen International*, 6 May, p. 6.
8   Vickery, Graham and Hawkins, Richard (2008) *Remaking the Movies: Digital Content and the Evolution of the Film and Video Industries*, OECD, Paris. Their value chain diagram is on p. 32. Indications that theirs is predominantly a studio model are that it does not differentiate between different players and organizations in the chain; it shows market research and p&a planning and cost at the same time as development and production (more applicable to studios with in-house marketing departments and distribution companies); and the authors emphasize film as an intermediate product to be supplemented by merchandizing and other secondary spin-off products. These issues are all more representative of Hollywood studio films, especially franchise movies and blockbusters, than independent European films.
9   This definition of an independent film has been adapted from the following sources: first, that an independent film is 'a film that is not a studio picture, and whose development and/or production finance is provided by more than one source' (Davies, Adam and Wistreich, Nicol (2007) *The Film Finance Handbook*, New Global Edition, Netribution, London, pp. 8–9, 449); and second, that it is a film 'that is developed without ties to a major studio, regardless of where subsequent production and/or distribution financing comes from', and/or where the producer shares some of the investment risk (Goodell (1998) p. xvii; cited in Vogel, H. (2007) *Entertainment Industry Economics – A Guide for Financial Analysis*, 7th edn, Cambridge University Press, Cambridge, pp. 90–1, 73–4.
10   It is important to point out that Porter's value chain and system model is intended to show that value is *added* to the product during production and distribution, and how companies cooperate to create a product; and does not

attempt to represent the flow of revenue back through the chain from the exploitation of the product nor show how profit is made or shared.

11 Porter (1985) op. cit., pp. 33–8.

12 Bloore (2009) op. cit. This paper also contains a full analysis of other film value chain models then in existence, and a more detailed rationale for the design of the proposed model.

13 Bloore (2009) op. cit., revised 2012.

14 Regarding the trend to name the film value system as a value chain, Swedish media academic Lucy Küng explains: 'The value chain has been a tool of preference for analysing convergence in the media industry for practitioners, consultants and academics (see for example Tapscott, 1996; Yoffie, 1997; Downes and Mui, 1998). However in the majority of examples it is not used in the "pure form" described above – where individual firm activities are disaggregated and analysed – but rather at industry level as a shorthand means of depicting graphically the various stages by which media products are created and delivered to the end consumer.' Küng, Lucy (2008) *Strategic Management in the Media: Theory to Practice*, Sage, London, p. 20.

15 Adapted from Davies and Wistreich (2007) op. cit., pp. 99–101, 154–74.

16 Source for the drop in value of the DVD market of 20 per cent in 2008: Epstein, E.J. (2010) *The Hollywood Economist: The Hidden Financial Reality Behind the Movies*, Melville House Publishing, New York, pp. 206–9.

17 For more analysis of the role of the sales agent and distributor and their role in selling and marketing films, including the role of film festivals, see ch. 8 of Kerrigan, Finola (2010) *Film Marketing*, Butterworth-Heinemann, Oxford, pp. 151–73.

18 For more on shrinking release windows, and the way Warner Brothers led the way with *Harry Potter* and *Batman*, see Epstein (2010) op. cit., pp. 182–5.

19 For example, IFC Films in New York has experimented with simultaneous release windows since 2006. Another route is to keep the cinema release but then collapse the following windows; for example, Warner Bros experimented on *Benjamin Button* in 2009, which after cinema then went to pay-per-view and iTunes at the same time as DVD and Blu-Ray. IFC Films also tried out VOD release simultaneous with DVD on some arthouse titles, but in 2012 it was reported that IFC Films were cutting back on this approach, because without the cinema release even arthouse audiences were not sufficiently aware of the films (Goodridge, Mike (2012) 'We Need Our Curators', *Screen International*, 16 February, available at http://www.screendaily.com/5038146.article, accessed 20.02.201).

20 Epstein, E.J. (2010) 'If You Are a Producer of Indie Movies …', *The Hollywood Economist Blogspot*, 5 February 2010, available at http://thehollywoodeconomist. blogspot.com/2010/02/if-you-are-producer-of-indie-movies.html, accessed 11.07.2011.

21 Vickery and Hawkins (2008) op. cit., pp. 106, 59.

22 Reception theory is a branch of cultural studies. Further reading: Hall, Stuart (1973) *Encoding and Decoding in the Television Discourse*, CCS, Birmingham; Jancovich, Mark, Faire, Lucy and Stubbings, Sarah (2003) *The Place of the Audience: Cultural Geographies of Film Consumption*, British Film Institute, London; Staiger, Janet (2000) *Perverse Spectators: The Practices of Film Reception*, New York University Press, New York. For a wider overview see Staiger, Janet (2005) *Media Reception Studies*, New York University Press, New York.

23 This relationship of risk to the value chain is discussed further by Vickery and Hawkins (2008) op. cit., p. 62.

24 For a historical explanation of how the British industry ended up in the situation of operating through a complex and fragmented value chain, see

Baillieu, Bill and Goodchild, John (2002) *The British Film Business*, John Wiley and Sons, Chichester, especially their concluding chapter 'Lessons from the Twentieth Century', pp. 151–80. This history echoes that of many other European countries where the distribution machine has been dominated by Hollywood for many years.

25   Finney, Angus (2010) *The International Film Business: A Market Analysis*; Routledge, Oxford, p. 12.

26   Lynch (2006) op. cit., pp. 417 and 465.

27   For more information see Jason Squire's *The Movie Business Book* (2006), 3rd edn, Simon & Schuster, New York, p. 113.

28   For more information on PolyGram Filmed Entertainment see Kuhn, Michael (2003) *One Hundred Films and a Funeral: PolyGram Films: Birth, Betrothal, Betrayal, and Burial*, Thorogood Publishing, London, p. 94.

29   Mintzberg, H., Lampel, J., Quinn, J.B. and Ghoshal, S. (2003) *The Strategy Process*, 4th edn, Pearson Prentice Hall, New Jersey.

30   Davies and Wistreich (2007) op. cit., pp. 154–74.

31   Following Michael Porter it has been conventional to show the value chain or value system as a series of arrows or lines going from left to right. Unfortunately this means that vertical integration is horizontally along the diagram, and horizontal integration is vertically across it, so in this figure the value chain is redrafted to go from top to bottom, to show the types of integration more clearly. Some elements of the full value chain in Fig. 2.4 have been left out due to lack of space.

32   The Film Policy Review recommended that 'Lottery funding would be used to incentivise distributors to invest in UK films by reducing their financial exposure at acquisition stage, and incentivise producers to bring distribution rigour and expertise into the financing stage, in return for a more equitable share of revenues. ... The interests of producer and distributor would be better aligned as they would be 50/50 partners in the film release venture.' Film Policy Review Panel (2012) *A Future For British Film: Report to Government by the Film Policy Review Panel*, published on behalf of the Film Policy Review Panel by the Department for Culture, Media and Sport (DCMS), London, pp. 41–5, the quotation from p. 44.

33   Bloye, Charlie (2011) Interview by Peter Bloore for the book *The Screenplay Business* [Interview – mp3 recording], Soho House, 27 April, 2011. Charlie Bloye is Chief Executive of the UK sales agent trade association: Film Export UK.

34   Ibid.

35   Hazelton, John (2011) 'Sellers Gain from Capital', *Screen International*, 6 May, pp. 12–13, available at http://www.screendaily.com/reports/in-focus/sellers-gain-from-capital/5026870.article, accessed 22.05.2012.

36   For more on this see Lynch (2006) op. cit., pp. 203–8. Lynch has also shown that two competitor companies may be using different suppliers from the value system, or sometimes some of the same suppliers, and therefore it is the *way* in which these suppliers are combined and the value added by the company itself that provides the differentiation. This is again relevant to the film industry, where similar projects using the same technical crew or talent may result in very different finished films.

37   Porter (1985) op. cit., pp. 36–52, 62–118, 130–46.

38   Source of 'a fictional example of an independent film budget investment and recoupment chart'. Davies and Wistreich (2007) op. cit., pp. 100 and 115. Davies and Wistreich argue that this fictional film would be regarded as 'in profit' once 71 per cent of the budget is recouped (in that equity is paid back and so-called profit shares can start). Therefore the vertical lines above 71 per

cent show the subdivision of the remaining 'profit'. However some soft money (usually subsidy or public money) might today be expected to recoup at the same time as equity.

39 Source of typical film recoupment chart figure: Finney (2010) op. cit., p. 71. The original was designed to be read from top to bottom, so it was adapted for this book to be read from bottom to top to make an easier comparison with the Davies and Wistreich diagram.

40 For a detailed overview of the different types of acquisition/pick-up and recoupment in the US studio system see Vogel (2007) op. cit., pp. 175–94.

41 Source of Fig. 2.9: Finney (2010) op. cit., p. 17; written by Finney 'with input from a range of industry sources.'

3 A new analysis of types of film and film development funding

1 The George Lucas quote is from Lane, R. (1996) 'The Magician', *Forbes Magazine*, 11 March; cited in Pardo, Alejandro (2010) 'The Film Producer as Creative Force', *Wide Screen* 2(2): 1–23, p. 19.

2 EuropaCorp have firm relationships with Lionsgate and Fox for US distribution, and on principle pre-sell 80 per cent of their production budgets. Between March and December 2008, EuropaCorp saw sales of $123.8m, of which $39.1m came internationally (being vertically integrated with a sales agent, about a third of EuropaCorp's revenues emanate from international sales). Source: Jaafar, Ali and Keslassy, Elsa (2009) 'France's EuropaCorp Strikes Gold', *Variety* (online), available at http://www.variety.com/article/VR1118003298?ref CatId=13, accessed 23.05.2012. One UK producer has suggested that it is easier for French producers to form integrated companies of this sort than their English counterparts, because they have access to better lines of credit due to the French subsidy system.

3 *Slumdog Millionaire* was greenlit and fully funded by Celador and Film4, and Warner's were not contractually signed up until the film had almost completed filming. Celador was the originator and producer of the TV series *Who Wants to be A Millionaire*, which inspired the original novel. Source: email correspondence by the author with Film4 and the following article: Ayres, C., Mostrous, A. and Teeman, T. (2009) 'Oscars for Slumdog Millionaire – the Film that Nearly Went Straight to DVD', *The Times*, 24 February, available online at http://entertainment.timesonline.co.uk/tol/arts_and_entertainment/film/oscars/article5793160.ece, accessed 11.02.2011.

4 The UK Film Council provided a detailed definition of specialist films in 2008 for the purposes of some of its subsidy funding and the Digital Screen Network. For distribution purposes this included acquired foreign films and US indies. Source: UK Film Council (2008) *Definition of Specialised Film*, http://www.ukfilmcouncil.org.uk/specialisedfilms, accessed 26.03.2011.

5 UK Film Council Research and Statistics Unit (2010) *UK Film Council Statistical Yearbook 2010*, UK Film Council, London, p. 40.

6 It is usual for movie buffs and broadsheet newspaper critics to dismiss Anglo-Hollywood films as being not British films, but many industry figures argue that they are a large source of employment for the industry (including studio hire, location work, facilities and post-production), and also internationally effective as cultural ambassadors for the UK. This film category is also discussed under the term 'British-Hollywood film' by Paul McDonald in a 2008 essay called 'Britain: Hollywood' in McDonald, P. and Wasko, J. (2008) *The Contemporary Hollywood Film Industry*, Blackwell, Oxford, pp. 220–31.

7   Walker, Tim (2009) 'All You Need to Know about *Slumdog Millionaire*', *Independent*, 21 January, available at http://www.independent.co.uk/arts-entertainment/films/features/all-you-need-to-know-about-slumdog-millionaire-1452119.html, accessed 01.01.2009

8   Box Office Mojo, http://www.boxofficemojo.com/movies/?id=slumdog millionaire.htm, accessed 10.2.2011.

9   UK Film Council/Stimulating World Research (2007) *A Qualitative Study of Avid Cinema-goers*, UK Film Council, London.

10   Ten per cent of people go only to blockbuster films, and 59 per cent go mainly to mainstream blockbusters, and prefer comedy and romantic comedies; 29 per cent go mainly to indie films, and are likely to view also by online streaming, and 2 per cent go only to indie films and prefer drama and foreign-language titles. The sample was of committed and 'engaged' film-goers, representing the top 40 per cent of cinema-goers and 80 per cent of admissions, sampling over 18,000 people; and the emphasis on mainstream would probably rise further with a more occasional cinema-going audience sample. These are similar category breakdowns to the Film Council research cited above. Source: Film3Sixty, as cited in Mitchell, Wendy (2012) 'Target Audience', *Screen International*, 27 January, available online at http://www.screendaily.com/reports/in-focus/target-audience/5037164.article, accessed 23.05.2012.

11   Sam Lavender (Head of Development at Film 4) is specific about the brand of the company being director-driven in its project choices: 'We are led by authorship, led by close work with writers and lots of concentration on developing original ideas, but at the end of the process we're also very director-led. I think the idea of backing and supporting directors is very important – so that would be the most important thing about the Film 4 brand in terms of development and production.' Source: Lavender, Sam (2011) Interview by Peter Bloore for the book *The Screenplay Business* [Interview – mp3 recording], Channel 4, Horseferry Road, Peter Bloore, 10.08.2011. Sam Lavender is Head of Development at Film4.

12   Some acquire, some fund production with equity, and some do both. Specialist US studio here means (at the time of writing) the likes of Universal's Focus Features, Sony Pictures Classics, Fox Searchlight. There used to be more options, but the space of a few months in 2008 saw the closure of specialist studios New Line Cinema, Miramax, Fine Line Features, Picturehouse, Warner Independent Films, Fox Atomic and Paramount Vantage. This was a result of the declining DVD market, the end of output deals with HBO and other pay-TV, and recession retrenchment by the parent companies.

13   The indicative development budgets in the table of development finance are based on outgoing payments to writers and freelance script editors, and other hard costs; and do not include development staff salaries, producer's fees, production company overheads and office costs (these would be factored into the final development line in the final shooting budget). One of the identified problems with development funding is that the producer often finds it hard to survive while keeping a project in development (see Chapter 14).

14   Gatekeepers could be defined as individuals or organizations that control access to resources or a communication medium, and may exert editorial control or influence.

15   Film Policy Review Panel (2012) *A Future For British Film: Report to Government by the Film Policy Review Panel*, published on behalf of the Film Policy Review Panel by the Department for Culture, Media and Sport (DCMS), London.

16   The UK is the second biggest exporter of television content in the world (after the far bigger US industry), and the world leader in certain types of television export, such as remake rights (known as format rights). Source: PACT (2010)

Rights of Passage, report by TRP for UKTI/Pact; cited in *Memorandum* submitted by PACT on 24.09.2010, PACT response to BIS Committee enquiry, available on PACT website at http://www.pact.co.uk/support/document-library/pact-response-to-bis-committee-enquiry-into-government/, accessed 03.03.2012.

4 The creative triangle

1 Jean-Luc Ormieres, speaking at the ACE (*Ateliers du Cinéma Européen*) Conference *Creative Producer* at the Times BFI London Film Festival at the Institut Francais on 24 October 2007.
2 A similar creative triangle could be proposed for television drama. However, the writer is often in a position of greater influence and there are different development relationships to consider, especially in the case of returning series and soaps where the triangle may be complicated by the important contributions of the executive producer (who may have been the originating writer and may determine the overall thrust of the series), the showrunner, the storylining team, the broadcaster channel commissioning editor, and so on.
3 Adler, Tim (2004) *The Producers: Money, Movies and Who Really Call the Shots*, Methuen, London, p. 147.
4 For a good accessible introduction to personality types and character traits see chs 2 and 3 in Chamorro-Premuzic, Tomas (2007) *Personality and Individual Differences*, Blackwell, Oxford.
5 All of these suggested writer's characteristics are also mentioned in Raymond Nickerson's list of 'personal characteristics necessary for creativity', in Nickerson, Raymond S. (1999) 'Enhancing Creativity', in Sternberg, R. (ed.) (1999) *Handbook of Creativity*, Cambridge University Press, Cambridge, pp. 419–20.
6 Goffee, Rob and Jones, Gareth (2007) 'Leading Clever People', *Harvard Business Review*, March: 72–9.
7 Csíkszentmihályi, Mihály (1990) *Flow: The Psychology of Optimal Experience*, Harper & Row, New York, p. 71. For more detail on his creativity research see Csíkszentmihályi, M. (1996) *Creativity: Flow and the Psychology of Discovery and Invention*, Harper Collins, New York.
8 Adapted from Epstein, E.J. (2006) *The Big Picture: The New Logic of Money and Power in Hollywood*. Random House, New York, pp. 271–4; and the quote is from p. 274. For more references to *auteur theory* see Chapter 1.
9 For more on transactional vs. transformational leaders see: Burns, J.M. (1978) *Leadership*, Harper & Row, New York; and Bass, B.M. and Avolio, B.J. (1994) *Improving Organizational Performance through Transformational Leadership*, Sage, Thousand Oaks, CA.
10 Adapted from: Conger, J. and Kunungo, R. (1988) *Charismatic Leadership*, Josey-Bass, San Francisco, CA; and Greenberg, J. and Barn, R. (2003) *Behaviour in Organisations*, 8th edn, Prentice Hall, New York.
11 Lubit, R. (2002) 'The Long-term Organizational Impact of Destructively Narcissistic Managers', *Academy of Management Executive* 16(1): 127–38, p. 128.
12 Ibid., pp. 127–38. Maccoby, M. (2000) 'Narcissistic Leaders: The Incredible Pros, the Inevitable Cons', *Harvard Business Review* (January–February): 69–77. Also more recently, Maccoby, M. (2007) *Narcissistic Leaders: Who Succeeds and Who Fails*, Harvard Business School Press, Boston, MA.
13 Nickerson (1999) op. cit., p. 414.
14 Extroversion or introversion? The extrovert's flow is directed outward towards people and objects, whereas the introvert's is directed inward towards concepts and ideas. In general, extroverts are action-oriented, while introverts are

thought-oriented; extroverts recharge and get their energy from spending time with people, while introverts recharge and get their energy from spending time alone. Tieger, Paul and Barron-Tieger, Barbara (1999) *The Art of SpeedReading People*, Little, Brown and Company, New York, p. 66.

15   The producer and business strategy: in terms of Mintzberg's strategy process schools, producers fit more into strategy schools like *environmental* (responding to wider industry dynamics beyond their control), *power* and *entrepreneurial* rather than the *planning, design* and *positioning* schools of strategy. For more on these categories see Mintzberg, H., Ahlstrand, B. and Lampel, J. (1998) *Strategy Safari*, The Free Press, Simon & Schuster, New York.

16   Shane, S. (2009) 'Entrepreneurship and the Big Five Personality Traits: A Behavioral Genetics Perspective', available at http://pdfcast.org/pdf/entrepreneurship-and-the-big-five-personality-traits-a-behavioral, accessed 22.05.2012. Also Nicolaou, N. et al. (2011) 'A Polymorphism Associated with Entrepreneurship: Evidence from Dopamine Receptor Candidate Genes', *Small Business Economics* 36(2): 151–5; Nicolaou, N., Shane, S., Cherkas, L. and Spector, T.D. (2008) 'The Influence Of Sensation Seeking in the Heritability of Entrepreneurship', *Strategic Entrepreneurship Journal* 2: 7–21; Zuckerman, M. (2007) *Sensation Seeking and Risky Behavior*, American Psychological Association, Washington DC.

17   Summarized and adapted from Burns, P. (2011) *Entrepreneurship and Small Business*, 3rd edn, Palgrave Macmillan, Basingstoke, pp. 33–42.

18   Adapted from Quinn, J.B. (1985) 'Managing Innovation: Controlled Chaos', *Harvard Business Review* 63(3): 73–84.

19   Adler (2004) op. cit..

20   Professor Allan Williams (now at London Metropolitan) and Professor Gareth Shaw at Exeter University developed the lifestyle entrepreneur concept through their study of tourism entrepreneurs from the late 1990s onward. For example: Williams, A.M., Shaw, G. and Greenwood, J. (1989) 'From Tourist to Tourism Entrepreneur, from Consumption to Production: Evidence from Cornwall, England', *Environment and Planning* A(21): 1639–53; and Shaw, G. and Williams, A. (2004) 'From Lifestyle Consumption to Lifestyle Production: New Forms of Tourism Entrepreneurship', in Thomas, R. (ed.) *Small Firms in Tourism: International Perspectives*, Elsevier, Amsterdam, pp. 99–113.

21   This research on lifestyle entrepreneurs comes from tourism and the food and accommodation industry, but is remarkably accurate when applied to some of the less successful independent producers in the UK. Box 4.4 is the edited version of a table from Peters, Mike, Frehse, Joerg and Buhalis, Dimitrios (2009) 'The Importance of Lifestyle Entrepreneurship: A Conceptual Study of the Tourism Industry', *Pasos Online* 7(2): 393–405, available at http://www.pasosonline.org/Publicados/7309special/PS0309_5.pdf, accessed 22.05.2012. The directly quoted excerpt is from p. 401.

22   Burns (2011) op. cit., pp. 19–20.

23   Source: Belbin, R.M. (1981) *Management Teams: Why They Succeed or Fail*, Butterworth Heinemann, Oxford; and revised (using above headings) in Belbin, R.M. (2004) *Management Teams*, 2nd edn, Butterworth Heinemann, Oxford, pp. 60–73.

24   To find out more about personality types and introversion/extroversion, see Carl Jung's 1921 book *Psychological Types*; and the work of Katharine Cook Briggs and her daughter Isabel Briggs Myers, who created the influential *Myers–Briggs personality-type tests* (published in 1962 and still widely used). Critics of Myers–Briggs tests and Belbin tests argue that they have not been tested with proper scientific experiments, and that they are prone to the *Forer effect* or *Barnum effect*, which suggests that people answering questionaires and

personality tests tend to falsify their answers and believe what they want to believe. For more on the Forer effect see Forer, B.R. (1949) 'The Fallacy of Personal Validation: A Classroom Demonstration of Gullibility', *Journal of Abnormal and Social Psychology* 44(1): 118–23.

25 Summary of Belbin's team roles, as applied to film development: Belbin (1981) op. cit., adapted with film emphasis by the author.

26 For more on the working relationship of producers Stephen Woolley and Nik Powell see Finney, A. (1996) *The Egos Have Landed: The Rise and Fall of Palace Pictures*, Heinemann, London.

27 De Winter, H. (2006) *What I Really Want to Do is Produce: Top Producers Talk Movies & Money*, Faber and Faber, London, p. 9.

28 Adler (2004) op. cit.; and De Winter (2006) op. cit..

29 Powdermaker, H. (1950) *Hollywood, the Dream Factory: An Anthropologist Looks at the Movie-Makers*, Secker & Warburg, London, pp. 164–6.

5 The reality of development

1 For further reading on power and influence, including theories of exchange and resource power, see Homans, G. (1961) *Social Behaviour*, Routledge & Kegan Paul, London; and for a good overview see Handy, C. (1985) *Understanding Organizations*, 3rd edn, Facts On File Publications, New York, pp. 120–53.

2 Sources: Handy (1985) op. cit., pp. 120–2; French, J. and Raven, B. (1959) in Cartwright, D. (ed.) *Studies in Social Power*, University of Michigan; cited in Handy (1985), pp. 120, 122, 438; and French, J. and Raven, B. (1968) 'The Bases of Social Power', in Cartwright, D. and Zander, A.F. (eds) *Group Dynamics: Research and Theory*, 3rd edn, Harper & Row, New York.

3 Tracey Josephs of Film4 emphasized that it was rare that Film4 embarks on development without a producer attached, saying: 'We are not set up to work in this way and do not have the manpower to micro manage projects, even if we wanted to, which we don't.' Christine Langan from BBC Films said it was unusual for them to option a property without a producer: 'I think there's a feeling here that if we [at BBC Films] were to attempt to option something that was being looked at by independent production companies, then you inflate the price (being asked for the option), or you get into a competitive situation with the person you should be working alongside, which is the producer.'

4 The Sidney Howard quote about optimism is taken from a letter to his wife. Source: Howard, Margaret and Urquhart, Sidney Howard (1995) 'Letters Home', reprinted in Boorman, John, Luddy, Tom, Thomson, David and Donohue, Walter (1995) *Projections 4: Film-Makers on Film-Making*, Faber and Faber, London.

5 Not a sparrow will fall from the sky. Source: 'Are not two sparrows sold for a farthing? and one of them shall not fall on the ground without your Father', *The Bible (King James Translation)*, Mt. 10.29.

6 Hetreed, O. (2009) 'Uneasy Bedfellows: Writers and Directors Working Together', keynote speech at the Screenwriters Festival 2009 launch event at Channel 4, 13 January.

7 Adapted from P. Bloore (2009), unpublished lecture notes, University of East Anglia.

8 Lavender, Sam (2011) Interview by Peter Bloore for the book *The Screenplay Business* [Interview – mp3 recording], Channel 4, Horseferry Road, Peter Bloore, 10.08.2011.

9 The commitment matrix is adapted for this book from Bloore, P. (2005) 'The Film Screen Academy Policy and the Effect on the National Film and Television School', unpublished MVA dissertation, London South Bank University, p. 56. The matrix was originally designed to provide a defining framework for organizational response to public policy initiatives, but is similarly applicable to levels of commitment to other projects, including in this instance film projects. The matrix design goes back to the Ansoff Matrix (1957), the Boston Consulting Group Matrix (1973) and the Mendelow Matrix (1991); but with the addition by the author of the central contingency box to highlight ambivalence. The Ansoff Matrix was first proposed in the article Ansoff (1957) 'Strategies for Diversification', *Harvard Business Review*.

6 The development executive and the script editor

1 For more on exchange power transactions versus position power and other forms of power and influence, see Chapter 5.
2 For more on the obligation to network in cultural industries see Hesmondhalgh, David and Baker, Sarah (2011) *Creative Labour: Media Work in Three Cultural Industries*, Routledge, London, pp. 108–11. They point out that the obligation to network can also threaten creative autonomy, especially when pitching to commissioners or powerful gatekeepers (however, their research was looking particularly at TV commissioning, rather than at film).
3 Kapadia, Asif (2005) Interview by Peter Bloore for Bournemouth Media MBA teaching session [Interview – informal], Regents College, London, Peter Bloore, 03.06.2005.

7 Defining creativity in the movie business

1 Theories about managing creative people in the workplace were developed initially from the research work of Robert Sternberg (1988, 1997, 1999); Margaret Boden (1990, 1994, 2004, 2010); Mihály Csíkszentmihályi (1988, 1996); Jane Henry (1991, 2001); and above all Teresa Amabile at Harvard (1983, 1996, 1998). This created an increasing body of evidence that supportive environments could encourage creative people in their work. Furthermore, these environments could be manipulated by understanding the distinctive psychology of creative people; the exploitation of intrinsic and extrinsic motivation; the encouragement of creative risk; and the creation of enabling organizational cultures and company structures. These ideas were developed by Davis and Scase (2000), and Boynton and Fischer (2005). With the exception of Bilton (2007), most books on media management only touch in passing on managing creativity (Björkegren 1996; Block 2001; Howkins 2001; Aris and Bughin 2006; Küng 2008); and none apply it to film in any detail.
2 Creativity reading list: There are endless books on creativity and its definition, so this is a personal selection to provide an overview and encourage further reading. For an approachable analysis of the history of concepts associated with creativity, novelty and artists, and the cultural and media studies context, see Negus, Keith and Pickering, Michael (2004) *Creativity, Communication and Cultural Value*, Sage, London. For a fascinating exploration of ideas around *ex nihilo* and boundary breaking, see D.N. Perkins' essay 'The Possibility of Invention', which can be found in the invaluable book Sternberg, R.J. (1988) *The Nature of Creativity: Contemporary Psychological Perspectives*, Cambridge University Press, Cambridge, pp. 362–85.

A thorough academic overview of creativity research is found in Albert and Runco's paper 'A History of Research on Creativity', published as ch. 2 of Sternberg's 1999 *Handbook of Creativity*; and the same book contains Raymond Nickerson's essay 'Enhancing Creativity', which analyses various definitions of creativity and asks whether creativity can be enhanced (pp. 392–429). A readable and therefore widely read book is Csíkszentmihályi, Mihály (1996) *Creativity: Flow and the Psychology of Discovery and Invention*, Harper Collins, New York. Although more polemical, Gordon Torr's recent book also provides an accessible introduction to creativity and its management (Torr, G. (2009) *Managing Creative People*, Wiley and Sons, London). To explore the thinking on the key concept of intrinsic and extrinsic motivation it is best to go back to Teresa Amabile's influential 1996 book *Creativity in Context*, Westview Press, Perseus Books, Boulder, CO; and Amabile, Teresa and Hennessey, Beth (1988) 'The Conditions of Creativity', in Sternberg, R.J. *The Nature of Creativity: Contemporary Psychological Perspectives*, Cambridge University Press, Cambridge, pp. 11–38.

This book has drawn regularly from Boden, Margaret (2004) *Creative Mind: Myths and Mechanisms*, 2nd edn, Routledge, London (her 2011 book *Creativity and Art: Three Roads to Surprise*, looks more closely at art and craft in particular); and from many articles and papers by Amabile (see the bibliography for a complete list; but her *Harvard Business Review* articles are accessible and enlightening).

Having the creative idea is only the start of the process, and recent business books have looked harder at the problematic area of effective implementation and entrepreneurial innovation, including Govindarajan, V. and Trimble, C. (2010) *The Other Side of Innovation: Solving the Execution Challenge*, HBS Press, Boston, MA; Berkun, Scott (2007) *The Myths of Innovation*, O'Reilly Media, Sebastopol, CA; and Bilton, Chris and Cummings, Stephen (2010) *Creative Strategy: Reconnecting Business and Innovation*, Wiley & Sons, Chichester. It could be argued that there is a distinction between innovation (the action of successfully introducing something new to an organization or market), which almost always requires teamwork and implementation, and creativity (coming up with a new idea, process or artefact), which may or may not require teamwork, and may or may not be implemented successfully. You can have creativity without innovation (if the idea is not adopted or implemented), but it is harder to have innovation without some element of creativity. However, in organizational terms not all innovations are the result of creativity within the organization – they may be adopted from elsewhere and still be new to the organization that is being changed.

3 Boden (2004) op. cit., p. 1. (Note that this definition is not in the 1990 first edition of the book.)
4 Ibid.
5 Figure 7.1 is based on a working model of the creative literary text shown as products and processes, as developed by the literature Professor and creativity expert Rob Pope, and adapted from a 1953 essay by M.H. Abrams. Original figure: Pope, Rob (2002) *The English Studies Book: An Introduction to Language, Literature and Culture*, 2nd edn, Routledge, London (1st edn, 1998), p. 77, adapted from Abrams (1953) 'Orientation of Critical Theories', in M.H. Abrams (1971) *The Mirror and the Lamp: Romantic Theory and the Critical Tradition*, Oxford University Press, London. Adapted by the author of this book.
6 Csíkszentmihályi, Mihály (1988) *A Systems Perspective on Creativity*, in Sternberg (1999) op. cit., pp. 313–35; and Csíkszentmihályi (1996) op. cit., pp. 27–50. The quote is from the latter, p. 28. Systems thinking places emphasis on holistic

cyclical relationships between problems, solutions and environment, rather than simple linear cause and effect.

7   Figure 7.2 and quote from Csíkszentmihályi (1988) op. cit., p. 315.

8   Csíkszentmihályi (1996) op. cit., p. 10.

9   Boden, Margaret (2000) *Creative Mind: Myths and Mechanisms*, 1st edn, George Weidenfeld & Nicolson, London, pp. 32–7; and Boden (2004) op. cit., pp. 43–7. Companies employ people who are capable of P-creative ideas, in the hope that some of those may eventually be H-creative too (ground-breaking).

10 Box 7.2 is summarized and adapted by the author from ibid., pp. 3–7. For a detailed review of the critical response to Boden's definition see Thornton, C. (2007) *A Quantitative Reconstruction of Boden's Creativity Theory*, University of Sussex, Brighton, available at http://citeseerx.ist.psu.edu/viewdoc/download?doi=10.1.1.62.6745&rep=rep1&type=pdf, accessed 22.05.2012.

11 Csíkszentmihályi distinguishes between (1) those who express unusual thoughts, (2) those who experience the world in novel, original ways, (3) those who effect significant changes in their culture, any act, idea or product that changes an existing domain: Csíkszentmihályi (1996) op. cit., p. 28. Gardner makes a similar distinction between 'little C' and 'big C' creativity: Gardner, H. (1993) 'Seven Creators of the Modern Era', in J. Brockman (ed.) *Creativity*, Simon & Schuster, New York; cited in Nickerson, Raymond S. (1999) *Enhancing Creativity*, in Sternberg (1999) op. cit., p. 399.

12 Guilford, J. (1950) 'Creativity', *American Psychologist* 5: 444–54; and Guilford, J. (1967) *The Nature of Human Intelligence*, McGraw-Hill, New York. Divergent thinking required: (1) fluency (a great number of ideas or problem solutions in a short period of time); (2) flexibility (simultaneously propose a variety of approaches to a specific problem); (3) originality; and (4) elaboration (ability to organize the details of an idea and carry it out).

13 Gardner (1993) op. cit., p. 399.

14 Bilton, Chris (2007) *Management and Creativity: From Creative Industries to Creative Management*, Blackwell, Oxford, p. 6. Convergent thinking dealing with continuity, focus and conscious processes and divergent thinking with random thoughts, removal of constraints and subconscious processes.

15 Csíkszentmihályi (1996) op. cit., p. 28.

16 Ekvall, G. (2006) 'Organisational Conditions and Levels of Creativity', in Henry, J. (2006) *Creative Management and Development*, Sage, London, pp. 141–2.

17 Kirton, M. (1984) 'Adaptors and Innovators: Why New Initiatives Get Blocked' (from Kirton, M. (1984) 'Adaptors and Innovators', *Long Range Planning* 17(2): 137–43), in Henry (2006) op. cit., p. 109. Adaptors stretch existing agreed definitions and seek likely solutions to 'do things better'; innovators work separately to the paradigm or customary viewpoint, seeking problems, and are less concerned with doing things better and more with doing things differently. Adaptors will sometimes cooperate well in a team with innovators, but may sometimes close down the innovators' radical ideas and ways of working.

18 Sternberg, R.J. (2006) 'The Nature of Creativity', *Creativity Research Journal* 18: 87–99; repr. in Kaufman, James and Grigorenko, Elena (2009) *The Essential Sternberg: Essays on Intelligence, Psychology and Education*, Springer, New York.

19 James Webb Young, in one of the most influential books on creative thinking in advertising, identified that creative ideas are 'the new combination of old elements': Young, J.W. (1960) *A Technique for Producing Ideas*, McGraw Hill, New York.

20 Altman, C. (1977) 'Towards a Theory of Genre Film', in 'A New Approach To Genre', *Purdue Film Studies Annual*, vol. 2, Purdue University, West Lafayette.

21   For example, creativity academic D.N. Perkins also places emphasis on the importance of creative people intentionally seeking to explore boundaries, either because of an intransigent problem that is not solvable within the existing boundaries; or an exhaustion of existing opportunities; or simply intentional 'boundary fiddling' (creative people are prone to struggle against the status quo, as we shall see). Perkins, D.N. (1988) 'The Possibility of Invention', in Sternberg (1988) op. cit., pp. 362–85.

22   For more on the action thriller sub-genre of 'hard-bodied masculinity' and its cultural context, see Tasker, Yvonne (1993) *Spectacular Bodies: Gender, Genre, and the Action Cinema*, Routledge, London; Jeffords, Susan (1993) *Hard Bodies: Hollywood Masculinity in the Reagan Era*, Rutgers University Press, New Jersey; and Tasker, Yvonne (ed.) (2004) *Action and Adventure Cinema*, Routledge, London.

23   For more detail on transmedia storytelling and the Wachowskis see Jenkins, Henry (2006) *Convergence Culture: Where Old and New Media Collide*, New York University Press, New York.

24   Rose, Steve (2011) 'The Droog Rides Again', *Guardian Film and Music Review*, 12 May, pp. 19–21.

8 Who creative people are and how to motivate them

1   Socrates, quoted in Plato's *Ion*; cited in Perkins, D.N. (1988) 'The Possibility of Invention', in Sternberg, Robert J. (1988) *The Nature of Creativity: Contemporary Psychological Perspectives*, Cambridge University Press, Cambridge, pp. 365 and 385.

2   For a thorough review of research into creative personality traits see Stein, M. (1974–5) *Stimulating Creativity* (vols 1–2), Academic Press, New York; or again Nickerson, Raymond (1999) 'Enhancing Creativity', in Sternberg, R. (ed.) (1999) *Handbook of Creativity*, Cambridge University Press, Cambridge, pp. 392–429; or for a quicker overview try the widely available Adair, J. (2007) *Leadership for Innovation: How to Organize Team Creativity and Harvest Ideas*, Kogan Page, London (a reissue of Adair, J. (1990) *The Challenge of Innovation*, Talbot Adair Press), pp. 71–83. In 1950 Guilford defined a personality as a unique pattern of traits and a trait as 'any relatively enduring way in which persons differ from one another. The psychologist is particularly interested in those traits that are manifested in performance; in other words, in behaviour traits ... aptitudes, interests, attitudes, and temperamental qualities.' Guilford, J.P. (1950) 'Creativity', *American Psychologist* 5: 444–54; cited in Amabile, Teresa (1996) *Creativity in Context* (update to the *Social Psychology of Creativity*), Westview Press, Perseus Books, Boulder, CO, p. 21. There are some limitations to the methodology of the character trait approach. Colin Martindale of the University of Maine has studied the biological bases of creativity and confirms that high creativity is a rare trait because it requires the *simultaneous* presence of a bundle of character traits which are not unusual in themselves, but rare when found together (Martindale, Colin (1999) 'Biological Bases of Creativity', in Sternberg, R. (ed.) (1999) *Handbook of Creativity*, Cambridge University Press, Cambridge, pp. 137–48). Mihály Csíkszentmihályi adds that creative people can also be chameleons and adapt their true natures to the social circumstances and situations:

> Creative people are characterised not so much by their single traits, as by their ability to operate through the entire spectrum of personality dimensions. ...Creative individuals are sensitive and aloof, dominant and

humble, masculine and feminine, as the occasion demands. What dictates their behaviour is not a rigid inner structure, but the demands of the interaction between them and the domain in which they are working.

(Csíkszentmihályi, M. (1988) 'A Systems Perspective on Creativity', in Sternberg (ed), see above, pp. 313–35)

The Harvard academic Teresa Amabile points out that whilst these clusters of character traits are found fairly consistently among people with high levels of creativity, they are not sufficient in themselves for creativity to happen: 'certainly, any given individual – even one exhibiting a particular "creative" personality-trait constellation – is not creative at all times or in all domains'. Amabile (1996), see above, p. 83. Different people may exhibit different degrees of these traits, and there are also other variables such as educational background; the age at which peak creativity is achieved in different domains; the levels of practice and expertise required in the craft; good old-fashioned luck; and above all the social and work environment, and its role in encouraging motivation.

3   The world of studying creative people and innovation is divided between two polarities, or positions on a continuum between those polarities: on one side the lone genius concept (where individuality and personal inspiration are vital and creative people are special), and, on the other side, active decrying of the genius 'myth' in favour of the management of teams and the use of processes that can exploit the hidden creativity in all people (because we are all creative if we learn how to unlock it). The see-saw between the lone genius and the team player has changed over time and is subject to socio-cultural influence. For an analysis of the historical context of the genius approach to creativity see Negus, Keith and Pickering, Michael (2004) *Creativity, Communication and Cultural Value*, Sage, London, pp. 138–61; and for more on the value of teamworking and the need to control and manage creativity see Bilton, Chris (2007) *Management and Creativity: From Creative Industries to Creative Management*, Blackwell, Oxford, pp. 23–44 and 66–90. A more forceful voice in favour of the team can be found in Robert W. Weisberg's (1986) *Creativity: Genius and Other Myths*, W.H. Freeman and Co., Gordonsville, VA, updated into *Creativity: Beyond the Myth of Genius* in 1993, and Berkun, Scott (2007) *The Myths of Innovation*, O'Reilly Media, Sebastopol, CA.

4   For example, Amabile, Teresa and Fisher, Colin (2009) 'Stimulate Creativity by Fuelling Passion', in Locke, E.A. (2009) *Handbook of Principles of Organizational Behaviour: Indispensable Knowledge for Evidence-Based Management*, Wiley, Chichester, p. 482. For a good introduction to various views about the link or otherwise between intelligence and creativity and personality traits, see Chamorro-Premuzic, Tomas (2007) *Personality and Individual Differences*, Blackwell, Oxford, pp. 131–7.

5   Nickerson is summing up his own research and that of other authors. Nickerson (1999) op. cit., pp. 419–20.

6   Majaro, Simon (1992) 'Managing Ideas for Profit', *Journal of Marketing Management* 8; cited in Burns, Paul (2011) *Entrepreneurship and Small Business*, 3rd edn, Palgrave Macmillan, Basingstoke, p. 112.

7   Source: Adair(1990) op. cit., pp. 71–83. In a review of other creativity research Barron and Harrington (1981) wrote that creative people have 'high valuation of aesthetic qualities in experience, broad interests, attraction to complexity, high energy, independence of judgment, autonomy, intuition, self-confidence, ability to resolve antimonies or to accommodate opposite or conflicting traits in one's self concept, and finally a firm sense of self as "creative".' Barron and

Harrington (1981) 'Creativity, Intelligence, and Personality', *Annual Review of Psychology* 32: 439–76, p. 453.

8　'The creative mind plays with the objects it loves' (Carl Jung (1875–1961)). Like some other Jung quotes this is attributed to him, but no precise citation has been found by the author.

9　For more discussion of ideas around de-focused attention, cortical arousal and left/right hemisphere research, see Martindale (1999) op. cit., pp. 137–48.

10　An early and influential proponent of applying Freudian primary and secondary process thought to creative inspiration was Kris, E. (1952) *Psychoanalytic Explorations in Art*, International Universities Press, New York.

11　Katz, A. (1997) 'Creativity in the Cerebral Hemispheres', in Runco, M. (ed.) *Creativity Research Handbook*, Hampton Press, New Jersey, pp. 203–26; cited in Chamorro-Premuzic (2007) op. cit., Blackwell, Oxford, p. 129.

12　Martindale (1999) op. cit., p. 148. Damage to the frontal lobes can also cause acute disinhibition, decreased socialization, peculiar sexual habits and diminished creativity and problem-solving.

13　According to the Indian neurologist Professor Vilayanur Ramachandran the cross-talking clue may rest in a condition called *synaesthesia*: the strange and apparently useless ability of some people's brains to automatically associate colours with numbers or days of the week, or musical notes. To a synaesthete the number 5 on a white page may look tinged with red, number 6 with green and so on. Ramachandran tells us that this condition is seven times more common among creative types. Famous examples include David Hockney, Vladimir Nabokov, Duke Ellington, Franz Liszt and Nikolai Rimsky-Korsakov. Synaesthesia runs in families, so it appears that a genetic influence on the creation of the brain causes an accidental cross-talk or cross-wiring between the parts of the brain where numbers and colours are processed, and as a result abstract notions become associated with sensory perceptions. The reason this condition is interesting is that it is similar to lateral thinking:

> What artists, poets and novelists all have in common is their skill at forming metaphors, linking seemingly unrelated concepts in their brain, as when Macbeth said 'Out out brief candle', talking about life. But why call it a candle? Is it because life is a long white thing? Obviously not. Metaphors are not meant to be taken literally (except by schizophrenics, which is another story altogether). But in some ways life is like a candle: it's ephemeral, it can be snuffed out, it illumines only very briefly.
>
> (Ramachandran, V. (2003) *The Emerging Mind: The Reith Lectures 2003*, BBC/Profile Books, London. The quote is from p. 83. Other relevant sections: pp. 70–86 and pp. 157–62)

Ramachandran suggests that the brains of creative people may have an unusual level of hyperconnectivity between different regions of the brain (what he calls *subpathological cross-modal interactions*), and this could be the beginning of an explanation of the crucial creative ability to think laterally and use metaphor (which is after all the ability to meaningfully link seemingly unrelated things) (Ramachandran, V. (2011) *The Tell-Tale Brain: Unlocking the Mystery of Human Nature*, William Heinemann, London, p. 108). However, not all creatives are synaesthetes; creativity and synaesthesia are just similar but possibly related processes:

Why isn't every synesthete highly gifted or every great artist or poet a synesthete? The reason may be that synesthesia might merely predispose you to be creative, but this does not mean other factors (both genetic and environmental) aren't involved in the full flowering of creativity. Even so I would suggest that similar – though not identical – brain mechanisms might be involved in both phenomena.

(Ibid., p. 107)

Since synaesthesia is known to be genetically transmitted it raises the unpopular notion that there is a genetic component to certain elements of high creativity.

14 Martindale (1999) op. cit., p. 138.
15 Kekulé is recounting his own account of the discovery of benzene (in a speech in 1890 as part of the celebrations of the twenty-fifth anniversary of his first benzene paper), so as with Coleridge's account of the writing of the poem 'Kubla Khan' there may be an element of intentional myth-making. For detailed discussions of the importance of the Kekulé case see Csíkszentmihályi, Mihály (1996) *Creativity: Flow and the Psychology of Discovery and Invention*, Harper Collins, New York, pp. 101–4; Boden, Margaret (2004) *Creative Mind: Myths and Mechanisms*, 2nd edn, Routledge, London, pp. 25–8 and 62–71; and Martindale (1999) op. cit., pp. 137–48.
16 Freud of course argued that creativity and lateral thinking were all about problems with sex: the result of a repressed memory of sexual awakening or trauma seeking resolution through misdirected curiosity.
17 Martindale (1999) op. cit., p. 149.
18 Cronin, Paul (2004) *Alexander Mackendrick on Film-making*, Faber and Faber, London, pp. 36–9. It seems possible that Mackendrick is specifically referring to Young's work, since the chapter is called 'A Technique for Producing Ideas', the same as Young's book.
19 Box 8.4 on the creative process is largely based on the five steps described in Young, J.W. (1960) *A Technique for Producing Ideas*, McGraw Hill, New York. The bold headings come from the four creative phases of Poincaré and Hadamard. Poincaré, Henri (1924) *The Foundations of Science*, University Press of America, Washington, DC; cited in Boden (2004) op. cit., pp. 29–35; and cited in Amabile (1996) op. cit., p. 99. Herman Von Helmholtz had just three phases: saturation, incubation and illumination. Wallas also has four steps; see Wallas, G. (1926) *The Art of Thought*, Harcourt, Brace, New York; cited in Amabile (1996) op. cit., p. 99. Amabile generally places less emphasis on the illumination stage: task identification, preparation, response generation, response validation (op. cit., p. 101 on illumination, and see her componential model diagram on p. 113). In reality the creative process is often not as sequential, and may involve revisiting the first two stages regularly before illumination (Isaksen, Scott G., Dorval, Brian K. and Treffinger, Donald J. (1994) *Creative Approaches to Problem Solving*, Kendal/Hunt Publishing Company; cited in Amabile (1996), p. 114). For a brief survey of different theories of the creative process also see Bilton, Chris (2006) *Management and Creativity: From Creative Industries to Creative Management*, Blackwell, Oxford, pp. 7–14. The team roles in step 5 are from Belbin (1981).
20 Young (1960) op. cit., p. 24.
21 Csíkszentmihályi and Nickerson agree on the value of the inquisitive mind, and Csíkszentmihályi notes that 'the first step toward a more creative life is the cultivation of curiosity and interest, that is the allocation of attention to things for their own sake'. Csíkszentmihályi (1996) op. cit., p. 346.
22 Nickerson (1999) op. cit., pp. 392–429.

23 Google 20 per cent time is cited in Adair (2007) op. cit. and Goffee, Rob and Jones, Gareth (2007) 'Leading Clever People', in *Harvard Business Review*, March: 72–9.

24 The excerpt on deadlines and meaningful urgency is from Amabile, T.M., Hadley, C.N. and Kramer, S.J. (2002) 'Creativity under the Gun', *Harvard Business Review*, August: 52–61.

25 For the original work on brainstorming see Osborn, Alex (1942) *How to 'Think Up'*, McGraw-Hill, New York; and Osborn, Alex (1953) *Applied Imagination: Principles and Procedures of Creative Problem Solving*, Charles Scribner's Sons, New York.

26 Critics of the effectiveness of brainstorming include: Torr, Gordon (2009) *Managing Creative People*, Wiley & Sons, London; Diehl, Michael and Stroebe, Wolfgang (1991) 'Productivity Loss in Idea-Generating Groups: Tracking Down the Blocking Effect', *Journal of Personality and Social Psychology* 61(3): 392–403; and Diehl, Michael and Stroebe, Wolfgang (1987) 'Productivity Loss in Brainstorming Groups: Toward the Solution of a Riddle', *Journal of Personality and Social Psychology* 53: 497–509.

27 Catton, Catherine (2008) *To Explore How A Production Company Should Manage Its Creative Teams in Order to Generate Successful Factual Entertainment Ideas*, unpublished MBA dissertation, Bournemouth University Media School, p. 69. Note that this study covered a single company over a specific period, and further research is needed in this field, especially within television. This dissertation was supervised by the author.

28 Op. cit., p. 63.

29 Part of Osborn's theory was that listening to the ideas of others may encourage more ideas; however, other research, including that of Diehl and Stroebe, indicates that the act of listening to other people may stifle creativity. Amabile's recent research shows that creatives would often work with one or two peers. This also applies to corporate life generally, as well as brainstorms: 'Our research suggests that managers should also encourage one-on-one collaborations and discussions, avoiding an excess of the obligatory group meetings that may contribute to feelings of fragmentation and wasted time.' Amabile et al. (2002) op. cit., p. 61.

30 On cortical arousal and brainstorming, see Martindale (1999) op. cit., p. 140.

31 Csíkszentmihályi summarizing the research of MacKinnon, D. (1963) 'Creativity and Images of the Self', in White, R.W. (ed.) *The Study of Lives*, Atherton, New York, pp. 251–78; Sternberg, R. (1985) 'Implicit Theories of Intelligence, Creativity and Wisdom', *Journal of Personality and Social Psychology* 49: 607–27; Westby, E. and Dawson, V. (1995) 'Creativity: Asset or Burden', *Creativity Research Journal* 8: 1–10; cited in Csíkszentmihályi (1996) op. cit., p. 403.

32 Creative people have a firm sense of themselves as creative: Barron and Harrington (1981) 'Creativity, Intelligence, and Personality', *Annual Review of Psychology* 32: 439–76, p. 453.

33 'Like herding cats' from Goffee and Jones (2007) op. cit.

34 Feist, Gregory (1998) 'The Influence of Personality on Artistic and Scientific Creativity', in Sternberg (1999) op. cit., p. 275. Another review of research into creative people included similar negative character traits such as argumentative, assertive, cynical, demanding, egotistical, hurried, idealistic, impulsive, rebellious, and specifically 'not conventional and not inhibited'. Barron and Harrington (1981) op. cit., p. 454.

35 The author, in informal conversation with screenwriters in the business, and at various universities and film schools.

36 'Sensation seeking is a trait defined by the seeking of varied, novel, complex, and intense sensations and experiences, and the willingness to take physical,

social, legal, and financial risks for the sake of such experience.' Zuckerman, Marvin (1994) *Behavioural Expressions and Biosocial Bases of Sensation Seeking*, Cambridge University Press, Cambridge, p. 27. For a detailed introduction to Zuckerman's research into the character traits of sensation-seekers it is worth reading his 1994 book, which includes several references to creativity. His most recent book places particular emphasis on risky behaviour such as sex and substance abuse. Zuckerman, Marvin (2007) *Sensation Seeking and Risky Behavior*, American Psychological Association, Washington DC.

37 Op. cit., pp. 107–68; and Zuckerman (1994) op. cit.
38 Rosenbloom, Tova (2003) 'Risk Evaluation and Risky Behavior of High and Low Sensation seekers', *Social Behavior and Personality* 31(4): 75–386. Nicolaou, Nicos et al. (2011) 'A Polymorphism Associated with Entrepreneurship: Evidence from Dopamine Receptor Candidate Genes', *Small Business Economics* 36(2): 151–5; Shane, S. (2009) 'Entrepreneurship and the Big Five Personality Traits: A Behavioral Genetics Perspective', available at http://pdfcast.org/pdf/entrepreneurship-and-the-big-five-personality-traits-a-behavioral, accessed 22.05.2012.
39 Ebstein, R.P. et al. (1996) 'Dopamine DR Receptor (DRD4): Exon III Polymorphism Associated with the Human Personality Trait of Sensation Seeking', *Nature Genetics* 12: 78–80; cited in Zuckerman (2007) op. cit., p. xiv.
40 Interview with Malcolm McDowell in Rose, Steve (2011) 'The Droog Rides Again', *Guardian Film and Music Review*, 12 May, pp. 19–21, on the occasion of the reissue of a restored print *Clockwork Orange* at the Cannes Film Festival 2011.
41 Regarding creative people and androgyny, see: Csíkszentmihályi, M., Rathunde, K. and Whalen, S. (1993) *Talented Teenagers*, Cambridge University Press, New York; and Spence, J. and Helmrich, R. (1978) *Masculinity and Femininity*, University of Texas Press, Austin; cited in Csíkszentmihályi (1996) op. cit. It is also discussed in Chamorro-Premuzic (2007) op. cit., p. 130.
42 Harlow, H.F. (1950) 'Learning and Satiation Response in Intrinsically Motivated Complex Puzzle Performance by Monkeys', *Journal of Comparative Physiological Psychology* 43: 289–94; cited in Amabile (1996) op. cit., pp. 108 and 282.
43 R. Crutchfield (1962) 'Conformity and Creative Thinking', in Gruber, H., Terrell, G. and Wertheimer, M. (eds) *Contemporary Approaches to Creative Thinking*, Atherton Press, New York; and Lepper, M., Greene, D. and Nisbett, R. (1973) 'Undermining Children's Intrinsic Motivation with Extrinsic Rewards: A Test of the Overjustification Hypothesis', *Journal of Personality and Social Psychology* 28(1): 129–37; both cited in Amabile (1996), op cit., pp. 108–9; Lepper et al. available at http://psycnet.apa.org/journals/psp/28/1/129/, accessed 22.05.2012.
44 Amabile (1996) op. cit., p. 15.
45 Csíkszentmihályi (1996) op. cit.
46 Adapted from Csíkszentmihályi (1996) op. cit., pp. 111–13. The quote is from p. 123.
47 Amabile (1996) op. cit., p. 16.
48 Enzle, M.A. and Ross, J.M. (1978) 'Increasing and Decreasing Intrinsic Interest with Contingent Rewards: A Test of Cognitive Evaluation Theory', *Journal of Experimental Social Psychology* 14(6): 588–97.
49 Amabile, T., Phillips, E. and Collins, M. (1994) 'Creativity by Contract: Social Influences on the Creativity of Professional Artists', unpublished manuscript, Brandeis University; cited in Amabile (1996) op. cit., p. 117.
50 For more discussion of intrinsic motivation and selecting the right people for the task, see Adair, J. (1990) op. cit., p. 76. More recently, American journalist Daniel Pink has set out to popularize intrinsic motivation theories for wider

business application: Pink, Daniel (2010) *Drive: The Surprising Truth About What Motivates Us*, Canongate Books, Edinburgh.

51 Technical aspects of performance do not decline as a result of the expectation of evaluation in the way that creative performance does. Amabile (1996) op. cit., pp. 149–50. The dangers of extrinsic motivation were identified prior to Amabile by McGraw, K. (1978) 'The Detrimental Effects of Reward on Performance: A Literature Review and a Prediction Model', in Lepper, M. and Greene, D. (eds) *The Hidden Costs of Reward*, Lawrence Erlbaum Associates, Hillsdale, NJ; cited in Amabile (1996), pp. 133 and 286.

52 Maslow, A. (1971) *Farther Reaches of Human Nature*, McGraw-Hill, New York, p. 300. Maslow put creativity (and the need for beauty) into *metamotivation*. Being American, Maslow has been accused of focusing too much on individual achievement in his model, following the individualistic perspective reflected by the American Dream and US/Western culture as opposed to the view of more collectivist societies. Hofstede, G. (1984) 'The Cultural Relativity of the Quality of Life Concept', *Academy of Management Review* 9(3): 389–98. It could also be argued that sex is part of the love and relationships need, and not a biological need.

53 McGregor, D.M. (1957) 'The Human Side of Enterprise', *Management Review* 46: 22–8. In McGregor's system creative people are hitting on the self-fulfilment and ego needs, not physiological or safety needs.

54 Adapted from Maslow, A.H. (1954) *Motivation and Personality*, Harper and Brothers, New York. The basic theory was originally proposed in Maslow, A.H. (1943) 'A Theory of Human Motivation', *Psychological Review* 50(4): 370–96.

55 Connolly, Cyril (1938) *Enemies of Promise*, Andre Deutsch, London, p. 116.

56 Alderfer, Clayton P., 'An Empirical Test of a New Theory of Human Needs', *Organizational Behaviour and Human Performance* 4(2): 142–75; cited in Chamorro-Premuzic (2007) op. cit., pp. 120–1.

57 Hesmondhalgh, David and Baker, Sarah (2011) *Creative Labour: Media Work in Three Cultural Industries*, Routledge, London, pp. 139–58. Their research is particularly looking at workers in television, magazine journalism and music, but some of the findings can also apply to film workers.

58 Hesmondhalgh and Baker (2011) op. cit., p. 158.

59 Source: Amabile (1996) op. cit., p. 119 (italics added).

60 Amabile's research has shown that *win-lose competition* between peers (as used, for example, with corporate sales staff) generally has a negative effect on creativity, although competition with outside groups may have a positive effect on work teams.

61 Source: ibid., p. 119. Only direct and primary influences are depicted in the figure. The text has also been informed by further recent discussion of different types of extrinsic motivation in Amabile, Teresa and Fisher, Colin (2009) 'Stimulate Creativity by Fuelling Passion', in Locke, E.A. (2009) *Handbook of Principles of Organizational Behaviour: Indispensable Knowledge for Evidence-Based Management*, Wiley, Chichester, p. 484.

62 The term *hack writer* was first used in the eighteenth century, when publishing was establishing itself as a business. Hack was apparently a shortening of *hackney* – a breed of horse that was often available for hire (a hackney carriage is the old name for a London taxi).

63 Schulberg, Budd (1954) *On the Waterfront: Screenplay*, Columbia Pictures Corporation/Sony Pictures Home Entertainment. Incidentally, most people know the lines were spoken by Marlon Brando in *On the Waterfront*, and film buffs may know that it was directed by the Turkish-born American director Elia Kazan and produced by Sam Spiegel – but how many people know the name of the screenwriter (Budd Schulberg, based on original research by New York

investigative journalist Malcolm Johnson)? This example also casts light on the role of the creative producer in the conception and development of the film, because it was Sam Spiegel who nagged Budd Schulberg into another year of rewrites, when the writer had previously thought the script finished. It was these extra rewrites that ended up creating this now famous scene. It was also Spiegel who suggested restructuring the original script to concentrate more on the relationship between the brothers (rather than the politics). For more see Adler, Tim (2004) *The Producers: Money, Movies and Who Really Call the Shots*, Methuen, London, pp. 14–16; and Sinclair, Andrew (1987) *Spiegel: The Man behind the Pictures*, Weidenfeld & Nicolson, London.

64   Hortense Powdermaker (1950) *Hollywood, the Dream Factory: An Anthropologist Looks at the Movie-Makers*, Little, Brown, Boston, MA: available at http://astro. temple.edu/~ruby/wava/powder/table.html, p. 149.

65   Adapted and summarized by the author, from Amabile (1996) op. cit., pp. 82–93 and 260. Amabile's later further division of these different components into specific application at different stages of the five-step creative process (p. 113) is perhaps over-simplistic or schematic, in that they are probably in use consciously or subconsciously throughout the process.

66   Sternberg's *investment theory of creativity* suggested that creative people are those who are willing to 'buy low and sell high' in the realm of ideas by pursuing ideas that are new, unknown or out of favour, and adapting them to modern needs (selling), before moving on to the next idea. Note that Sternberg places emphasis on creative people *choosing* to do these things, rather than being compelled or forced by genetic predisposition. If these are conscious decisions then they can be encouraged by a work environment that encourages creativity or these ways of working. For more details see Appendix A. Sternberg, Robert J. (2006) 'The Nature of Creativity', *Creativity Research Journal* 18: 87–99; repr. in Kaufman, James and Grigorenko, Elena (2009) *The Essential Sternberg: Essays on Intelligence, Psychology and Education*, Springer, New York. It is a development of the paper Sternberg, R. and Lubart, T. (1991) 'An Investment Theory of Creativity and Its Development', *Human Development*, 34: 1–31. It is compared by Amabile to her own componential theory in Amabile (1996) op. cit., pp. 124–5.

9 Managing creative people and film development

1   David Puttnam, cited in Howkins, John (2001) *The Creative Economy*, Allen Lane/Penguin, London, p. 160.

2   Adapted from Amabile, Teresa (1996) *Creativity in Context* (update to *Social Psychology of Creativity*, 1983), Westview Press, Perseus Books, Boulder, CO, pp. 261–2.

3   Amabile, T. and Khaire, M. (2008) 'Creativity and the Role of the Leader', *Harvard Business Review* 86(10): 100–9, p. 102.

4   Tannenbaum, R. and Schmidt, W. (1958) 'How to Choose a Leadership Pattern', *Harvard Business Review* 36(2): 95–101. The application of the model is also discussed in Adair, J. (1990) *Understanding Motivation*, Talbot Adair Press, reissued as Adair, J. (2006) *Leadership and Motivation*, Kogan Page, London, p. 16.

5   Aris, A. and Bughin, J. (2006) *Managing Media Companies: Harnessing Creative Value*, John Wiley, Sussex, fig. on p. 376; for detailed discussion of people management in creative companies see pp. 373–97.

6   Summarized from Amabile, Teresa (1988) 'A Model of Creativity and Innovation in Organisations', *Research in Organizational Behaviour* 10: 123–67;

Amabile, Theresa (1997) 'Motivating Creativity in Organisations', *California Management Review* 40 (1): 39–58; and Amabile, Hadley and Kramer (2002) 'Creativity under the Gun', *Harvard Business Review*, August.

7 Amabile, T.M., Hadley, C.N. and Kramer, S.J. (2002) 'Creativity under the Gun', *Harvard Business Review*, August: 52–61.

8 Amabile, Teresa (1998) 'How to Kill Creativity', *Harvard Business Review*, September: 77–8.

9 Amabile and Khaire (2008) op. cit.

10 Csíkszentmihályi (1996) *Creativity: Flow and the Psychology of Discovery and Invention*, Harper Collins, New York, p. 11.

11 Goffee, Rob and Jones, Gareth (2007) 'Leading Clever People', *Harvard Business Review*, March: 72–9.

12 Kirton, M. (1984) 'Adaptors and Innovators: Why New Initiatives Get Blocked' (from Kirton, M. (1984) 'Adaptors and Innovators', *Long Range Planning* 17(2): 137–43), in Henry, J. (ed.) (2006) *Creative Management and Development*, Sage, London, p. 109.

13 Kirton, Michael (1984) 'Adaptors and Innovators: A Description and Measure', *Journal of Applied Psychology* 61: 622–9, reproduced and cited in Kirton (1984) op. cit., p. 111.

14 For more on the conflict between adaptive and innovative creative people see Ekvall, G. (1997) *Organisational Conditions and Levels of Creativity*, in Henry, J. (2006) *Creative Management and Development*, Sage, London, p.135; and Kirton (1984) op. cit., pp. 141–2.

15 For more on external pressures that prevent creativity, see Amabile, Teresa and Fisher, Colin (2009) 'Stimulate Creativity by Fuelling Passion', in Locke, E.A. (2009) *Handbook of Principles of Organizational Behaviour: Indispensable Knowledge for Evidence-Based Management*, Wiley, Chichester, p. 481. This includes detailed citations of each of the experiments proving these links.

16 For research findings on staff retention of creative people, see Amabile and Fisher (2009) op. cit., p. 483.

17 Summarized from Amabile (1983) *The Social Psychology of Creativity*, Westview Press, Perseus Books, Boulder, CO; Amabile (1996, 1998) op. cit., and also Goffee and Jones (2007) op. cit.; and West, M.A. and Sacramento, C.A. (2004) 'Flourishing in Teams: Developing Creativity and Innovation', in Henry, Jane (ed.) (2006) *Creative Management and Development*, 3rd edn, Sage, London; and Boynton, Andy and Fischer, Bill (2005) *Virtuoso Teams: Lessons from Teams that Changed their Worlds*, Pearson, Edinburgh.

10 The script meeting

1 Garnett, Tony (2009) 'Tony Garnett's email on BBC drama', *Guardian*, 15 July, available at http://www.guardian.co.uk/media/2009/jul/15/tony-garnett-email-bbc-drama, accessed 23.05.2012.

2 Further reading: there are many books on how to write screenplays, but often cited are *The Screenwriter's Workbook* by Syd Field (1987), *Story* by Robert McKee (1999), *The Writer's Journey* by Christopher Vogler (1996), *How to Make Money Scriptwriting* by Julian Friedmann (2000), *Screenwriting* by Lew Hunter (1994), and *The Art and Science of Screenwriting* by Phil Parker (2000). Books on analysing screenplays for a living include Lucy Scher's insightful *Reading Screenplays*, and from an American perspective: *Reading for a Living: How to Be a Professional Story Analyst for Film and Television* by T.L. Katahn; *Screenplay Story Analysis* by Asher Garfinkel; and *Animation Writing and Development: From Script Development to Pitch* by Jean Ann Wright.

3 Writer-director Radu Mihaileanu (*Train de vie, Vis et Deviens*) speaking at the ACE (Ateliers du Cinéma Européen) Conference Creative Producer at the Times BFI London Film Festival at the Institut Francais, 24 October 2007.

4 Adapted from Travis, Mark (2002) *Directing Feature Films: The Creative Collaboration between Directors, Writers and Actors*, Michael Weise Productions, Los Angeles, pp. 43–68.

5 Kelman, H.C. (1958) 'Compliance, Identification, and Internalization: Three Processes of Attitude Change', *Journal of Conflict Resolution* 2(1): 51–60, available at http://scholar.harvard.edu/hckelman/files/Compliance_identification_and_internalization.pdf, accessed 23.04.2012.

6 Handy, Charles (1985) *Understanding Organizations*, 3rd edn, Facts On File Publications, New York, pp. 138–40.

7 Ibid., p. 139.

8 Radu (2007) op. cit.

9 Source: Adapted from Rudkin, D., Allan, D. and Murrin, K. (2002) *Sticky Wisdom: How to Start a Creative Revolution at Work*, Capstone Publishing, Chichester, pp. 54–5.

10 Ibid., p. 61.

11 Rollnick, S., Miller, W. and Butler, C. (2006) *Motivational Interviewing in Health Care*, Guilford Press, New York, pp. 44–53. To read more about these techniques in therapy and healthcare see also Rollnick, S. and Miller, W. (2002) *Motivational Interviewing*, 2nd edn, Guilford Press, New York; and Rosengren, D. (2009) *Building Motivational Interviewing Skills: A Practitioner Workbook*, Guilford Press, New York.

12 Ibid., p. 47.

13 Rollnick et al. (2006) op. cit., pp. 44–53.

14 The first two phrases are from Ruane, Janet (2005) *Essentials of Research Methods: A Guide to Social Science Research*, Blackwell, Malden, pp. 152–3; and the third is from p. 132. For further examination of question types see Seidman, I.E. (1991) *Interviewing as Qualitative Research*, Teachers College Press, New York.

15 Ruane (2005) op. cit., pp. 152–3.

16 On the technique of summarizing: Rollnick et al. (2002) op. cit., pp. 74–6.

17 Ruane (2005) op. cit., p. 154.

18 The roadblocks to listening quotation comes from Rollnick et al. (2008) op. cit., p. 69. It has in turn been adapted from Thomas Gordon's twelve roadblocks. Gordon, Thomas (1970) *Parent Effectiveness Training*, Wyden, New York; cited in Rosengren (2009) op. cit., p. 32.

19 Source: Davenport, T., Prusack, L. and Wilson, H. (2003) 'Who's Bringing You Hot Ideas (and How are You Responding)?', *Harvard Business Review* 81(2): 58–64. They went on to develop their thinking in a book: Davenport, T. Prusack, L. and Wilson, H. (2003) *What's the Big Idea: Creating and Capitalizing on the Best Management Thinking*, Harvard Business School Press, Boston, MA.

11 Strengthening the development team culture and building a sustainable creative company

1 For more on effective teamwork see Katzenbach, Jon and Smith, Douglas (1993) *The Wisdom of Teams: Creating the High-Performance Organization*, Harvard Business School Press, Boston, MA; Belbin, R.M. (2010) *Management Teams: Why They Succeed or Fail*, 3rd edn, Butterworth Heinemann, Oxford (original version published in 1981).

2   Organizational culture: 'the way we do things round here'. Cited in Deal, T.E. and Kennedy, A.A. (1982) *Corporate Cultures: The Rites and Rituals of Corporate Life*, Penguin, Harmondsworth, p. 4.

3   Source: Robbins, S. and Barnwell, N. (2002) *Organisation Theory*, 4th edn, Prentice Hall, Pearson, Sydney, p. 8; Schein, Edgar (2010) *Organizational Culture and Leadership*, 4th edn, Jossey-Bass, San Francisco, CA, p. 18; originally proposed in 1985. Mintzberg, Henry (1989) *Mintzberg on Management: Inside Our Strange World of Organizations*, Free Press/Collier Macmillan, New York and London, p. 221.

4   Schein (2010) op. cit., pp. 200–1.

5   Ibid., p. 199, citing his own research in 1999.

6   Ibid., p. 202.

7   SMART is an acronym standing for a widely used business objectives, progress and evaluation system: Specific, Measurable, Achievable, Relevant, and Time-bound. Unfortunately, this is less applicable to film development.

8   Adair, J. (2006) *Leadership and Motivation*, Kogan Page, London, p. 11 (first published in 1990 as *Understanding Motivation*).

9   For more on pros and cons of the working culture of the film and TV industry see Hesmondhalgh, David and Baker, Sarah (2011) *Creative Labour: Media Work in Three Cultural Industries*, Routledge, London; and for more on the culture of film shoots see Caldwell, John (2008) *Production Culture: Industrial Reflexivity and Critical Practice in Film and Television*, Duke University Press, Durham, NC; and Caldwell, J., Mayer, V. and Banks, M. (eds) (2009) *Production Studies: Cultural Studies of Media Industries*, Routledge, Abingdon.

10 Catmull, Ed (2008) 'How Pixar Fosters Collective Creativity', *Harvard Business Review*, September: 65–72, p. 72, available at http://hbr.org/2008/09/how-pixar-fosters-collective-creativity/ar/1, accessed 23.05.2012.

11 Ibid., pp. 66, 69.

12 Sources: Tuckman, Bruce W. (1965) 'Developmental Sequence in Small Groups', *Psychological Bulletin* 63: 384–99 (the article was reprinted in *Group Facilitation: A Research and Applications Journal* 3 (2001)); and Mullins, Laurie (2005) *Management and Organisational Behaviour*, 7th edn, Prentice Hall, London, p. 532. 'Adjourning' was added in Tuckman, Bruce and Jensen, Mary Ann (1977) 'Stages of Small-Group Development Revisited', *Group & Organization Studies* 2: 419–27.

13 Boynton, Andy and Fischer, Bill (2005) *Virtuoso Teams: Lessons from Teams that Changed their Worlds*, Pearson, Edinburgh.

14 The description of Brad Bird's arrival at Pixar is from Bunn, Austin (2004) 'Welcome to Planet Pixar', *Wired*, 12 June, available at http://www.wired.com/wired/archive/12.06/pixar.html?pg=2&topic=pixar&topic_set, accessed 23.04. 2012. For an excellent detailed description of Pixar's culture see Purkayastha, D. (2006) *Pixar's Incredible Culture*, Case Study, 406-077-1 ICFAI, Centre for Management Research, available at ECCH at http://www.icmrindia.org/casestudies/catalogue/Human%20Resource%20and%20Organization%20Behavior/HROB082.htm, accessed 23.05.2012.

15 Mullins (2005) op. cit., p. 533.

16 The table is by the author. The reference to the marketing mix refers to a popular but an unattributable list of elements that allegedly enables successful marketing. These were originally 4 Ps: *Product, Price, Promotion, Place*, but over time others have been added, such as *People, Process* and *Physical Evidence*. In his 1994 and 1997 books *Successful Charity Marketing* Ian Bruce added another P: that of *Philosophy*, to encompass a charity's or company's mission and way of behaving (1997, p. 50). He had to continue the tyranny of the first letter P, but Philosophy and People are both close to or heavily affected by culture. Since

the mid-1990s an ordinary company's philosophy and culture has become as important to marketing and public perception as it is for a charity.

17   Source: Schein (2010) op. cit., pp. 23–33; originally proposed in 1985.

18   Ibid., p. 236.

19   Ibid., pp. 219 and 235–58.

20   For more on culture change see ibid., pp. 299–362; Dyer, W.G. (1986) *Culture Change in Family Firms*, Jossey-Bass, San Francisco, CA; and Kotter, J.P. (1996) *Leading Change*, Harvard Business School Press, Boston, MA.

21   There are many influential books on organizational culture, and the contentious field of identifying and analysing it. For example: Martin, Joanne (2002) *Organizational Culture: Mapping the Terrain*, Sage, Thousand Oaks, CA; Handy, C. (1985) *Understanding Organizations*, 3rd edn, Facts On File Publications, New York; Senge, Peter (1990) *The Fifth Discipline*, Doubleday/Currency, New York; Kotter, J. P. (1992) *Corporate Culture and Performance*, The Free Press, New York; and of course Schein (2010) op. cit., with pp. 115–93 concentrating on the complexity of observing and deciphering culture. A quick introduction to overall thinking on culture can be found in Martin, Joanne (2004) 'Organizational Culture: Pieces of the Puzzle', in Shafritz, J.M., Ott, J.S. and Jang, Y.S. (eds), *Classics of Organizational Theory*, 6th edn, Wadsworth Publishing, Belmont, CA, pp. 393–414.

22   Luft, J. and Ingham, H. (1950) 'The Johari Window, a Graphic Model of Interpersonal Awareness', in *Proceedings of the Western Training Laboratory in Group Development*, UCLA, Los Angeles; cited in Stacey, R. (1996) *Strategic Management and Organisational Dynamics*, 2nd edn, Pitman, London, p. 193; cited in Block, P. (ed.) (2001) *Managing in the Media*, Focal Press, Oxford, p. 192.

23   The Sixteen Films case study was assembled from interviews for this book with producers Rebecca O'Brien and Camilla Bray, and the author's observations when working with the company in the early 2000s.

24   Fuller, Graham (ed.) (1998) *Loach on Loach*, Faber, London, p. 96. For more on Loach's working practice as a director see Hill, John (2011) *Ken Loach: The Politics of Film and Television*, Palgrave Macmillan/British Film Institute, London.

25   For a detailed account of the development and production in 1993 of the film *Shallow Grave* and MacDonald's role as producer, see Adler, Tim (2004) *The Producers: Money, Movies and Who Really Call the Shots*, Methuen, London, pp. 126–30. After casting, the triumverate even lived with the three lead actors for a week, talking about the project and watching relevant films together, to make sure they were all making the same type of film.

12 Working with the Hollywood studio system

1   Further reading: for books about the development process in Hollywood, and especially case studies of what goes wrong and right, it is worth reading *Tales from Development Hell* (2004) by David Hughes, and *The Best Screenplay Goes to …* (2008) by Linda Seeger. For more on studio development and the first look deal see the development chapter of Jeffrey Ulin's 2010 book *The Business of Media Distribution*, and the accompanying online resources, and Edward Epstein's (2006) *The Big Picture*, chs 6 and 24. Although it is now a bit out of date it is worth reading Thom Taylor's *The Big Deal: Hollywood's Million-Dollar Spec Script Market* (1999). The cases may be old but the principles are the same, even if high prices are harder to come by nowadays. And of course the two William Goldman books: *Adventures in the Screen Trade* (1983), and *Which Lie Did I Tell? More Adventures in the Screen Trade* (2001).

2   For more information on the distribution drivers of the studios see Ulin, J. (2010) *The Business of Media Distribution: Monetizing Film, TV, and Video Content*, Focal Press/Elsevier, Boston, MA/Amsterdam; and Epstein, E.J. (2010) *The Hollywood Economist: The Hidden Financial Reality Behind the Movies*, Melville House Publishing, New York.

3   Source: The Hollywood Creative Directory, Studio Report: Film Development in conjunction with BaselineStudioSystems; cited in Cones, John W. (2009) *Introduction to the Motion Picture Industry: A Guide for Filmmakers, Students & Scholars*, Marquette Books, Washington DC, p. 7.

4   Cones (2009) op. cit., p. 7.

5   BRICS nations already account for a quarter of the world's economic output. Source: McClintock, Pamela (2011) 'Foreign Rescue for Homegrown Duds', *Hollywood Reporter*, 5 May, http://www.hollywoodreporter.com/news/foreign-rescue-homegrown-duds-185072 accessed on 23.05.2012; and Szalai, Georg (2011) 'CBS Corp Touts Financial Upside of Emerging Businesses', *Hollywood Reporter*, 24 February, available at http://www.hollywoodreporter.com/news/cbs-corp-touts-financial-upside-161216, accessed 23.05.2012.

6   Goodridge, Mike (2011) 'Paramount to Shut Down Worldwide Acquisitions Group', *Screen International*, 3 June, available at http://www.screendaily.com/5028423.article, accessed 06.06.2011.

7   Epstein, E.J. (2006) *The Big Picture: The New Logic of Money and Power in Hollywood*, Random House, New York, p. 136.

8   Ulin, J. (2010) *The Business of Media Distribution: Monetizing Film, TV, and Video Content: Online Supplementary Material*, Focal Press/ElsevierAmsterdam/Boston, available at http://www.elsevierdirect.com/companions/9780240812007/casestudies/Online_Supplement.pdf, accessed on: 11.04.2011, p. 4.

9   Epstein (2006) op. cit., p. 131.

10 Regarding the recent perceived rise in spec. scripts in Hollywood: 'The good news is that people are not acting day to day out of fear as much as they did maybe six months ago,' says producer Mark Gordon, whose Source Code, a spec. written by Ben Ripley, had its world premiere at South by Southwest. 'The studio heads were so frozen because they didn't quite know what to do. The DVD market was going to hell; they were figuring out what was going to replace it; the costs were going up. They were able to rely on their older development and the things that they had in their trunks, but now it's caught up with them, and they need to start buying things.' Fernandez, Jay and Kit, Borys (2011) 'The Return of the Spec Script Buyer: Original Material is Hot Again', *Hollywood Reporter*, 25 March, available at http://www.hollywoodreporter.com/news/return-spec-script-buyer-167555, accessed 23.05.2012, p. 20.

11 Most recently this was publicly admitted by Andrew Cripps (president of Paramount Pictures International – the worldwide marketing and distributing arm of Viacom-owned studio Paramount) at the British Screen Advisory Council Conference in London in 2011. Following the distribution success of lower budget niche films like *Never Say Never* and *Paranormal Activity*, he said that films being greenlit by Paramount in 2011 were evolving towards either the mass blockbuster that catered to worldwide audiences or else the cheaper film that was 'less risky'. Source: British Screen Advisory Council (2011) *BSAC Eighth Annual Film Conference Report 2011*, BSAC, London, p. 8.

13 The writer

1   Grisoni, Tony (2011) Keynote speech to the London Film School on 14 December 2011, unpublished, reproduced with permission of Tony Grisoni.

2   Swain, Dwight (1976) *Film Scriptwriting: A Practical Manual*, Focal Press, Butterworth, London and Boston, MA, p. 19.
3   Swain (1976) op. cit., pp. 198–9.
4   Director John Madden quoted in Seeger, Linda (2008) *And the Best Screenplay Goes to ... Sideways, Shakespeare in Love, Crash: Learning from the Winners*, Michael Wiese Productions, Los Angeles, p. 165. Her book contains an excellent account of the development of the project and the changes made to the script.
5   This interview case is the result of a BAFTA keynote event at the 2009 Screenwriters' Festival in Cheltenham, where the author interviewed Simon Beaufoy onstage. Prior to that interview there were phone conversations and a meeting, and this case is gleaned from all three sources. Where credited (see below) there are also excerpts from published third-party interviews. The whole completed case has been seen and approved by him.
6   Beaufoy, Simon (2009) BBC Writers Room/Story Engine Screen Writing Conference, Darlington, available at http://www.bbc.co.uk/writersroom/insight/simon_beaufoy_4.shtml, accessed 15.05.2009.
7   Beaufoy (2009) op. cit.

14 Into the future

1   Carroll, Lewis (1871) *Through the Looking Glass*, Macmillan, London, ch. 5.
2   Macnab, Geoffrey (2009) 'Can the Writers Change the Script?', *Screen International*, 22 October, available at http://www.screendaily.com/territories/europe/can-the-writers-change-the-script/5007243.article, accessed 23.05.2012.
3   While encouraging diversity of gatekeepers the Review advised against setting up separate development funds, but preferred to keep development and production funds integrated. Film Policy Review Panel (2012) *A Future For British Film: Report to Government by the Film Policy Review Panel*, published on behalf of the Film Policy Review Panel by the Department for Culture, Media and Sport (DCMS), London, p. 94.
4   In 2010 the UK government called on BSkyB to invest in film. Minister Ed Vaizey said he could not understand why Sky did not make films: 'as one of the country's most innovative broadcasters, they would bring a new dynamic force to the table that would lift everybody's game' (Source: Brown, M. (2010) 'British Film Institute to take over from UK Film Council', *Guardian*, 29 November, available at http://www.guardian.co.uk/film/2010/nov/29/bfi-takes-over-from-ukfc, accessed 23.05.2012). This was also encouraged by the 2012 Film Policy Review, which recommended that the government established Memorandums of Understanding with the BBC, ITV, Channel 4, Channel 5 and BSkyB, setting out agreed commitments to support British film, and otherwise including film-related licence requirements in the new Communications Act (for an overview of broadcaster involvement, see Film Policy Review (2012) op. cit., pp. 51–8, and for the recommendation see p. 55).
5   Source: UK Film Council (2009) *UK Film Council Statistical Yearbook 2009*, UK Film Council, London, p. 151.
6   UK Film Council Research and Statistics Unit (2010) *UK Film Council Statistical Yearbook 2010*, UK Film Council, London, p. 148.
7   Film Policy Review (2012) op. cit., p. 95.
8   Levine, Robert (2011) *Free Ride: How the Internet is Destroying the Culture Business*, Bodley Head, London, pp. 1–13.
9   Mike Kelly/Northern Alliance/UK Film Council (2008) *Low and Micro-Budget Film Production in the UK*, UK Film Council, London.

10   In 2011 the UK Film Policy Review added its voice to complaints about the high cost of the *virtual print fee* (VPF) reducing independent and arthouse distribution, stating that 'the VPF model as currently formulated means that, for independent distributors, the cost of getting their films on screen is often considerably higher than before, and that this is limiting the availability of certain titles to a broader audience', and recommending that 'the studios, third party consolidators and exhibitors find a new Virtual Print Fee model that puts the independent distributor in an economic position which is as good as or better than the 35mm model. This is in accordance with the Panel's objective of expanding audiences for independent British and specialized films,' Film Policy Review (2012) op. cit., p. 31.

11   Anderson, Chris (2006) *The Long Tail: How Endless Choice is Creating Unlimited Demand (The New Economics of Culture and Commerce)*, Random House, London. However long tail theory is questioned by some academics, including Elberse, Anita (2008) 'Should you Invest in the Long Tail', *Harvard Business Review*, July, available at http://hbr.org/2008/07/should-you-invest-in-the-long-tail/ar/1, accessed 23.05.2012, pp. 88–96.

12   Vogel, H. (2007) *Entertainment Industry Economics: A Guide for Financial Analysis*, 7th edn, Cambridge University Press, Cambridge, p. 92.

13   Also in 2010 the Miramax library was put up for sale and received offers in the $400–$500m range (instead of the $700m being asked for by Disney); and Viacom got the DreamWorks SKG library for $400m (it had been sold in 2006 for $900m). There is more detailed discussion of declining library values in Hazelton, John (2010) 'Why Libraries are Losing Value', *Screen International*, 14 April, available at http://www.screendaily.com/reports/in-focus/why-libraries-are-losing-value/5012738.article, accessed 08.12.2011. MGM library sale source: Barnes, Brooks and Cielpy, Michael (2010) 'In Hollywood, Grappling with Studios' Lost Clout', *New York Times*, 18 January; cited in Levine (2011) op. cit., pp. 2, 174 and 258.

14   Vickery, Graham and Hawkins, Richard (2008) *Remaking the Movies: Digital Content and the Evolution of the Film and Video Industries*, OECD, Paris, p. 106. Graham Vickery is Head of the Information Economy Group at OECD and Richard Hawkins is Professor at the University of Calgary.

15   Finney, Angus (2010) *The International Film Business: A Market Analysis*, Routledge, Oxford, p. 15. For more on Finney's thinking about the future of the value chain see Finney, Angus (2010) *Value Chain Restructuring in the Global Film Industry*, a paper presented at the 4th Annual Conference on Cultural Production in a Global Context, Grenoble Ecole de Management, France, available at http://ec.europa.eu/culture/media/programme/docs/public_cons_media2010/44.pdf, accessed 23.05.2012.

16   Source: *The Economist* (2008) 'Coming Soon: Hollywood and the Internet', 23 February, available at http://www.economist.com/node/10723360, accessed 28.05.2012.

17   For a more detailed analysis of the distinctions between the deconstruction, disintermediation and fragmentation of value, see Küng, Lucy (2008) *Strategic Management in the Media: Theory to Practice*, Sage, London, pp. 20–4; and Evans, P. and Wurster, T.S. (2000) *Blown to Bits: How the New Economics of Information Transform Strategy*, Harvard Business School Press, Boston, MA; cited in Küng (2008) op. cit., pp. 20–3.

18   Goldman, William (1983) *Adventures in the Screen Trade: A Personal View of Hollywood and Screenwriting*, Warner Books, New York.

19   Mamet, David (1991) *On Directing Film*, Viking Penguin, New York, p. 61.

20   It seems fitting to end the notes to the main part of this book on this quote about money, especially since it is so often misquoted. King James' Bible, 1

Timothy, 6.10: 'For the love of money is the root of all kinds of evil: which while some coveted after, they have erred from the faith, and pierced themselves through with many sorrows.'

Appendix A

1   'Each sci-fi film depicts a border area, just outside the known world, giving the spectator the opportunity to let his imagination go, to enter into worlds which seem unattainable, forbidden, or unimaginable.' Altman, Charles (1977) 'Towards a Theory of Genre Film in a New Approach to Genre', *Purdue Film Studies Annual*, vol. 2, Purdue University, West Lafayette.

2   First three columns adapted from Sternberg, R.J. (2006) 'The Nature of Creativity', *Creativity Research Journal* 18: 87–99; repr. in Kaufman, James and Grigorenko, Elena (2009) *The Essential Sternberg: Essays on Intelligence, Psychology and Education*, Springer, New York. Adapted into a table by the author, with added film examples with help from Keith Johnston, author of *Science Fiction Film: A Critical Introduction* (2011).

3   In film and TV what Sternberg refers to as 'the crowd' can also be segmented into the different responses of industry peers, critics, specialist audiences (who may want to be challenged), and mainstream audiences (who want to be entertained but not challenged).

4   Sternberg (2006) op. cit. This is a development of the paper by Sternberg, R. and Lubart, T. (1991) 'An Investment Theory of Creativity and Its Development', *Human Development* 34: 1–31.

5   Csíkszentmihályi argues that creativity only occurs when the intent of the creative person is matched by its adoption: 'Creativity is any act, idea, or product that changes an existing domain into a new one. And the definition of a creative person is: someone whose thoughts or actions change a domain, or establish a new domain. It is important to remember, however, that a domain cannot be changed without the explicit or implicit consent of a field responsible for it.' Csíkszentmihályi, Mihály (1996) *Creativity: Flow and the Psychology of Discovery and Invention*, Harper Collins, New York, p. 28.

6   Adapted into a table by the author, from Sternberg (2006) op. cit.

7   Key meta-componential skills are used to define the problem, represent the problem, plan how the problem should be solved, monitor the selected problem-solving strategy, and evaluate its success. Sternberg, R.J. (1979). 'The Nature of Mental Abilities', *American Psychologist* 34(3): 214–30.

8   Amabile, Teresa (1983) *The Social Psychology of Creativity*, Westview Press, Perseus Books, Boulder, CO; Csíkszentmihályi (1996) op. cit.

Bibliography

Original interviews for this book

Anonymized director (2011) Interview by Peter Bloore for the book *The Screenplay Business* [no recording], Shoreditch House, Peter Bloore, 23 May 2011. The contributor chose to be anonymous.

Anonymized media lawyer (2010) Interview by Peter Bloore [Interview – informal], Groucho Club, Peter Bloore, Inns of Court, 10 February. The contributor chose to be anonymous.

Anonymized screenwriter 1 (2011) Interview by Peter Bloore for the book *The Screenplay Business* [no recording], Groucho Club, Peter Bloore, 3 March. The contributor chose to be anonymous.

Anonymized screenwriter 2 (2011) Interview by Peter Bloore for the book *The Screenplay Business* [no recording], Soho House, Peter Bloore, 4 June. The contributor chose to be anonymous.

Anonymized screenwriter and director 3 (2011) Interview by Peter Bloore for the book *The Screenplay Business* [no recording], Groucho Club, Peter Bloore, 3 September. The contributor chose to be anonymous.

Baines, Julie (2011) Interview by Peter Bloore for the book *The Screenplay Business* [Interview – mp3 recording], Dan Films, Kings Cross, London, 29 September.

Beaufoy, Simon (2011) BAFTA keynote event: the screenwriter as a diplomat, negotiator, and psychiatrist, interview by Peter Bloore at the 2009 Screenwriters Festival in Cheltenham [Interview], Cheltenham, 27 October.

Bloye, Charlie (2011) Interview by Peter Bloore for the book *The Screenplay Business* [Interview – mp3 recording], Soho House, 27 April. Charlie Bloye is Chief Executive of the UK sales agent trade association: Film Export UK.

Bray, Camilla (2011) Interview by Peter Bloore for the book *The Screenplay Business* [Interview – mp3 recording], Sixteen Films, 15 July.

Ettedgui, Peter (2011) Interview by Peter Bloore for the book *The Screenplay Business* [Interview – mp3 recording], Waterstones Piccadilly, London, 30 September.

Friedmann, Julian (2011) Interview by Peter Bloore for the book *The Screenplay Business* [Interview – mp3 recording], offices of Blake Friedmann, London, 6 June.

Golding, Sarah (2011) Interview by Peter Bloore for the book *The Screenplay Business* [Interview – mp3 recording], 28 February.

Goodridge, Mike (2011) Interview by Peter Bloore for the book *The Screenplay Business* [Interview – mp3 recording], EMAP offices, London, 1 August. Mike Goodridge is Editor of *Screen International.*

Grisoni, Tony (2011) Interview by Peter Bloore for the book *The Screenplay Business* [Interview – mp3 recording], Stoke Newington, London, 6 June.

Hetreed, Olivia (2011) Interview by Peter Bloore for the book *The Screenplay Business* [Interview – mp3 recording], North London, 10 March.

Josephs, Tracey (2011) Interview by Peter Bloore for the book *The Screenplay Business* [Interview – mp3 recording], Channel 4, Horseferry Road, Peter Bloore, 10 August. Tracey Josephs is Head of Production at Film4.

Langan, Christine (2011) Interview by Peter Bloore for the book *The Screenplay Business* [Interview – mp3 recording], BBC Television Centre, Peter Bloore, 23 September. Christine Langan is Head of BBC Films.

Lavender, Sam (2011) Interview by Peter Bloore for the book *The Screenplay Business* [Interview – mp3 recording], Channel 4, Horseferry Road, Peter Bloore, 10 August. Sam Lavender is Head of Development at Film4.

Lawrence, Kate (2011) Interview by Peter Bloore for the book *The Screenplay Business* [Interview – mp3 recording], Number 9 Films, London, 1 November.

Leys, Kate (2011) Interview by Peter Bloore for the book *The Screenplay Business* [Interview – mp3 recording], Groucho Club, London, 9 December.

MacKinnon, Ivana (2011) Interview by Peter Bloore for the book *The Screenplay Business* [Interview – mp3 recording], Paddington Station, London, 25 November.

O'Brien, Rebecca (2011) Interview by Peter Bloore for the book *The Screenplay Business* [Interview – mp3 recording], Sixteen Films, 15 July.

Paterson, Andrew (2011) Interview by Peter Bloore for the book *The Screenplay Business* [Interview – mp3 recording], North London, 10 March.

Peplow, Neil (2011) Interview by Peter Bloore for the book *The Screenplay Business* [Interview – mp3 recording], Skillset, London, 8 September.

Sprackling, Rob (2011) Interview by Peter Bloore for the book *The Screenplay Business* [Interview – mp3 recording], Marylebone, London, 9 December.

Wethered, Ed (2011) Interview by Peter Bloore for the book *The Screenplay Business* [Interview – mp3 recording], BBC Television Centre, Peter Bloore, 23 September 2011. Ed Wethered is Development Editor at BBC Films.

Woolley, Steven (2011) Interview by Peter Bloore for the book *The Screenplay Business* [Interview – mp3 recording], Number 9 Films, London, 16 November.

Other interviews and events

Beaufoy, Simon (2009) BBC Writers Room/Story Engine Screen Writing Conference, Darlington, available at http://www.bbc.co.uk/writersroom/insight/simon_beaufoy_4.shtml, accessed 15.05.2009.

Grisoni, Tony (2011) Keynote speech to the London Film School on 14 December 2011, unpublished, used with permission of Tony Grisoni.

Hetreed, Olivia (2009) 'Uneasy Bedfellows: Writers and Directors Working Together', Keynote speech at the Screenwriters' Festival 2009 launch event at Channel 4 on 13 January.

Kapadia, Asif (2005) Interview by Peter Bloore for Bournemouth Media MBA teaching session [Interview – informal], Regents College, London, Peter Bloore, 03.06.2005.

Mihaileanu, Radu (2007) Speaking at the ACE (Ateliers du Cinéma Européen) Conference Creative Producer at the Times BFI London Film Festival at the Institut Francais on 24 October.

Books and articles

Abrams, M.H. (1953) 'Orientation of Critical Theories', in Abrams, M.H. (1971) *The Mirror and the Lamp: Romantic Theory and the Critical Tradition*, Oxford University Press, London; cited in Pope (1998), p. 77.

Adair, J. (1990) *Understanding Motivation*, Talbot Adair Press, reissued as Adair (2006).

—— (2006) *Leadership and Motivation*, Kogan Page, London (first published in 1990 as *Understanding Motivation*).

—— (2007) *Leadership for Innovation*, Kogan Page, London (first published in 1990 as *The Challenge of Innovation*, Talbot Adair Press).

Adler, Tim (2004) *The Producers: Money, Movies and Who Really Call the Shots*, Methuen, London.

Albert, R.S. and Runco, M.A. (1999) 'A History of Research on Creativity', in Sternberg, R. (ed.) (1999) *Handbook of Creativity*, Cambridge University Press, Cambridge, pp. 16–31.

Alderfer, Clayton P. (1969) 'An Empirical Test of a New Theory of Human Needs', *Organizational Behaviour and Human Performance* 4(2): 142–75; cited in Chamorro-Premuzic (2007), pp. 120–1.

Altman, C. (1977) 'Towards a Theory of Genre Film', in 'A New Approach To Genre', *Purdue Film Studies Annual*, vol. 2, Purdue University, West Lafayette.

Amabile, T.M. (1983) *The Social Psychology of Creativity*, Springer, New York.

—— (1996) *Creativity in Context* (update to *Social Psychology of Creativity*, 1983), Westview Press, Perseus Books, Boulder, CO.

—— (1998) 'How to Kill Creativity', *Harvard Business Review*, September: 77–8.

Amabile, Teresa and Fisher, Colin (2009) 'Stimulate Creativity by Fuelling Passion', in Locke, E.A. (2009) *Handbook of Principles of Organizational Behaviour: Indispensable Knowledge for Evidence-Based Management*, Wiley, Chichester.

Amabile, T.M. and Gryskiewicz, N.D. (1989) 'The Creative Environment Scales: The Work Environment Inventory', *Creativity Research Journal* 2: 231–54.

Amabile, T. and Hennessey, B. (1988) 'The Conditions of Creativity', in Sternberg (1988), pp. 11–38.

Amabile, T. and Khaire, M. (2008) 'Creativity and the Role of the Leader', *Harvard Business Review* 86(10): 100–9.

Amabile, T.M. and Sensabaugh, S.J. (1992) *High Creativity versus Low Creativity: What Makes the Difference?*, in Gryskiewicz, Stanley and Hills, David (eds) (1992) *Readings in Innovation*, Center for Creative Leadership, Greensboro, NC.

Amabile, T.M., Hadley, C.N. and Kramer, S.J. (2002) 'Creativity under the Gun', *Harvard Business Review*, August: 52–61.

Amabile, T.M., Phillips E. and Collins, M.A. (1993). *Personality and Environmental Determinants of Creativity in Professional Artists*, Brandeis University, Waltham, MA.

Anderson, Chris (2006) *The Long Tail: How Endless Choice is Creating Unlimited Demand (The New Economics of Culture and Commerce)*, Random House, London.

Ansoff, I.H. (1957) 'Strategies for Diversification', *Harvard Business Review* 35(2): 113–24.

Appleton, Dina and Yankelvits, Daniel (2010) *Hollywood Dealmaking: Negotiating Talent Agreements for Film, TV and New Media*, Allworth Press, New York.

Aris, A. and Bughin, J. (2006) *Managing Media Companies: Harnessing Creative Value*, John Wiley, Chichester.

Ayres, C., Mostrous, A. and Teeman, T. (2009) 'Oscars for Slumdog Millionaire – the Film that Nearly Went Straight to DVD', *The Times*, 24 February, available online at http://entertainment.timesonline.co.uk/tol/arts_and_entertainment/film/oscars/article5793160.ece, accessed 11.02.2011.

Baillieu, Bill and Goodchild, John (2002) *The British Film Business*, John Wiley & Sons, Chichester.

Barnes, Brooks and Cielpy, Michael (2010) 'In Hollywood, Grappling with Studios' Lost Clout', *New York Times*, 18 January; cited in Levine (2011).

Barron and Harrington (1981) 'Creativity, Intelligence, and Personality', *Annual Review of Psychology* 32: 439–76.

Bass, B.M. and Avolio, B.J. (1994) *Improving Organizational Performance through Transformational Leadership*, Sage, Thousand Oaks, CA.

Bazalgette, Peter (2005) *Billion Dollar Game*, Time Warner Books, London.

Belbin, R.M. (1981) *Management Teams: Why They Succeed or Fail*, Butterworth Heinemann, Oxford; 2nd edn (2004); 3rd edn (2010).

Ben-Zvi, L. (2006) 'Staging the Other Israel: The Documentary Theatre of Nola Chilton', *The Drama Review* 50(3): 42–55.

Berkun, Scott (2007) *The Myths of Innovation*, O'Reilly Media, Sebastopol, CA.

Bilton, Chris (2006) 'Cultures of Management: Cultural Policy, Cultural Management and Creative Organisations' (a draft paper), London School of Economics, available at www.lse.ac.uk/collections/geographyAndEnvironment/research/Bilton-june28.doc, accessed 23.05.2012.

—— (2007) *Management and Creativity: From Creative Industries to Creative Management*, Blackwell, Oxford.

Bilton, Chris and Cummings, Stephen (2010) *Creative Strategy: Reconnecting Business and Innovation*, Wiley & Sons, Chichester.

Biskind, Peter (2004) *Down and Dirty Pictures. Miramax, Sundance, and the Rise of Independent Film*, Simon & Schuster, New York.

Björkegren, D. (1996) *The Culture Business*, Routledge, London.

Block, P. (2001) *Managing in the Media*, Focal Press, Oxford.

Bloore, Peter (2005) 'The Film Screen Academy Policy and the Effect on the National Film and Television School', unpublished MVA dissertation, London South Bank University.

—— (2009) 'Re-defining the Independent Film Value Chain' (online), UK Film Council, London, available at http://industry.bfi.org.uk/media/pdf/h/b/Film_Value_Chain_Paper.pdf, accessed 22.05.2012.

Blume, Steven (2006) 'The Revenue Streams: An Overview', in Squire, Jason E. (ed.) (2006) *The Movie Business Book*, 3rd edn, Simon & Schuster, New York.

Boden, Margaret (1990) *Creative Mind: Myths and Mechanisms*, 1st edn, George Weidenfeld & Nicolson, London.

—— (ed.) (1994) *Dimensions of Creativity*, MIT Press, Cambridge, MA.

—— (2004) *Creative Mind: Myths and Mechanisms*, 2nd edn, Routledge, London.

—— (2010) *Creativity and Art: Three Roads to Surprise*, Oxford University Press, Oxford.

Bournemouth University (2008) 'Curricula: Unit Guide: Media MBA, Film Business Module', unpublished internal document.

Boynton, A. and Fischer, B. (2005) *Virtuoso Teams: Lessons from Teams that Changed their Worlds*, Pearson, Edinburgh.

Boynton, Andy and Fischer, Bill (2005) 'Virtuoso Teams', *Harvard Business Review* 83(7/8): 116–23.

British Screen Advisory Council (2011) *BSAC Eighth Annual Film Conference Report 2011*, BSAC, London.

Brown, M. (2010) 'British Film Institute to take over from UK Film Council', *Guardian*, 29 November, available at http://www.guardian.co.uk/film/2010/nov/29/bfi-takes-over-from-ukfc, accessed 23.05.2012.

Bruce, Ian (1997) *Successful Charity Marketing*, 2nd edn, ICSA, London.

Bunn, Austin (2004) 'Welcome to Planet Pixar', *Wired*, 12 June, available at http://www.wired.com/wired/archive/12.06/pixar.html?pg=2&topic=pixar&topic_set, accessed 23.04.2012.

Burns, Paul (2011) *Entrepreneurship and Small Business*, 3rd edn, Palgrave Macmillan, Basingstoke.

Burns, J.M. (1978) *Leadership*, Harper & Row, New York.

Caldwell, John (2008) *Production Culture: Industrial Reflexivity and Critical Practice in Film and Television*, Duke University Press, Durham, NC.

Caldwell, J., Mayer, V. and Banks, M. (eds) (2009) *Production Studies: Cultural Studies of Media Industries*, Routledge, Abingdon.

Carroll, Lewis (1871) *Through the Looking Glass*, Macmillan, London.

Cass Business School (2006) 'Curricula: MSc in Film Business', Film Business Academy, Cass Business School, unpublished internal document.

Catmull, Ed (2008) 'How Pixar Fosters Collective Creativity', *Harvard Business Review*, September: 65–72, available at http://hbr.org/2008/09/how-pixar-fosters-collective-creativity/ar/1, accessed 23.05.2012.

Catton, Catherine (2008) *To Explore How A Production Company Should Manage Its Creative Teams in Order to Generate Successful Factual Entertainment Ideas*, unpublished MBA dissertation, Bournemouth University Media School.

Chamorro-Premuzic, Tomas (2007) *Personality and Individual Differences*, Blackwell, Oxford.

Cini, Marie A. (2001) 'Group Newcomers: From Disruption to Innovation', *Group Facilitation Journal*, Spring 2001, available at http://www.learning-org.com/01.05/0111.html, accessed 25.05.2012.

Cones, John W. (1992) *Film Finance and Distribution: A Dictionary of Terms*, Silman-James Press, Los Angeles.

—— (2009) *Introduction to the Motion Picture Industry: A Guide for Filmmakers, Students & Scholars*, Marquette Books, Washington DC.

Conger, J. and Kunungo, R. (1988) *Charismatic Leadership*, Josey-Bass, San Francisco, CA.

Connolly, Cyril (1938) *Enemies of Promise*, Andre Deutsch, London.

Cronin, Paul (2004) *Alexander Mackendrick on Film-making*, Faber and Faber, London.

Crutchfield, R. (1962) 'Conformity and Creative Thinking', in Gruber, H., Terrell, G. and Wertheimer, M. (eds) (1962) *Contemporary Approaches to Creative Thinking*, Atherton Press, New York, pp. 120–40.

Csíkszentmihályi, Mihály (1988) 'A Systems Perspective on Creativity', in Sternberg (1999), pp. 313–35.

—— (1990) *Flow: The Psychology of Optimal Experience*, Harper & Row, New York.

—— (1996) *Creativity: Flow and the Psychology of Discovery and Invention*, Harper Collins, New York.

Csíkszentmihályi, M., Rathunde, K. and Whalen, S. (1993) *Talented Teenagers*, Cambridge University Press, New York; cited in Csíkszentmihályi (1996).

D'Agostino, G. (2010) *Copyright, Contracts, Creators: New Media, New Rules*, Edward Elgar, Cheltenham.

Davenport, T., Prusack, L. and Wilson, H. (2003) *What's the Big Idea: Creating and Capitalizing on the Best Management Thinking*, Harvard Business School Press, Boston, MA.

—— (2003) Who's Bringing You Hot Ideas (and How are You Responding)?', *Harvard Business Review* 81(2): 58–64.

Davies, Adam and Wistreich, Nicol (2007) *The Film Finance Handbook*, New Global Edition, Netribution, London.

Davis, H. and Scase, R. (2000) *Managing Creativity: The Dynamics of Work and Organisation*, Oxford University Press, Oxford.

De Winter, H. (2006) *What I Really Want to Do is Produce: Top Producers Talk Movies & Money*, Faber and Faber, London.

Deal, T.E. and Kennedy, A.A. (1982) *Corporate Cultures: The Rites and Rituals of Corporate Life*, Penguin, Harmondsworth.

Diehl, Michael and Stroebe, Wolfgang (1987) 'Productivity Loss in Brainstorming Groups: Toward the Solution of a Riddle', *Journal of Personality and Social Psychology* 53: 497–509.

—— (1991) 'Productivity Loss in Idea-Generating Groups: Tracking Down the Blocking Effect', *Journal of Personality and Social Psychology* 61(3): 392–403.

Downes L. and Mui, C. (1998) *Unleashing the Killer Application: Digital Strategies*, Harvard Business School Press, Boston, MA; cited in Küng (2008).

Dyer, W.G. (1986) *Culture Change in Family Firms*, Jossey-Bass, San Francisco, CA.

Ebstein, R.P. et al. (1996) 'Dopamine DR Receptor (DRD4): Exon III Polymorphism Associated with the Human Personality Trait of Sensation Seeking', *Nature Genetics* 12: 78-80; cited in Zuckerman (2007), p. xiv.

Economist, The (2008) 'Coming Soon: Hollywood and the Internet', 23 February, available at http://www.economist.com/node/10723360, accessed 28.05.2012.

Ekvall, G. (2006) 'Organisational Conditions and Levels of Creativity', in Henry, J. (2006) *Creative Management and Development*, Sage, London.

Elberse, Anita (2008) 'Should you Invest in the Long Tail', *Harvard Business Review*, July, available at http://hbr.org/2008/07/should-you-invest-in-the-long-tail/ar/1, accessed 23.05.2012.

Eliashberg, Jehoshua, Elberse, Anita and Leenders, Mark (2006) 'The Motion Picture Industry: Critical Issues in Practice, Current Research, and New Research Directions', *Marketing Science* 25(6): 638–61.

Enzle, M.A. and Ross, J.M. (1978) 'Increasing and Decreasing Intrinsic Interest with Contingent Rewards: A Test of Cognitive Evaluation Theory', *Journal of Experimental Social Psychology* 14(6): 588–97.

Epstein, E.J. (2006) *The Big Picture: The New Logic of Money and Power in Hollywood*, Random House, New York.

—— (2010) *The Business of Media Distribution: Monetizing Film, TV, and Video Content: Online Supplementary Material*, Focal Press/ElsevierAmsterdam/Boston, MA, available at http://www.elsevierdirect.com/companions/9780240812007/case studies/Online_Supplement.pdf, accessed 23.05.2012.

—— (2010) *The Hollywood Economist: The Hidden Financial Reality Behind the Movies*, Melville House Publishing, New York.

—— (2010) 'If You Are a Producer of Indie Movies ...', *The Hollywood Economist Blogspot*, 5 February 2010, available at http://thehollywoodeconomist.blogspot.com/2010/02/if-you-are-producer-of-indie-movies.html, accessed 11.07.2011.

Evans, P. and Wurster T.S. (2000) *Blown to Bits: How the New Economics of Information Transform Strategy*, Harvard Business School Press, Boston, MA; cited in Küng (2008), pp. 20–3.

Feist, Gregory (1998) 'The Influence of Personality on Artistic and Scientific Creativity', in Sternberg (1999), pp. 273–96.

Fernandez, Jay and Kit, Borys (2011) 'The Return of the Spec Script Buyer: Original Material is Hot Again', *Hollywood Reporter*, 25 March, available at http://www.hollywoodreporter.com/news/return-spec-script-buyer-167555, accessed 23.05.2012.

Field, Syd (1987) *The Screenwriter's Workbook*, Dell Trade, Random House, New York.

Film Policy Review Panel (2012) *A Future For British Film: Report to Government by the Film Policy Review Panel*, published on behalf of the Film Policy Review Panel by the Department for Culture, Media and Sport (DCMS), London.

Finney, A. (1996) *The Egos Have Landed: The Rise and Fall of Palace Pictures*, Heinemann, London.

—— (1996) *The State of European Cinema: A New Dose of Reality*, Cassell, London.

—— (2010) *The International Film Business: A Market Analysis*, Routledge, Oxford.

—— (2010) 'Value Chain Restructuring in the Global Film Industry', paper presented at the 4th Annual Conference on Cultural Production in a Global Context, Grenoble Ecole de Management, France, available at http://ec.europa.eu/culture/media/programme/docs/public_cons_media2010/44.pdf, accessed 23.05.2012.

Forer, B.R. (1949) 'The Fallacy of Personal Validation: A Classroom Demonstration of Gullibility', *Journal of Abnormal and Social Psychology* 44(1): 118–23.

Fosbrook, Deborah and Laing, Adrian (2009) *The Media Contracts Handbook*, 4th rev. edn, Sweet and Maxwell, London.

French, J. and Raven, B. (1959) in Cartwright, D. (ed.) *Studies in Social Power*, University of Michigan; cited in Handy (1985), pp. 120–2, 438.

—— (1968) 'The Bases of Social Power', in Cartwright, D. and Zander, A.F. (eds) *Group Dynamics: Research and Theory*, 3rd edn, Harper & Row, New York.

Friedmann, Julian (2000) *How to Make Money Scriptwriting*, Intellect Books, Bristol.

Fuller, Graham (ed.) (1998) *Loach on Loach*, Faber, London.

Gardner, H. (1993) 'Seven Creators of the Modern Era', in J. Brockman (ed.) *Creativity*, Simon & Schuster, New York; cited in Nickerson, Raymond S. (1999) *Enhancing Creativity*, in Sternberg (1999), p. 399.

Garfinkel, Asher (2007) *Screenplay Story Analysis*, Allworth Press, New York.

Garnett, Tony (2009) 'Tony Garnett's email on BBC drama', *Guardian*, 15 July, available at http://www.guardian.co.uk/media/2009/jul/15/tony-garnett-email-bbc-drama, accessed 23.05.2012.

Girard, René (1961) *Mensonge romantique et vérité romanesque*, Grasset, Paris; English translation: (1966) *Deceit, Desire and the Novel: Self and Other in Literary Structure*, Johns Hopkins University Press, Baltimore, MD.

Goffee, Rob and Jones, Gareth (2007) 'Leading Clever People', *Harvard Business Review*, March: 72–9.

Goldman, William (1983) *Adventures in the Screen Trade: A Personal View of Hollywood and Screenwriting*, Warner Books, New York; 2nd rev edn (1996) Abacus, New York.

—— (2001) *Which Lie Did I Tell? More Adventures in the Screen Trade*, new edn, Bloomsbury Publishing, London.

Goodell, G. (1998) *Independent Feature Film Production*, St Martins Griffin, New York; cited in Vogel (2007).

Goodridge, Mike (2011) 'Paramount to Shut Down Worldwide Acquisitions Group', *Screen International*, 3 June, available at http://www.screendaily.com/5028423. article.

—— (2011) 'Taking the Stage: Cross Creek Pictures', *Screen International*, 9 February, available at http://www.screendaily.com/reports/interviews/taking-the-stage/5023327.article, accessed 23.05.2012.

—— (2012) 'We Need Our Curators', *Screen International*, 16 February, available at http://www.screendaily.com/5038146.article, accessed 20.02.2012.

Gordon, Thomas (1970) *Parent Effectiveness Training*, Wyden, New York; cited in Rosengren (2009), p. 32.

Govindarajan, Vijay and Trimble, Chris (2010) *The Other Side of Innovation: Solving the Execution Challenge*, HBS Press, Boston, MA.

Greenberg, J. and Barn, R. (2003) *Behaviour in Organisations*, 8th edn, Prentice Hall, New York.

Guilford, J. (1950) 'Creativity', *American Psychologist* 5: 444–54.

—— (1967) *The Nature of Human Intelligence*, McGraw-Hill, New York.

Hall, Stuart (1973) *Encoding and Decoding in the Television Discourse*, CCS, Birmingham.

Hamilton, E. and Cairns, H. (eds) (1961) *The Collected Dialogues of Plato*, Princeton University Press, Princeton, NJ.

Handy, C. (1985) *Understanding Organizations*, 3rd edn, Facts On File Publications, New York.

Harlow, H.F. (1950) 'Learning and Satiation Response in Intrinsically Motivated Complex Puzzle Performance by Monkeys', *Journal of Comparative Physiological Psychology* 43: 289–94; cited in Amabile (1996), pp. 108 and 282.

Hatch, M.J. (2006) *Organisation Theory. Modern, Symbolic, Postmodern*, Oxford University Press, Oxford.

Hazelton, John (2010) 'Why Libraries are Losing Value', *Screen International*, 14 April, available at http://www.screendaily.com/reports/in-focus/why-libraries-are-losing-value/5012738.article, accessed 08.12.2011.

—— (2011) 'Sellers Gain from Capital', *Screen International*, 6 May, available at http://www.screendaily.com/reports/in-focus/sellers-gain-from-capital/5026870.article, accessed 22.05.2012.

Henry, Jane (1991) *Creative Management*, Sage, London.

—— (2001) *Creativity and Perception in Management*, Sage, London.

—— (ed.) (2006) *Creative Management and Development*, 3rd edn, Sage, London.

Henry, J. and Mayle, D. (eds) (2002) *Managing Innovation and Change*, Open University and Sage, London.

Hesmondhalgh, David (2007) *The Cultural Industries*, 2nd edn, Sage, London.

Hesmondhalgh, David and Baker, Sarah (2011) *Creative Labour: Media Work in Three Cultural Industries*, Routledge, London

Hill, John (2011) *Ken Loach: The Politics of Film and Television*, Palgrave Macmillan/ British Film Institute, London.

Hofstede, G. (1984) 'The Cultural Relativity of the Quality of Life Concept', *Academy of Management Review* 9(3): 389–98.

Homans, G. (1961) *Social Behaviour*, Routledge & Kegan Paul, London.

Howard, Margaret and Urquhart, Sidney Howard (1995) 'Letters Home', reprinted in Boorman, John, Luddy, Tom, Thomson, David and Donohue, Walter (1995) *Projections 4: Film-Makers on Film-Making*, Faber and Faber, London.

Howkins, John (2001) *The Creative Economy*, Allen Lane/Penguin, London.

Hughes, David (2004) *Tales from Development Hell: Hollywood Film-Making the Hard Way*, Titan Books, London.

Hume, D. (1740) *A Treatise of Human Nature*, Section XI (Of The Love of Fame), Smith, Dublin, available at Project Gutenberg, http://www.gutenberg.org/ files/4705/4705-h/4705-h.htm, accessed 29.05.2012.

Hunter, Evan (1997) *Me and Hitch*, Faber and Faber, London.

Hunter, Lew (1994) *Screenwriting*, Hale Publishing, London.

Isaksen, S., Dorval, K., Noller, R. and Firestien, R. (1993) 'The Dynamic Nature of Creative Problem-Solving', in Gryskiewicz, S. (ed.) (1993) *Discovering Creativity*, Centre for Creative Leadership, pp. 155–62; cited in Amabile (1996), pp. 114 and 298.

Isaksen, Scott G., Dorval, Brian K. and Treffinger, Donald J. (1994) *Creative Approaches to Problem Solving*, Kendal/Hunt Publishing Company; cited in Amabile, T. (1996) *Creativity in Context* (update to *Social Psychology of Creativity*, 1983), Westview Press, Perseus Books, Boulder, CO, p. 114.

Jaafar, Ali and Keslassy, Elsa (2009) 'France's EuropaCorp Strikes Gold', *Variety* (online), available at http://www.variety.com/article/VR1118003298?refCat Id=13, accessed 23.05.2012.

Jancovich, Mark, Faire, Lucy and Stubbings, Sarah (2003) *The Place of the Audience: Cultural Geographies of Film Consumption*, British Film Institute, London.

Janssen, M. and Sol, H. (2000) 'Evaluating the Role of Intermediaries in the Electronic Value Chain', *Internet Research* 10(5): 406–417.

Jeffcut, Paul and Pratt, Andy (2002) 'Managing Creativity in the Cultural Industries', *Creativity and Innovation Management* 11(4): 225–33.

Jeffords, Susan (1993) *Hard Bodies: Hollywood Masculinity in the Reagan Era*, Rutgers University Press, New Jersey.

Jenkins, Henry (2006) *Convergence Culture: Where Old and New Media Collide*, New York University Press, New York.

Johnston, Keith (2011) *Science Fiction Film: A Critical Introduction*, Berg, London.

Katahn, T.L. (1990) *Reading for a Living: How to Be a Professional Story Analyst for Film and Television*, Blue Arrow Books, Wallington.

Katz, A. (1997) 'Creativity in the Cerebral Hemispheres', in Runco, M. (ed.) *Creativity Research Handbook*, Hampton Press, New Jersey, pp. 203–26; cited in Chamorro-Premuzic (2007), p. 129.

Katzenbach, Jon and Smith, Douglas (1993) *The Wisdom of Teams: Creating the High-Performance Organization*, Harvard Business School Press, Boston, MA.

Kelman, H.C. (1958) 'Compliance, Identification, and Internalization: Three Processes of Attitude Change', *Journal of Conflict Resolution* 2(1): 51–60, available at http://scholar.harvard.edu/hckelman/files/Compliance_identification_and_internalization.pdf, accessed 23.04.2012.

Kerrigan, Finola (2010) *Film Marketing*, Butterworth-Heinemann, Oxford.

Kirton, M. (1984) 'Adaptors and Innovators: Why New Initiatives Get Blocked' (from Kirton, M. (1984) 'Adaptors and Innovators', *Long Range Planning* 17(2): 137–43), in Henry (2006).

Kirwan, Michael (2004) *Discovering Girard*, Darton, Longman & Todd, London.

Kotter, J.P. (1992) *Corporate Culture and Performance*, The Free Press, New York.

—— (1996) *Leading Change*, Harvard Business School Press, Boston, MA.

Kotter, John and Cohen, Dan (2002) *The Heart of Change*, Harvard Business School Press, Boston, MA.

Kris, E. (1952) *Psychoanalytic Explorations in Art*, International Universities Press, New York.

Kuhn, Michael (2003) *One Hundred Films and a Funeral: PolyGram Films: Birth, Betrothal, Betrayal, and Burial*, Thorogood Publishing, London.

Küng, Lucy (2008) *Strategic Management in the Media: Theory to Practice*, Sage, London.

Küng, L., Leandros, N., Picard, R., Schroeder, R. and van der Wurff, R. (2008) 'Impact of the Internet on Media Organisation Structures', in Küng, L., Picard, R. and Towse, R. (2008) *The Internet and the Mass Media*, Sage, Los Angeles, CA.

Kurtzberg, T.R. and Amabile, T.M. (2000) 'From Guilford to Creative Synergy: Opening the Black Box of Team Level Creativity', *Creativity Research Journal* 13(3/4): 285–94.

Lampel, Joseph, Shamsie, Jamal and Lant, Theresa (2006) *The Business of Culture: Strategic Perspectives on Entertainment and Media*, Lawrence Erlbaum, Mahwah, NJ.

—— (2006) 'Toward a Deeper Understanding of Cultural Industries', in Lampel, Shamsie and Lant (2006), pp. 3–14.

Lane, R. (1996) 'The Magician', *Forbes Magazine*, 11 March; cited by Pardo (2010).

Lepper, M., Greene, D. and Nisbett, R. (1973) 'Undermining Children's Intrinsic Motivation with Extrinsic Rewards: A Test of the Overjustification Hypothesis', *Journal of Personality and Social Psychology* 28(1): 129–37, available at http://psycnet.apa.org/journals/psp/28/1/129/, accessed 22.05.2012.

Lessig, L. (2004) *Free Culture: The Nature and Future of Creativity*, Penguin, London.

Levine, Robert (2011) *Free Ride: How the Internet is Destroying the Culture Business*, The Bodley Head, London.

Lubit, R. (2002) 'The Long-term Organizational Impact of Destructively Narcissistic Managers', *Academy of Management Executive* 16(1): 127–38.

Luft, J. and Ingham, H. (1950) 'The Johari Window, a Graphic Model of Interpersonal Awareness', *Proceedings of the Western Training Laboratory in Group Development*, UCLA, Los Angeles; cited in Stacey, R. (1996) *Strategic Management and Organisational Dynamics*, 2nd edn, Pitman, London, p. 193; cited in Block (2001), p. 192.

Lynch, Richard (2006) *Corporate Strategy*, 4th edn, Financial Times/Prentice Hall, London.

—— (2009) *Strategic Management*, 5th edn (rev. edn of *Corporate Strategy*, 4th edn), Pearson Education, Harlow.

McClintock, Pamela (2011) 'Foreign Rescue for Homegrown Duds', *Hollywood Reporter*, 5 May, http://www.hollywoodreporter.com/news/foreign-rescue-homegrown-duds-185072 accessed 23.05.2012.

Maccoby, M. (2000) 'Narcissistic Leaders: The Incredible Pros, the Inevitable Cons', *Harvard Business Review* (January–February): 69–77.

—— (2007) *Narcissistic Leaders: Who Succeeds and Who Fails*, Harvard Business School Press, Boston, MA.

McDonald, P. (2008) 'Britain: Hollywood', in McDonald, P. and Wasko, J. (eds) *The Contemporary Hollywood Film Industry*, Blackwell, Oxford, pp. 220–31.

McDonald, P. and Wasko, J. (eds) (2008) *The Contemporary Hollywood Film Industry*, Blackwell, Oxford.

McGraw, K. (1978) 'The Detrimental Effects of Reward on Performance: A Literature Review and a Prediction Model', in Lepper, M. and Greene, D. (eds) *The Hidden Costs of Reward*, Lawrence Erlbaum Associates, Hillsdale, NJ; cited in Amabile (1996), pp. 133 and 286.

McGregor, D.M. (1957) 'The Human Side of Enterprise', *Management Review* 46: 22–8.

McKee, Robert (1999) *Story*, Methuen, London.

MacKinnon, D. (1963) 'Creativity and Images of the Self', in White, R.W. (ed.) (1963) *The Study of Lives*, Atherton, New York, pp. 251–78; cited in Csíkszentmihályi (1996).

Macnab, Geoffrey (2009) 'Can the Writers Change the Script?', *Screen International*, 22 October, available at http://www.screendaily.com/territories/europe/can-the-writers-change-the-script/5007243.article, accessed 23.05.2012.

—— (2011) 'New European Studio', *Screen International*, 6 May, available at http://www.screendaily.com/reports/in-focus/the-new-european-studios/5026865.article, accessed 25.05.2012.

Majaro, Simon (1992) 'Managing Ideas for Profit', *Journal of Marketing Management* 8; cited in Burns (2011), p. 112.

Mamet, David (1991) *On Directing Film*, Viking Penguin, New York, p. 61.

Martin, Joanne (2002) *Organizational Culture: Mapping the Terrain*, Sage, Thousand Oaks, CA.

—— (2004) 'Organizational Culture: Pieces of the Puzzle', in Shafritz, J.M., Ott, J.S. and Jang, Y.S. (eds) *Classics of Organizational Theory*, 6th edn, Wadsworth Publishing, Belmont, CA, pp. 393–414.

Martindale, Colin (1999) 'Biological Bases of Creativity', in Sternberg (1999), pp. 137–48.

Maslow, A. (1943) 'A Theory of Human Motivation', *Psychological Review* 50(4): pp. 370–96.

—— (1954) *Motivation and Personality*, Harper and Brothers, New York.

—— (1971) *Farther Reaches of Human Nature*, McGraw-Hill, New York.

Mendelow, A. (1991) 'Stakeholder Mapping', *Proceedings of the 2nd International Conference on Information Systems*, Cambridge, MA.

Mike Kelly/Northern Alliance/UK Film Council (2008) *Low and Micro-Budget Film Production in the UK*, UK Film Council, London.

Mintzberg, Henry (1975) 'The Manager's Job: Folklore and Fact', *Harvard Business Review* 53(4): 49–61.

—— (1989) *Mintzberg on Management: Inside Our Strange World of Organizations*, Free Press/Collier Macmillan, New York and London.

Mintzberg, H., Ahlstrand, B. and Lampel, J. (1998) *Strategy Safari*, The Free Press, Simon & Schuster, New York.

Mintzberg, H., Lampel, J., Quinn, J.B. and Ghoshal, S. (2003) *The Strategy Process*, 4th edn, Pearson Prentice Hall, New Jersey.

Mitchell, Wendy (2012) 'Target Audience', *Screen International*, 27 January, available online at http://www.screendaily.com/reports/in-focus/target-audience/5037164.article, accessed 23.05.2012.

Motion Picture Association of America, MPAA (2011) Theatrical Market Statistics, MPAA, Washington, available at http://www.mpaa.org/Resources/93bbeb16-0e4d-4b7e-b085-3f41c459f9ac.pdf, accessed 01.03.2012.

Mullins, Laurie (2005) *Management and Organisational Behaviour*, 7th edn, Prentice Hall, London.

Nardonne, J. (1982) 'Is the Movie Industry Contracyclical?', *Cycles* 33(3); cited in Vogel (2007), pp. 101 and 575.

NAWE (National Association of Writers in Education) Higher Education Committee (2008) 'A Subject Benchmark for Creative Writing', September.

—— (2008) 'Creative Writing Research Benchmark Statement', October.

Negus, Keith and Pickering, Michael (2004) *Creativity, Communication and Cultural Value*, Sage, London.

Nickerson, Raymond S. (1999) 'Enhancing Creativity', in Sternberg (1999), pp. 392–429.

Nicolaou, N., Shane, S., Cherkas, L. and Spector, T.D. (2008) 'The Influence of Sensation Seeking in the Heritability of Entrepreneurship', *Strategic Entrepreneurship Journal* 2: 7–21.

Nicolaou, N. et al. (2011) 'A Polymorphism Associated with Entrepreneurship: Evidence from Dopamine Receptor Candidate Genes', *Small Business Economics* 36(2): 151–5.

Nishimoto, S. et al. (2011) 'Reconstructing Visual Experiences from Brain Activity Evoked by Natural Movies', *Current Biology* 21(19): 1641–6.

Oberman, L.M., Hubbard, E.M., McCleery, J.P., Altschuler, E.L., Ramachandran, V.S. and Pineda, J.A. (2005) 'EEG Evidence for Mirror Neuron Dysfunction in Autism Spectrum Disorders', *Brain Res Cogn Brain Res* 24 (2): 190–8.

Osborn, Alex (1942) *How to 'Think Up'*, McGraw-Hill, New York.

—— (1953) *Applied Imagination: Principles and Procedures of Creative Problem Solving*, Charles Scribner's Sons, New York.

Oxford Economics (2010) *The Economic Impact of the UK Film Industry*, UK Film Council, London.

PACT (2010) *Rights of Passage*, a report by TRP for UKTI/Pact; cited in *Memorandum* submitted by PACT on 24.09.2010, PACT response to BIS Committee inquiry, available on PACT website at http://www.pact.co.uk/support/document-library/pact-response-to-bis-committee-enquiry-into-government/, accessed 03.03.2012.

Pardo, Alejandro (2010) 'The Film Producer as Creative Force', *Wide Screen* 2(2): 1–23.

Parker, Phil (2000) *The Art and Science of Screenwriting*, Intellect Books, Bristol.

—— (2009) 'Where Have All the Screenwriters Gone?', *Screen International*, 24 September, available at http://www.screendaily.com/news/opinion/where-have-all-the-screenwriters-gone/5006085.article, accessed 25.05.2012.

Pasley, B.N., David, S.V., Mesgarani, N., Flinker, A., Shamma, S.A., et al. (2012) 'Reconstructing Speech from Human Auditory Cortex', *PLoS Biology* 10(1), available at http://www.plosbiology.org/article/info:doi/10.1371/journal. pbio.1001251, last accessed 21.05.2012.

Perkins, D.N. (1988) 'The Possibility of Invention', in Sternberg (1988).

Peters, Mike, Frehse, Joerg and Buhalis, Dimitrios (2009) 'The Importance of Lifestyle Entrepreneurship: A Conceptual Study of the Tourism Industry', *Pasos Online* 7(2): 393–405, available at http://www.pasosonline.org/Publicados/ 7309special/PS0309_5.pdf, accessed 25.05.2012.

Pink, Daniel (2010) *Drive: The Surprising Truth About What Motivates Us*, Canongate Books, Edinburgh.

Poincaré, Henri (1924) *The Foundations of Science*, University Press of America, Washington DC; cited in Boden (2004), pp. 29–35.

Pope, Rob (2002) *The English Studies Book: An Introduction to Language, Literature and Culture*, 2nd edn, Routledge, London (1st edn 1998).

—— (2005) *Creativity: Theory, History, Practice*, Routledge, London.

Porter, Michael E. (1980) *Competitive Strategy*, Free Press, Macmillan, New York.

—— (1985) *Competitive Advantage: Creating and Sustaining Superior Performance*, Free Press, Macmillan, New York.

—— (2001) 'Strategy and the Internet', *Harvard Business Review*, March: 62–78.

Porter, Michael. E. and Millar, Victor, E. (1985) 'How Information Gives You Competitive Advantage: The Internet Revolution is Transforming the Nature of Competition', *Harvard Business Review*, July–August: 149–60.

Powdermaker, Hortense (1950) *Hollywood, the Dream Factory: An Anthropologist Looks at the Movie-Makers*. Boston, MA: Little, Brown, available at http://astro.temple. edu/~ruby/wava/powder/table.html.

Purkayastha, D. (2006) *Pixar's Incredible Culture*, Case Study, 406-077-1 ICFAI, Centre for Management Research, available at ECCH at http://www.icmrindia.org/ casestudies/catalogue/Human%20Resource%20and%20Organization%20 Behavior/HROB082.htm, accessed 23.05.2012.

Quinn, James Brian (1985) 'Managing Innovation: Controlled Chaos', *Harvard Business Review* 63(3): 73–84.

Ramachandran, V. (2003) *The Emerging Mind: The Reith Lectures 2003*, BBC/Profile Books, London.

—— (2011) *The Tell-Tale Brain: Unlocking the Mystery of Human Nature*, William Heinemann, London.

Rizzolatti, Giacomo and Siniglalglia, Corrado (2008) *Mirrors in the Brain – How our Minds Share Actions and Emotions*, translated by Anderson, Frances, Oxford University Press, Oxford.

Robbins, S. and Barnwell, N. (2002) *Organisation Theory*, 4th edn, Prentice Hall, Pearson, Sydney.

Rollnick, S. and Miller, W. (2002) *Motivational Interviewing*, 2nd edn, Guilford Press, New York.

Rollnick, S., Miller, W. and Butler, C. (2006) *Motivational Interviewing in Health Care*, Guilford Press, New York.

Rose, Steve (2011) 'The Droog Rides Again', *Guardian Film and Music Review*, 12 May, pp. 19–21.

Rosenbloom, Tova (2003) 'Risk Evaluation and Risky Behavior of High and Low Sensation Seekers', *Social Behavior and Personality* 31(4): 375–86.

Rosengren, David (2009) *Building Motivational Interviewing Skills: A Practitioner Workbook*, Guilford Press, New York.

Ruane, Janet (2005) *Essentials of Research Methods: A Guide to Social Science Research*, Blackwell, Malden.

Rudkin, D., Allan, D. and Murrin, K. (2002) *Sticky Wisdom: How to Start a Creative Revolution at Work*, Capstone Publishing, Chichester.

Runco, Mark (2006) *Creativity: Theories and Themes: Research, Development, and Practice*, Academic Press, Burlington, MA.

Shafritz, J.M., Ott, J.S. and Jang, Y.S. (eds), *Classics of Organizational Theory*, 6th edn, Wadsworth Publishing, Belmont, CA.

Schatz, Tom (2008) 'The Studio System and Conglomerate Hollywood', in McDonald and Wasko (2008), pp. 11–42.

Schein, Edgar (1993) *Organizational Culture and Leadership*, 2nd edn, Jossey-Bass, San Francisco, CA; 3rd edn (2004); 4th edn (2010).

Scher, Lucy (2011) *Reading Screenplays*, Creative Essentials, London.

Schulberg, Budd (1954) *On the Waterfront: Screenplay*, Columbia Pictures Corporation/Sony Pictures Home Entertainment.

Seeger, Linda (2008) *And the Best Screenplay Goes to … Sideways, Shakespeare in Love, Crash: Learning from the Winners*, Michael Wiese Productions, Los Angeles.

Seidel, V. (2006) 'An Evolutionary Process Theory of Radical Product Development: Concepts as Coordination Totems', working paper presented at the Academy of Management, 16 August.

Seidman, I.E. (1991) *Interviewing as Qualitative research*, Teachers College Press, New York.

Senge, Peter (1990) *The Fifth Discipline*, Doubleday/Currency, New York.

Shane, S. (2009) 'Entrepreneurship and the Big Five Personality Traits: A Behavioral Genetics Perspective', available at http://pdfcast.org/pdf/entrepreneurship-and-the-big-five-personality-traits-a-behavioral, accessed 22.05.2012.

Shaw, G. and Williams, A. (2004) 'From Lifestyle Consumption to Lifestyle Production: New Forms of Tourism Entrepreneurship', in Thomas, R. (ed.) *Small Firms in Tourism: International Perspectives*, Elsevier, Amsterdam, pp. 99–113.

Sinclair, Andrew (1987) *Spiegel: The Man Behind the Pictures*, Weidenfeld & Nicolson, London.

Spence, J. and Helmrich, R. (1978) *Masculinity and Femininity*, University of Texas Press, Austin; cited in Csíkszentmihályi (1996).

Squire, Jason E. (ed.) (2006) *The Movie Business Book*, 3rd edn, Simon & Schuster, New York.

Staiger, Janet (2000) *Perverse Spectators: The Practices of Film Reception*, New York University Press, New York.

—— (2005) *Media Reception Studies*, New York University Press, New York.

Stalk, G. and Stern, C.W. (1973) *Perspectives on Strategy: From the Boston Consulting Group*, Wiley, New York.

Stein, M. (1974–5) *Stimulating Creativity* (vols 1–2), Academic Press, New York.

Sternberg, R. (1985) 'Implicit Theories of Intelligence, Creativity and Wisdom', *Journal of Personality and Social Psychology* 49: 607–27, cited in Csíkszentmihályi (1996), p. 403.

—— (1988) *The Nature of Creativity: Contemporary Psychological Perspectives*, Cambridge University Press, Cambridge.

—— (ed.) (1999) *Handbook of Creativity*, Cambridge University Press, Cambridge.

—— (2006) 'The Nature of Creativity', *Creativity Research Journal* 18: 87–99; repr. in Kaufman, James and Grigorenko, Elena (2009) *The Essential Sternberg: Essays on Intelligence, Psychology and Education*, Springer, New York.

Sternberg, R. and Lubart, T. (1991) 'An Investment Theory of Creativity and Its Development', *Human Development* 34: 1–31.

Styhre, A. and Sundgren, M. (2005) *Managing Creativity in Organizations: Critique and Practices*, Palgrave Macmillan, Basingstoke.

Sutton, R.I. (2001) 'The Weird Rules of Creativity', *Harvard Business Review*, September: 94–103.

Swain, Dwight (1976) *Film Scriptwriting: A Practical Manual*, Focal Press, Butterworth, London and Boston, MA.

Szalai, Georg (2011) 'CBS Corp Touts Financial Upside of Emerging Businesses', *Hollywood Reporter*, 24 February, available at http://www.hollywoodreporter. com/news/cbs-corp-touts-financial-upside-161216, accessed 23.05.2012.

Tallis, Raymond (2008) 'The Neuroscience Delusion: Neuroaesthetics is Wrong about our Experience of Literature – and it is Wrong about Humanity', *Times Literary Supplement*, 9 April.

—— (2011) *Aping Mankind: Neuromania, Darwinitis and the Misrepresentation of Humanity*, Acumen Publishing, London.

Tannenbaum, R. and Schmidt, W. (1958) 'How to Choose a Leadership Pattern', *Harvard Business Review* 36(2): 95–101.

Tapscott, D. (1996) *The Digital Economy*, McGraw Hill, New York; cited in Küng (2008), p. 20.

Tasker, Yvonne (1993) *Spectacular Bodies: Gender, Genre, and the Action Cinema*, Routledge, London.

—— (ed.) (2004) *Action and Adventure Cinema*, Routledge, London.

Taylor, Thom (1999) *The Big Deal: Hollywood's Million-Dollar Spec Script Market*, Quill Books, William Morrow, New York.

Thornton, Chris (2007) *A Quantitative Reconstruction of Boden's Creativity Theory*, University of Sussex, Brighton, available at http://citeseerx.ist.psu.edu/viewdoc/download?doi=10.1.1.62.6745&rep=rep1&type=pdf, accessed 22.05.2012.

Tieger, Paul and Barron-Tieger, Barbara (1999) *The Art of Speedreading People*, Little, Brown & Co, New York.

Torr, G. (2009) *Managing Creative People: Lessons in Leadership for the Ideas Economy*, Wiley & Sons, London.

Townley, Barbara and Beech, Nic (eds) (2010) *Managing Creativity: Exploring the Paradox*, Cambridge University Press, Cambridge.

Travis, Mark (2002) *Directing Feature Films: The Creative Collaboration Between Directors, Writers and Actors*, Michael Weise Productions, Los Angeles, CA.

Tuckman, Bruce W. (1965) 'Developmental Sequence in Small Groups', *Psychological Bulletin* 63: 384–99 (the article was reprinted in *Group Facilitation: A Research and Applications Journal* 3 (2001)); and Mullins, Laurie (2005) *Management and Organisational Behaviour*, 7th edn, Prentice Hall, London).

Tuckman, Bruce and Jensen, Mary Ann (1977) 'Stages of Small-Group Development Revisited', *Group & Organization Studies* 2: 419–27.

UK Film Council (2008) *Definition of Specialised Film*, http://www.ukfilmcouncil.org.uk/specialisedfilms, accessed 26.03.2011.

—— (2009) *UK Film Council Statistical Yearbook 2009*, UK Film Council, London.

UK Film Council Research and Statistics Unit (2008) *Film in the UK: A Briefing Paper*, draft dated 21.08.2009, UK Film Council, London.

—— (2010) *UK Film Council Statistical Yearbook 2010*, UK Film Council, London.

UK Film Council/Skillset/Attentional (2007) *Study of Feature Film Development*, UK Film Council, London.

UK Film Council/Stimulating World Research (2007) *A Qualitative Study of Avid Cinema-goers*, UK Film Council, London.

Ulin, J. (2010) *The Business of Media Distribution: Monetizing Film, TV, and Video Content*, Focal Press/Elsevier, Boston, MA/Amsterdam.

Vickery, Graham and Hawkins, Richard (2008) *Remaking the Movies: Digital Content and the Evolution of the Film and Video Industries*, OECD, Paris.

Vogel, H. (2007), *Entertainment Industry Economics: A Guide for Financial Analysis*, 7th edn, Cambridge University Press, Cambridge.

Vogler, Christopher (1996) *The Writer's Journey: Mythic Structure for Storytellers and Screenwriters*, Boxtree Ltd, London.

Wallas, G. (1926) *The Art of Thought*, Harcourt, Brace; cited in Amabile, T. (1996), p. 99.

Watson, T.J. (2002) *Organising and Managing Work*, Prentice Hall, Harlow.

Weisberg, Robert W. (1986) *Creativity: Genius and Other Myths*, W.H. Freeman & Co, Gordonsville, VA (updated into *Creativity: Beyond the Myth of Genius* in 1993).

West, M.A. and Sacramento, C.A. (2004) 'Flourishing in Teams: Developing Creativity and Innovation', in Henry (2006), pp. 25–43.

Westby, E. and Dawson, V. (1995) 'Creativity: Asset or Burden', *Creativity Research Journal* 8: 1–10; cited in Csíkszentmihályi (1996), p. 403.

Williams, A.M., Shaw, G. and Greenwood, J. (1989) 'From Tourist to Tourism Entrepreneur, from Consumption to Production: Evidence from Cornwall, England', *Environment and Planning* A(21): 1639–53.

Williams, Melanie (2007) 'The Creative Producer: Frank Godwin Interviewed by Melanie Williams', *Journal of British Cinema and Television* 4(1): 140–9.

Wright, Jean Ann (2005) *Animation Writing and Development: From Script Development to Pitch*, Focal Press, London.

Yoffie, D. (ed.) (1997) *Competing in the Age of Digital Convergence*, Harvard Business School Press, Boston, MA; cited in Küng (2008), p. 20.

Young, J.W. (1960) *A Technique for Producing Ideas*, McGraw Hill, New York.

Zerdick, A. et al. (2000) *E-conomics: Strategies for the Digital Marketplace*, European Communication Council Report, Springer, Berlin.

Zuckerman, M. (1994) *Behavioural Expressions and Biosocial Bases of Sensation Seeking*, Cambridge University Press, Cambridge.

—— (2007) *Sensation Seeking and Risky Behavior*, American Psychological Association, Washington DC.

Index

Note: for the purposes of the index a studio has been defined as an integrated business regularly funding development, production, international sales, and supplying a permanently owned or semi-owned distribution network. Subsidiary companies that are part of a studio have also been labelled as a studio. Other companies have been defined by their primary activity.